BASIC READING INVENTORY

Kindergarten through Grade Twelve and Early Literacy Assessments

— Twelfth Edition —

JERRY L. JOHNS
Distinguished Teaching Professor Emeritus
Northern Illinois University, DeKalb

LAURIE ELISH-PIPER
Dean of the College of Education
Northern Illinois University, DeKalb

BETH JOHNS
Writer and Editor
Seattle, Washington

Kendall Hunt
publishing company

Book Team

Chairman and Chief Executive Officer   Mark C. Falb
President and Chief Operating Officer   Chad M. Chandlee
Vice President, Higher Education   David L. Tart
Director of Publishing Partnerships   Paul B. Carty
Vice President, Operations   Timothy J. Beitzel
Senior Development Coordinator   Angela Willenbring
Permissions Editor   Tammy Hunt
Cover Designer   Faith Walker

Author Information for Correspondence and Workshops

Jerry L. Johns, Ph.D.
Consultant in Reading
jjohns@niu.edu
Fax: 815-899-3022

Laurie Elish-Piper, Ph.D.
Dean of the College of Education
Northern Illinois University, DeKalb
laurieep@niu.edu

Beth Johns
Writer and Editor
bjohns012@gmail.com

Ordering Information

Address: Kendall Hunt Publishing Company
4050 Westmark Drive, P.O. Box 1840
Dubuque, IA 52004-1840

Telephone: 800-247-3458, ext. 6

Web site: www.kendallhunt.com/readingresources

Brief Contents

Contents

Expert Noticing Notes for Elyse and Answers for Practice Exercises

Performance Booklets & Individual and Class Summary Sheets

History of the Informal Reading Inventory

Annotated Bibliography

Figures and Tables

About the Authors

The author team: Beth, Jerry, and Laurie

Jerry L. Johns

Jerry L. Johns has been recognized as a distinguished teacher, writer, outstanding teacher educator, and professional development speaker for schools, school districts, and conferences. He has taught students from kindergarten through graduate school and also served as a reading teacher. Jerry spent his career at Northern Illinois University. He served in leadership positions at the local, state, national, and international levels. He has been president of the International Literacy Association, the Illinois Reading Council, the Association of Literacy Educators and Researchers, and the Northern Illinois Reading Council. He also served on the board of directors for each of these organizations, as well as the American Reading Forum. Jerry has authored or co-authored nearly 300 articles, monographs, and research studies as well as over 40 professional books and instructional materials for students.

Jerry has been the recipient of numerous awards for his contributions to various professional organizations. He received the Outstanding Service Award from the Association of Literacy Educators and Researchers and was honored by the Illinois Reading Council (IRC) with induction into the IRC Reading Hall of Fame. Other recognitions include the Alpha Delta Literacy Award for Scholarship, Leadership, and Service to Adult Learners, the A.B. Herr Award for outstanding contributions to the field of reading, and the Laureate Award for life-long contributions to the field of reading presented by the Association of Literacy Educators and Researchers. The International Literacy Association renamed the Outstanding Teacher Educator in Reading Award in his honor. Most recently he was elected to the international Reading Hall of Fame and selected to receive the William S. Gray Citation of Merit from the International Literacy Association.

Laurie Elish-Piper

Laurie Elish-Piper, Ph.D., is Dean of the College of Education at Northern Illinois University. She also holds the titles of Presidential Engagement Professor and Distinguished Teaching Professor in the Department of Literacy and Elementary Education at Northern Illinois University. Laurie served as the Director of the Jerry L. Johns Literacy Clinic for 15 years and as Co-Director of the Center for the Interdisciplinary Study of Language and Literacy for eight years. Laurie has served as the President of the Association of Literacy Educators and Researchers, and she is currently on the Board of Directors of the International Literacy Association.

Laurie's scholarship and teaching focus on literacy leadership, literacy coaching, teacher professional development, literacy assessment, and struggling readers. She has co-authored 10 books and over 75 articles in refereed professional journals and professional yearbooks. She is a regular presenter at international, national, state, and local conferences. Prior to starting her career in higher education, Laurie was an elementary teacher and a middle school language arts/reading teacher in Indiana.

Beth Johns

Beth Johns is a writer and editor who lives in Seattle, Washington. She has grown up with the Basic Reading Inventory, assisting her father (author Dr. Jerry L. Johns) with presentations at Northern Illinois University and the University of Victoria in British Columbia as an example test student. For the last two editions of the Basic Reading Inventory, she has been instrumental in field-testing many new and revised passages. Her contributions for this edition focus primarily on refining and strengthening the materials for grades 3–12, while adding fresh insight to the project as a whole. She is a current member of the International Literacy Association, the Washington Organization for Reading Development, the Seattle Reading Council, and the Seattle Women's Hockey Club.

We wish you great success with the Basic Reading Inventory!

Acknowledgments

Appreciation is extended to the following groups who contributed directly or indirectly to the twelfth edition:

Colleagues. Countless professors and instructors in the United States and Canada have directly or indirectly influenced the Basic Reading Inventory. Teaching the inventory to preservice and inservice teachers at both the undergraduate and graduate levels has provided an important basis for informal feedback when we meet at conferences or professional meetings. Your writing and research about the reading process, assessment, instructional practices, progress monitoring, and response to intervention continues to inform my work. Your contributions have made a difference in our efforts to make instruction more responsive to the needs of individual students.

Students. A fundamental purpose of the Basic Reading Inventory is to use the results to develop individual literacy plans and interventions for students to enhance reading achievement. Thousands and thousands of students have been given the reading inventory. It is our hope that the results have been used to help them become better readers. Based on many conversations with teachers, specialists, and interventionists, it is clear that the Basic Reading Inventory is contributing to the goal of helping students reach their potential as readers.

Teachers and Specialists. Thousands of teachers have used the Basic Reading Inventory over the years, and I want to express my grateful appreciation to each of you. Special thanks are given to teachers and specialists who assisted by sharing ideas, raising questions, fieldtesting, and/or providing support and encouragement. Our workshops with the Basic Reading Inventory in schools and school districts throughout the United States and in Canada have been stimulating events resulting in the rich sharing of ideas. Emails, conference calls, and numerous telephone conversations have provided an opportunity to respond personally to individual questions. Thanks for your partnership.

We are grateful for many useful contributions to this edition.

Special thanks to the following individuals, as well as many others who have supported and facilitated our work.

Kristen Alger
Katie Allison
Katie Balajthy
Gail Barker
Joan Bereman
Kristina Blakely
Nancy Bonkowski
Georgia Botsford
Betsy Brantner
Scott Braswell
Benita Bruster
Michael Buckner
Steve Carlson
James Cohen
Brooke Condon
Kari Countryman
Linda Cox
Kristi Crawford
Jim Cunningham
Mayra Daniel
Drewe Davey
Marissa Dobie
Bobette Dodson
Natalie Dunnegan
Tracy Egerman
Roseanne Feldmann
Leah Fern
Lou Ferroli
Veronica Fife-Demski
Joyce Fine
Mary Beth Fletcher
Karen Ford
Vickie Foster
Mary Gardner
Stacie Garrett
Terisa Golding
Anne Gregory

Helen Hadley
Kelly Hardesty
Ashley Hatteberg
Laura Heitritter
Jennifer Heth
Jeffery Hillmer
Suzi Hinrichs
Allyson Holder
Laurie Jacobson
Virginia Jamnicki
Ryan Janisch
Annette Johns
Debbi Joyce
Cindy Kaiser
Mary Keil
Amy Kennedy
Lucy Killian
Bridget Klein
Debbie Kruzus
Jodi Lampi
Marie Leahy
Samantha Lebouef
Sue Lenski
Lorena Lule
Anne Marie Magliari
Mike Manderino
Kelly May
Jennifer McCormick
Becky Mecca
Clay Meier
Lynne Miller
Beth Morgano
Jacalyn Morton
Lynn Mullenbruck
Linda Mullins
Veronica Origel
Ashley Orth

Jennifer Oswald
Kim Payne
Sue Pelikan
Leslie Pergament-Nenia
Vicki Phelps
Leslie Ann Prosak-Beres
Patricia Rieman
Tifanny Ryan
Rich Samo
Mary Ellen Sanders
Rachel Scheiner
Jennifer Schroeder
Gwen Senokossoff
Rita Shafer
Ellie Shaffer
Carmen Siragusa
Angela Slack
Carol Slutz
Norm Stahl
Steven Stephens
Jami Thompson
Carol Untch
Ginny Van Wingerden
Rachel Vidales
Lindsy Vincent
Jolene Ward
Kelly Wardle
Joyce Warner
Pam Webb
Missy Wehrmeister
Donna Werderich
Diane Wesley
Dan Wheeler
Whitney Wheeler
Adam Williams
Stacie Williar

Preface

The twelfth edition of the *Basic Reading Inventory* continues with the well-received "two book" approach. Initially, these two books resulted from the suggestions of teachers, reading specialists, and coaches who desired to have the student word lists, passages, and student materials from the Early Literacy Assessments in a separate book so it would be easier to manage and use during the administration of the Basic Reading Inventory.

The larger of the two books contains all you need to know to administer, score, and interpret the Basic Reading Inventory. We have devoted our efforts to refining those components that warranted revision, clarification, expansion, and updating. Special thanks to all teachers, colleagues, reading specialists, interventionists, and reading coaches who have offered help, ideas, constructive criticism, and encouragement. Below we highlight the new features of the twelfth edition:

- The largest change involves a redesigned approach to assessing reading in kindergarten and first grade. Because students in kindergarten and first grade are expected to make significant growth in reading, their progress is often documented through a gradient of text levels (e.g., Beaver & Carter, 2011; Fountas & Pinnell, 2010). To support this common practice in many schools, we developed three passages for kindergarten and three passages for first grade in Forms A, B, C, D, and E. These passages correlate with expectations at the beginning, middle, and end of kindergarten and first grade. By providing three passages in kindergarten and three passages in first grade, we seek to help teachers more precisely determine their students' reading levels, enabling progress monitoring, and most importantly, matching students with appropriate texts. There are also three word lists for kindergarten in each of forms A–C.

- Many of the passages throughout the inventory have been replaced, reworked, or updated. Users familiar with the inventory will likely notice many of these changes during administration. A number of questions and answers have also been changed.

- A writing component and a scoring rubric are now provided for every passage to enable you to assess student writing ability. The writing prompts are loosely based on the passages.

- A dedicated website provides many resources beyond those contained in the manual. You will find video clips, a comprehensive bibliography on informal reading inventories, answers to practice exercises, and other helpful resources. Website information and access code is located on the inside back cover of this manual.

- Connections to the common core and an updated Instructional Interventions Grid are provided to help you target instruction based on student needs.

We also want to highlight a few items that can make the Basic Reading Inventory even more useful to you:

- There is a page with tabs in the back of this manual that you can cut out and fasten to the appropriate pages to make finding information easier. Tabs are also provided at the back of the Student Book that can be placed on appropriate pages to more easily locate the word lists, passages, and Early Literacy Assessments.

- Helpful guides for administering the inventory are found inside the front cover and on page 439 of this manual.

The Basic Reading Inventory has seven forms and seven Early Literacy Assessments. A dedicated website contains video clips to help you learn administration procedures, the performance booklets for all seven forms of the inventory, the record booklets for the two forms of the Early Literacy Assessments, numerous summary sheets, answers to practice exercises, and a large annotated bibliography of research and resources related to informal reading inventories.

The twelfth edition makes us thankful for your partnership over the years. We hope you, whether veteran or first-time user, will find the Basic Reading Inventory helpful in your work with all students and especially with those students who find reading difficult. Together, in partnership, we strive to continue helping students strengthen their reading.

Jerry, Laurie, and Beth

PART ONE

Basic Reading Inventory Manual

Overview

High-quality instruction enhances reading achievement.

Making Instruction Responsive

"Effective reading instruction begins with assessment" (Cooter & Perkins, 2007, p. 6). For more than fifty years, the informal reading inventory has been regarded as "the comprehensive assessment instrument of choice" (Walpole & McKenna, 2006, p. 592). With the impact of Reading First (Cummins, 2006), the emphasis on Response to Intervention (RTI) (Fuchs, Fuchs, & Vaughn, 2008), and the Common Core Standards (NGA Center & CCSSO, 2010), there is a need for instructionally helpful diagnostic information. With the new Common Core assessments, Shanahan (2014, p. 186) poses and answers an appropriate question: "Will these new assessments be able to provide the kind of specific diagnostic information that past tests could not? In a word, no."

Informal assessments like the Basic Reading Inventory help to identify students who are struggling in reading. In addition, the Basic Reading Inventory can be used in the progress-monitoring process to assess student performance and growth and diagnose specific weaknesses in word recognition, fluency, and comprehension (Mahdavi & Haager, 2007). Furthermore, the results of the Basic Reading Inventory can serve as the basis for determining appropriate instructional interventions in classrooms, resource rooms, and special education settings. These interventions often focus on the five areas identified by the report of the National Reading Panel (2000): phonemic awareness, phonics, fluency, vocabulary, and comprehension. Table 1.3 on page 8 provides a concise overview of how the Basic Reading Inventory can help assess these five important areas. Allington (2005) and others have added to these five areas. Fink (2006, p. 131), for example, notes that informal reading inventories "can determine both the level and type of instruction likely to be most beneficial for each student." She also stresses that estimates of each student's three reading levels (independent, instructional, and frustration) make "planning instruction easier and more effective" (p. 131). If students are to reach their potential, teachers must provide responsive instruction. A fundamental principle of responsive instruction is attention to individual differences, and teachers are the critical core in making a difference in reading achievement (International Reading Association, 2007). Teachers can differentiate instructional interventions to help students make significant progress in reading. While methods come and go, teachers are the core in providing quality reading instruction that is responsive to their students. Responsive instruction has many qualities, and a fundamental principle is attention to individual differences.

Students have the right to be evaluated with appropriate reading assessments (Bass, Dasinger, Elish-Piper, Matthews, & Risko, 2008). A position statement of the International Reading Association (2000), titled *Making a Difference Means Making It Different*, notes that students "have a right to reading assessment that identifies their strengths as well as their needs . . ." (p. 7). The Basic Reading Inventory is one resource to help gather information for instructional decision making in reading. It can be used to estimate the student's instructional level—the level at which the student is challenged but not overwhelmed. It is the level where the student can profit from reading instruction (Spiegel, 1995). If students are placed in instructional materials where they are able to pronounce approximately 95 percent of the words, they tend to be successful readers who are on task (Adams, 1990). Unfortunately, many students are placed in materials that are too difficult for them (Johnston & Allington, 1991). These students fail to benefit much from lessons using grade-level texts (O'Connor, Bell, Harty, Larkin, Sacker, & Zigmond, 2002).

Responsive instructional interventions are more likely to be provided if teachers can use assessment tools to determine a student's strengths and weaknesses in reading (International Reading Association, 2007; Kibby, 1995). According to Manning (1995), valuable information can be obtained by noting the behaviors of students as they read orally in instructional materials. The Basic Reading Inventory provides one means through which teachers can systematically gain insights into a student's reading. Teachers can study and analyze a student's abilities in word identification, fluency, and comprehension. The information gained can be an important basis for responsive instruction and high-quality instructional decisions. Taylor, Pearson, Clark, and Walpole (2002) noted that systematic assessment of student progress figured prominently in their findings of effective schools. "Assessment practices should enrich teaching and learning" (Tierney, 1998, p. 388). The Basic Reading Inventory can help teachers "to become better informed and make better decisions" (Tierney, 1998, p. 388). Such decisions can be used to help develop individual literacy plans for students (Felknor, 2000), resulting in students becoming more efficient and effective readers.

In an attempt to ensure that all students are effective readers who are college- and career-ready, the Common Core State Standards have been adopted by nearly all of the 50 states (Council of Chief State School Officers & National Governors Association, 2010). These standards will have a significant impact on the field of education in the coming years. The Common Core State Standards for reading are organized as a staircase of increasing difficulty for the fundamental skills of phonics, word recognition, and fluency as well as comprehension skills for both literary (narrative) and informational (expository) texts. These standards align closely with areas assessed by the Basic Reading Inventory.

Components of the Basic Reading Inventory

The Basic Reading Inventory is an individually administered informal reading test. Composed of a series of graded word lists and graded passages, the inventory helps teachers gain insights into students' reading behavior from kindergarten through grade twelve. Inventory results will help support the daily instructional decisions teachers need to make (Farr, 1992; Gillet & Temple, 2000; Gunning, 2006; Johns, 1996; McCormick, 2007; Walker, 2004). Five types of comprehension questions follow each passage at and above the middle of first grade: topic, fact, inference, evaluation, and vocabulary. This section explains the purposes of the Basic Reading Inventory, gives directions for administering and scoring the inventory, and provides concrete assistance for interpreting the findings of the inventory so that the results can be used to improve students' reading. The development of the Basic Reading Inventory is described in Section 6.

There are seven forms (A, B, C, D, E, LL, LI) of the Basic Reading Inventory.

- Forms A, B, and C contain word lists ranging from kindergarten through grade twelve and passages ranging from the kindergarten level through the eighth grade.

- Form D contains passages ranging from kindergarten through eighth grade and is designed specifically for silent reading.

- Form E contains informational (expository) passages ranging from kindergarten through eighth grade.

- Forms LL and LI contain passages of 250 words ranging in difficulty from third grade to twelfth grade.

Table 1.1 contains the code for the seven forms.

Table 1.1

Code of Grade Levels for the Seven Forms of the Basic Reading Inventory

| Grade Level | Form of the Basic Reading Inventory | | | | | | |
	A	B	C	D	E	LL	LI
Beginning K	A Kb	B Kb	C Kb	D Kb	E Kb	—	—
Middle K	A Km	B Km	C Km	D Km	E Km	—	—
End K	A Ke	B Ke	C Ke	D Ke	E Ke	—	—
Beginning 1	A 7141b	B 7141b	C 7141b	D 7141b	E 7141b	—	—
Middle 1	A 7141m	B 7141m	C 7141m	D 7141m	E 7141m	—	—
End 1	A 7141e	B 7141e	C 7141e	D 7141e	E 7141e	—	—
2	A 8224	B 8224	C 8224	D 8224	E 8224	—	—
3	A 3183	B 3183	C 3183	D 3183	E 3183	LL 3183	LI 3183
4	A 5414	B 5414	C 5414	D 5414	E 5414	LL 5414	LI 5414
5	A 8595	B 8595	C 8595	D 8595	E 8595	LL 8595	LI 8595
6	A 6867	B 6867	C 6867	D 6867	E 6867	LL 6867	LI 6867
7	A 3717	B 3717	C 3717	D 3717	E 3717	LL 3717	LI 3717
8	A 8183	B 8183	C 8183	D 8183	E 8183	LL 8183	LI 8183
9	A 4959	B 4959	C 4959	D 4959	E 4959	LL 4959	LI 4959
10	A 1047	B 1047	C 1047	D 1047	E 1047	LL 1047	LI 1047
11	A 1187	B 1187	C 1187	D 1187	E 1187	LL 1187	LI 1187
12	A 1296	B 1296	C 1296	D 1296	E 1296	LL 1296	LI 1296

Kindergarten and First-Grade Levels

There are three passages in Forms A–E for kindergarten and first grade. The kindergarten levels are designated by two upper-case letters and one lower-case letter. The initial capital letter indicates the form. The K indicates that the passage is for kindergarten. The lower-case letters indicate the placement within kindergarten:

- The "b" designates the beginning of kindergarten, the "m" designates middle kindergarten, and the "e" designates the end of kindergarten. For example, A Km refers to the middle of kindergarten in Form A.

For first grade, there are also three passages for each of Form A–E.

- Similar to kindergarten, the lower-case letters indicate beginning, middle, or end of the year for first grade. The capital letter indicates the form, and the two identical numerals in 7141 designate that the passage is at the first-grade level. For example, C 7141e designates a first-grade passage in Form C at the end of the year.

Grade Levels 2–9

For the remaining levels through grade nine, you can determine the grade level of the word list or passage by determining which two numerals are identical.

In Table 1.1, for example, A 8224 indicates that the word list or passage in Form A is at the second-grade level because there are two 2's. The code B 8183 indicates the word list or passage in Form B is at the eighth-grade level because there are two 8's. A similar procedure is followed for the remaining word lists and passages. When two numerals are the same within each grade level, those two numerals represent the grade level.

Grade Levels 10–12

For the word lists and passages at grades ten, eleven, and twelve, the first two numerals indicate the grade level.

BRI Forms

Seven forms of the Basic Reading Inventory are included so that a variety of purposes can be achieved.

- Forms A and B assess and help to monitor the student's oral reading. Teachers often use Form A as an initial assessment. Form B may be used to help monitor progress. It is especially important that students above the primary grades engage in silent reading (see Form D).

- Form C can be used as an initial assessment. It can also be used to help assess growth in reading (progress monitoring). The passages in Form C can also be used for additional oral or silent reading opportunities to better estimate the student's reading levels or to further study the student's reading behavior. This form can also be used to estimate the student's listening level.

- Form D is specifically designed for assessing silent reading. It can help assess the student's ability to read informational (expository) passages at and above grade two.

- Form E is specifically designed for assessing informational (expository) reading.

- Forms LL and LI, because of their length (250 words), permit a more in-depth appraisal of the student's ability to read literary or narrative (LL) and informational or expository (LI) materials. The passages in these two forms may be read orally and/or silently. Each form spans grades three through twelve.

Table 1.2 contains suggestions for how the various forms of the Basic Reading Inventory may be used. This same table can also be found inside the front cover of the student book.

Table 1.2

Uses of Basic Reading Inventory Forms

Form	Primary Uses	Other Uses
A	Oral Reading Initial Assessment	Silent Reading Listening Level
B	Oral Reading Later Assessment	Silent Reading Listening Level Progress Monitoring
C	Oral Reading Initial Assessment	Silent Reading Listening Level Progress Monitoring
D	Silent Reading (Informational*)	Oral Reading Progress Monitoring
E	Oral Reading (Informational*)	Silent Reading Progress Monitoring
LL	Silent Reading (Literary)†	Oral Reading Progress Monitoring
LI	Silent Reading (Informational)†	Oral Reading Progress Monitoring

* beginning with grade two
† longer passages for grades three through twelve

Early Literacy Assessments

Two forms of early literacy assessments are included in Part 3 of this manual. These assessments are especially useful for students who find the easiest word lists and passages difficult and who could be called emergent or beginning readers. Separate Record Booklets for each form, directions, and the following seven assessments are found in Part 3:

1. Alphabet Knowledge
2. Writing
3. Literacy Knowledge
4. Wordless Picture Reading
5. Auditory Discrimination
6. Phoneme Segmentation
7. Phoneme Awareness (Spelling)

Purposes of the Basic Reading Inventory

On the basis of the student's performance on the word lists and graded passages, you can gain insights into the student's:

- **independent reading level**—the level at which the student reads fluently with excellent comprehension.

- **instructional reading level**—the level at which the student can make maximum progress in reading with your instructional guidance.

- **frustration level**—the level at which the student is unable to pronounce many of the words and/or is unable to comprehend the material satisfactorily.

- **strategies for word identification**—you can evaluate the student's sight vocabulary and ability to use phonic analysis, context clues, and structural analysis to pronounce words.

- **fluency**—you can determine the student's rate of reading (in words per minute), assess accuracy in word identification, and make observational judgments about phrasing and expression.

- **strengths and weaknesses in comprehension**—you can evaluate the student's ability to answer various types of comprehension questions.

- **listening level**—you can determine the highest level of material that the student can comprehend when it is read to him or her.

Observations can also be made regarding the student's interests, attitudes, self-monitoring strategies, general approach to various tasks, and reading behavior (such as engagement and persistence). In addition, a new feature includes writing prompts for all of the passages. The use of these prompts is described in Section 2.

Assessing Five Core Components of Reading with the Basic Reading Inventory

The three forms (A, B, and C) of the graded word lists and the seven forms (A, B, C, D, E, LL, and LI) of passages, coupled with two forms of the seven Early Literacy Assessments, can help assess five core components of effective reading instruction identified by the National Reading Panel (2000): phonemic awareness, phonics, fluency, vocabulary, and comprehension. Table 1.3 lists the five core components and identifies the assessments that can be used to assess these areas so that responsive instructional interventions can be provided. A helpful grid of instructional interventions can be found on page 89.

Table 1.3

Core Areas from the National Reading Panel (NRP) Report Keyed to the Basic Reading Inventory (BRI)

NRP Core Area	BRI Early Literacy Assessments (Location in BRI Manual)	BRI Word Lists and Passages (Pages in Student Book)
Phonemic Awareness	Phoneme Segmentation, 376 Phoneme Awareness (Spelling), 377	
Phonics	Auditory Discrimination, 375 Writing, 372	Word Lists: A (2–8), B (24–30), C (46–52) Passages: A (10–22), B (32–44), C (54–66), D (68–80), E (82–94), LL (96–105), LI (108–117)
Fluency		Word Lists: A (2–8), B (24–30), C (46–52) Passages: A (10–22), B (32–44), C (54–66), D (68–80), E (82–94), LL (96–105), LI (108–117)
Vocabulary	Wordless Picture Reading, 374	Passages: A (10–22), B (32–44), C (54–66), D (68–80), E (82–94), LL (96–105), LI (108–117)
Comprehension		Passages: A (10–22), B (32–44), C (54–66), D (68–80), E (82–94), LL (96–105), LI (108–117)

Table 1.3 reveals that the graded word lists and passages provide important information in all areas except phonemic awareness (where there are two Early Literacy Assessments for this purpose). You can observe the student's behavior while reading the word lists and passages and then analyze responses to gain insights. Below is a brief overview of some ways teachers, specialists, and interventionists have used the word lists, passages, and Early Literacy Assessments in the Basic Reading Inventory to assess phonemic awareness, phonics, fluency, vocabulary, and comprehension.

Phonemic Awareness

Refer to "Phoneme Segmentation" and "Phoneme Awareness (Spelling)" in the Early Literacy Assessments for two assessments to gain insights in this area.

Phonics

When miscues are made on the graded word lists and passages, you can note the miscues and analyze them to determine areas for instruction and intervention. See "Determining Word Identification Strategies" in Section 4 of this manual for two ways to analyze the student's miscues in order to gain information about the student's phonic skills. Section 4 also contains some suggestions for instructional interventions. For three additional assessments related to phonics, refer to "Phoneme Awareness (Spelling)," "Alphabet Knowledge," and "Auditory Discrimination" in the Early Literacy Assessments.

Fluency

As a student reads word lists, you can assess the automaticity with which the words are pronounced. If a student has considerable difficulty pronouncing words on a grade-level list, it is quite possible that the student may have difficulty reading the passage at that level in a fluent manner. When the student reads graded passages, you can note phrasing, expression, and automaticity. Rate or speed of reading can also be determined by timing the student's reading and using the oral reading norms that are provided. See "Rate of Reading" in Section 2 of this manual for two ways to determine reading rate and to view norms for oral and silent reading rates. "Fluency Considerations" in Section 4 provides a concise overview of what fluency embodies and offers some instructional interventions to help with several common problems in fluency.

Vocabulary

There are different types of vocabulary. Sight vocabulary refers to words that the student recognizes immediately. As the student reads word lists and passages, you can note if words are mostly recognized at sight.

Meaning vocabulary refers to words that the student understands. You can evaluate the student's ability to answer the V (vocabulary) questions after passages are read as one assessment of meaning vocabulary. The student's responses to the comprehension questions can also be used to evaluate vocabulary. Some students are much more expressive than other students. You can also informally assess the quality of the student's vocabulary when using the retelling strategy.

Comprehension

After the student reads a graded passage, comprehension can be assessed with questions, retelling, or a combination of the two. If you use the questions, there are five different types (topic, fact, inference, experience/evaluation, and vocabulary) and analysis by question type can be done. Another way to analyze comprehension is by lower-level comprehension and higher-level comprehension. Refer to Section 4 in this manual for explanations and examples for conducting these analyses. Appendix A contains different ways to elicit and evaluate passage retellings.

The Basic Reading Inventory contains passages that are literary (narrative/stories) and informational (expository), so you can assess the student's ability to understand these two major types of discourse.

Background Information on Reading Levels and the Listening Level

A major function of the Basic Reading Inventory is to identify a student's three reading levels: independent, instructional, and frustration. The framework of reading levels offers a helpful structure for matching students with texts. You "should use it with the full awareness of its limitations and of additional factors that can lead to variations in reading behaviors" (Halladay, 2012, p. 61). Numerous questions have been raised about standards for evaluating a student's performance on reading inventories (Johns, 1976; 1990a). Although some research (Anderson & Joels, 1986; Johns & Magliari, 1989; Powell, 1971) indicates that the original criteria suggested by Betts (1946) are too high for determining the instructional level for students in the primary grades, other studies (Hays, 1975; Homan & Klesius, 1985; Morris, 1990; Pikulski, 1974) report contradictory findings. Other researchers (Morris, Bloodgood, Perney, Frye, Kucan, Trathen, Ward, & Schlagal, 2011; Morris, Trathen, Frye, Kucan, Ward, Schlagal, & Hendrix, 2013) have offered evidence supporting the traditional Betts criteria. You should remember that the numerical criteria for reading levels are not absolute standards; they are *guidelines* to help you evaluate a student's reading in conjunction with observational data. Each of the three reading levels presented here will be considered from two viewpoints: the teacher's and the student's. The listening level will also be discussed. Note that each reading level is characterized by both quantitative (numerical) and qualitative (behavioral) data.

What Is the Independent Reading Level?

Level	Characteristics	Types of Reading
Independent (Easy)	Excellent comprehension (90%+) Excellent word recognition (99%+) Few or no repetitions Very fluent	All schoolwork and reading expected to be done alone Pleasure reading Informational reading

Student's Viewpoint Because most students have never heard of the various reading levels, they would not refer to the percentages and related behavioral characteristics described below. A student might, however, describe the independent reading level in these terms: "I can read this book by myself, and I understand what I read. I like reading books like this; they're easy."

Teacher's Viewpoint The independent reading level is that level at which the student can read fluently without teacher assistance. In other words, the student can read the materials independently with excellent comprehension. This is the level of supplementary and recreational reading. The material should not cause the student any difficulty. If the student reads orally, the reading should be expressive with accurate attention to punctuation. When reading silently, the student's reading should be free from finger pointing, vocalizing, lip movement, poor phrasing, and other indications of general tension or problems with the reading material.

In order to be considered at the student's independent level, materials should be read with near-perfect accuracy in terms of word recognition. Even in a situation of oral reading at sight, the student should generally not make more than one significant miscue in each 100 running words. With respect to comprehension,

Students enjoy reading at their independent level.

the student's score, when 10 comprehension questions of various types are asked, should be no lower than 90 percent. In short, the student should be able to fully understand the material.

If a retelling strategy is used, a student "will be able to reflect most of the content of a selection and will reflect it in an organized fashion." In a narrative passage, the student will recount events in the proper order. In expository passages, the student's retelling will reflect the text structure or organization of that material. For example, a passage with the main idea followed by supporting details will usually be retold in the same manner (Johnson, Kress, & Pikulski, 1987, p. 14).

It is important that the above criteria for determining a student's independent reading level be applied with careful judgment. The criteria, especially the near-perfect accuracy for word recognition, may have to be a bit more liberal when evaluating a student's reading in grades one and two. The younger reader, for example, may frequently substitute *a* for *the* and vice versa while reading. An older student may omit or substitute a number of words that do not seriously interfere with fluency and/or a good understanding of the passage. Miscues of this nature should be regarded as acceptable; they are not significant. If the teacher has correctly determined the student's independent reading level, the student will experience little difficulty with materials that are written at or below that particular level.

Caution

What Is the Instructional Reading Level?

Level	Characteristics	Types of Reading
Instructional (Just right; comfortable)	Good comprehension (75–85%) Good word recognition (95%+) Fluent A few unknown words Some repetitions	Guided reading Texts used for instruction

Student's Viewpoint A student might describe the instructional level in these terms: "Some of the words are hard, but after the teacher gives me some help, the story is easy to read. I can understand what I am reading."

Teacher's Viewpoint The instructional reading level is that level at which the student can, theoretically, make maximum growth in reading. It is the level at which the student is challenged but not frustrated. Many teachers are interested in finding the student's instructional level so they can provide classroom reading materials at that level (Felknor, Winterscheidt, & Benson, 1999; McTague, 1997). Allington (2005, 2012) considers matching students with materials at their instructional levels critical for students who are behind in reading. This is the level of materials used in guided reading groups. At the instructional level, the student should be free from externally observable symptoms of difficulty, such as finger pointing, produced by the reading materials. Although the student might experience some difficulties when reading classroom materials at sight, most of these difficulties should be overcome after the student has had an opportunity to read the same material silently. In other words, oral rereading should be definitely improved over oral reading at sight. If the student is to make maximum progress from instruction, he or she should encounter no more difficulty in reading materials than can be adequately dealt with through good teaching.

In order to be considered at the student's instructional level, materials should be read with no more than 5 miscues in each 100 words in terms of word recognition. According to Adams (1990, p. 113), "there is evidence that achievement in reading is improved by placement in materials that a student can read orally with a low error rate (2 percent to 5 percent), and that students placed in materials that they read with greater than 5 percent errors tend to be off-task during instruction." Additional research by Berliner (1981), Gambrell, Wilson, and Gantt (1981), and Morris, Trathen, Frye, Kucan, Ward, Schlagal, and Hendrix (2013) also support the 95 percent criterion. In addition, Enz (1989) found that placing students using these standards resulted in greater engagement, higher success rates, and more positive attitudes toward reading. O'Connor, Bell, Harty, Larkin, Sacker, and Zigmond (2002) found that students who read materials at their reading (instructional) level made greater gains in fluency compared to students who read grade-level materials. Although some difficulties will probably arise in word recognition, the student should be able to use contextual cues, phonics, and other strategies to decode most unknown words. In terms of comprehension, the student should miss fewer than 3 of 10 comprehension questions.

If a retelling strategy is used, a student responding to instructional level materials will "reflect less content than at an independent level. The organization of the passage will be less complete and some minor misinterpretations and inaccuracies may begin to appear." In essence, the student is able to share the overall sense and content of the passage (Johnson, Kress, & Pikulski, 1987, p. 17).

It is at the instructional level that the student will have the best opportunity to build new reading strategies and solidify those skills and strategies already taught. This is the level at which guided reading instruction is likely to be most successful (Lenski, 1998). Teachers need to be sure that books used for reading instruction are at students' instructional levels (Burkins & Croft, 2010).

To summarize, "a number of studies have demonstrated that texts used for instruction that can be read with at least 95% accuracy produce greater gains [in reading] than harder texts," and we recommend that the traditional oral reading accuracy of 95% or higher be used by teachers (Allington, McCuiston, & Billen, 2015, p. 499).

What Is the Frustration Level?

Level	Characteristics	Types of Reading
Frustration (Too hard)	Weak comprehension (≤50%) Weak word recognition (≤90%) Word-by-word reading Many unknown words Rate is likely to be slow Lack of expression Fluency lacking Fidgeting	Materials for some diagnostic purposes Avoid instructional materials at this level Occasional self-selected material when interest and background knowledge are high

Student's Viewpoint Because reading materials at this level are too difficult for the student, it is likely that the frustration level would be described in these terms: "This book is too hard. I hate to read when books are this hard. I hardly know any of the words." Other students will say nothing when books are too difficult for them to read, but the perceptive teacher will note when books are at a student's frustration level. The teacher can then provide or suggest other materials that are at the student's independent or instructional levels.

Teacher's Viewpoint The frustration level is that level at which the student should not be given materials to read. A serious problem in many classrooms is that a large number of students are asked to read books at their frustration levels (Allington, 2012). Students at their frustration levels are unable to deal effectively with the reading material. Numerous behavioral characteristics may be observed if students are attempting to read materials that are too difficult for them. Some students may actually refuse to continue reading their books. Other students may exhibit lack of expression in oral reading, lip movement during silent reading, difficulty in pronouncing words, word-by-word reading, and/or finger pointing. A study by Jorgenson (1977) found that as reading material became more difficult, teachers judged their students as becoming more impatient, disturbing to the classroom, and reliant on persons other than themselves for directions.

The criteria for the frustration level, in addition to the behavioral characteristics just noted, are 10 or more miscues in every 100 words (90 percent or less) and comprehension scores of 50 percent or less. For example, a student who could not correctly pronounce 90 or more words in a 100-word selection and who could not answer at least half of the questions asked by the teacher is likely trying to read material that is too difficult.

If a retelling strategy is used, "materials at a frustration level are recalled incompletely or in a rather haphazard fashion. Bits of information may be recalled, but they are not related in any logical or sequential order." Questions asked by the teacher tend to go unanswered. In addition, behaviors such as finger pointing and tenseness may appear (Johnson, Kress, & Pikulski, 1987, p. 20).

What Is the Listening Level?

The listening level is the *highest* level at which the student can understand material that is read *to* him or her. Determining this level can help you ascertain whether a student has the potential to improve as a reader. When a substantial difference exists between the student's instructional level and listening level (generally a year or more), it usually indicates that the student should be able to make significant growth in reading achievement with appropriate instruction. The larger the difference, the more reason for you to believe that the student can profit from instruction that is responsive to the student's needs in reading. Many students who struggle with reading can improve if they are given quality instruction, placed in reading materials at their instructional levels, and have their progress monitored regularly.

The criterion for the listening level are a minimum comprehension score of at least 70 percent. In other words, the student should miss no more than 3 of 10 comprehension questions. It is also important for you to informally assess whether the student's vocabulary and language structure in conversations are as complex as that used in the reading passage.

Schell (1982), after reviewing several studies relating to the listening level, cautioned teachers not to use the procedure with students in grades one through three. He argued that reading comprehension and listening comprehension are not the same for students in the primary grades; moreover, neither grow at approximately equal rates until about sixth grade. For these reasons, you should not use the listening level procedure with students in the primary grades.

`Caution`

Preparation for Assessment

Understand the Procedures

To prepare for assessment, you first need to be familiar with the procedures for administering and scoring the Basic Reading Inventory. These procedures are fully discussed and explained in Section 2. What is needed for assessment? There are four basic items:

1. This manual or the summary of administration and scoring procedures on page 47 or inside the front cover of this manual.

2. The separate student book containing the word lists and passages (and seven Early Literacy Assessments).

3. A performance booklet in which you will record the student's responses. These performance booklets are in this manual and on the website.

4. A desk or table and two chairs located in an area reasonably free from excessive noise and distractions. If you are right-handed, seat the student to your left. If you are left-handed, do the opposite.

Selecting Word Lists and Passages

The student will read from selected pages in the separate student book. To aid in locating word lists and passages, consult the Quick Reference Guide printed on the inside front cover of the student book. You may want to attach the pre-printed tabs found in the back of the student book at the beginning of the word lists and passages to help locate the different forms.

While the student reads, you record the student's performance and make notes on the graded word lists and the graded passages in a performance booklet.

Permission is granted to users of the Basic Reading Inventory to reproduce all, or any part, of the seven performance booklets that follow the student copies of the reading inventory. These performance booklets are also on the website.

The validity of a student's performance on the Basic Reading Inventory is related to how completely and accurately you are able to record the student's reading performance and answers to the comprehension questions. An audio or digital recorder is recommended as a method of self-checking until your recording of the student's performance becomes automatic and swift.

Brief Overview of Administration and Scoring Procedures

To evaluate a student's reading, it is recommended that you administer the reading tests included in the Basic Reading Inventory in the following manner. More detailed directions and examples can be found in Section 2.

Word Recognition in Isolation

Select a graded word list at a reading level in the student book that will be easy for the student. Ask the student to pronounce the words at a comfortable rate. Record the student's responses in the sight column beside the corresponding word in the performance booklet. If the student miscalls a word and immediately corrects it, the recommended procedure is to put a plus (+) in the analysis column with a "sc" (self-correction) notation.

Return to mispronounced or unknown words for a second attempt and note the student's responses in the analysis column. Administer successive word lists until the student is no longer able to achieve a total of at least 14 words correct or until the student becomes frustrated. Examples of student and teacher copies of word lists are shown in Figure 1-1. To view the student copies of the word lists, consult the Quick Reference Guide printed on the inside front cover of the student book.

Scoring Word Recognition in Isolation

Total the correct responses in the sight and analysis columns. Consult the criteria in the scoring guide at the bottom of the word lists in the performance booklet to determine a rough estimate of the reading level achieved on each graded word list. Record the number-correct scores and the reading levels in the Word Recognition, Isolation column on the summary sheet of the performance booklet. See page 26 for a partially completed summary sheet example.

Figure 1-1 (Left) Sample Student Copy of Graded Word Lists from Student Book; (Right) Sample Teacher Copy of Word Lists from Performance Booklet

List A 7141		List A 8224	
1. here		1. ten	
2. down		2. poor	
3. then		3. city	
4. how		4. teacher	
5. saw		5. turn	
6. pocket		6. fight	
7. hello		7. because	
8. aunt		8. soft	
9. never		9. open	
10. puppy		10. winter	
11. could		11. joke	
12. after		12. different	
13. hill		13. say	
14. men		14. quiet	
15. gone		15. sister	
16. ran		16. above	
17. gave		17. seed	
18. or		18. thought	
19. way		19. such	
20. coat		20. chase	

List A 7141 (Grade 1)	Sight	Analysis	List A 8224 (Grade 2)	Sight	Analysis
1. here*	_____	_____	1. ten*	_____	_____
2. down*	_____	_____	2. poor	_____	_____
3. then*	_____	_____	3. city	_____	_____
4. how*	_____	_____	4. teacher	_____	_____
5. saw*	_____	_____	5. turn*	_____	_____
6. pocket	_____	_____	6. fight	_____	_____
13. hill	_____	_____	13. say*	_____	_____
14. men	_____	_____	14. quiet	_____	_____
15. gone*	_____	_____	15. sister	_____	_____
16. ran*	_____	_____	16. above	_____	_____
17. gave*	_____	_____	17. seed	_____	_____
18. or*	_____	_____	18. thought*	_____	_____
19. way	_____	_____	19. such	_____	_____
20. coat	_____	_____	20. chase	_____	_____

*denotes high-frequency word from Revised Dolch List

Number Correct _____ _____

Total _____

*denotes high-frequency word from Revised Dolch List

Number Correct _____ _____

Total _____

Scoring Guide for Graded Word Lists			
Independent	Instructional	Inst./Frust.	Frustration
20 19	18 17 16	15 14	13 or less

Word Recognition in Context (Passages)

Ask the student to read aloud the graded passage **one level below** the highest independent level achieved on the graded word lists. As the student reads the passage from the student book, record miscues on the corresponding copy of the passage found in the performance booklet. A miscue occurs when the student's oral reading of a passage differs from the printed passage. For example, a miscue results if the student says *wood* when the word in the passage is *good*. Substituting *wood* for *good* is called a miscue. Other major types of miscues are omissions, insertions, and mispronunciations. A suggested method for recording a student's miscues can be found in Figure 2-3 on page 28. Examples of student and teacher passages are shown in Figure 1-2 on page 16. To view the student copies of the passages, consult the Quick Reference Guide printed on the inside front cover of the student book.

Scoring Word Recognition in Context (Passages)

To find the word recognition in context score, count the number of miscues (total or significant) in each graded passage in the performance booklet and record the numeral in the appropriate box (total or significant). To determine reading levels, consult the appropriate set of criteria in the scoring guide at the bottom of the passage in the performance booklet. Then record the number of miscues and the corresponding reading levels in the Word Recognition, Context column on the summary sheet of the performance booklet.

Sample Student Copy

B 8224

Bill at Camp

It was the first time Bill went to camp. He was very happy to be there. Soon he went for a walk in the woods to look for many kinds of leaves. He found leaves from some maple and oak trees. As Bill walked in the woods, he saw some animal tracks. At that moment, a mouse ran into a small hole by a tree. Bill wondered if the tracks were made by the mouse. He looked around for other animals. He did not see any. The last thing Bill saw was an old bird nest in a pine tree.

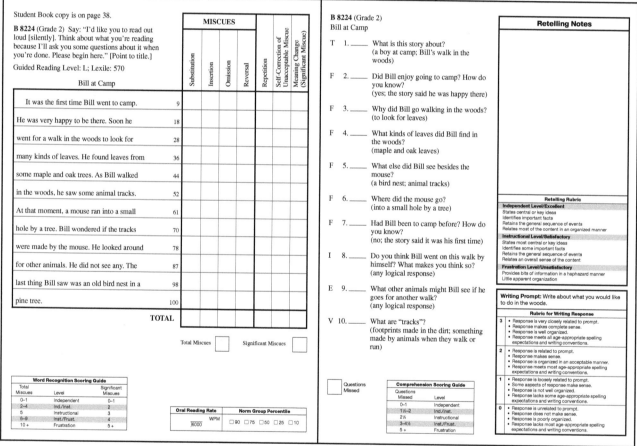

Sample Teacher Copy of Graded Passage   Sample Teacher Copy of Comprehension Questions

Comprehension Questions

Ask the comprehension questions that accompany the passage in the performance booklet and record the student's responses. Continue administering graded passages until the student is unable to answer half of the comprehension questions or makes so many miscues that frustration is apparent. Also, watch for behaviors associated with frustration: lack of expression, word-by-word reading, excessive fidgeting, and so on. **Discontinue assessment when frustration is evident.**

Scoring the Comprehension Questions

To find the student's comprehension score for each passage, count the number of comprehension questions answered incorrectly. Then record the numeral in the box provided.

To convert the comprehension scores into reading levels, consult the criteria on the scoring guide at the bottom of the page in the performance booklet. Then record the number of questions missed and the corresponding reading levels for oral and silent reading in the appropriate Comprehension columns on the summary sheet of the performance booklet.

You must exercise judgment at the kindergarten and first-grade levels because the limited number of questions may not permit precise measurement of achievement. At this level, a retelling of the passage by the student instead of the comprehension questions may be a better indicator of the student's reading ability.

`Caution`

How to Use This Manual

Those who have limited knowledge of reading inventories will profit by reading Sections 1–4 in the manual carefully. It is written to permit self-study and includes numerous practice exercises.

If you are already familiar with reading inventories, read sections of interest and use the remainder of the manual as needed. Because reading inventories differ in their orientation, Sections 3 and 4 may be especially helpful.

Working with a colleague can be helpful in learning how to use the BRI.

Guide to Understanding the Basic Reading Inventory*

Your comprehension can often be enhanced by posing questions about the Basic Reading Inventory manual *before* you actually begin reading it. With this in mind, the following tips are suggested as you read Sections 2–4 of this manual:

1. Read the questions for each section.

2. Look for the answers to the questions as you read the section.

3. Make a notation when you discover an answer for one of the questions (write notes in the margin or tag the page).

Keep in mind that the answers to *all* of these questions are explicitly stated in the text. That is, answers are "right there." Nonetheless, for some of them you might have to "think and search" because the answers may be in separate sentences or paragraphs.

Questions to Aid Understanding of the Basic Reading Inventory

Section 2

Graded Word Lists

1. What can be gained by establishing rapport?

2. What are five purposes for administering the graded word lists?

3. Why do you need to use the graded word lists with caution?

4. What do you need to administer the graded word lists?

5. What are the two scores that can be derived from the graded word lists?

6. How many word lists do you have the student read?

Graded Passages (Oral Reading)

1. What is a miscue?

2. How are miscues recorded?

3. Why might a warm-up passage be helpful?

4. With which passage should you begin?

5. What is your major task while the student reads?

6. What do you do after the student finishes reading a passage?

7. How accurate do responses to comprehension questions need to be?

8. When should you have the student stop reading the passages?

*Shared by Michael F. Opitz and adapted with permission. From Jerry L. Johns, Laurie Elish-Piper, and Beth Johns, *Basic Reading Inventory* (12th ed.). Copyright © 2017 by Kendall Hunt Publishing Company (1-800-247-3458, ext. 6). May be reproduced for noncommercial educational purposes. Website: www.kendallhunt.com

Determining Reading Levels from the Word Recognition in Context Scores

1. What do you need to consider as you go about determining a student's three reading levels?
2. How is a student's word recognition score found?
3. What are *significant* miscues?
4. How should you count significant miscues on the kindergarten and first-grade passages?
5. How is the percentage found?

Determining Reading Levels from the Comprehension Questions

1. What is the comprehension score?
2. How is the comprehension score derived?
3. How is the comprehension score determined for the kindergarten and first-grade passages?

Determining Reading Levels from Silent Reading

1. Explain which passage should be used to begin silent reading.
2. What do you do as the student reads silently?
3. What do you do after the passage has been read?
4. What is the student asked to reread orally?
5. What does the oral rereading enable you to assess?
6. How many passages does the student read?

Determining Rate of Reading

1. Where would you find the formula for determining a student's rate of reading?
2. What is the other way to determine a student's rate of reading?
3. How many words per minute (WPM) would the average third grader read orally in the fall of the year?
4. What would be an estimate of a third grader's silent reading rate?

Determining Listening Level

1. What does a student's listening level convey?
2. What procedure do you use to determine a student's listening level?
3. What are some limitations for using the listening level as an indicator of reading potential?

Section 3

1. Is it possible for some students to have a range of several grades within the instructional level?
2. What should you use when making decisions about students' reading levels?
3. Are the reading levels determined by using this inventory entirely accurate?

Section 4

Determining Strengths and Weaknesses in Word Identification

1. What are some questions that can be used to guide your analysis?
2. What is Advanced Qualitative Analysis and how can it be used?

Determining Strengths and Weaknesses in Comprehension

1. What are some questions you can use to assess the student's comprehension?
2. What are five types of comprehension questions used in the BRI?
3. What is Analysis by Question Type and how can it be used?

Fluency Considerations

1. What are the four components of fluency?
2. What is probably the most important foundation for fluency?
3. What are some factors that can impact fluency?

Administration
and Scoring Procedures

Working closely with students helps teachers build rapport.

Because the Basic Reading Inventory is an informal test, there is no set of procedures that must be followed rigidly. You must, nevertheless, be thoroughly familiar with the recommended procedures for administration prior to asking a student to read the graded word lists and passages. The Basic Reading Inventory will take longer to administer initially until greater familiarity with the procedures is achieved. After you are comfortable with the procedures, the inventory flows smoothly and will take less time to administer. Facility improves greatly after five or six administrations.

Before giving the Basic Reading Inventory, it is helpful to have a general idea of the student's reading ability. You can gather this information by:

- consulting the student's cumulative record from the previous year to note the level at which the student was reading.

- noting the student's reading performance in the classroom.

- examining the results of other reading assessments.

- conferring with colleagues who may have potentially helpful insights.

Regardless of the method used to decide where to begin administration of the inventory, it is important that the student experiences success with the initial graded word lists and passages. You should begin administering the inventory at a level where the student is likely to find the material easy.

The recommended procedure for administering and scoring the reading inventory is given in this section. Frequently asked questions along with answers are provided at the end of the section.

Establishing Rapport and Gaining Insights

View Laurie (teacher) establishing rapport with Jimmy (student) on the website.

If the reading inventory is to yield valid, reliable, and useful results, it is necessary to obtain the student's cooperation. In an effort to establish rapport, you may wish to give the student some idea about how his or her reading will be evaluated. You may also want to explore the student's interests and answer questions about the assessment procedure. This brief discussion may help to reduce the anxiety that often accompanies an assessment. Remember that rapport is not always fully established before the administration of a reading inventory begins. In some cases, rapport is steadily increased throughout the assessment. In other cases, interaction between you and the student may become strained during the assessment. If this occurs, make efforts to reestablish rapport.

During the early stages of establishing rapport, as well as throughout the administration of the reading inventory, you have the opportunity to gain valuable diagnostic information in several areas. You can appraise the student's oral language, vocabulary, and background knowledge through informal conversation and observe how well the student responds to specific comprehension questions that are asked after the graded passages are read. You may also gain insight into how the student attempts to decode unknown words by asking, "What do you do when you come to unknown words?" or "What did you do to finally figure out that word?" Questions such as, "What is reading?" and "What do you do when you read?" may give you insights into how the student views the reading process. When you feel that adequate rapport has been established, it is generally advisable to begin the reading inventory with the graded word lists.

Some students, especially young ones or readers who struggle, may become tired during the administration of the inventory. In such instances, "refresher" breaks can be used or the assessment can be spread over two periods. For example, the graded word lists can be given during one sitting and the graded passages can be given at another sitting. Because the graded word lists and passages increase in difficulty, it is permissible to explain this fact to the student before assessment begins. Some teachers encourage students to say "pass," "skip it," "not yet," or "I don't know" when difficult words or questions are encountered.

Graded Word Lists

There are at least five reasons for giving the graded word lists:

- First, the word lists will provide the approximate level at which the student should begin reading the graded paragraphs.

- Second, you will be able to study some of the student's word identification strategies such as structural analysis and phonics.

- Third, the word lists can be used to informally classify the student's word recognition ability as above, at, or below grade level.

- Fourth, you can assess the extent of the student's sight vocabulary and knowledge of high-frequency words. Many of the words on lists from kindergarten and first grade are high-frequency words.

- Fifth, you can use the easiest word list to determine if a student has some ability to pronounce words or to help decide if the Early Literacy Assessments in Part 3 are more likely to provide helpful information.

High-frequency words on the graded word lists are indicated with an asterisk (*). These words are found on the Revised Dolch List (Johns & Lenski, 2014) and comprise over 50 percent of the running words found in all types of printed materials.

Because the word lists are not a natural reading situation, exercise extreme caution. In addition, you cannot examine all word identification strategies through the student's performance on the graded word lists. Phonics, structural analysis, and sight vocabulary are the three most common areas that can be observed. Because the words are presented in isolation, it is not possible to explore the student's overall word identification strategies and the balance between phonics and context. All aspects of a student's word identification repertoire, however, deserve careful attention, because they can provide potential insights for instruction. The best judgments about the student's word identification strategies result from a careful analysis of the student's oral reading of the graded passages coupled with insights from the graded word lists.

The graded word lists do not assess the student's ability to comprehend and are, therefore, an inappropriate measure of overall reading ability. Goodman (1965) has demonstrated that students decode much more readily when words appear in context than when they appear in lists. Also, Marzano and others (1978) have cautioned teachers about basing assessment solely on a word recognition test.

Administering Graded Word Lists

To administer the graded word lists, you will need the word lists in the student book and the performance booklet in which the student's responses will be recorded. The recommended procedure for administering the graded word lists is to present the student with the graded list of words and ask him or her to pronounce them at a comfortable rate. If a student reads a word correctly within one second, it is defined as a sight word (Leslie & Caldwell, 1995). Morris (2015), however, suggests exposing each word individually for half a second. As the student reads down each list of words, you should record the student's responses in a performance booklet. The word list initially selected should, if at all possible, be very easy for the student (i.e., at the student's independent level).

View Laurie (teacher) administering a fourth-grade word list to Elyse (student) on the website.

It is important for you to note and record the student's responses promptly because any delays are likely to result in incorrect reporting. The use of an audio or digital recorder may prove quite helpful so you can review the accuracy of your notations during your first few administrations. The graded word lists are continued until the student is no longer able to achieve a total score of at least 14 correct words or when you observe that the task has become frustrating for the student. Your judgment plays an important role in the administration of the entire inventory. At the kindergarten level, note that the limited number of words on those lists makes it more difficult to reach a decision about the appropriateness of the score.

Scoring Graded Word Lists

Three scores are derived for each graded word list administered to the student (see Figure 2-1). One score represents the student's immediate responses to the words and is called the *sight* score. The second score represents the student's correction of any words missed during the sight presentation or words immediately self-corrected during the initial attempt. The opportunity for the student to study each word missed in an attempt to pronounce it is called the *analysis* score. If the student does not know or mispronounces any words on the first attempt without immediate self-correction (that is, at sight), you should return to each of these words after the student has finished the list and provide the student with an opportunity to analyze the word in an attempt to arrive at its correct pronunciation. The student's *immediate* responses are recorded in the sight column. The responses the student makes when given an opportunity to study the words missed are recorded in the analysis column. The third score is the total of the sight and analysis scores. The total score can be used as a rough indicator of reading levels at and above first grade.

Scoring Jeff's Graded Word Lists

To show how the graded word lists are scored, Figure 2-1 contains Jeff's performance on the first- and second-grade word lists. An empty space next to a word means that Jeff pronounced it correctly. Some teachers put a plus (+) or check mark (✓) for each correct word, because it lessens students' perceptions of when they get a word wrong. Miscues in word recognition are noted as follows: "DK" indicates that he said "I don't know." Single letters or phonetic symbols represent Jeff's attempt to pronounce the word. The plus (+) in the analysis column indicates that he corrected a miscalled word. When Jeff said a word which was different from the stimulus word, it is noted in the appropriate column. In the sight column, the "sc" indicates that the word was self-corrected immediately. A plus is then placed in the analysis column. Other pertinent comments that might have diagnostic significance (for example, skips unknown words; uses phonic knowledge; knows high-frequency words; quite persistent; gives up easily) can also be noted.

Jeff's scores are shown at the bottom of each column of words. For the first grade word list, the score of 15 indicates that he correctly pronounced 15 of the 20 words on the sight presentation. These 15 words were known automatically. The 5 words not correctly pronounced during the sight presentation were numbers 3, 8, 12, 17, and 18. From his score on the *analysis* column, you can note that Jeff corrected 4 of his initial miscues (numbers 3, 8, and 12), thereby achieving a total score of 19 correct words. (Word 17 was immediately self-corrected, so a + was put in the analysis column.) At the second-grade level, Jeff achieved a score of 15 on the sight presentation and a total score of 18 because he corrected 3 (numbers 2, 11, and 14) of his initial miscues.

You can use the total number of words Jeff correctly pronounced on each graded word list for a very rough estimate of his reading levels. To convert total scores to a rough estimate of the various reading levels, compare the total number of correct words for each list of words to the scoring guide at the bottom of the word lists in the performance booklet. This scoring guide is also reproduced in Table 2.1. This scoring guide is used at and above first grade. At the kindergarten level, your judgment must be used; refer to the Qualitative Analysis of Word List Responses for the kindergarten lists in the performance booklet.

Table 2.1

Scoring Guide for Graded Word Lists

Independent	Instructional	Inst./Frust.	Frustration
20 19	18 17 16	15 14	13 or less

Determining Reading Levels—Graded Word Lists

From Jeff's responses in Figure 2-1, note that he achieved a total score of 19 correct words on the first-grade list. According to the scoring guide below the word lists, a score of 19 would indicate an independent level. The total score of 18 for the second-grade word list indicates an instructional level. From the results reported thus far, it is not possible to estimate Jeff's frustration level. You would need to continue with additional word lists until Jeff mispronounced 7 words, appeared to be having considerable difficulty, or was extremely slow in pronouncing the words. When this point is reached, you would stop administering the graded word lists and proceed to the graded passages. Keep in mind that reading levels estimated with word lists represent only rough indications of reading ability. The inadequacies of graded word lists are recognized by teachers, specialists, and interventionists who know that some students can identify words in isolation that cause difficulty in reading materials. Other students who have difficulty with words in isolation can identify words in reading materials. It is important, therefore, to recognize the

Figure 2-1 Jeff's Performance on Two Graded Word Lists

Form B • Graded Word Lists • Performance Booklet • Student Book copy is on page 25.

List B 7141 (Grade 1)	Sight	Analysis	List B 8224 (Grade 2)	Sight	Analysis
1. little*			1. feel		
2. next*			2. drink	*drank*	+
3. reads	*read*	+	3. wave		
4. my*			4. gray		
5. make*			5. start*		
6. old*			6. horn		
7. mother			7. across*		
8. bed	*bad*	+	8. warm*		
9. grow*			9. bad		
10. laugh			10. even*		
11. near*			11. feed	*fed*	+
12. before*	*bef-*	+	12. always*		
13. lamb			13. round*		
14. ride			14. country	*county*	+
15. store			15. enough*		
16. high*			16. able		
17. began*	*begin* SC	+	17. should*		
18. made*	*make*	*make*	18. bottom	*bo-*	*bot-*
19. cry			19. crawl		
20. her*			20. machine	*DK*	*machine*

*denotes high-frequency word from Revised Dolch List   *denotes high-frequency word from Revised Dolch List

Number Correct   _15_   _4_   Number Correct   _15_   _3_

Total   _19_   Total   _18_

Scoring Guide for Graded Word Lists			
Independent	Instructional	Inst./Frust.	Frustration
20 19	18 17 16	15 14	13 or less

limitations of graded word lists and to use this knowledge when scoring and interpreting inventory results.

✎ Recording Jeff's Word Recognition Scores for Graded Word Lists

Figure 2-1 shows that Jeff achieved a **total** score of 19 on the first-grade list and 18 on the second-grade list. These scores should then be entered on the summary sheet similar to that shown in Figure 2-2 and reproduced on the cover of the performance booklets for Forms A, B, C, D, and E. To determine the reading levels corresponding to these two scores, consult Table 2.1 or the scoring guide at the bottom of the word lists. Using these criteria, Jeff achieved an independent level on the first-grade word list and an instructional level on the second-grade word list. Note that the abbreviations *Ind.* and *Inst.* are written on the summary sheet to indicate the levels achieved.

You should check your understanding of this procedure by finding the reading levels that correspond to Jeff's performance on the third- through fifth-grade word lists as noted in Figure 2-2. This task can be accomplished by taking the total score given in Figure 2-2 for the third-grade word list (20) and finding the corresponding reading level from the scoring guide (Table 2.1 on page 24). The reading level should then be entered next to the number of words correct. This procedure can be repeated for the scores on the fourth-grade and fifth-grade word lists.

Graded Passages

Prior to actually administering the graded passages, you must develop some system for recording the student's responses. There are numerous systems and techniques for coding reading miscues (Barr, Blachowicz, Bates, Katz, & Kaufman, 2007; Block, 2003; Gillet, Temple, & Crawford, 2004; Goodman, Watson, & Burke, 1987; Gunning, 2006; Jennings, Caldwell, & Lerner, 2006; Johnson, Kress, & Pikulski, 1987; Manzo & Manzo, 1993; McCormick, 2007; McKenna & Stahl, 2003). A miscue is "an oral reading response that differs from the expected response to the written text" (Harris & Hodges, 1981, p. 199). Miscues "provide a rich source of information for analyzing language and reading development" (Harris & Hodges, 1995, p. 155). Figure 2-3 on page 28 contains examples of miscues and a suggested method for recording them during oral reading. You should carefully study and learn or adapt the suggested procedure so that it can be used and referred to later when actual examples of a student's oral reading are presented.

TIP **It is generally recommended to begin administering the graded passages at least one level below the student's highest independent level on the graded word lists.** If a student, for

Figure 2-2 Summary Sheet for Jeff's Performance on the Basic Reading Inventory

Grade	Word Recognition						Comprehension	
	Isolation (Word Lists)				Context (Passages)		Form B	
	Sight	Analysis	Total	Level	Miscues*	Level	Questions Missed	Level
1	15	4	19/20	*Ind.*	0	*Ind.*	0	
2	15	3	18/20	*Inst.*	5		1½	
3	16	4	20/20		2		0	
4	14	2	16/20		5		2½	
5	9	2	11/20		10		5	

*Refers to *total* miscues in this example

example, achieved independent levels on the word lists at the first- and second-grade levels, it is recommended that you select a graded passage at the first-grade level. If the student is unable to read that passage at the independent level, go to the next lower level and continue to move down until an independent level is found or a kindergarten passage is reached. Then return to the starting point and proceed until the student reaches a frustration level. In the event that a kindergarten passage is too difficult for the student to read, selected Early Literacy Assessments in Part 3 may be used.

Administering Graded Passages

Select a graded passage in the student book. Do not describe what the passage is about or explain key concepts, because the student's comprehension may be artificially enhanced. Use the instructions on the performance booklet page to introduce the passage. Note that the instructions for the student vary slightly according to the grade level.

> View Laurie (teacher) administering a third-grade passage to Elyse (student) on the website.

- For kindergarten through the end of first-grade passages, the general directions are as follows: Point to each word in the title as you read it. Then say: "Read this story about a _____. I'll ask you some questions about it when you're done."

- For grade 2 and above, the general directions are as follows: Say: "I'd like you to read out loud [silently]. Think about what you're reading because I'll ask you some questions about it when you're done. Please begin here." [Point to title.]

Recording Miscues during Oral Reading and Timing the Reading

While the student is reading from the graded passage in the student book, use a performance booklet to keep a careful record of the exact way in which the student reads the passage. Some students may need to be told a word if they pause for more than five seconds; however, the recommended procedure is to encourage students to read the graded passages using their own strategies for word identification without any assistance. The suggested method for recording a student's oral reading, presented in Figure 2-3, should be a valuable aid for anyone who has not yet developed a system for recording. Your major task is to record the manner in which the student reads the passage by noting omissions, insertions, substitutions, and other miscues. In addition, note hesitations, word-by-word reading, finger pointing, monitoring strategies, and so on. If desired, time the student's reading

A careful record is kept of the student's oral reading.

using a stopwatch or a watch with a second hand. There is a place in the performance booklet to note the number of seconds it takes the student to read passages at and above the middle of first grade. Performing division will result in the student's rate of reading in words per minute (WPM). Any timing should be done in an inconspicuous manner because some students, if they see they are being timed, do not read in their usual way. In addition, some students may focus more on pronouncing words quickly than trying to understand the passage (Johns, 2007). Further discussion of how to determine rate of reading is found under Rate of Reading on page 40.

`Caution`

Figure 2-3 A Suggested Method for Recording a Student's Oral Reading Miscues

SUBSTITUTIONS

Jim saw ~~the~~ boy. *(a above "the")*

OMISSIONS

Poor little ~~Baby~~ Bear could not move from the tall tree.

INSERTIONS

He strolled along the path and soon ^he was deep in the forest.

REVERSALS

Are they twins? *(Are / they reversal marks)*

REPETITIONS

A. Plain repetition

Jim saw a bear. *(underlined: a bear)*

B. Correcting a miscue

Baby Bear did not know where he was. *(Ⓒ see above "know")*

C. Abandoning a correct word said correctly initially

He stayed alone in the pine tree all night. *(Ⓐⓒ along above "alone")*

D. Unsuccessfully attempting to correct an intial miscue (attempts are numbered)

He had slept hard all night. *(Ⓤⓒ 1. heavy 2. ha- above "hard")*

ADDITIONAL MARKINGS

A. partial words

The hunters rescued the boys. *(res- above "rescued")*

B. Nonword substitutions

people on the frontier had shooting contests. *($ frontmer above "frontier")*

C. Punctuation ignored

. . . from some maple and oak trees⌄As Bill

D. Intonation

He played a record that was his favorite. *(rē´cord above "record")*

E. Word pronounced by examiner

Men on the frontier often had shooting contests. *(p above "frontier")*

F. Dialect

He went home. *(ⓓ goed above "went")*

G. Lip movement

place LM in margin

H. Finger pointing

place FP above word

I. Vocalization

place V in text

From Jerry L. Johns, Laurie Elish-Piper, and Beth Johns, *Basic Reading Inventory* (12th ed.). Copyright © 2017 by Kendall Hunt Publishing Company (1-800-247-3458, ext. 6). May be reproduced for noncommercial educational purposes. Website: www.kendallhunt.com

Four Ways to Assess Comprehension

After the student finishes reading the passage, assess comprehension by asking the comprehension questions, integrating the concept of engagement with the questions, using retelling, or combining retelling with the questions. Initially, you may prefer to ask the comprehension questions, at least in the first several administrations of the reading inventory.

Ask Comprehension Questions. Each reading passage above the beginning first-grade level contains 10 comprehension questions of various types: topic, fact, inference, experience/evaluation, and vocabulary. The general procedure is to ask the student the comprehension questions and write the student's verbatim responses to the comprehension questions or underline the "answers" given in the performance booklets. Noting the student's responses will make scoring the questions much easier. You will also be able to analyze the reasoning used by the student. **The student's answers to the comprehension questions need not conform exactly to the answers in the performance booklets;** responses similar in meaning to the printed answer should be scored as correct. In addition, some students may need to be told that the answers to some questions (vocabulary, evaluation, and inference) are not stated directly in the passage. For these questions, always give credit for responses that demonstrate understanding and/or logical thinking. **"Answers" in parentheses that are separated by semicolons mean that only one of the answers must be given for full credit (unless indicated otherwise).** When you ask the first question, some student's responses will answer one or more subsequent questions. When this occurs, mark those questions correct without asking them.

Do not help the student arrive at the correct answers to the questions (use a + for questions answered correctly). If a comprehension question is answered incorrectly (use a –), note the student's response and go on to the next question. You may, however, ask for clarification if the answer for a particular question is not clear. Neutral probes such as "Tell me more," "What else?" or "Explain that further" often help students elaborate on partial answers. Half credit (use ½) may be given for partial answers. Some students might look back in the text for answers to questions. Allowing look-backs may provide useful information about the student's inability to remember what was read. Such look-backs can be noted on the appropriate record sheet in the performance booklet. You may wish to code such look-backs next to the corresponding question with an L and give half credit when correct. Look-backs are seldom used in the primary grades; in the middle and upper grades, look-backs become more frequent, especially for the factual questions. We suggest several approaches and considerations for look-backs:

- You could use the comprehension score without look-backs to calculate the student's score, especially in determining whether that passage is at the student's instructional level.

- Generally, look-backs that result in the correct answer should be given half credit. Five or more look-backs in a single passage may be an informal indication that the student is having difficulty remembering the passage content.

- For the passages in grades nine and above, it may be appropriate to use comprehension scores with look-backs to determine the student's instructional level (Leslie & Caldwell, 2011).

Continue with subsequent passages until the student is unable to answer at least half of the comprehension questions satisfactorily or makes many miscues.

Integrate the Concept of Engagement with the Questions. Manzo and Manzo (1993) have suggested the "engagement" concept to enhance comprehension assessment by determining whether the student's responses to comprehension questions are congruent or incongruent. All correct responses are congruent. Incorrect responses "may be congruent (related but incorrect) or incongruent (unrelated as well as incorrect). An increase of congruent responses is a sound sign that the student is engaged" (Manzo & Manzo, 1993, p. 92). Unfortunately, so-called remedial students answer 55 to 80 percent of teachers' questions with totally incongruent responses (Manzo & Manzo, 1995).

If you wish to integrate the engagement concept while asking the comprehension questions, follow these guidelines:

- All comprehension questions scored as correct (+) are a sign of engagement. For correct responses that are "especially full, fresh, or elaborated in some meaningful and appropriate way," circle the numeral beside the comprehension question (Manzo & Manzo, 1993, p. 467).

- For comprehension questions scored as incorrect (–), a decision needs to be made: Is the incorrect response congruent (related to the passage in some meaningful way) or incongruent (not related to the passage in some meaningful, logical way)? Incorrect responses that are congruent may indicate engagement. For incorrect responses that are incongruent, place an X on the numeral beside the comprehension question.

General guidelines for evaluating engagement can be found in Section 4 of this manual. More extensive information can be found in an inventory developed by Manzo, Manzo, and McKenna (1995).

Use Retelling. Retelling is sometimes referred to as free recalls plus probes (questions or imperative statements). McCormick (1995, p. 174) notes several advantages to using retellings or free recalls plus probes. They can assist the teacher in "determining whether students have noted important information, whether they can reproduce it in a manner that makes sense, and whether their background knowledge has an effect on the way they interpret the substance of the text." You can also informally assess the student's short-term retention. In retelling, the student is asked to orally recall a passage after it has been read. You could say something like the following: "After you have read the passage, you will be asked to retell it in your own words."

Other ways to initiate the retelling include the following probes:

- Tell me what the passage (story/text) is about.
- Tell me as much as you can about what you have just read.
- What is the passage (story/text) about?

Goodman, Watson, and Burke (1987) have offered suggestions to teachers who are interested in gaining proficiency in using a retelling strategy to assess a student's comprehension. A few of their suggestions for those who want to use retelling procedures include:

- familiarity with the passage,
- not giving the student information from the passage,
- asking open-ended questions, and
- retaining any nonwords or name changes given by the student.

Once you become familiar with the graded passages, it is possible to use a retelling strategy to assess comprehension. First, invite the student to tell everything about the passage that has just been read. Then ask specific questions without giving the student information that has not already been mentioned. Using Jeff's reading of the second-grade passage in Figure 2-4 for illustration, you would first ask him to describe or explain what he read. Suppose Jeff said that the passage is about a boy who went to camp for the first time. You could encourage Jeff to relate further events and also ask him the boy's name. Through experience, you will gain confidence in extracting the main ideas and important details in the passages without asking the comprehension questions.

There are some probes that teachers have found especially useful. Consider adapting and using the following probes (Lipson & Wixson, 1991, p. 198):

- Tell me more about what you have read.
- Tell me more about what happened.
- Tell me more about the people you just read about.
- Tell me more about where this happened.

Lipson and Wixson (2000, pp. 283–284) have suggested prompts in the form of questions asked by the teacher. Prompts vary for literary (narrative) and informational (expository) text. Some sample prompts for the two major types of text follow.

Prompts for Eliciting Literary (Narrative) Retellings

- How is the setting in the story important?
- What happens to get the story started?
- What is the main problem the characters face?
- How do the characters solve the main problem?

Prompts for Eliciting Informational (Expository) Retellings

- What is the big idea in this selection?
- Why do you think the author wrote this piece?
- How does the author organize the information to share the major ideas?
- What are the main ideas and important details?

To judge student retelling, the categories *excellent* (independent level), *satisfactory* (instructional level), and *unsatisfactory* (frustration level) may be used in conjunction with the evaluation criteria in Figure 2-4 to help assess the quality and accuracy of student retellings. There is space for retelling notes beside the comprehension questions in the performance booklet. The rubric in Figure 2-4 provides the specific criteria for evaluating the accuracy and quality of student retellings.

Figure 2-4 Retelling Evaluation Criteria

Level	Description
Independent Level/Excellent	States central or key ideas Identifies important facts Retains the general sequence of events Relates most of the content in an organized manner
Instructional Level/Satisfactory	States most central or key ideas Identifies some important facts Retains the general sequence of events Relates an overall sense of the content
Frustration Level/Unsatisfactory	Provides bits of information in a haphazard manner Little apparent organization

While retelling is a viable option, it "is not an easy procedure for students, no matter what their ages" (Morrow, 1988, p. 128). In addition, retelling requires considerable teacher judgment, and there is no widely used, generally accepted criteria for judging student retellings of passages.

Harris and Sipay (1990) also note that retellings place a heavy demand on the student's ability to retrieve and organize information in the passage. Johnson, Kress, and Pikulski (1987) believe that it is somewhat premature to recommend retelling for widespread practical use. Those interested in pursuing this strategy in greater depth will find examples and tips in Appendix A for using retelling. Hansen (2004) also provides helpful developmentally appropriate retelling strategies.

Combine Retelling with the Questions. In actual practice, you may feel more comfortable combining the retelling strategy with some of the comprehension questions. This procedure gives you the necessary flexibility to gather the information needed to make an accurate assessment of the student's understanding of the passage. The recommended procedure is to invite retelling, during which time an asterisk or R (for retelling) is used to note the comprehension questions answered. The remaining questions or selected questions are asked after the retelling. This technique capitalizes on the strengths of both assessment procedures while minimizing their weaknesses.

Scoring Jeff's Graded Passage

Figure 2-5 on page 33 contains Jeff's oral reading performance on a second-grade passage. The notations indicate that he substituted *Bob* for *Bill*, *so* for *soon*, *was* for *saw*, and *minute* for *moment*. These four substitutions were not corrected. He also inserted *trees*. Based on a total (quantitative) count, Jeff made 5 miscues. The numeral 5 is recorded in the "Total Miscues" box at the bottom of the page. The miscue tallies in the chart should not be done until after the assessment has been completed. Jeff's reading was also timed with a stopwatch. It was done inconspicuously, and the time in seconds was noted at the bottom of the page as the divisor (65).

On the 10 comprehension questions shown in Figure 2-6 on page 34, Jeff responded freely and demonstrated the ability to answer various types of questions (+ indicates correct responses; a – indicates incorrect responses; underlining indicates his responses). Jeff didn't know why Bill went walking (so he earned no credit) and could not remember the name of the other kind of leaf Bill found in the woods so he was asked "What else?" Jeff couldn't remember (hence he received half credit). His understanding of the passage, nevertheless, was quite good. From the general criteria for the three reading levels at the bottom of Figure 2-6, it would appear that this passage is at Jeff's instructional level, because he made 5 *total* miscues, had comprehension in the *Ind./Inst.* range (see the Comprehension Scoring Guide in Figure 2-6), and a reading rate of 92 wpm which is average for a second grader in the spring of the school year when the assessment was done (see Table 2.5 on page 43).

Determining Reading Levels—Graded Passages

You can determine whether the passage is at the student's independent, instructional, or frustration level by considering: (1) the accuracy with which the student reads; and (2) the student's behavior and fluency while reading. In order to determine the accuracy with which the student reads the passage, determine the student's word recognition score. The word recognition score is found by determining the number of either *total* or *significant* miscues the student makes during the oral reading of the graded passages. Depending on your philosophy, you can count miscues in one of two ways: total miscues or significant miscues.

Word Recognition

Counting Total Miscues

Determining the word recognition in context score by counting the student's total miscues is a *quantitative* analysis of oral reading behavior. You would count all miscues, regardless of type,

Figure 2-5 Jeff's Performance on a Graded Passage

Student Book copy is on page 38.

B 8224 (Grade 2) Say: "I'd like you to read out loud [silently]. Think about what you're reading because I'll ask you some questions about it when you're done. Please begin here." [Point to title.]

Guided Reading Level: L; Lexile: 570

Bill at Camp

		MISCUES						
		Substitution	Insertion	Omission	Reversal	Repetition	Self-Correction of Unacceptable Miscue	Meaning Change (Significant Miscue)
Bob It was the first time Bill went to camp.	9	1						
So He was very happy to be there. Soon he	18	1						
went for a walk in the woods to look for	28							
many kinds of leaves. He found leaves from	36							
trees some maple ⌄and oak trees. As Bill walked	44		1					
was in the woods, he saw some animal tracks.	52				1			
minute At that moment, a mouse ran into a small	61	1						
hole by a tree. Bill wondered if the tracks	70							
were made by the mouse. He looked around	78							
for other animals. He did not see any. The	87							
last thing Bill saw was an old bird nest in a	98							
pine tree.	100							
TOTAL		3	1	0	1			

good phrasing and intonation

Total Miscues [5]   Significant Miscues [ ]

Word Recognition Scoring Guide		
Total Miscues	Level	Significant Miscues
0–1	Independent	0–1
2–4	Ind./Inst.	2
5	Instructional	3
6–9	Inst./Frust.	4
10 +	Frustration	5 +

Oral Reading Rate	Norm Group Percentile
65)6000 → 92 WPM	☐ 90 ☐ 75 ☐ 50 ☐ 25 ☐ 10

Figure **2-6** Jeff's Performance on Comprehension Questions

B 8224 (Grade 2)

Bill at Camp

T   1. _+_   What is this story about?
(a boy at camp; Bill's walk in the
woods)   *Bill at camp*

F   2. _+_   Did Bill enjoy going to camp? How do
you know?
(yes; the story said he was happy there)

F   3. _—_   Why did Bill go walking in the woods?
(to look for leaves)
to find animals

F   4. _½_   What kinds of leaves did Bill find in
the woods?
(maple and oak leaves)
What else? I don't know

F   5. _+_   What else did Bill see besides the
mouse?
(a bird nest; animal tracks)

F   6. _+_   Where did the mouse go?
(into a small hole by a tree)

F   7. _+_   Had Bill been to camp before? How do
you know?
(no; the story said it was his first time)

I   8. _+_   Do you think Bill went on this walk by
himself? What makes you think so?
(any logical response)   *Yes, he
didn't talk to anyone*

E   9. _+_   What other animals might Bill see if he
goes for another walk?
(any logical response)
deer and squirrels

V   10. _+_   What are "tracks"?
(footprints made in the dirt; something
made by animals when they walk or
run)

_1½_ Questions Missed

Comprehension Scoring Guide	
Questions Missed	Level
0–1	Independent
1½–2	Ind./Inst.
2½	Instructional
3–4½	Inst./Frust.
5 +	Frustration

Retelling Notes

Retelling Rubric

Independent Level/Excellent
States central or key ideas
Identifies important facts
Retains the general sequence of events
Relates most of the content in an organized manner

Instructional Level/Satisfactory
States most central or key ideas
Identifies some important facts
Retains the general sequence of events
Relates an overall sense of the content

Frustration Level/Unsatisfactory
Provides bits of information in a haphazard manner
Little apparent organization

Writing Prompt: Write about what you would like to do in the woods.

	Rubric for Writing Response
3	• Response is very closely related to prompt. • Response makes complete sense. • Response is well organized. • Response meets all age-appropriate spelling expectations and writing conventions.
2	• Response is related to prompt. • Response makes sense. • Response is organized in an acceptable manner. • Response meets most age-appropriate spelling expectations and writing conventions.
1	• Response is loosely related to prompt. • Some aspects of response make sense. • Response is not well organized. • Response lacks some age-appropriate spelling expectations and writing conventions.
0	• Response is unrelated to prompt. • Response does not make sense. • Response is poorly organized. • Response lacks most age-appropriate spelling expectations and writing conventions.

and use this total to help determine the student's reading level. In this procedure, all miscues are given equal weight in scoring the student's oral reading. You may find it easier to count total miscues during the actual administration of the reading passages. After the Basic Reading Inventory has been administered, further analysis, if desired, may be undertaken to determine significant miscues and to complete the miscue tally in the chart to the right of the passage.

Various guidelines have been offered for counting total miscues. After a review of five studies, Morris (1990) found that investigators counted miscues differently; nevertheless, there was consensus on certain types of miscues. Based on this information, a careful review of the literature, and input from teachers, it is recommended that you count the following for total miscues:

- substitutions (sometimes called mispronunciations)
- omissions (words and punctuation)
- insertions
- examiner aid (however, giving aid is not recommended)
- self-corrections (see comments below)

In counting total miscues, some special considerations are warranted. They are noted below. It is important that all this information be considered carefully when analyzing the student's word identification and comprehension strategies.

- Self-corrections provide evidence that the student is monitoring his or her reading, and some teachers prefer not to count such miscues. Numerous self-corrections, however, impact fluency and rate of reading. If such miscues are not counted, they should still be considered as a qualitative source of information in the overall determination of the student's reading levels.
- Dialect variations (such as *goed* for *went*), hesitations, and repetitions should not be included in the count of total miscues although they may be recorded for later study and analysis. Hesitations and repetitions impact fluency and may offer clues to helpful instructional interventions.
- The *consistent* mispronunciation of a word more than once in a passage should only be counted once. For example, if a student reads *Bob* for *Bill* repeatedly in the passage, it should be counted as only one miscue. This same guideline also applies to situations where a particular word is used for a proper name or any other word.
- If a student omits an entire line, it should be counted as one miscue.

Counting Significant Miscues

Determining the word recognition in context score by counting only significant miscues is a *qualitative* analysis of oral reading behavior. Some evidence (Goodman, 1972; Goodman & Marek, 1996; Lipton, 1972; Recht, 1976) suggests that certain substitutions, insertions, omissions, and the like do not seriously damage the student's understanding of the passage; hence, such miscues should not be counted as significant. Teachers have also made similar observations.

It must be remembered that accurate recognition is not the major objective in reading. *The goal is always meaning.* Because even proficient readers make errors on unfamiliar material, teachers must resist the temptation to meticulously correct all inconsequential mistakes. They must always ask whether a particular miscue really makes a difference (Goodman, 1971, p. 14).

Perhaps the best advice for counting significant miscues is to include those omissions, insertions, substitutions, mispronunciations, and other miscues that appear to affect comprehension. In short, significant miscues alter the meaning of the passage. To determine which miscues are significant, evaluate each miscue in the passage to judge the extent to which the meaning of the sentence or passage is altered by the miscue. For example, the miscue in this sentence (*blank* for *black*) is significant because it changes the meaning of the sentence. "Everyone turned to stare as a *blank* hooded figure whizzed by on a skateboard." See Frequently Asked Question 9 (page 51) for a more detailed discussion of how to determine if miscues are significant. The following method is suggested:

1. Count the **total** number of miscues in the passage.

2. Find the total of all dialect miscues, all corrected miscues, and all miscues that do not change the meaning.

3. Subtract this number from the total miscues. The result is the number of significant miscues.

A comprehensive, chronological annotated bibliography of miscue analysis has been compiled by Brown, Goodman, and Marek (1996). In addition, Wilde (2000) has provided numerous helpful and practical suggestions for conducting a miscue analysis so the results can be used for instruction. The miscue chart provided with each graded passage makes it quite easy to determine the number, type, and significance of miscues.

Scoring Jeff's Oral Reading

From Jeff's oral reading of a second-grade passage, as recorded in Figure 2-5, it is apparent that he made five total miscues. If you decided to count *total* miscues to determine Jeff's score in word recognition, you would record the numeral 5 in the "Total Miscues" box and circle the corresponding level (Instructional) in the Word Recognition Scoring Guide (see Table 2.2). Then, the numeral and the level would be written on the summary sheet of the performance booklet. The same procedure would be used to determine the word recognition score for the other graded passages.

If you decided to count *significant* miscues, each of the five miscues would be evaluated within the context of the passage to determine whether the meaning of the passage was affected. After such an analysis, three of the miscues Jeff made (*Bob*, *so*, and *was*) appear to be significant. You would record the numeral 3 in the "Significant Miscues" box and circle the corresponding level (Instructional) in the Word Recognition Scoring Guide. Then the numeral and the level would be recorded on the summary sheet of the performance booklet.

Figure 2-2 on page 26 contains various scores based on counting *total* miscues. By consulting Table 2.2 or the appropriate section of the Word Recognition Scoring Guide at the bottom of each passage, you should determine the reading levels that correspond to the various scores and place the appropriate levels in Figure 2-2. For example, at the first-grade level, Jeff's *total* miscue count was 0. This score corresponds to a reading level of "Independent" which is written as *Ind.* in the appropriate column of Figure 2-2. For practice, write in the appropriate levels for first, second, third, fourth, and fifth grade. Remember to use "Total Miscues" from the Word Recognition Scoring Guide.

Table 2.2

Scoring Guide for Words in Context for Forms A, B, C, D, and E*

Total Miscues	Level	Significant Miscues
0–1	Independent	0–1
2–4	Ind./Inst.	2
5	Instructional	3
6–9	Inst./Frust.	4
10 +	Frustration	5 +

*At and above the middle of first-grade passages

Miscue counts of total and significant miscues may not always result in the same reading level. In such instances, reflect on the student's reading and use qualitative judgments to make the best possible appraisal. For example, a student may have a large miscue count that approaches frustration, but only a few of the uncorrected miscues result in a significant change in meaning. You may note, however, that the student appeared to be very nervous and frustrated. In addition, the student's rate of reading was quite labored and slow. Using this qualitative information will enable you to make a better judgment. In this example, it is doubtful that the passage was at the student's independent level. The passage is more likely instructional or frustration, depending on the student's comprehension.

Observation of Reading Behaviors and Other Evidence

In addition to counting miscues, pay attention to and note other evidence that may be helpful in determining the appropriateness of the passage:

- finger pointing
- expression (prosody)
- phrasing (good, adequate, poor)
- rate of reading in words per minute (WPM) and/or words correct per minute (WCPM)
- flushed face or anxiety
- frustration
- refusals
- attitude
- persistence
- monitoring strategies
- background knowledge
- overall engagement

Teachers who have used the Basic Reading Inventory report that such behaviors and observations (qualitative data) are often as helpful as actual miscue counts and comprehension scores (quantitative data) in helping to determine whether a particular passage is easy, about right, or too difficult for the student. At the very least, these observations can provide additional information as tentative judgments are made regarding a student's oral reading and reading levels.

Using Expert Noticing Skills to Observe Student Reading Behaviors

View Elyse (student) reading a third-grade passage on the website.

You can also use a more structured approach to observe student reading behaviors. Through applying expert noticing skills (Ross & Gibson, 2010), you can use a series of questions to guide your observations of student reading behaviors. Expert noticing skills help you to cue into patterns in students' reading and metacognitive behaviors so that you can make appropriate instructional decisions. To develop expert noticing skills, you can engage in a two-step process. First, using the video clip on the website, you can practice your expert noticing skills while observing Elyse orally read a third-grade passage. As you watch the video clip, record your notes in Figure 2-7. Then, compare your notes to those provided on the website.

After completing the expert noticing process with the video on the website, you can use the questions provided in Figure 2-7 to focus on your own students while administering the Basic Reading Inventory and during instruction. By developing and using expert noticing skills in tandem with the Basic Reading Inventory, you can enhance your understanding of your students' reading.

Figure 2-7 Expert Noticing Video Observation Guide

Question	Your Notes
What did you see the student do?	
Why is this important?	
What did you notice about the way the student responded to reading/writing/discussion activities in terms of the knowledge, strategies, and dispositions necessary to perform the tasks?	
Why do you think the student responded this way?	
What do the student's responses tell you about how well the student understood the tasks?	
What did you learn about the student that will be helpful in planning an appropriate lesson or intervention?	

Determining Reading Levels—Comprehension Questions or Retelling

The comprehension score is determined by counting the number of questions missed. To convert this score into one of the three reading levels, consult Table 2.3 or the scoring guide at the bottom of each passage. For example, if Jeff missed five comprehension questions, that passage would be at his frustration level.

Table 2.3

Scoring Guide for Comprehension*

Questions Missed	Level
0–1	Independent
1½–2	Ind./Inst.
2½	Instructional
3–4½	Inst./Frust.
5 +	Frustration

*At and above the middle of first grade

The above procedure, however, is not directly applicable to the kindergarten and beginning first-grade passages, because they contain only five questions. You must exercise judgment in determining the student's comprehension score. If you decide that the score from these levels does not accurately reflect the student's achievement, use the Qualitative Analysis of Comprehension chart on the kindergarten and beginning first-grade pages in the performance booklet.

If you choose to use the retelling strategy to assess comprehension, you may (1) determine a percent score from the student's retelling or (2) identify the passage as one of the three reading levels without noting a specific percent of comprehension. When using retelling, you may circle *excellent* (independent), *satisfactory* (instructional), or *unsatisfactory* (frustration) in the retelling rubric below the space for retelling notes in the performance booklet. The main issue to keep in mind is whether the student's comprehension of the passage is judged to be at the independent, instructional, or frustration level.

`Caution`

Recording Jeff's Comprehension Scores for the Graded Passages

Figure 2-2 on page 26 contains Jeff's scores for the comprehension questions for the mid-first through fifth-grade levels. Consult Table 2.3 or the scoring guide below each passage to determine the reading level that corresponds to each comprehension score and place these levels in Figure 2-2. When a student's scores fall between the reading levels, your judgment must be used. The recommended procedure is to record *Ind./Inst.* or *Inst./Frust.* on the summary sheet and circle the level closest to the actual score. If the score is exactly between two levels, circle the slash (/). The gray areas in the scoring guide indicate areas that require your judgment. The determination of reading levels that require your judgment is discussed in Section 3.

Determining Reading Levels—Silent Reading

Select a form of the Basic Reading Inventory that the student did not read orally. Form D is specifically designed for silent reading. **It is recommended that you begin the silent reading at the highest passage where the student achieved an independent level during oral reading.** If this procedure does not result in an independent level for silent reading, proceed to easier passages until an independent level is determined or the easiest kindergarten passage is read. Then, return to the original starting point and continue until the student reaches a frustration level.

As the student reads the passage silently, time the student's reading and note behavioral characteristics such as lip movement, vocalization, and finger pointing. Following silent reading, the student's comprehension is assessed with comprehension questions, a retelling strategy, or a combination of the two.

Then the student is asked to locate and orally reread a sentence in the passage that answers the question located below the passage in Form D of the performance booklet. The correct sentence in the passage is printed in bold type. According to Johnson, Kress, and Pikulski (1987), the oral rereading permits assessment of the student's ability to (1) skim for specific information, (2) read for specific information and stop when that purpose has been achieved, and (3) demonstrate oral reading ability after the material has been read silently. Generally, oral rereading following silent reading should be better than the oral reading at sight from another passage at the same level of difficulty. For example, if a student reads a third-grade passage orally and a different third-grade passage silently, the sentence orally reread from the silent passage should generally be read more accurately and fluently than the passage read at sight.

When the student finds and rereads the sentence orally, record the reading in the same manner as was done on the passages read orally at sight. You can also note how the student located the sentence that was read (for example, skimmed to locate the information; reread the passage from the beginning; seemed confused).

Have the student continue to read increasingly difficult passages until a frustration level is determined. The various scores and corresponding reading levels should be entered at the appropriate place on the summary sheet. These silent reading levels can be used in conjunction with the student's oral reading performance to arrive at estimations of the three reading levels.

Rate of Reading

A formula for determining a student's rate of reading is provided on each graded-passage in the performance booklet at and above the middle of first grade. The 6,000 for these graded passages in Forms A, B, C, D, and E was determined by multiplying the number of words per selection (100) by 60. This procedure permits the resulting division to be in words per minute (WPM). For Forms LL and LI, a similar procedure was used (multiplying the 250 words in each passage by 60 seconds). To determine a student's rate of reading, use the formula provided. Merely record as the divisor of the formula the time (in seconds) the student takes to read the passage. Perform the necessary division, and the resulting numeral will be a rough estimate of the student's rate in words per minute (WPM). For example, suppose a middle-grade student took 70 seconds to read the fourth-grade selection on Form A. You would divide 6,000 by 70. The result is a reading rate of approximately 86 words per minute (WPM) as shown in the sidebar.

$$
\begin{array}{r}
85.7 \text{ WPM} \\
70{\overline{\smash{\big)}\,6000}} \\
\underline{560} \\
400 \\
\underline{350} \\
500 \\
\underline{490} \\
\end{array}
$$

Another way to determine words per minute is provided by the numerals at the end of each line of the teacher's passage (see Figure 2-8). These numerals represent the cumulative total of words to that point in the passage. Time the student's reading for one minute and draw a line or slash after the last word read by the student at the end of that minute. Then count the number of words not read on that line and subtract this numeral from the numeral at the end of the line. The result will be the number of words read in one minute. The line or slash in Figure 2-8 shows that the student read to the word *by* in one minute. By subtracting the four words not read from 77, the result is 73 words per minute (WPM). Some teachers have used "one-minute reads" in their classrooms. The above procedure permits teachers to use passages from the Basic Reading Inventory in a similar manner.

Both of the above procedures determine words per minute (WPM). If you prefer to calculate words correct per minute (WCPM), the following may be done after one of the above procedures is used to determine WPM. Merely subtract the number of miscues made by the student from the WPM score. The result will be words correct per minute (WCPM). There are no universally accepted standards for which miscues to count. **It is recommended that mispronunciations, substitutions, omissions, and reversals be counted. Insertions, repetitions, and self-corrections are generally not counted in determining WCPM.** Using the example in Figure 2-8,

Figure 2-8 Example of a One-Minute Timed Reading

Bill at Camp	
Bob It was the first time Bill went to camp.	9
So He was very happy to be there. Soon he	18
went for a walk in the woods to look for	28
many kinds of leaves. He found leaves from	36
trees some maple⌄and oak trees. As Bill walked	44
was in the woods, he saw some animal tracks.	52
minute At that moment, a mouse ran into a small	61
hole by a tree. Bill wondered if the tracks	70
(end of one minute) were made by⁄the mouse. He looked around	78
for other animals. He did not see any. The	87
last thing Bill saw was an old bird nest in a	98
pine tree.	100

there are five miscues: *Bob, so, trees, was,* and *minute*. Following the above recommendations, *trees* would not be counted because it is an insertion. The other four miscues, however, would be subtracted from the total number of words read (73), resulting in 69 WCPM.

You are encouraged to make general notes about a student's rate (for example, read very quickly; read slowly but accurately; seems to think that fast is best). A slow rate beyond second grade is usually an indication that the student lacks a large sight vocabulary and effective word identification strategies.

A more comprehensive estimate of a student's reading rate can be determined by averaging the rates for those passages where the student misses three or fewer comprehension questions. This procedure has the advantage of using a larger sample of behavior and taking comprehension into account. It should also be remembered that reading rate can vary according to the material being read, the student's interest and familiarity with the material, the purpose for which it is being read, and whether reading is done orally or silently. Oral and silent reading rates should be averaged separately (see Table 2.4 on page 42).

Combining Reading Rates for Shorter and Longer Passages

The passages in Forms A, B, C, D, and E each contain 100 words (except for the kindergarten and beginning first-grade passages) and differ in length from the longer passages (250 words) in Forms LL and LI. If you wish to combine the results from passages in both forms (for example, Form A and Form LL), the following procedure should be used:

1. Select passages at and above the middle of first grade where the student missed three or fewer comprehension questions. Keep oral and silent reading separate in the calculations.

2. Add the total number of words read for all the passages where the student missed three or fewer questions and multiply by 60. The resulting numeral becomes the dividend.

3. Add the times it took the student to read each passage. This numeral is used as the divisor.

4. Complete the necessary division to determine the approximate reading rate.

For example, the data in Table 2.4 is from Terell who read seven passages orally. His resulting reading rate is approximately 80 words per minute (WPM).

Table 2.4

Data for Terell's Reading Rate

Level of Passage	Number of Words	Time (in Seconds)
4 (A 5414)	100	70
5 (A 8595)	100	80
6 (A 6867)	100	90
4 (LL 5414)	250	160
5 (LL 8595)	250	190
6 (LL 6867)	250	180
7 (LL 3717)	250	200
	1300	970
	× 60	
	78000	

$$\begin{array}{r} 80.4\text{ WPM} \\ 970 \overline{)78000} \\ \underline{7760} \\ 4000 \\ \underline{3880} \end{array}$$

A Note about Oral and Silent Reading

"Studies have demonstrated that beginning and poor readers typically comprehend text better after reading orally rather than silently, whereas more advanced readers tend to show superior understanding after silent reading" (Prior & Welling, 2001, p. 1). In the study, however, students in grades three and four achieved significantly higher comprehension scores after oral reading; therefore, exercise caution when generalizing about which mode of reading (oral or silent) is likely to result in higher comprehension scores.

Caution

Norms for Oral and Silent Reading Rates

The norms in Table 2.5 are based on four sources of information. The first was a five-year study (Forman & Sanders, 1998) that established norms for first-grade students. Over 3,500 scores were obtained from students who took part in their study. These students were from a large suburban school district whose students generally score considerably above average on state and national reading assessments. Norms were provided for three points of the school year.

The second source was a study by Hasbrouck and Tindal (1992). Their study involved over 7,000 scores from students in grades two through five who read passages at sight for one minute from their grade-level texts, regardless of the students' instructional levels. Because most classrooms have students who represent a range of reading levels, their procedure resulted in some students reading passages that were very easy (independent level), while other students were asked to read passages that would be too difficult (frustration level). The norms provide words correct per minute at the 75th, 50th, and 25th percentiles for students in grades two through five at three points (fall, winter, and spring) in the school year.

Table 2.5

Oral Reading Norms for Students in Grades One through Eight

Grade (N)	Percentile	Fall N	Fall WCPM	Winter N	Winter WCPM	Spring N	Spring WCPM
1 (74,623)	90	22,847	32	33,366	75	38,410	105
	75		14		43		78
	50		7		22		50
	25		2		11		27
	10		1		6		14
2 (99,699)	90	29,634	102	33,683	124	36,382	141
	75		77		99		116
	50		50		72		89
	25		24		44		62
	10		12		19		34
3 (96,460)	90	29,832	128	32,371	145	34,257	161
	75		100		119		137
	50		72		91		107
	25		46		60		78
	10		24		36		47
4 (87,436)	90	29,609	144	27,373	165	30,454	180
	75		119		139		152
	50		94		111		124
	25		69		86		99
	10		42		60		72
5 (82,073)	90	28,510	165	25,229	181	28,334	194
	75		137		155		167
	50		109		126		138
	25		85		98		108
	10		60		73		81
6 (57,575)	90	18,923	177	17,668	194	20,984	204
	75		153		166		178
	50		127		140		150
	25		98		111		122
	10		67		81		93
7 (29,135)	90	10,687	176	7,313	188	11,135	200
	75		154		162		176
	50		127		134		150
	25		102		108		122
	10		79		86		97
8 (24,105)	90	8,674	183	5,986	193	9,445	198
	75		160		168		176
	50		130		142		151
	25		104		112		124
	10		79		84		97

N = number of student scores
WCPM = words correct per minute

From Jerry L. Johns, Laurie Elish-Piper, and Beth Johns, *Basic Reading Inventory* (12th ed.). Copyright © 2017 by Kendall Hunt Publishing Company (1-800-247-3458, ext. 6). May be reproduced for noncommercial educational purposes. Website: www.kendallhunt.com

The third source of data was reading fluency data that was gathered beginning in 1999 and ending with the 2002–2003 school year (www.edformation.com). Over 240,000 scores for students in grades one through eight who read passages for one minute were analyzed. The passages were at grade level, which meant that they were easy for some students and difficult for other students. Separate norms were calculated for each of the four school years. The resulting norms for each year provide words correct per minute at the 90th, 75th, 50th, 25th, and 10th percentiles at three points (fall, winter, and spring) of the school year.

The fourth source of data was a follow-up study by Hasbrouck and Tindal (2006) using over 297,000 scores obtained from students in grades one through eight. Students represented all achievement levels, including those identified as gifted or reading disabled. English Language Learners (ELLs) who were receiving reading instruction in a regular classroom were also included in the data. Schools and districts from 23 states used curriculum based measures (CBMs) for the assessment. This procedure resulted in some students reading materials at their frustration levels. Norms were complied for students performing at the 90th, 75th, 50th, 25th, and 10th percentiles at three points throughout the school year (fall, winter, and spring) with the exception of grade one (which reported students' fluency norms for only the winter and spring).

All these data were thoughtfully studied, analyzed, and compiled into Table 2.5. The resulting table is intended to provide helpful information to teachers who desire to have some guidelines for students' reading rates. Because the norms are in words correct per minute (WCPM), comparing them to words per minute (WPM) as suggested in the Basic Reading Inventory means that there is a slightly different basis for comparison. Comparisons can still be done and used to make informal appraisals regarding students' rates of reading. Just remember that the rates in Table 2.5 are more conservative than the rates determined by the WPM method. The percentiles within each grade level can be used by teachers, if desired, to informally track and monitor student progress in rate throughout the school year.

In recent years, there has been mention of desired reading rates for various instructional levels for students in various grades. Using the four sources of information previously described, Table 2.6 was developed to provide average rates for students at three points in the school year (fall, winter, and spring). These figures are less than the "challenging" rates created by Carnine, Silbert, Kame'enui, and Tarver (2004, pp. 192–93) based on students who were performing very well on standardized tests. They argue that helping students achieve high rates of fluency in the early grades leads to more reading by the student and makes school a more enjoyable experience. Keep in mind that the averages are best used to informally determine students' progress in comparison with so-called average students. Note in grade six and beyond that the rate for the spring of the year stays at 150 words correct per minute. Because of individual differences in student ability and learning rates, expecting all students to reach the target is unrealistic. Finally, do not consider rate to be the same as fluency (Johns & Berglund, 2010). See "Fluency Considerations" in Section 4 (page 87) for an important discussion of the core elements of fluency.

Caution

Table 2.6

Mean Words Correct per Minute* for Average Students in Grades One through Eight

Grade	Fall	Winter	Spring
1	Not Applicable	20	50
2	50	70	90
3	70	90	110
4	95	110	125
5	110	125	140
6	125	140	150
7	125	140	150
8	130	140	150

*Reported in "round" numbers

Carver (1989, p. 165) has provided information on *silent* reading rates for students in grades one through twelve that "may be helpful to teachers who administer informal reading inventories." The figures he presents are the average rates of students in that *particular* grade who can *understand* material at *that* grade level. Although Carver's figures are in standard word lengths, they may be useful as a rough indication of the average rates at which average students in a particular grade read with understanding. Users of the Basic Reading Inventory, then, can use the figures presented in Table 2.7 to help evaluate a student's silent reading rate. We also provide in parentheses silent reading rates from a recent study by Spichtig, Hiebert, Vorstius, Pascoe, Pearson, and Radach (2016). The ranges for sixth grade reveal that, by grade eight, students' reading rates begin to decline. This decline continued to the end of their high school careers. There seems to be a significant decline in comprehension-based silent reading rates among high school students.

Table 2.7

Silent Reading Rates for Students in Various Grades Who Understand the Material

Grade	1	2	3	4	5	6	7	8
WPM	<81	82–108 (110–120)	109–130	131–147 (143–152)	148–161	162–174 (159–171)	175–185	186–197 (161–170)

	9	10	11	12
	198–209	210–224 (178–192)	225–240	241–255 (186–198)

The Listening Level

In addition to the three reading levels, you may wish to get a rough estimate of the student's listening level or potential for substantial growth in reading. Intelligence tests are sometimes used to estimate potential for reading; however, their limitations have led some teachers to read graded passages to a student and determine the highest level of material that the student can understand. Undertaking such a procedure is known as determining the student's listening level. This procedure should **not** be used with students in the primary grades (Schell, 1982).

 ## Determining the Listening Level

Select a form of the Basic Reading Inventory that was not used for either oral or silent reading. The listening level is determined after *you* read increasingly difficult passages to the student. You should first read the title and develop a purpose for listening to the passage. For example, you could invite the student to predict what the passage will be about and then have the student *listen* to the content in the passage as you read it *to* the student. After the passage has been read, assess the student's comprehension with the questions, a retelling strategy, or a combination of the two. The criteria for estimating the student's listening level is a comprehension score of three or fewer questions missed. You should also informally note the student's ability to use vocabulary and language structures as complex as those used in the passage read.

It is recommended that you begin reading a passage that is not higher than the student's instructional level. Then continue reading more difficult passages until the student misses more than three comprehension questions. The *highest* passage at which the student misses three or fewer questions is his or her listening level.

✎ Scoring Tom's Listening Level

Suppose, for example, that Tom is a fifth-grade student who has a fourth-grade instructional level for oral and silent reading. To determine his listening level or potential, you should choose a passage at the fourth-grade level from a form of the Basic Reading Inventory that Tom has not read orally or silently. After you read the passage aloud, Tom responds to the comprehension questions. If Tom misses three or fewer questions, continue reading increasingly difficult passages until Tom misses more than three questions. The highest level at which Tom meets this criterion is identified as his listening level. To illustrate this procedure, consider the data in Table 2.8.

Table 2.8

Data for Tom's Listening Level

Level of Passage	Comprehension Questions Missed
4 (C 5414)	0
5 (C 8595)	2
6 (C 6867)	3
7 (C 3717)	4

Based on these data, Tom's listening level would be sixth grade, because that was the highest level at which he missed three or fewer questions. Because his listening level (sixth grade) is higher than his instructional level (fourth grade), there is reason to believe that Tom has the potential to increase his reading ability. Harris and Sipay (1990) suggest a two-year discrepancy between the listening level and the instructional level as a rough criterion for practical significance. In this instance, Tom's listening comprehension can be viewed as a favorable prognostic sign; namely, Tom should be able to understand material at the sixth-grade level once he acquires the necessary reading competence.

There are some limitations for using the listening level as an indicator of reading potential. Limitations within the assessment process as well as a student's auditory handicaps and/or unfamiliarity with standard English reduce the importance that should be attached to a listening level. In addition, bright students in the middle and upper grades may have reading abilities that exceed their listening abilities. For these reasons, consider the listening level as a rough estimate of reading potential that needs to be supported from observation and the results of measures of intellectual capacity.

`Caution`

Figure 2-9 (page 47) provides a summary of procedures for administering and scoring the Basic Reading Inventory. You will also find a helpful quick guide inside the front cover of this manual. The quick guide provides an easy-to-use reference with page numbers that will facilitate your administration of the Basic Reading Inventory.

Writing Prompts

This optional component of the Basic Reading Inventory was added to address the expectation that students write about their responses to text as part of the Common Core and other new standards. Writing prompts for each of the graded passages can help facilitate an informal assessment of student writing fluency, spelling and use of conventions, organization, and relevance to the prompt. It is important to note, however, that the writing prompts are not intended as measures of comprehension per se, because the comprehension questions and retelling options connected with the reading passage are already designed to assess comprehension. Each writing prompt is inspired by the topic or key ideas in the passage, but allows students to express their own insights or experiences rather than recount content directly from the passage.

Figure 2-9 Basic Reading Inventory Administration and Scoring Procedures

Basic Reading Inventory Administration and Scoring Procedures

To determine a student's independent, instructional, and frustration levels, administer the graded word lists and graded passages included in the Basic Reading Inventory as follows:

WORD RECOGNITION IN ISOLATION: Select a graded word list at a reading level that will be easy for the student. Ask the student to pronounce the words at a comfortable rate. Record the student's responses in the sight column beside the corresponding word list in the performance booklet. The website provides downloadable versions of all performance booklets.

Return to mispronounced or unknown words for an attempt at analysis and note the student's responses in the analysis column. Administer successive word lists until the student is no longer able to achieve a total score of at least 14 correct words or until the student becomes frustrated.

Scoring: Total the correct responses in the sight and analysis columns. Consult the criteria on the scoring guide at the bottom of the word lists to determine a rough estimate of the reading level achieved on each graded word list. Judgment must be exercised at the kindergarten levels because of the limited number of words. Record the number-correct scores and the reading levels on the summary sheet of the performance booklet.

WORD RECOGNITION IN CONTEXT: Ask the student to read aloud the passage graded one level below the highest independent level achieved on the graded word lists. If desired, time the student's reading. As the student reads the passage, record all miscues such as omissions, repetitions, substitutions, and the like on the corresponding copy of the passage found in the performance booklet.

Scoring: Count the number of total miscues or significant miscues (those that affect meaning) in each graded passage.

To determine reading levels from the word recognition in context scores, consult the criteria on the scoring guide at the bottom of the passage. Judgment must be exercised at the kindergarten and beginning first-grade levels because of the limited number of words in these passages. Record the score and the reading levels on the summary sheet of the performance booklet.

COMPREHENSION: Ask the comprehension questions that accompany the passage in the performance booklet and record the student's responses. Continue administering graded passages until the student has many word recognition miscues or is unable to answer half the comprehension questions. Also, watch for behavior associated with frustration: lack of expression, word-by-word reading, excessive anxiety, and so on.

Scoring: Count the number of comprehension questions missed.

To convert these scores into reading levels, consult the criteria on the scoring guide at the bottom of the questions. Judgment must be exercised at the pre-primer levels because the limited number of questions may not permit precise measurement of comprehension. Record the scores and the reading levels on the summary sheet of the performance booklet.

Teachers may choose to have students respond to the writing prompt for each passage they read; they may determine that one writing exercise during the administration of the Basic Reading Inventory is sufficient; or they may choose not to use the writing prompts at all. Because writing prompts are included for all grade levels, including kindergarten and first grade, teachers of young children or those with emergent level literacy skills are encouraged to have students use both writing and drawing to craft their responses.

The rubric for evaluating the student's writing is shown below. It is also found on the performance booklet pages with questions for Forms A–E and in Appendix B. Using both the Rubric for Writing Response and your professional judgment, you can determine if students are able to write a response that is related to the prompt, makes sense, is organized in a logical manner, and reflects age-appropriate expectations for spelling and mechanics. These assessment results can help you plan targeted instruction in writing to meet students' needs and to build on their strengths.

Figure 2-10 Rubric for Evaluating Students' Written Responses

Rubric for Writing Response	
3	• Response is very closely related to prompt. • Response makes complete sense. • Response is well organized. • Response meets all age-appropriate spelling expectations and writing conventions.
2	• Response is related to prompt. • Response makes sense. • Response is organized in an acceptable manner. • Response meets most age-appropriate spelling expectations and writing conventions.
1	• Response is loosely related to prompt. • Some aspects of response make sense. • Response is not well organized. • Response lacks some age-appropriate spelling expectations and writing conventions.
0	• Response is unrelated to prompt. • Response does not make sense. • Response is poorly organized. • Response lacks most age-appropriate spelling expectations and writing conventions.

1. **Must every student be given the Basic Reading Inventory?**

    Many teachers use the inventory with all their students so they can differentiate instruction, provide suitable reading materials, and monitor progress. Other teachers use the inventory with those students they believe need further assessment in reading: students who score very high or very low on state tests, other standardized reading tests, or students who need assessment of their word identification, fluency, or comprehension skills. The Basic Reading Inventory has also been used in response to intervention programs to help assess progress. It is also useful with students who have transferred into your school. Remember that the basic assessment strategy described in this manual can be used with instructional materials in your classroom (such as trade books, literature-based readers, and language experience stories) to help make your instruction more responsive to students' needs.

2. **Can the Basic Reading Inventory be used for progress monitoring in Response to Intervention (RTI)?**

    Yes, the Basic Reading Inventory can be an excellent tool as part of the progress-monitoring process in RTI. Depending on the schedule for progress monitoring for a specific student, the Basic Reading Inventory can be used in three different ways. First, because the Basic Reading Inventory has seven forms to help assess word identification, fluency, and comprehension, it can be used as a helpful tool for progress monitoring for students who need to be assessed regularly. Second, the Basic Reading Inventory can be used in conjunction with other assessments such as Curriculum Based Measures (CBMs). CBMs may be administered weekly, and the Basic Reading Inventory can be administered on a quarterly basis to provide a more complete assessment of the student's reading and progress. The Basic Reading Inventory may also be used as a pre-assessment and post-assessment to informally determine student growth related to reading interventions.

3. **Why do students sometimes have difficulty with the kindergarten and beginning first-grade passages?**

    Generally, students at the early stages of reading, especially those taught with intensive phonic programs, literature-based readers, or trade books, are most familiar with the vocabulary used in such books. Because the Basic Reading Inventory is not designed for use with specific reading programs or materials, differences in vocabulary may exist, particularly in the kindergarten and beginning first-grade passages. You should take this information into consideration when you assess reading to determine the student's three levels. You may also find the Early Literacy Assessments (ELA) in Part 3 to be especially helpful with emergent readers. Take a moment to look over these assessments (see page 369). You may find the following Early Literacy Assessments especially helpful with emergent and beginning readers: Literacy Knowledge and Wordless Picture Reading.

4. **How should I assess the reading of students who are unable to read the easiest word lists and passages?**

    Remember that emergent readers and older students experiencing difficulty in reading may find the easiest word lists and passages difficult. When this situation occurs, the language experience approach (LEA) is recommended. A concrete object, photograph, or experience is used to engage the student in discussion. Then the teacher writes down the student's dictation and has the student read the LEA story. This strategy can be used to probe what students have learned about how the reading process works. Walker (2004, pp. 266–67), Gillet, Temple, and Crawford (2004, pp. 413–15), McCormick (2007), and Lipson and Wixson (2000, pp. 488–91) offer some concise assistance for launching, maintaining, and using dictated stories. You may want to use Wordless Picture Reading in Part 3 (page 374) as the stimulus for a language experience story.

Part 3 of this manual contains a variety of Early Literacy Assessments. Included are informal ways to assess literacy knowledge, phoneme segmentation awareness, auditory discrimination, alphabet knowledge, wordless picture reading, and so on. The informal assessment devices will be especially useful for students who are unable to read the easiest word lists and passages.

5. Why do illustrations accompany only the kindergarten and beginning first-grade passages of the reading inventory?

Illustrations can make reading material attractive. They can also capture the interest of a student. Pictures, however, sometimes provide clues to help the student understand the passage. Because the Basic Reading Inventory is designed to assess how a student uses language cues to construct meaning from print, illustrations are restricted to the kindergarten and beginning first-grade passages.

6. Why are some passages literary (narrative) and others informational (expository)?

Literary passages generally tell a story. Informational passages inform by presenting information. Both types of literature are commonly found in schools, and students need to be able to read both types of texts. In recent years, informational books have become much more common in the primary grades.

Forms A, B, and LL of the Basic Reading Inventory contain literary passages. Form C contains mostly literary passages. Form D, starting in grade two, contains informational passages. Form A is designed for oral reading, and you can assess the student's ability to deal with literary discourse. Form LL contains longer literary passages (250 words) than Form A (100 words). You can use Form LL for oral or silent reading.

In the upper grades, the content areas become more important, so Forms D and LI contain informational passages at and above the second-grade level. Form E contains all informational passages. Because students often read their content area texts silently, Form D assesses silent reading with informational materials. Form LI contains longer informational passages and may be used for oral or silent reading. With these various forms, you have the resources to help you gain a more complete picture of the student's reading. Both teachers and research have found that informational (expository) passages can cause students greater difficulty. McCormick (1999) notes that informational text structures are commonly more difficult to comprehend than the story structures of literary materials. One reason such a situation exists may be a student's lack of experience with informational materials. Another reason may be the differences in structure between the two types of literature. If, for example, a student has more difficulty with the informational passages, you may have gained valuable knowledge to use in your instructional program.

7. Should I help students with words they don't know?

Every time a student is told an unknown word is one less opportunity to gain insights into the student's reading strategies. There will probably be some instances where you tell a student a word; nevertheless, the recommended procedure is to remain silent or to say, "Do the best you can." Then you can note the strategies (or lack of them) that the student uses frequently, occasionally, or not at all. There is some evidence (McNaughton, 1981) that students were less accurate and self-corrected a smaller proportion of their miscues when they received immediate, as compared with delayed, correction. You may, therefore, want to be very selective about telling students unknown words when administering the Basic Reading Inventory.

8. What should I do when the student mispronounces proper nouns?

First, do not include multiple mispronunciations of the same word in counting miscues. Count only one miscue. Second, encourage the student to use strategies to pronounce the word by saying, "Just do the best you can." Third, use the student's pronunciation if the word appears in a question. Finally, in some instances you may pronounce the word for the student because of the frustration that is evident. Be sure you make a note about the student's behavior (for example, "unable to go on until I pronounced the word;" "tried several pronunciations;" "is aware that the word is mispronounced but seems to have the basic meaning").

9. What are miscues and what's the difference between total miscues and significant miscues?

Miscues occur when a student's oral reading of the passage results in a version that differs from the printed passage. Common miscues include substitutions, omissions, and insertions. A miscue can be as minor as substituting *a* for *the* in the following sentence: I saw the squirrel run up *the* tree. Other miscues can be significant: substituting *horse* for *house* in the sentence, Dad parked the car in the garage and walked into the *house*. It is important to remember that miscues are a natural part of the reading process.

The number of miscues a student makes can merely be counted; this procedure is called quantitative analysis or total miscues. Such analysis does not take into account the quality of the student's miscues; therefore, all miscues are given equal weight.

A qualitative analysis counts significant miscues. It is a search to gain insights into a student's reading by making judgments about the student's miscues. In a qualitative analysis, some miscues are rated of higher quality than others. To determine significant miscues, evaluate each miscue in the passage in which it occurs and judge the extent to which the meaning of the sentence or passage is altered. Generally, significant miscues change the meaning of the passage. Whether you choose to count total miscues or significant miscues is up to you. The scoring guide contains both options. Consult page 35 for a method to determine which miscues are considered significant. Also, see question 10.

Below are some examples of miscues that teachers **considered significant** because of the change in meaning was substantial.

Student:	Here comes a *cat*.
Text:	Here comes a *car*.
Student:	While gathered *above* the council fire . . .
Text:	While gathered *about* the council fire . . .
Student:	The summer had been a dry one, *usual* . . .
Text:	The summer had been a dry one, *unusual* . . .
Student:	The flower got its name from its *stage* habit . . .
Text:	The flower got its name from its *strange* habit . . .
Student:	They threw leaves into the *yard*.
Text:	They threw leaves into the *air*.
Student:	He unlocked the *bank* door.
Text:	He unlocked the *back* door.
Student:	He *sniffled* slowly down the street.
Text:	He *shuffled* slowly down the street.
Student:	Jim put the *bird* on the snow.
Text:	Jim put the *bread* on the snow.
Student:	Only she would know the amount in each dose.
Text:	Only she would know the *correct* amount in each dose.

Here are some examples of miscues that were **not considered significant** because the essential meaning of the phrase or sentence was retained.

Student: . . . sailing over the *middle* line . . .
Text: . . . sailing over the *midline* . . .

Student: . . . and scored. *The* game ended.
Text: . . . and scored *as* the game ended.

Student: *Ooh!* What fun!
Text: *Wow!* What fun!

Student: She went with her parents to the pet *store*.
Text: She went with her parents to the pet *shop*.

Student: . . . trees fell *on* the ground.
Text: . . . trees fell *to* the ground.

Student: Dale *was* the strongest player on the team *and* was up first.
Text: Dale, the strongest player on the team, was up first.

Student: The Tigers and *the* Jets were playing . . .
Text: The Tigers and Jets were playing . . .

Finally, here are some **"gray area" examples** for which greater teacher judgment is needed to determine whether the miscues are significant.

Student: The *kick* went sailing . . .
Text: The *ball* went sailing . . .

Student: The children helped by *carrying* bits of wood.
Text: The children helped by *carting* bits of wood.

Student: This is *funny*.
Text: This is *fun*.

Student: . . . some would take *the* wood and start . . .
Text: . . . some would take *this* wood and start . . .

10. What guidelines should be used if I decide to count only significant miscues?

Miscues are generally significant when:

1. the meaning of the sentence or passage is significantly changed or altered, and the student does not correct the miscue.
2. a nonword is used in place of the word in the passage.
3. only a partial word is substituted for the word or phrase in the passage.
4. a word is pronounced for the student.
5. a word is omitted and the omission changes the meaning.

Miscues are generally *not* significant when:

1. the meaning of the sentence or passage undergoes no change or only minimal change.
2. they are self-corrected by the student.
3. they are acceptable in the student's dialect (*goed home* for *went home*, *idear* for *idea*).
4. they are later read correctly in the same passage.

11. Are the answers provided with the comprehension questions the only acceptable answers?

No. You may decide that some students' responses are both logical and reasonable even though they differ from the "answer" in the parentheses under the question. In such cases, give the student credit. The age and grade of the student should also be taken into consideration when you are scoring responses. In essence, use your knowledge of students when scoring the comprehension questions.

TIP   Some "answers" in parentheses for the comprehension questions are separated by a semicolon. When two or more answers are separated by a semicolon, only one of the answers is necessary for full credit (unless other guidelines are specified).

12. What should I do if a student uses his or her experience instead of information in the passage to correctly answer a factual question even though it is not the answer in parentheses?

After you acknowledge the student's response, ask the student what the passage said. You might say, "That's right, but what did it say in the passage?" In essence, the student's answers to factual questions should be tied to information presented in the passage. If the student is unable to remember and the initial response (based on experience) was correct, you may want to give half credit. If the student looks back in the passage and gives the correct answer, put L (look-back) beside the number of the question and give half credit.

13. What should I do when students fail to see that they should use their experience along with information in the passage to answer an inference or evaluative question?

Gently remind students that, based on what they read, you want to know what they think. When the student says, "It didn't say," you might respond, "That's right, but I want to know what you think." Feel free to encourage students to use their experience in conjunction with information in the passage (see question 16).

14. Is it acceptable to reword questions that the student doesn't seem to understand?

Yes. You should not, however, provide information that will help the student answer the question. In addition, if you find that many students experience difficulty with a particular question, you may want to develop a replacement question of your own.

15. May I change some comprehension questions?

If you find that a particular comprehension question is consistently confusing to students, feel free to change or clarify it by using different wording. Sometimes minor rewording will resolve the problem. You could also develop a new question that you believe is more important in assessing the student's comprehension. How you conceptualize the nature of comprehension will likely influence the types of questions you ask. The authors' view is that if comprehension is assessed with questions, an effort should be made to tap the student's ability to recall the literal information *and* to reason beyond the information given in the passages. That is why evaluation and inference questions are also included.

16. Do some comprehension questions tap the student's background and experience?

For most of the questions in the Basic Reading Inventory, the student must recall or use information from the passage to answer the question. These types of questions are called passage dependent. Some questions, however, are not totally passage dependent. The most notable ones are the vocabulary questions. Two other types of questions (inference and experience/evaluation) encourage students to use their knowledge, background, and experience in conjunction with the information presented in the passage to engage in what some reading authorities identify as higher-level thinking. Raphael and Au (2005) refer to such questions as author and you. Such questions invite students to make explicit connections between the ideas in the passage and their own background knowledge and experience. Teachers are generally pleased with the variety of questions contained in the Basic Reading Inventory.

17. When I ask the first comprehension question, the student also answers other questions in his or her response. What should I do?

Just put a plus (+) next to the questions answered. There is no need to ask them again.

18. What should I do if a student mispronounces a word in the passage that happens to be the word used in the vocabulary question?

Ask the question as it is printed. You can then determine whether the student has meaning for the word even if he or she did not pronounce it correctly in the passage.

19. What should I do if a student finds a particular passage extremely easy or difficult?

The diversity of students' experiences and backgrounds may make a particular passage easier or more difficult than its assigned level. You can generally note this issue when the student's reading of a particular passage is much better or worse than would be predicted from the student's performance on previous passages. When you believe that a passage is inappropriate, the recommended procedure is to substitute a passage at the same level from a different form of the reading inventory. If this passage is still too difficult for the student to read, you may discontinue the assessment at that time.

20. Is it acceptable to give the student a break during administration of the Basic Reading Inventory?

Yes, if the student appears tired, bored, or frustrated, you can give the student a break. Doing so will help to ensure that the student is focused and performing to his or her true ability on the Basic Reading Inventory. For younger students or students who struggle a great deal, you may wish to plan to administer the Basic Reading Inventory over brief periods of two or three days, with one day for the word lists, and one to two days for the passages and accompanying comprehension questions.

21. Are informal reading inventory (IRI) results appropriate additions to my students' portfolios?

Certainly. One of the guiding principles for literacy portfolios is that assessment should be a multifaceted process (Valencia, 1990). Results and insights (both yours and the student's) from the Basic Reading Inventory can help chronicle reading development. You can record or make a DVD of the student's reading and responses to the comprehension questions and include the recording or DVD in the portfolio. Teachers have used multiple indications of performance for many years. Continue using observations, your judgments, running records, daily work, and other informal and formal assessments.

22. What do I do when the student's scores (word list, passage reading, and comprehension) don't indicate the same level?

McKenna and Stahl (2003) use the term *borderline results* to describe the situation and note that such results are a natural consequence of using reading inventories. The term *gray areas* also can be used to describe the situation. Basically, you have to make an overall judgment when results are in the gray areas as shown below.

Word Identification Percentages

100	99	98	97	96	95	94	93	92	91	90	<90
Ind.		Ind./Inst.			Inst.		Inst./Frust.			Frust.	

| 100 | 90 | 85 | 80 | 75 | 70 | 60 | 50 | <50 |

Comprehension Percentages

Section 3 contains examples of determining a student's reading levels when there are gray areas in the results. You should find that information helpful. There are also practice exercises in Section 3 that you can use to gain greater competence. The completed exercises can be found on the website. The important point to remember is that your judgment must be used when there are gray areas. Some teachers also like to share and discuss their results with colleagues to help gather additional insights and perspectives.

A teacher in a Basic Reading Inventory workshop shared an idea for the gray areas. When scores fall in the ind./inst. or inst./frust. areas, circle the level closest to the numerical score. If the numerical score is in the middle, circle the slash (/). This procedure will help you know at a glance the level to which the numerical score was closest and should help you make a more informed decision as you determine the student's three reading levels.

23. Can students have a range of reading levels?

Yes and no. A student's instructional level can sometimes span two or more grades. The independent and frustration levels are always designated by a single number. For example, if a student is independent at first and second grade, you would record the student's **highest** independent level. On the other hand, if the student is frustrated at the fifth and sixth grades, you would record the **lowest** grade as the student's frustration level. For this particular student, third and fourth grade could be recorded as the instructional level range. The student's three reading levels would be: independent—second grade, instructional—third and fourth grade, and frustration—fifth grade. The reading levels you record should have no gaps or missing grades.

24. What other tips might be helpful as I learn to administer the Basic Reading Inventory (BRI)?

You need to be patient with yourself! Even with a careful reading and study of this manual, you may feel overwhelmed during your first administration. Cut yourself some slack! After a few administrations, you will gain greater confidence and competence. Below are some tips you may find useful.

- Gather all the materials you will need for the administration of the BRI.

- Arrange the materials in the order that they will be used.

- Review the directions for administration.

- Make a copy of page 47 which contains a concise summary of BRI administration and scoring procedures.

- Enjoy your time with the student—even if things get confusing from time to time.

- Refer to the examples in the manual as you determine the student's three reading levels and analyze his or her miscues and comprehension.

- Learn from your experiences, and you will be on your way to becoming a BRI pro!

Note: In addition to the above questions, Felknor, Winterscheidt, and Benson (1999) and Paris and Carpenter (2003) provide thoughtful answers to many questions related to selecting, administering, scoring, and using informal reading inventories.

Determining the Student's Three Reading Levels

Is this book at the appropriate instructional level for this student?

Assimilating Jeff's Results

After you have summarized the results for graded word lists, words in context, and passage comprehension, estimates of the student's independent level, instructional level, and frustration level can be determined. Figure 3-1 contains a summary of Jeff's performance on Form B of the Basic Reading Inventory. The various scores and levels should correspond to your efforts to complete the examples that were presented in Figure 2-2 (page 26). You should check your results from Figure 2-2 with Figure 3-1 (page 58), check your answers, and resolve any discrepancies. Note that the circled items in Figure 3-1 indicate the level closest to Jeff's actual scores.

From the data presented in Figure 3-1, Jeff has independent levels at first and third grade. Because the independent level is the *highest* level at which Jeff can read books by himself, third grade would be his independent level. Second and fourth grades were both scored as instructional level, but less emphasis was placed on second grade because of Jeff's independent scores in all five areas at third grade. Fourth-grade materials would be an appropriate place to begin instruction for Jeff. With teacher guidance, he is likely to make good progress. The fifth-grade level, according to the criteria, is clearly his frustration level. In summary, Jeff's three reading levels are: independent—third grade, instructional—fourth grade, and frustration—fifth grade.

Examples: Reading Levels for Bob and Pablo

It should be noted that most summary sheets, unlike Figure 3-1, will not provide such clear distinctions among the three reading levels. When discrepancies arise, you must use your judgment in conjunction with the results to determine the student's three reading levels. Frequently, it is wise to consider the student's performance *preceding and following* the level in question, as well as the student's performance *within* a particular passage.

Figure 3-1 Summary of Jeff's Performance on Form B of the Basic Reading Inventory

| Grade | Word Recognition | | | | | | Comprehension | |
| | Isolation (Word Lists) | | | | Context (Passages) | | Form B | |
	Sight	Analy-sis	Total	Level	Miscues*	Level	Questions Missed	Level
1	15	4	19/20	Ind.	0	Ind.	0	Ind.
2	15	3	18/20	Inst.	5	Ind.	1½	(Ind.)/Inst.
3	16	4	20/20	Ind.	2	(Ind.)/Inst.	0	Ind.
4	14	2	16/20	Inst.	5	Inst.	2½	Inst.
5	9	2	11/20	Frust.	10	Frust.	5	Frust.

*Refers to *total* miscues in this example

Generally, the recommended procedure is to place a bit more emphasis on comprehension if word identification on the graded word lists and in context is clearly instructional level or better. **Remember that the goal of reading is constructing meaning from print.** The ability to pronounce words automatically *is* important; nevertheless, word identification must always be judged with regard to the student's ability to understand the passage. In addition, give greater emphasis to silent reading comprehension in the upper grades.

It is also important to take reading rates (judged in words per minute and/or words correct per minute) and the behavioral characteristics of the student at each reading level into consideration to aid in proper placement. A student, for example, may have percentages high enough to read independently at a certain level of difficulty; however, the student may read very slowly, lack fluency, appear to be quite nervous, and/or exhibit other behavioral characteristics that lead you to conclude that such a level is too difficult for independent reading. It is prudent to exercise extreme care in determining a student's three reading levels. It is always best to give a student easier material than to give or recommend a book to the student that might be difficult and frustrating.

In most cases the three reading levels serve as a starting point for effective reading instruction. Because the reading levels are determined in a relatively short period of time, they may not be entirely accurate. You should not, therefore, consider a student's three reading levels to be rigid and static. If, in working with the student, you find that the student's various reading levels are not accurate, make the necessary adjustments. Keep in mind that the passages in the Basic Reading Inventory provide a limited sample of student reading behavior and that the assessment was done one on one. Adjustments, based on classroom performance and other relevant information, should be made when necessary.

Estimating Bob's Reading Levels

Interpreting the summary of Bob's reading, presented in Figure 3-2 on the next page, requires some judgment. The circled levels in Figure 3-2 indicate the levels to which the scores are closest. Note that *total* miscues are recorded for word recognition in context.

All the scores for the first- and third-grade levels present no problems because the numerals correspond to those given in Tables 2.1, 2.2, and 2.3. At the second-grade level, however, word recognition in context is below the criteria in Table 2.2 for a clear independent level. Because Bob's other two scores at the second-grade level are marked independent with strong scores, you

Figure 3-2 Summary of Bob's Performance on Form A of the Basic Reading Inventory

| Grade | Word Recognition | | | | | | Comprehension | |
| | Isolation (Word Lists) | | | | Context (Passages) | | Form A | |
	Sight	Analysis	Total	Level	Miscues*	Level	Questions Missed	Level
1	20	0	20/20	Ind.	1	Ind.	1	Ind.
2	19	1	20/20	Ind.	3	Ind./(Inst.)	0	Ind.
3	13	3	16/20	Inst.	5	Inst.	2½	Inst.
4	8	3	11/20	Frust.	8	Inst./(Frust.)	6	Frust.

*Refers to *total* miscues in this example

may hypothesize that second grade is probably his independent level. For the fourth-grade level, Bob achieved the instructional/frustration level for word recognition in context and this score was closer to frustration than instructional. In addition, his scores for word recognition in isolation and comprehension are at the frustration level. Bob is unable to comprehend the material satisfactorily, so fourth grade is likely to be Bob's frustration level. Now, by analyzing Bob's performance *within* a given graded passage and *between* the four graded passages, you can verify earlier hypotheses and make a judgment that his three reading levels are: independent—second grade, instructional—third grade, and frustration—fourth grade.

You should also note that it is possible for some students to have a range of several grades within the instructional level. If, for example, Bob's scores in Figure 3-2 were changed so that the comprehension score at the second-grade level was two questions missed, his three reading levels would probably be: independent—first grade, instructional—second grade and third grade, and frustration—fourth grade. Given a range of instructional levels, where should Bob be placed for instruction? Place him in second-grade reading materials and carefully monitor his progress. If he does well at this level, you should consider a temporary placement in third-grade reading materials and monitor his reading at this level. Generally, it is easier to move a student to a higher level than to a lower level.

Estimating Pablo's Reading Levels

Another summary sheet that requires judgment is shown in Figure 3-3. Study the percentages and make a judgment with regard to Pablo's independent, instructional, and frustration levels before continuing. Remember that the circled levels in Figure 3-3 indicate the levels to which scores are closest. Note that *total* miscues are recorded for word recognition in context.

At the fourth-grade level, you must resolve Pablo's word recognition score in context. Two significant miscues could be either independent or instructional; however, by examining the other scores *within* that level, you should judge fourth grade as his independent level because of his near-perfect scores for word recognition in isolation and silent reading comprehension. The fifth-grade level requires judgment in oral reading comprehension. Because the score in comprehension is near the independent level and the other three scores at this grade level are independent, you should conclude that the fifth-grade level is also independent. At the sixth-grade level, the two significant miscues for word recognition in context are probably best identified as instructional (even though his word recognition is strong) because Pablo's other three scores are instructional.

Figure 3-3 Summary of Pablo's Performance on Form A and Form D of the Basic Reading Inventory

| Grade | Word Recognition | | | | | | Comprehension | | | |
| | Isolation (Word Lists) | | | | Context (Passages) | | Form A | | Form D | |
	Sight	Analy-sis	Total	Level	Mis-cues*	Level	Ques-tions Missed	Level	Ques-tions Missed	Level
4	20	0	20/20	Ind.	2	(Ind.)/Inst.	0	Ind.	1	Ind.
5	19	1	20/20	Ind.	1	Ind.	1½	(Ind.)/Inst.	1	Ind.
6	16	2	18/20	Inst.	2	(Ind.)/Inst.	2½	Inst.	2½	Inst.
7	16	1	17/20	Inst.	8	Inst.(Frust.)	4½	Inst.(Frust.)	5	Frust.
8	10	4	14/20	Inst.	5	Inst.	5	Frust.	6	Frust.

*Refers to *total* miscues in this example

The seventh-grade level requires judgment in two areas: word recognition in context and oral reading comprehension. Both of these scores, according to the scoring guide, appear to be nearer the frustration level, so a tentative judgment for the seventh-grade level is frustration. Judgment is required at the eighth-grade level because the words in isolation score and the words in context score are both instructional. Both comprehension scores, however, are clearly frustration. In addition, because the seventh-grade level was judged to be frustration, the eighth-grade level, by definition, would also be frustration.

You must now decide on Pablo's reading levels. From the earlier judgments, his three reading levels would probably be independent—fifth grade, instructional—sixth grade, and frustration—seventh grade. Although Pablo is quite good at pronouncing words at the seventh- and eighth-grade levels, considerable emphasis was placed on comprehension and these levels were considered to be too difficult.

Contrasting Examples: Reading Levels for Aaron and Hem

Those who have given reading inventories have noticed that some students make many miscues but are still able to answer many of the comprehension questions. Other students are able to recognize most of the words but have difficulty answering the comprehension questions. How are the reading levels of such students best estimated?

Estimating Aaron's Reading Levels

Aaron's reading performance is presented in Figure 3-4. Look at his performance in word recognition. It is clear in grades five and six that he is having difficulty pronouncing words in the word lists and graded passages. His comprehension, however, is not clearly frustration at grades five or six. Aaron appears to have great difficulty in word recognition, but his comprehension could be characterized as near instructional level at grade five and clearly instructional or better at grade six. Because the goal of reading is comprehension, some teachers may tend to emphasize Aaron's ability to comprehend in spite of many miscues. There is a problem with this sort of emphasis—it fails to acknowledge that both word recognition and comprehension must be taken into account when determining reading levels. An over-emphasis on comprehension may lead to placement in materials where Aaron would make many miscues, lack fluency, and likely regard reading as a frustrating experience. He would have to work so hard to construct meaning that the potential joys of reading would be lost.

Figure 3-4 Summary of Aaron's Performance on Form A of the Basic Reading Inventory

| Grade | Word Recognition | | | | | | Comprehension | |
| | Isolation (Word Lists) | | | | Context (Passages) | | Form A | |
	Sight	Analysis	Total	Level	Miscues*	Level	Questions Missed	Level
3	18	2	20/20	Ind.	1	Ind.	0	Ind.
4	15	3	18/20	Inst.	5	Inst.	2½	Inst.
5	11	2	13/20	Frust.	10	Frust.	3	(Inst.)/Frust.
6	9	1	10/20	Frust.	11	Frust.	2	Ind./(Inst.)

*Refers to *total* miscues in this example

Reflective teachers will recognize the need to help Aaron strengthen his sight vocabulary and word identification skills. Based on the data in Figure 3-4, Aaron's independent reading level is third grade. His instructional level is best characterized as grade four because his scores for words in isolation, words in context, and comprehension are all instructional level. Grade five would be Aaron's frustration level because of his great difficulty with word recognition. The teacher should realize that Aaron has the ability to comprehend at higher levels—possibly because his background knowledge and/or intelligence allow him to compensate for his limited abilities in word recognition. A systematic analysis of Aaron's miscues could provide the basis for specific instruction that is responsive to Aaron's needs. Responsive instruction, coupled with plenty of reading materials at Aaron's instructional level, will likely result in strengthening his sight vocabulary, fluency, and overall confidence in reading. It might then be appropriate to try materials at the fifth-grade level that are of interest to Aaron.

Estimating Hem's Reading Levels

In contrast to Aaron, Hem has the ability to recognize words (see Figure 3-5). His scores for words in isolation and words in context never reach the frustration level. Comprehension, however, is an entirely different matter. He has no clear independent level in comprehension. Even at second grade, Hem is experiencing difficulties with comprehension. Those difficulties persist with each of the subsequent passages Hem reads. The ability to pronounce words without adequate comprehension is often characterized as word calling or barking at print. Situations of this type suggest that a student may have limited background experiences, limited vocabulary knowledge, lowered mental abilities, and/or limited oral language skills in English.

Hem's teacher should explore possible explanations for his reading behavior. It is possible that his background experiences are limited. Based on the data available, Hem does not have a clear independent level, but second grade might be his independent level as long as he has the necessary background knowledge for the selection being read or the necessary background is built prior to reading. Third grade could be Hem's instructional level, but his teacher must be sure that needed concepts and ample background are built before reading. Materials at grades four and five should not be used for instruction unless adequate attention is devoted to ensure that Hem has the necessary background experiences. Hem's teacher will probably need to help him expand his meaning vocabulary, teach him that the goal of reading is comprehension, and develop strategies he can use for comprehension monitoring. See Johns and Lenski (2014) for teaching strategies in these areas. Plenty of easy reading in materials where Hem possesses the necessary background knowledge, coupled with retellings and discussions about the material, should help Hem strengthen his reading.

Figure 3-5 Summary of Hem's Performance on Form A of the Basic Reading Inventory

| Grade | Word Recognition | | | | | | Comprehension | |
| | Isolation (Word Lists) | | | | Context (Passages) | | Form A | |
	Sight	Analysis	Total	Level	Miscues*	Level	Questions Missed	Level
2	20	0	20/20	Ind.	0	Ind.	3	Inst./Frust.
3	19	1	20/20	Ind.	1	Ind.	4	Inst./Frust.
4	17	2	19/20	Ind.	2	Ind./Inst.	5	Frust.
5	16	1	17/20	Inst.	3	Ind./Inst.	5	Frust.

*Refers to *total* miscues in this example

Practice Exercises in Determining Reading Levels

To give you an opportunity to practice determining students' reading levels, Figures 3-6 (Nick), 3-7 (Antonio), and 3-8 (Corey) have been adapted from the research of Johns and L'Allier (2004). Two additional practice exercises (Figures 3-9 and 3-10) are also included. You should complete the three practice exercises by filling in the numerical and reading level data where necessary. In Figure 3-6, for example, Nick's grade two total for words in isolation and the corresponding reading level need to be determined. Nick's reading level for grade two comprehension and the grade three words in context also need to be determined. Then all the data should be carefully considered as you estimate Nick's three reading levels and write them in the space provided. You can check your results by looking on the website for the Answers for Practice Exercises in Determining Reading Levels for Figures 3-6 through 3-10.

The practice exercises in Figures 3-7, 3-8, 3-9, and 3-10 each have more information that you need to complete before reading levels can be determined. The answers for these practice exercises can be found on the website. These practice exercises consider only quantitative information; hence there is no opportunity to observe the students' behaviors and gather useful qualitative information. These exercises, nevertheless, should help you gain additional expertise in scoring the Basic Reading Inventory.

Conferring with colleagues provides support when determining a student's reading levels.

Figure 3-6 Practice Exercise to Determine Nick's Reading Levels

Twelfth Edition

BASIC READING INVENTORY PERFORMANCE BOOKLET

Form A

Jerry L. Johns, Laurie Elish-Piper, and Beth Johns

Student _Nick_

Grade _____ Gender M F   Date of Test _____

School _____   Examiner _____   Date of Birth _____

Address _____   Current Book/Level _____   Age _____

SUMMARY OF STUDENT'S READING PERFORMANCE

| Grade | Word Recognition | | | | | | Comprehension | | Reading Rate | |
| | Isolation (Word Lists) | | | | Context (Passages) | | Form A | | | |
	Sight	Analysis	Total	Level	Miscues	Level	Questions Missed	Level	Words per Minute (WPM)	Norm Group Percentile
Kb			/ 6							
Km			/ 9							
Ke	10	1	11 /12	Ind.	0	Ind.	0	Ind.		
1b	16	4	20 /20	Ind.	0	Ind.	½	Ind.		
1m					1	Ind./Inst.	1	Ind.		
1e					2	Inst.	1½	Ind./Inst.		
2	14	2	/20		5	Inst.	2½			Fill in.
3	9	2	11 /20	Frust.	10		5	Frust.		
4			/20							
5			/20							
6			/20							
7			/20							
8			/20							
9			/20							
10			/20							
11			/20							
12			/20							

ESTIMATE OF READING LEVELS

Independent _____   Instructional _____   Frustration _____   Fill in.

Word Recognition Scoring Guide

Total Miscues	Level	Significant Miscues
0–1	Independent	0–1
2–4	Ind./Inst.	2
5	Instructional	3
6–9	Inst./Frust.	4
10 +	Frustration	5 +

Comprehension Scoring Guide

Questions Missed	Level
0–1	Independent
1½–2	Ind./Inst.
2½	Instructional
3–4½	Inst./Frust.
5 +	Frustration

Scoring Guide for Graded Word Lists

Independent	Instructional	Inst./Frust.	Frustration
20 19	18 17 16	15 14	13 or less

1. Complete the summary where necessary.
2. Study the overall results.
3. Estimate reading levels. Fill in the chart.
   Remember:
   - Reading levels generally go in order.
   - Only the instructional level can have a range of two or more levels.

Figure **3-7** Practice Exercise to Determine Antonio's Reading Levels

Twelfth Edition

BASIC READING INVENTORY PERFORMANCE BOOKLET

Form A

Jerry L. Johns, Laurie Elish-Piper, and Beth Johns

Student _Antonio_

School _____

Address _____

Grade _____ Gender M F

Examiner _____

Current Book/Level _____

Date of Test _____

Date of Birth _____

Age _____

SUMMARY OF STUDENT'S READING PERFORMANCE

Grade	Word Recognition — Isolation (Word Lists)				Context (Passages)		Comprehension Form A		Reading Rate	
	Sight	Analysis	Total	Level	Miscues	Level	Questions Missed	Level	Words per Minute (WPM)	Norm Group Percentile
Kb			/ 6							
Km			/ 9							
Ke			/12							
1b	20	0	20 /20	Ind.						
1m										
1e					1	Ind.	2	Ind./Inst.		
2	19	1	/20		4		1			⟵ Fill in.
3	13	2	15 /20	Inst./Frust.	5	Inst.	2½	Inst.		
4	9	4	/20		8		5½			
5	6	2	8 /20	Frust.						
6			/20							
7			/20							
8			/20							
9			/20							
10			/20							
11			/20							
12			/20							

ESTIMATE OF READING LEVELS

Independent _____   Instructional _____   Frustration _____ ⟵ Fill in.

Word Recognition Scoring Guide

Total Miscues	Level	Significant Miscues
0–1	Independent	0–1
2–4	Ind./Inst.	2
5	Instructional	3
6–9	Inst./Frust.	4
10 +	Frustration	5 +

Comprehension Scoring Guide

Questions Missed	Level
0–1	Independent
1½–2	Ind./Inst.
2½	Instructional
3–4½	Inst./Frust.
5 +	Frustration

Scoring Guide for Graded Word Lists

Independent	Instructional	Inst./Frust.	Frustration
20 19	18 17 16	15 14	13 or less

1. **Complete the summary where necessary.**
2. **Study the overall results.**
3. **Estimate reading levels. Fill in the chart. Remember:**
   - Reading levels generally go in order.
   - Only the instructional level can have a range of two or more levels.

From Jerry L. Johns, Laurie Elish-Piper, and Beth Johns, *Basic Reading Inventory* (12th ed.). Copyright © 2017 by Kendall Hunt Publishing Company (1-800-247-3458, ext. 6). May be reproduced for noncommercial educational purposes. Website: www.kendallhunt.com

Figure **3-8** Practice Exercise to Determine Corey's Reading Levels

Twelfth Edition	BASIC READING INVENTORY PERFORMANCE BOOKLET	Form A

Jerry L. Johns, Laurie Elish-Piper, and Beth Johns

Student _Corey_

Grade _____ Gender M F Date of Test _____

School _____ Examiner _____ Date of Birth _____

Address _____ Current Book/Level _____ Age _____

SUMMARY OF STUDENT'S READING PERFORMANCE

Grade	Word Recognition						Comprehension Form A		Reading Rate	
	Isolation (Word Lists)				Context (Passages)		Questions Missed	Level	Words per Minute (WPM)	Norm Group Per- centile
	Sight	Analy- sis	Total	Level	Mis- cues	Level				
Kb			/ 6							
Km			/ 9							
Ke			/12							
1b			/20							
1m										
1e										
2	18	1	/20							
3	18	2	/20		2		1			
4	15	3	/20		6		2			
5	11	2	/20		10		4			
6	9	1	/20		12		6			
7			/20							
8			/20							
9			/20							
10			/20							
11			/20							
12			/20							

Fill in. (Grade 2 row)

Fill in. (Estimate of Reading Levels)

ESTIMATE OF READING LEVELS

Independent _____ Instructional _____ Frustration _____

Word Recognition Scoring Guide

Total Miscues	Level	Significant Miscues
0–1	Independent	0–1
2–4	Ind./Inst.	2
5	Instructional	3
6–9	Inst./Frust.	4
10 +	Frustration	5 +

Comprehension Scoring Guide

Questions Missed	Level
0–1	Independent
1½–2	Ind./Inst.
2½	Instructional
3–4½	Inst./Frust.
5 +	Frustration

Scoring Guide for Graded Word Lists

Independent	Instructional	Inst./Frust.	Frustration
20 19	18 17 16	15 14	13 or less

1. Complete the summary where necessary.
2. Study the overall results.
3. Estimate reading levels. Fill in the chart. Remember:
   - Reading levels generally go in order.
   - Only the instructional level can have a range of two or more levels.

Figure 3-9 Practice Exercise to Determine Marcus' Reading Levels

Twelfth Edition

BASIC READING INVENTORY PERFORMANCE BOOKLET

Jerry L. Johns, Laurie Elish-Piper, and Beth Johns

Form A

Student _Marcus_ _____ Grade _____ Gender M F Date of Test _____

School _____ Examiner _____ Date of Birth _____

Address _____ Current Book/Level _____ Age _____

SUMMARY OF STUDENT'S READING PERFORMANCE

Grade	Word Recognition						Comprehension Form A		Reading Rate	
	Isolation (Word Lists)				Context (Passages)		Questions Missed	Level	Words per Minute (WPM)	Norm Group Percentile
	Sight	Analysis	Total	Level	Miscues	Level				
Kb			/ 6							
Km			/ 9							
Ke			/12							
1b	19	1	/20							
1m					3		0			
1e					3		1½			
2	17	1	/20		4		1			
3	14	3	/20		7		1½			
4	11	2	/20		11		4			
5			/20							
6			/20							
7			/20							
8			/20							
9			/20							
10			/20							
11			/20							
12			/20							

Fill in.

ESTIMATE OF READING LEVELS

Independent _____   Instructional _____   Frustration _____

Fill in.

Word Recognition Scoring Guide		
Total Miscues	Level	Significant Miscues
0–1	Independent	0–1
2–4	Ind./Inst.	2
5	Instructional	3
6–9	Inst./Frust.	4
10 +	Frustration	5 +

Comprehension Scoring Guide	
Questions Missed	Level
0–1	Independent
1½–2	Ind./Inst.
2½	Instructional
3–4½	Inst./Frust.
5 +	Frustration

Scoring Guide for Graded Word Lists			
Independent	Instructional	Inst./Frust.	Frustration
20 19	18 17 16	15 14	13 or less

1. **Complete the summary where necessary.**
2. **Study the overall results.**
3. **Estimate reading levels. Fill in the chart. Remember:**
   - Reading levels generally go in order.
   - Only the instructional level can have a range of two or more levels.

Figure 3-10 Practice Exercise to Determine Kyle's Reading Levels

Twelfth Edition	**BASIC READING INVENTORY PERFORMANCE BOOKLET**	Form A

Jerry L. Johns, Laurie Elish-Piper, and Beth Johns

Student __Kyle__ Grade _____ Gender M F Date of Test _____

School _____ Examiner _____ Date of Birth _____

Address _____ Current Book/Level _____ Age _____

SUMMARY OF STUDENT'S READING PERFORMANCE

Grade	Word Recognition						Comprehension		Reading Rate	
	Isolation (Word Lists)				Context (Passages)		Form A		Words per Minute (WPM)	Norm Group Per-centile
	Sight	Analy-sis	Total	Level	Mis-cues	Level	Ques-tions Missed	Level		
Kb	4	1	/ 6		0		1			
Km	6	1	/ 9		1		1			
Ke	6	2	/12		3		2			
1b	8	1	/20		4		2			
1m										
1e										
2			/20							
3			/20	Use your judgment.						
4			/20							
5			/20							
6			/20							
7			/20							
8			/20							
9			/20							
10			/20				ESTIMATE OF READING LEVELS			
11			/20							
12			/20				Independent ____ Instructional ____ Frustration ____			

Fill in.

Fill in.

Word Recognition Scoring Guide for Kb		
Total Miscues	Level	Significant Miscues
0	Independent	0
—	Ind./Inst.	—
—	Instructional	—
1	Inst./Frust.	1
2 +	Frustration	2 +

Word Recognition Scoring Guide for Km		
Total Miscues	Level	Significant Miscues
0	Independent	0
—	Ind./Inst.	—
—	Instructional	—
1	Inst./Frust.	1
2 +	Frustration	2 +

Comprehension Scoring Guide	
Questions Missed	Level
0	Independent
1	Ind./Inst.
1½	Instructional
2	Inst./Frust.
2½ +	Frustration

Word Recognition Scoring Guide for Ke		
Total Miscues	Level	Significant Miscues
0	Independent	0
—	Ind./Inst.	—
—	Instructional	—
1	Inst./Frust.	1
2 +	Frustration	2 +

Word Recognition Scoring Guide for 1b		
Total Miscues	Level	Significant Miscues
0	Independent	0
—	Ind./Inst.	—
—	Instructional	—
1	Inst./Frust.	1
2 +	Frustration	2 +

1. **Complete the summary where necessary.**
2. **Study the overall results.**
3. **Estimate reading levels. Fill in the chart. Remember:**
   - **Reading levels generally go in order.**
   - **Only the instructional level can have a range of two or more levels.**

Note: Be sure to use the correct scoring guide for the appropriate level!

Instructional Uses
of Inventory Results

Determining students' reading levels facilitates grouping for instruction.

In addition to using the Basic Reading Inventory to estimate a student's three reading levels, the results can also be used to study the student's reading behavior in order to provide responsive interventions (Haager, Klingner, & Vaughn, 2007; Johns, L'Allier, & Johns, 2012). Kibby (1995) notes that a key question in a diagnostic decision-making model is determining which reading strategies and skills are strengths and limitations for the student. Careful evaluation of a student's performance on reading inventories provides an unsurpassed wealth of useful diagnostic data. Three strategies for evaluating inventory results are suggested for word identification. Two strategies are provided for analyzing the student's comprehension. Fluency is also considered.

Determining Word Identification Strategies

Any system of analyzing the student's word identification strategies should be guided by a careful and thoughtful analysis of oral reading performance. Conrad and Shanklin (1999) suggest helpful ways to use miscues to understand the student's reading. In addition, Johnson, Kress, and Pikulski (1987) provide several questions that may help guide the overall analysis:

- Does the student's oral reading reflect a balanced use of sight vocabulary, context clues, phonics, structural analysis, and syntactic clues? Do weaknesses appear to exist in any of these areas?

- Is the student's oral reading fluent or is the student's reading hesitant or word by word?

- To what extent do the student's miscues alter or interfere with the meaning of the passages read?

- When miscues occur, does the student appear to be monitoring his or her reading by rereading, correcting unacceptable miscues (those that adversely affect meaning), and/or noting that the passage is difficult? Are the miscues influenced by the student's dialect?

- Does the student's limited vocabulary, background, or concept development appear to be affecting oral reading?

- Are any patterns suggested by analyzing the student's miscues and oral reading behavior?

Strategy

 Simple Error Analysis

Three Strategies for Evaluating Inventory Results

1—Simple Error Analysis: to quickly identify general patterns in a student's miscues for instructional interventions.

2—Miscue Analysis Tally: to analyze the patterns in miscues to determine areas where a student is likely to benefit from instruction.

3—Advanced Qualitative Analysis: to provide an in-depth analysis of a student's miscues to determine types of miscues, graphic similarity, acceptability in context, and self-corrections to help focus instruction.

Simple error analysis is one method for analyzing the miscues made during oral reading in an effort to find patterns. These patterns may indicate certain tendencies in word identification or general reading behavior. By recording a student's miscues from the reading inventory on a sheet similar to that in Figure 4-1, you may make hypotheses about a student's needs in reading. A reproducible master for your use is found in Appendix B. The recommended procedure is to **use miscues from passages that are at the student's independent, instructional, and instructional/frustration levels.** Suppose, for example, that Sam's errors from the oral reading passages revealed the information contained in Figure 4-1. Based on these data, it would appear that Sam is able to apply the initial sounds in the words he has difficulty pronouncing. He has difficulty, however, with the middle of words. After further analysis of his medial errors, it would seem that a lack of vowel knowledge may be contributing to his difficulties in word recognition. It is also evident that many of these miscues distort the meaning of the reading selection (*ran* for *rain*, *well* for *will*, *barn* for *burn*, and so on). Sam may be helped with the strategy lessons from Scenario 5 in Section 5 on page 121. Sam has also made several other substitutions; however, these substitutions (*a* for *the*; *road* for *street*, and so on) do not result in significant changes in the meaning of the passage and do not require any instruction. The repetitions Sam made may indicate a problem that requires the attention of the teacher or the implementation of an effective reading strategy. Evaluate such repetitions within the context of Scenario 1 in Section 5 on page 117.

A different student may show weaknesses in other areas. Pete, for example, may have many words under the section "Omissions." Perhaps he does not attempt to pronounce many of the words he does not recognize immediately. Pete may need instruction in developing more effective strategies for anticipating words through the use of contextual and syntactic cues (see Scenarios 2 and 3 in Section 5 on pages 118–119).

Still another student may fail to recognize many word endings. Such miscues may be indicative of a possible problem in structural analysis (*s, es, ed, ing,* and so on). Remember, however, that some speakers of a particular dialect may omit word endings. Miscues of this type, as long as they make sense in the reader's dialect, should not be regarded as significant; furthermore, they do not require instructional intervention.

When analyzing word recognition by charting miscues, be careful to base conclusions on patterns of miscues, not just a few miscues in any given category. Remember that only miscues at the student's independent and instructional levels should be charted for analysis; the frustration level indicates that the reading process has broken down. Miscues noted at the student's frustration level may be used to verify tendencies noted at the student's independent and instructional levels. The graded word lists, if used in this type of analysis, should be kept separate because research (Allington & McGill-Franzen, 1980) has revealed that students made different miscues when reading the same words in a random order instead of in context.

Caution

Figure 4-1 Summary of Sam's Oral Reading Performance

SUBSTITUTIONS			
Different Beginnings	**Different Middles**	**Different Endings**	**Different in Several Parts**
	ran for rain *naw – now* *well – will* *walk – work* *barn – burn*	*fly for flew* *had – have* *big – bigger* *in – into*	*a for the* *road – street* *big – huge*
Insertions	**Omissions**	**Repetitions**	**Miscellaneous**
big *always*	*she* *spider⑤* *many*	*/ / / /*	

Your hypotheses regarding a student's tendencies in word identification should be considered tentative and verified or discounted through classroom instruction, observations, and other formal and informal assessment results. Also remember that word identification is not an end in itself; it is a means for constructing meaning of the text. It is often possible for a student to construct meaning from reading material even when he or she makes several miscues. Instruction in word identification, therefore, should be based on strategies that will help the student comprehend text and develop greater automaticity in word recognition.

Strategy

2 Miscue Analysis Tally

The teacher's passages for Forms A, B, C, D, and E have provisions to tally miscues and other reading behaviors as shown in Figure 4-2. The generic sheet for use with Forms LL and LI can be found in Appendix B. The tallies should be completed after the assessment session with the student has been completed.

The example in Figure 4-2 on the following page is based on Jeff's oral reading in Figure 2-5 (page 33). Each miscue should be considered and tallied accordingly. Jeff substituted *Bob* for *Bill* so a tally mark is placed in the substitution column. Because this miscue resulted in a meaning change, a tally mark is also placed under the meaning change column. The same columns were also marked for the miscue *so* because it was a substitution miscue that also changed the meaning. The miscue *trees* is an insertion, so a tally mark is placed in the insertion column on the appropriate line of the text. Jeff's teacher judged that this miscue did not change the meaning, so no other column is marked. The miscue *was* is a reversal, and a tally mark is placed in the reversal column. This miscue resulted in a meaning change, and a tally mark was placed

Figure 4-2 Jeff's Miscue Tally and Reading Behavior on a Graded Passage

Student Book copy is on page 38.

B 8224 (Grade 2) Say: "I'd like you to read out loud [silently]. Think about what you're reading because I'll ask you some questions about it when you're done. Please begin here." [Point to title.]

Guided Reading Level: L; Lexile: 570

Bill at Camp

		Substitution	Insertion	Omission	Reversal	Repetition	Self-Correction of Unacceptable Miscue	Meaning Change (Significant Miscue)
		MISCUES						
Bob It was the first time Bill went to camp.	9	1						1
So He was very happy to be there. Soon he	18	1						1
went for a walk in the woods to look for	28							
many kinds of leaves. He found leaves from	36							
trees some maple and oak trees. As Bill walked	44		1					
was in the woods, he saw some animal tracks.	52				1			1
minute At that moment, a mouse ran into a small	61	1						
hole by a tree. Bill wondered if the tracks	70							
were made by the mouse. He looked around	78							
for other animals. He did not see any. The	87							
last thing Bill saw was an old bird nest in a	98							
pine tree.	100							
TOTAL		3	1	0	1	0	0	3

good phrasing and intonation

Note: Only total miscues were used in scoring.

Total Miscues [5]   Significant Miscues [3]

Word Recognition Scoring Guide

Total Miscues	Level	Significant Miscues
0–1	Independent	0–1
2–4	Ind./Inst.	2
5	Instructional	3
6–9	Inst./Frust.	4
10 +	Frustration	5 +

Oral Reading Rate	Norm Group Percentile
$\dfrac{92}{65\,)\,6000}$ WPM	☐ 90 ☐ 75 ☒ 50 ☐ 25 ☐ 10

in the meaning change column corresponding to the appropriate line of text. The miscue *minute* for *moment* was a substitution that his teacher felt did not result in a significant meaning change; therefore, a tally mark was only placed in the substitution column corresponding to the line of text where the miscue was made.

Once the tallies for miscues and other reading behaviors are completed for **all** the passages read by the student, they can be summarized on the two sample charts shown below in Figure 4-3. These charts are also contained in Appendix B for reproduction and use.

After completing the Miscue Tally and Reading Behavior Summary Charts, look for patterns in order to hypothesize areas where the student might profit from strategy lessons. In the sample charts shown in Figure 4-3, the student appears to have a pattern of omissions. You might offer responsive instruction for omissions by considering some of the ideas in Scenario 3 in Section 5 on page 119. The student in this example also corrected a number of miscues that changed the meaning. Behavior of this sort should be seen as a reading strength, and the student should be praised for monitoring reading and using correction strategies. Some effort should be made to increase the student's sight vocabulary to build greater automaticity with words encountered during reading.

Figure 4-3 Sample Miscue Tally and Reading Behavior Summary Charts

Total Miscues Across Passages Read	Type of Miscue			
	Substitution	Insertion	Omission	Reversal
	3	2	8	0

Other Reading Behaviors (Totals)	Repetition	Self-Correction of Unacceptable Miscues	Meaning Change
	2	6	2

Strategy

 3 Advanced Qualitative Analysis

A more advanced system for analyzing miscues has been developed by Christie (1979) and is presented in Figure 4-4 on page 74. A reproducible master is found in Appendix B. This system draws upon the work of Goodman, Watson, and Burke (1987) and the suggestions of Williamson and Young (1974). The following qualitative analysis has been adapted, with permission, from Christie. For convenience, the procedure is presented in the following five-step outline.

Step 1—Select Miscues for Analysis

 A. Select miscues from oral passages at the student's **independent** and **instructional** levels only. Record the following types of miscues on the Analysis Sheet:
    1. substitutions
    2. omissions
    3. insertions
    4. word-order reversals
    5. nonwords

Figure 4-4 System for the Qualitative Analysis of Miscues

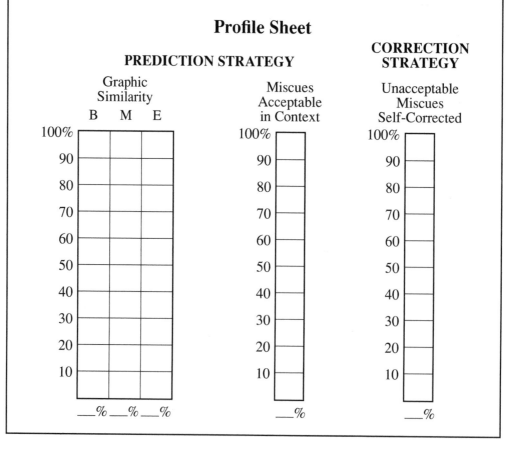

MISCUE	TEXT	GRAPHIC SIMILARITY			CONTEXT		Self-Correction of Unacceptable Miscues
		Beginning	Middle	End	Acceptable	Unacceptable	
Column Total							
Number of Miscues Analyzed							
Percentage							

Profile Sheet

PREDICTION STRATEGY

Graphic Similarity
B   M   E

100%
90
80
70
60
50
40
30
20
10

___% ___% ___%

Miscues Acceptable in Context

100%
90
80
70
60
50
40
30
20
10

___%

CORRECTION STRATEGY

Unacceptable Miscues Self-Corrected

100%
90
80
70
60
50
40
30
20
10

___%

B. Do *not* use the following types of miscues:
1. repetitions
2. hestitations
3. prompts
4. disregard for punctuation
5. omissions of entire lines of text
6. variations in pronunciation involving dialect
7. partial words

Step 2—Record Miscues on the Analysis Sheet

A. Record each type of miscue as follows:

1. substitutions

glad
The girl was very sad.

MISCUE	TEXT
glad	sad

2. omissions

He went to ~~the~~ church.

MISCUE	TEXT
————	the

3. insertions

very
The road was ∧narrow.

MISCUE	TEXT
very	————

4. word order reversals

at her desk quietly
Jill sat quietly at her desk.

MISCUE	TEXT
at her desk quietly	quietly at her desk

5. nonwords

redon
The region was large.

MISCUE	TEXT
redon	region

B. Special Rules
1. Record identical substitutions only once.
2. If the reader makes several attempts at a word, record the first complete word or nonword substitution.

Example: He went up
2. *stars*
1. *st-*
the stairs.

MISCUE	TEXT
stars	stairs

3. If a miscue causes the reader to immediately make another miscue in one apparent thought, record as one complex miscue.

have danced
Example: He could∧dance all night.

have danced	dance

A. Graphic Similarity

1. Miscues to Analyze
   a. Only substitutions of a single word or nonword for a single text item should be analyzed for graphic similarity.
   b. Do *not* analyze omissions, insertions, reversals, or substitutions that involve more than one word. In these cases, draw *Xs* through the three boxes under GRAPHIC SIMILARITY.
   c. Example:

   went
   He walked to ~~the~~ school.

MISCUE	TEXT	**GRAPHIC SIMILARITY** Beginning	Middle	End
went	walked	√		
————	the	✕	✕	✕

2. Judging Graphic Similarity
   a. Compare the sequence and shape of the letters in the miscue with those in the text item. Place a check in the appropriate box if the beginning, middle, and/or end of the miscue is graphically similar to the corresponding part of the text item.
   b. Guidelines for judging graphic similarity
      (1) divide the miscue and text item into corresponding thirds.
      (2) Use the following criteria for judging the different thirds as being graphically similar:
         (a) *Beginning*—the first letter of the miscue and the first letter of the text item must be identical.
         (b) *Middle* and *End*—the letters in the miscue and text item need only be similar in sequence and configuration.
      (3) Special cases
         (a) Two-letter text items—place an *X* in the "Middle" box and judge only for beginning and ending similarity.
         (b) One-letter text items—place an *X* in the "Middle" and "End" boxes and judge only for beginning similarity.

c. Examples for judging graphic similarity:

MISCUE	TEXT	Beginning	Middle	End
men	man	√	√	√
here	said		√	
his	this		√	√
walk	walked	√	√	
cub	carry	√		
meal	material	√		√
be	by	√	✗	
if	it	√	✗	
the	a		✗	✗
an	on		✗	√

GRAPHIC SIMILARITY

B. Acceptability in Context
   1. Judge all miscues recorded on the Analysis Sheet for acceptability in context. Refer to the graded passages that were coded to make these judgments.
   2. To judge the acceptability of a miscue, take the following two factors into consideration:
      a. *Syntax*—Is the miscue grammatically acceptable in the manner in which the sentence was read?
      b. *Semantics*—Does the miscue make sense in the context of the sentence and the preceding portion of the passage?
   3. Marking the Analysis Sheet
      a. If the miscue meets **both** criteria, check the box in the "Acceptable" column.
      b. If either criterion is not met, check the box in the "Unacceptable" column.
      c. If the unacceptable miscue is successfully self-corrected by the reader, place a check in the "Self-Correction of Unacceptable Miscues" column.

	Acceptable	Unacceptable	Self-Correction of Unacceptable Miscues
Acceptable in context; no self-correction	√		
Unacceptable in context; no self-correction		√	
Unacceptable in context; self-correction		√	√

CONTEXT

A. Graphic Similarity
   1. Count the number of checks in each column (Beginning, Middle, and End) and place the totals in the boxes marked Column Total.
   2. For each column, count the number of boxes that do not have Xs in them. Place each total in the box marked Number of Miscues Analyzed.
   3. Determine the percentage for each column by dividing each Column Total by the Number of Miscues Analyzed and then multiplying by 100.

B. Acceptability in Context
   1. Count the number of checks in the "Acceptable" column and enter the total in the appropriate Column Total box.
   2. "Acceptable" column *only*
      a. Enter the total number of miscues analyzed for acceptability in context in the box marked Number of Miscues Analyzed. (This should equal the total number of miscues recorded on the Analysis Sheet.)
      b. Determine the percentage of miscues acceptable in context by dividing the Column Total by the Number of Miscues Analyzed and then multiplying by 100.

C. Percentage of Unacceptable Miscues That Were Self-Corrected
   1. Count the number of checks in the "Unacceptable" column and enter the total in the appropriate Column Total box.
   2. Count the number of miscues in the "Unacceptable" Column that were self-corrected. Be sure to count only self-corrections for **Unacceptable** miscues. Place this total in the Column Total box in the "Self-Correction of Unacceptable Miscues" column.

		GRAPHIC SIMILARITY			CONTEXT		
MISCUE	TEXT	Beginning	Middle	End	Acceptable	Unacceptable	Self-Correction of Unacceptable Miscues
men	man	✓	✓	✓		✓	✓
here	said		✓			✓	✓
his	this		✓	✓		✓	
walk	walked	✓	✓		✓		
cub	carry	✓				✓	✓
meal	material	✓		✓		✓	
be	by	✓	X			✓	✓
if	it	✓	X			✓	
the	a		X	X	✓		
an	on		X	✓		✓	✓
Column Total		6	4	4	2	8	5
Number of Miscues Analyzed		10	6	9	10		
Percentage		60	67	44	20		63

3. Determine the percentage of unacceptable miscues that were self-corrected by dividing the Column Total of "Self-Correction of Unacceptable Miscues" by the Column Total of "Unacceptable" miscues and then multiplying by 100. Place this percentage in the Percentage Column under "Self-Correction of Unacceptable Miscues."

Step 5—Complete Profile Sheet

A. Transfer the percentages from the Analysis Sheet to the blanks below the appropriate bar graphs as shown here.
B. Darken in the bar graphs.

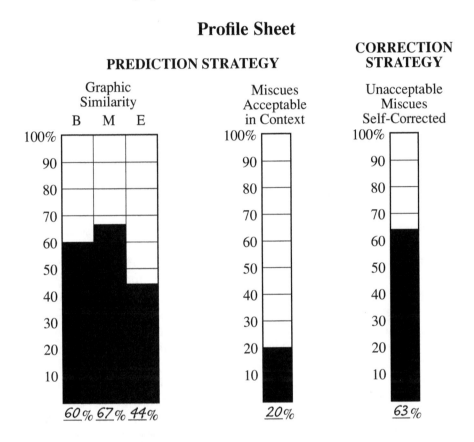

Profile Sheet

Once the three parts of the Profile Sheet are completed, reading strategy lessons and interventions can be developed. The two Prediction Strategy graphs help to determine whether the student is relying on graphic cues, context cues, or both in predicting upcoming text and decoding unknown words. When both graphs are similar, the student has a balanced prediction strategy. If, on the other hand, the two graphs show a marked difference, the student may be depending excessively on one type of cue.

If the Graphic Similarity graph is high and the Context graph is low, the student may be relying excessively on graphic (letter) cues. If this is the case, intervention lessons that emphasize the use of context cues may be warranted. See Scenarios 3 (page 119) and 6 (page 123) in Section 5.

When the Graphic Similarity graph is low and the Context graph is high, the student may be relying heavily on context cues. Intervention lessons could include asking the student a question like, "What word do you know that begins like _____ that would make sense?"

The Correction Strategy graph shows the percentage of unacceptable miscues that were self-corrected by the student. When a large percentage of unacceptable miscues are not corrected (when the Correction Strategy graph is low), the student may need to be taught strategies for monitoring his or her reading. Intervention lessons to help the reader develop a sensitivity to correcting miscues that disrupt meaning may also be needed. Scenario 5 in Section 5 on page 121 contains some useful suggestions. Several additional instructional interventions can be found in the work of Johns and Lenski (2014).

Analyzing Comprehension

To guide the overall assessment of the student's comprehension, the following questions should be considered:

- Does the student appear to know that comprehension is the goal of reading?
- Does the student appear to possess the background (concepts and vocabulary) necessary for understanding the passage?
- Are there significant differences between the student's oral and silent comprehension?
- Do significant comprehension differences exist between literary (narrative) and informational (expository) passages?
- Are there significant differences in comprehension between the shorter passages and the longer passages?
- Does the student appear to have difficulties with specific types of comprehension questions?
- What does the student do when comprehension becomes difficult?
- Does the student monitor his or her reading and use appropriate fix-up strategies?

Two Strategies for Analyzing Comprehension

1—Analysis of Comprehension by Question Type

2—Analysis by Level of Comprehension

At and above the middle of grade one, the Basic Reading Inventory contains five different types of comprehension questions coded as follows: (F) fact, (T) topic, (E) experience/evaluation, (I) inference, and (V) vocabulary. Two strategies are suggested for analyzing comprehension performance. For each strategy, **only comprehension questions at the student's independent, instructional, and instructional/frustration levels should be analyzed**. Comprehension questions at the student's frustration level may be used to verify tendencies at the student's independent and instructional levels.

Caution

These categories of comprehension questions, although widely used, have little or no empirical support (Schell & Hanna, 1981). In other words, many reading tests claim to measure comprehension skills that authorities cannot show to exist. Although such analysis lacks empirical support, Johnson, Kress, and Pikulski (1987) believe such a procedure is useful to help identify general tendencies in comprehension. Spache (1976) notes that comprehension is composed of three essential elements: (1) a word meaning factor, (2) a relationships-among-ideas factor, and (3) a reasoning factor. He goes on to say that "when the reading teacher has determined by repeated observations that the student apparently does not use a certain type of essential thinking, the remedial course is quite obvious. She may repeatedly ask the student to attempt to answer questions that appear to sample the missing cognitive process" (p. 269). The following strategies described for determining strengths and weaknesses in comprehension offer two systematic ways to gather preliminary evidence indicating that some aspect of a student's comprehension may need attention. You can then support or refute this tentative need through the student's performance in classroom activities, observations, and other assessment data. If a need exists, you can develop appropriate intervention lessons. Remember that the scheme for analyzing comprehension performance is intended to be used informally. It should aid your judgment, not replace it.

Analysis of Comprehension by Question Type

You can analyze comprehension after recording the number and types of questions the student misses on each passage read at the independent, instructional, and instructional/frustration levels. An example of this procedure, using Dan's comprehension scores, is shown in Figure 4-5. A reproducible master for your use is found in Appendix B. Using such a procedure may enable you to discern patterns of possible difficulty in comprehension. Dan's performance on the comprehension questions marked in Figure 4-5 indicates possible strengths in answering topic and vocabulary questions. Areas of possible weakness include answering fact, evaluation, and inference questions. Because of the limited data upon which these hypotheses are based, Dan's silent reading should also be considered. These hypotheses should then be verified or discounted through observation, instruction, and other relevant data.

Figure 4-5 Summary of Dan's Comprehension Performance in Oral Reading

Grade	Fact (F-6)* Oral	Topic (T-1) Oral	Evaluation (E-1) Oral	Inference (I-1) Oral	Vocabulary (V-1) Oral
3	2/6	0/1	0/1	0/1	0/1
4	1/6	0/1	0/1	0/1	0/1
5	3/6	0/1	0/1	1/1	0/1
6	2/6	0/1	1/1	1/1	0/1
Ratio Missed	8/24	0/4	1/4	2/4	0/4
Percent Missed	33%	0%	25%	50%	0%

*Indicates the type of question and the number of questions in each graded paragraph. For example, F indicates a fact question and 6 signifies that each graded passage contains six F questions.

Now, consider Tony's errors on the comprehension questions. To determine Tony's tendencies in comprehension, complete Figure 4-6 by determining the ratios of comprehension questions missed and the corresponding percentages. First, record the number of questions missed for each question type. Second, determine the percent of errors by dividing the number of errors by the total number of that question type and multiplying by 100. For example, Tony responded to 30 fact questions and missed 4 of them. His error rate for the fact questions was 13 percent ($4 \div 30 = .13; .13 \times 100 = 13\%$). What are Tony's possible strengths and weaknesses in comprehension?

During oral reading, Tony missed 4 of 30 fact questions (13%), 3 of 5 topic questions (60%), 1 of 5 evaluation questions (20%), 1 of 5 inference questions (20%), and 2 of 5 vocabulary questions (40%). Based on these percentages, answering topic questions may be hypothesized as an area of weakness. A possible strength is in the area of recalling facts. It seems most appropriate

Figure 4-6 Tony's Comprehension Performance in Oral Reading

Grade	Fact (F-6) Oral	Topic (T-1) Oral	Evaluation (E-1) Oral	Inference (I-1) Oral	Vocabulary (V-1) Oral
4	1/6	0/1	0/1	0/1	0/1
5	0/6	0/1	1/1	1/1	0/1
6	1/6	1/1	0/1	0/1	0/1
7	0/6	1/1	0/1	0/1	1/1
8	2/6	1/1	0/1	0/1	1/1
Ratio Missed	4/30	__/__	__/__	__/__	__/__
Percent Missed	13%	__%	__%	__%	__%

from this analysis to identify topic questions as a possible weakness and responses to fact questions as a possible strength. Whether the areas of evaluation, inference, and vocabulary warrant instructional interventions should be based on additional information gained from classroom observations and relevant performance on reading tasks.

When a student reads orally and silently, it is recommended that the results be combined for both sets of graded passages. This procedure enables you to use a larger sample of behavior on which to make hypotheses. Remember that the student may not always read the same number or level of oral and silent passages. A reproducible master is found in Appendix B. Figure 4-7 contains Tony's comprehension performance from the graded passages that were analyzed previously, as well as his silent reading performance on a different set of graded passages from the Basic Reading Inventory. Complete Figure 4-7 by determining the ratio of questions answered incorrectly and the corresponding percentages. First, total the ratio of questions missed for oral reading and silent reading separately. For the fact questions, Tony missed 4 of 30 questions in oral reading and 6 of 30 questions in silent reading. Second, add these numerals to complete the "Total Ratio Missed" column. Tony missed 10 of the 60 fact questions. Third, determine the percent of fact questions missed. (10 ÷ 60 = .16; .16 × 100 = 16%). After determining Tony's comprehension performance for topic, evaluation, inference, and vocabulary questions, compare the results to Table 4.1 on page 83.

A comparison of Tony's oral and silent reading comprehension is shown in Table 4.1. Check your work and resolve any discrepancies. Because the number of questions upon which the total percentages are calculated has increased, the hypotheses about Tony's strengths and weaknesses should have greater validity. His answers to fact, evaluation, and inference questions appear to be areas of strength. Errors on topic and vocabulary questions may be hypothesized as areas of weakness. Because these findings are generally consistent with those based on Tony's oral reading, the combined analysis should give the teacher greater confidence in the hypotheses made. See Johns and Lenski (2014) for over 75 teaching strategies and over 120 practice and reinforcement activities to strengthen general comprehension and reading both fictional texts and informational texts.

Grade	Fact (F-6) Oral	Silent	Topic (T-1) Oral	Silent	Evaluation (E-1) Oral	Silent	Inference (I-1) Oral	Silent	Vocabulary (V-1) Oral	Silent
4	1/6	0/6	0/1	0/1	0/1	0/1	0/1	1/1	0/1	0/1
5	0/6	0/6	0/1	0/1	1/1	0/1	1/1	0/1	0/1	0/1
6	1/6	1/6	1/1	1/1	0/1	0/1	0/1	0/1	0/1	1/1
7	0/6	3/6	1/1	0/1	0/1	0/1	0/1	0/1	1/1	0/1
8	2/6	2/6	1/1	1/1	0/1	0/1	0/1	0/1	1/1	1/1
Ratio Missed	4/30	6/30	3/5	_/_	1/5	_/_	1/5	_/_	2/5	_/_
Percent Missed	13%	20%	60%	_%	20%	_%	20%	_%	40%	_%
Total Ratio Missed	10/60		_/_		_/_		_/_		_/_	
Total Percent Missed	16%		_%		_%		_%		_%	

Table 4.1

Summary of Tony's Comprehension Performance in Oral and Silent Reading

	Fact Oral	Silent	Topic Oral	Silent	Evaluation Oral	Silent	Inference Oral	Silent	Vocabulary Oral	Silent
Ratio Missed	4/30	6/30	3/5	2/5	1/5	0/5	1/5	1/5	2/5	2/5
Percent Missed	13%	20%	60%	40%	20%	0%	20%	20%	40%	40%
Total Ratio Missed	10/60		5/10		1/10		2/10		4/10	
Total Percent Missed	16%		50%		10%		20%		40%	

Strategy

2 Analysis by Level of Comprehension

A second way to analyze comprehension performance is by classifying the various types of comprehension questions into logical categories. Numerous classification schemes have been developed (Raphael, 1986; Tatham, 1978). It is recommended that two levels of comprehension be used. Category one, lower-level comprehension, is composed of the six fact questions. Category two, higher-level comprehension, is composed of topic, evaluation, inference, and vocabulary questions. The logic behind the two categories is that the first is based on literal or explicit information, whereas the second is based on thinking beyond the ideas stated in the graded passages. The student's ability to reason and use experiences is assessed in the latter category. Although the evaluation, inference, and vocabulary questions may not be completely passage dependent, they can be used to help evaluate a student's vocabulary and ability to reason beyond the printed text. Even some of the factual questions may not be totally passage dependent, depending on student's prior knowledge. Viewed from this perspective, comprehension is only partially contextual. Johnston (1983, p. 34) argues strongly that "since no two individuals will have identical prior knowledge, the construction of tests which are free of bias at the individual level is impossible. Furthermore, it can be argued that it would be undesirable in any case since a reading comprehension test uninfluenced by prior knowledge would certainly not be measuring comprehension as it is understood theoretically."

Other classification schemes are also possible; you are encouraged to modify the scheme suggested to conform to your own conception of comprehension. The two categories of comprehension suggested make it possible for comprehension to be viewed more holistically when planning instruction for students. Table 4.2 contains the results of such an analysis for Tony's scores that were reported earlier. A reproducible master is found in Appendix B.

The results of the global analysis reveal that Tony's major difficulties are in the higher-level comprehension area. Johns and Lenski (2014) provide instructional strategies for this area of comprehension. If a more detailed analysis of this area is desired, the comprehension questions may be arranged by type and analyzed as described previously.

Table 4.2

Summary of Tony's Two-Level Comprehension Performance

	Lower-Level Comprehension (Fact Questions Only)		Higher-Level Comprehension (All Other Questions)	
	Oral	Silent	Oral	Silent
Ratio Missed	4/30	6/30	7/20	5/20
Total Ratio	10/60		12/40	
Total Percent Missed	16%		30%	

Integrating the Concept of Engagement

Another way to enhance comprehension assessment is to use the "engagement" concept (Manzo & Manzo, 1993). In short, you determine whether the student's responses to comprehension questions are congruent or incongruent. All correct responses are congruent. Incorrect responses "may be congruent (related but incorrect) or incongruent (unrelated as well as incorrect). An increase of congruent responses is a sound sign that the student is engaged" (Manzo & Manzo, 1993, p. 92).

Those who plan to integrate the engagement concept while asking comprehension questions should follow two guidelines to record relevant data:

- All comprehension questions scored as correct (+) are a sign of engagement. For correct responses that are "especially full, fresh, or elaborated in some meaningful and appropriate way," circle the numeral beside the comprehension question (Manzo & Manzo, 1993, p. 467).

- For comprehension questions scored as incorrect (−), a decision needs to be made: Is the incorrect response congruent (related to the passage in some meaningful way) or incongruent (not related to the passage in some meaningful, logical way)? Incorrect responses that are congruent may indicate engagement. For incorrect responses that are incongruent, place an X on the numeral beside the comprehension question.

If these two pieces of data have been recorded on appropriate pages of the performance booklet, they can be used to informally assess engagement. A reproducible master is found in Appendix B. An example of this procedure, using Kendrick's responses to comprehension questions, is shown in Table 4.3. Kendrick had one response to the questions at the fourth-grade level that was elaborated in some meaningful and appropriate way. None of the questions on the fifth-grade passage were elaborated; however, one response was rated as incongruent. For the sixth-grade passage, two questions were elaborated. Kendrick had four incongruent responses for the seventh-grade passage.

Table 4.3

Summary of Kendrick's Comprehension Engagement

	Grade Level of Passage			
	4	5	6	7
Correct responses especially full, fresh, or elaborated (numerals circled)*	1	0	2	0
Incongruent incorrect responses **unrelated** to the passage in some meaningful, logical way (numerals with Xs)*	0	1	0	4

*Refers to numerals beside the comprehension questions in the performance booklet.

To evaluate a student's responses, the following guidelines should be used. First, more than one elaboration per passage may be "taken as evidence of an alert mind that is engaged and being driven by meaning" (Manzo & Manzo, 1993, p. 467). Second, more than three incongruent responses (illogical, far out) "is an indication that engagement was weak and nonproductive" (Manzo & Manzo, 1993, p. 467). Based on these guidelines, Kendrick was quite engaged for the sixth-grade passage. For the seventh-grade passage, Kendrick's engagement was weak. You can use this information along with other qualitative criteria and observations to better understand a student's overall comprehension.

Now, consider Juan's engagement based on the data presented in Table 4.4. Using the guidelines just presented, what tentative conclusions regarding Juan's engagement are appropriate? For the second- and third-grade passages, Juan was engaged; however, on the fourth-grade passage, Juan's engagement was weak. No specific conclusions regarding engagement are appropriate for the fifth-grade passage.

According to Manzo and Manzo (1993, p. 467), "it is too soon to say if any significant meanings can be attached to the absence of elaborations." While future research is being conducted on the concept of engagement, teachers are encouraged to use the simple recording system in order to possibly add a richer interpretation of factors that may influence comprehension.

Table 4.4

Summary of Juan's Comprehension Engagement

	Grade Level of Passage				
	1	2	3	4	5
Correct responses especially full, fresh, or elaborated (numerals circled)*	0	2	3	0	1
Incongruent incorrect responses **unrelated** to the passage in some meaningful, logical way (numerals with Xs)*	0	0	0	4	2

*Refers to numerals beside the comprehension questions in the performance booklet.

Using Retelling to Evaluate Comprehension

You can also use the student's retelling to evaluate his or her comprehension. Retelling offers insight into the student's ability to recall specific information, to determine what is important, and to organize ideas from the text. A sample retelling rubric for a fifth-grade student, Maria, is provided in the figure below.

Figure 4-8 Maria's Retelling Performance

Level	Description	Retelling Notes
Independent Level Excellent	States central or key ideas Identifies important facts Retains the general sequence of events Relates most of the content in an organized manner	
Instructional Level Satisfactory	States most central or key ideas Identifies some important facts Retains the general sequence of events Relates an overall sense of the content	*Main idea, mystery figure, and solution included* *Included some facts, but forgot names* *Beginning, middle, and end accurate* *Included all big ideas— she clearly understood passage*
Frustration Level Unsatisfactory	Provides bits of information in a haphazard manner Little apparent organization	

To evaluate Maria's retelling, consider each of the criteria listed in the rubric and make an overall assessment of her level of comprehension by synthesizing her performance on each aspect of the retelling. Maria's retelling included the main idea of the passage, illustrated by her comment, "It is a mystery about a skateboarder." She also provided the solution to the mystery by explaining, "The kids found a skateboard and black hooded jacket by her house and a skateboard tricks book on her desk." The teacher noted this by recording her comments in the right column on the rubric. For the remaining criteria on the rubric, the teacher recorded Maria's performance by writing brief notes. Overall, Maria's retelling was satisfactory or instructional level because she included all of the key events, remembered some important facts, followed the general sequence of events, and demonstrated an overall sense of the content in the passage. Areas where Maria could use further instruction and development relate to identifying specific characters and settings.

Fluency Considerations

In recent years, the concept of fluency has been undergoing a much-needed transition. That transition has involved moving from a primary emphasis on accuracy and rate to one that also embodies expression (prosody) and comprehension. This more comprehensive view of fluency has been reflected in the Common Core Reading Foundational Skills (NGA Center & CCSSO, 2010). The Basic Reading Inventory offers an excellent means to gain insights into the student's reading fluency. A study by Morris, Trathen, Frye, Kucan, Ward, Schlagal, and Hendrix (2013) led the authors to conclude that fluency should always be considered in establishing a student's instructional level. Johns and Berglund (2010) note that fluency is comprised of four components: rate, accuracy, expression, and comprehension. How you can gain insights in each of these four areas is explained below.

Rate refers to speed of reading. When the student begins reading a graded passage orally or silently, you can time the student's reading using a stopwatch or a watch with a second hand. There are two ways to determine the student's rate or speed of reading. These two methods are described in detail on pages 40–42. In short, the first method determines the number of seconds it takes the student to read the passage and uses the formula at the bottom of the passage to get the student's rate in words per minute (WPM). Then the student's rate can be compared to the norms in Table 2.5 on page 43. Figure 4-9 contains an example for Ethan, a third-grade student.

Figure 4-9 Ethan's Oral Reading Rate

Oral Reading Rate	Norm Group Percentile
$120\overline{)6000}$ = 50 WPM	☐ 90 ☐ 75 ☐ 50 ☒ 25 ☐ 10

The second way to determine reading rate is described on page 40. That method determines the student's reading for one minute. A line or slash is drawn after the last word read by the student at the end of one minute. An example of this procedure is shown in Figure 2-8 (page 41).

Once the student's oral rate of reading is determined with either of these methods, consult Table 2.5 (page 43) and check the percentile that most closely corresponds to the student's rate in WPM. Table 2.6 (page 44) could also be used to help determine how the student's reading rate compares to average students at various points in the school year. For Ethan, it can be seen that his rate is near the 25th percentile on a third-grade passage in the fall of the school year. Figure 4-9 shows Ethan's reading rate (50 WPM) and percentile rank (25).

Accuracy refers to the facility with which the student recognizes words. In terms of the Basic Reading Inventory, the word recognition in context score gives some indication of the student's automaticity with words. You can also observe the student's ability to pronounce words and the ease with which the student moves through the passage. Obviously, a student who makes many miscues (misses one word in ten) would likely be trying to read a passage that is too difficult. The word lists can also be used to assess the student's ability to pronounce words at sight (automatically).

Appropriate expression "means that the student uses phrasing, tone, and pitch so that oral reading sounds conversational" (Johns & Berglund, 2010, p. 3). As the student reads, you can note the appropriateness of the oral reading in flow, emphasis, and phrasing. There are also more formal fluency rubrics that can be used if desired (see Johns & Berglund, 2010).

Comprehension is the essence of reading and refers to understanding the passage. Comprehension of passages on the Basic Reading Inventory is typically assessed with questions, retelling, or a combination of the two. Without comprehension, the student is merely word calling. There are some students who are very good at pronouncing words who are not actively constructing meaning. On the surface, these students may seem like excellent readers because they sound so good. Unfortunately, these readers are really automatic word callers (Valencia & Buly, 2004). Ideas for such students can be found later in this section titled "Targeting Interventions and Instruction for Struggling Readers." Refer to Cluster 1—Automatic Word Callers on page 92.

Important Points to Remember about Fluency

Fluency is dependent upon a variety of factors; the most important is probably an adequate sight vocabulary. Slow, choppy reading can be the result of not knowing a number of the words in the passage. It has been noted that "inefficiency in identifying individual words is the most important factor in accounting for individual differences in text reading fluency in samples of students with reading disabilities" (Torgesen, 2004, p. 376). Viewed from this perspective, fluency is symptomatic of poor reading rather than the cause of it. Many students improve their fluency when they are given books to read where they can recognize 95 percent or more of the words (Allington, 2012). The interest and background the student has about the topic or content of the reading material can also impact fluency.

If a student's reading is not fluent, hypothesize the most basic reasons for the behavior. Those hypotheses should then be used as the basis for initial responsive instruction and interventions. For example, one student may have weak word identification skills and a limited sight vocabulary. These areas would be the logical focus for instruction. Another student may have accurate, slow reading with adequate comprehension. For this student, instruction to increase rate may be appropriate. A third student may use improper phrasing and ignore punctuation. This student could profit from Scenario 8 in Section 5.

Through experience with the Basic Reading Inventory and a careful analysis of the student's reading, you will learn to differentiate the need for instruction in fluency from other, more casual factors for the lack of fluent reading (e.g., limited sight vocabulary and inadequate skills for word identification). It should also be noted that after third grade, the number of less frequent words increases rapidly, so it is difficult for students who struggle in reading to catch up with average students (Torgesen, 2004). Many of these students would likely profit from focused instruction in needed areas and extensive periods of practice with easy materials.

Instructional Interventions Grid

To help make instruction more responsive to the student's needs using the results of the Basic Reading Inventory, classroom observations, and the student's daily work, there are numerous sources for ideas. Several easy-to-use books to assist a wide range of professionals in their quest to enhance student achievement in reading are described below.

Improving Reading: Strategies, Resources, and Common Core Connections (Johns & Lenski, 2019) contains a wealth of teaching strategies, practice activities, games, and reproducible materials to use with students—nearly 500 pages. The ideas in this resource book support a wide range of learners. Teachers from kindergarten through high school have used the strategies to energize their instruction with average students as well as with students who struggle in reading. The sixth edition of *Improving Reading* contains more strategies than earlier editions and has many resource materials that can be duplicated and readily used with students. A website makes it even easier to use the reproducibles and resources. Refer to the instructional interventions grid on page 89 for a comprehensive overview of the areas included in *Improving Reading*.

Interventions Grid for Responsive Instruction

General Area Specific Interventions	Resource Book *Improving Reading* (6th ed.)	General Area Specific Interventions	Resource Book *Improving Reading* (6th ed.)
1. Motivation, Engagement, Interests, and Attitudes		**4. Fluency and Effective Oral Reading** *(continued)*	
Lack of Motivation and Engagement	1.1	Nonmeaning-Changing Substitutions	4.9
Negative Attitude Toward Reading	1.2	Nonword Substitutions	4.10
Limited Reading Interests	1.3	Meaning-Changing Omissions	4.11
Low Confidence in Reading Ability	1.4	Nonmeaning-Changing Omissions	4.12
Reluctant to Set Goals	1.5	Excessive Use of Phonics	4.13
2. Oral Language, Phonemic Awareness, and Beginning Reading		Excessive Use of Experience	4.14
Oral Language	2.1	**5. Vocabulary Acquisition and Use**	
Concepts About the Nature and Purpose of Reading	2.2	Learning Individual Word Meanings	5.1
Alphabet Knowledge	2.3	Developing Academic Vocabulary	5.2
Auditory Discrimination	2.4	Using Context Clues to Predict Meanings of Unknown Words or Phrases	5.3
Concept of a Word	2.5	Using Word Parts to Determine Word Meanings	5.4
Rhyming	2.6	Understanding Multi-Word Expressions (MWEs)	5.5
Syllabic Awareness	2.7	Differentiating between Word Meanings	5.6
Alphabetic Principle	2.8	Using New Words in Speaking and Writing	5.7
Onsets and Rimes	2.9	**6. Comprehension Strategies**	
Phonemic Awareness	2.10	Purpose for Reading	6.1
Visual Discrimination	2.11	Activating Prior Knowledge	6.2
Letter and Word Reversals	2.12	Making Predictions	6.3
Sense of Story	2.13	Sequence	6.4
3. Phonics, Decoding, and Word Identification		Monitoring Reading	6.5
Phonics: Consonants	3.1	Questioning	6.6
Phonics: Vowels	3.2	Making Inferences	6.7
Word Patterns and Word Building	3.3	Drawing Conclusions	6.8
Structural Analysis	3.4	Making Connections	6.9
High-Frequency Words	3.5	Visualizing	6.10
Sight Vocabulary	3.6	Reading Flexibly	6.11
Using Context to Predict Known Words	3.7	Reading Closely	6.12
Dictionary: Word Pronunciation	3.8	**7. Comprehending Fictional Texts**	
Dictionary: Word Meaning	3.9	Using Fictional Text Structure for Comprehension	7.1
Lack of Flexible Word-Identification Strategies	3.10	Understanding Characters in Fiction	7.2
Ineffective Use of Word-Identification Strategies	3.11	Determining Theme in Fiction	7.3
4. Fluency and Effective Oral Reading		Determining Point of View in Fiction	7.4
General Lack of Fluency	4.1	**8. Comprehending Informational Texts**	
Lack of Fluency: Poor Phrasing and Expression	4.2	Using Informational Text Structures	8.1
Lack of Fluency: Ignoring Punctuation	4.3	Identifying Main Ideas and Details	8.2
Lack of Fluency: Repetitions of Words or Phrases	4.4	Identifying and Evaluating Textual Evidence	8.3
Lack of Expression	4.5	Summarizing Ideas	8.4
Overemphasis on Speed and Accuracy	4.6	Evaluating Arguments	8.5
Failure to Attempt Unknown Words	4.7		
Meaning-Changing Substitutions	4.8		

Teaching Reading Pre-K–Grade 3 (Elish-Piper, Johns, & Lenski, 2006) contains 28 different assessments in areas such as literacy knowledge, phoneme segmentation, phonics, decoding, re-telling, sight words, fluency, passage reading, and writing. These assessments can be used with students who are emergent readers up to third grade. A unique feature of the book is the presentation of over 300 teaching strategies, ideas, and activities that are linked to the assessments. Also included are ideas to send home to help practice and reinforce needed skills and strategies. These home-school connections are presented in English and Spanish. A number of tips for English language learners are highlighted in an easy-to-use chart. To make this resource even easier to use, a CD is included. It contains a bonus chapter on writing and spelling, 40 instructional reproducibles, home-school connections, selected resources, and assessment record sheets.

Essential Comprehension Strategies for the Intermediate Grades (Johns, Lenski, & Berglund, 2011) contains over 20 comprehension strategies. A quick reference guide helps determine the text type, when to use the strategy, the group size, and which of the seven areas of comprehension are enhanced with each strategy. A step-by-step lesson that can be adapted follows the teaching goals related to expected student outcomes. There are one or more examples for each strategy along with ready-to-use reproducible masters for students.

Comprehension and Vocabulary Strategies for the Elementary Grades (Johns, Lenski, & Berglund, 2006) contains over 40 comprehension and vocabulary strategies neatly organized with a Quick Reference Guide that shows when, why, and how to use the strategies. Also shown is the type of text (narrative and/or informational) with which the strategy is most useful. Teaching is enhanced with a step-by-step lesson format and numerous examples. Reproducible masters, which you can use for instructional purposes, are provided with each strategy. A CD contains over 120 of these reproducibles plus bonus reproducibles for selected strategies.

Fluency: Differentiated Interventions and Progress-Monitoring Assessments (Johns & Berglund, 2010) provides answers to questions teachers often ask about fluency and offers over 30 strategies to strengthen fluency. A brief description is provided for each strategy, followed by a numbered set of procedures on how to use the strategy with students. A unique and helpful feature is a chart that aligns the various fluency strategies to six types of readers so that interventions can be targeted to specific students.

Visualization: Using Mental Images to Strengthen Comprehension (Zeigler & Johns, 2005) offers answers to some basic questions about visualization and provides 60 lessons to help students realize what visualization is, understand how to use it, and then apply it in various subject areas. Also included are assessments with scoring rubrics.

Content Area Learning: Bridges to Disciplinary Literacy (Manderino, Berglund, & Johns, 2014) contains 28 strategies accompanied with reproducibles. The strategies are keyed to the anchor standards in the Common Core and also include technology applications. These applications will help support schools and districts moving toward 1:1 computing environments. Like the other resources described above, the lessons are well organized and presented in easy-to-use steps. A Quick Reference Guide links the strategies to narrative and informational texts and includes disciplinary considerations such as close reading, comparing claims and propositions across texts, and posing discipline-relevant questions.

Reading and Learning Strategies (Lenski, Wham, Johns, & Caskey, 2011) is also a user-friendly book that contains approximately 140 strategies that focus on reading engagement, vocabulary, word study, comprehension, critical reading, and studying. The strategies are aimed at helping students learn more effectively in the content areas where informational (expository) text is often used. An included CD contains over 200 reproducibles and content area examples.

Targeting Interventions and Instruction for Struggling Readers

A study of 108 students who scored below standard on a state reading test given at the end of fourth grade was undertaken by Valencia and Buly (2004). Approximately two hours were spent with each student over several days to administer additional assessments, including an informal reading inventory. After an analysis of all the data, the students' scores "fell into three statistically distinct and educationally familiar categories: word identification (word reading in isolation and context), meaning (comprehension and vocabulary), and fluency (rate and expression)" (Valencia & Buly, 2004, p. 522). In addition, six clusters characterized the students who scored below standard on the state test:

1. Automatic Word Callers (18% of the sample)
2. Struggling Word Callers (15%)
3. Word Stumblers (17%)
4. Slow Comprehenders (24%)
5. Slow Word Callers (17%)
6. Disabled Readers (9%)

Beginning on page 92, six clusters are described with particular focus on informal reading inventory results and instructional interventions that can be found in *Improving Reading: Strategies, Resources, and Common Core Connections* (Johns & Lenski, 2019).

An investigation was undertaken by Lutes (2004) to study the impact of implementing numerous strategies from the third edition of *Improving Reading: Strategies and Resources*. Fifteen second graders enrolled in a Title I program participated in the study. There were twelve boys and three girls who received instruction twice a week over a four-month period. The Basic Reading Inventory was used as a pretest and posttest. Statistically significant ($p<.001$) gains were reported for word recognition, oral comprehension, and silent comprehension. Lutes (2004) noted that most students were reading at the kindergarten or beginning first-grade levels at the beginning of the study and at first- or second-grade levels at the conclusion of the study. While acknowledging the small sample size, the researcher noted that students can learn specific reading and writing strategies; moreover, teaching strategies can help strengthen comprehension.

As the results from the Basic Reading Inventory are analyzed for students in the upper grades who struggle with reading, it should become apparent which clusters characterize various students. Students who have similar needs can then be instructed together using some of the intervention strategies for that cluster (Johns, L'Allier, & Johns, 2012). Be cautious and flexible in this approach so students receive the type of instruction they need to become better readers. The cluster approach should be thought of as a beginning to high-quality, differentiated instruction. The six clusters may also be used with students in the primary grades to help identify instructional needs and interventions.

Caution

Cluster 1

Automatic Word Callers (18%)

Word Identification (Isolation & Context)	Meaning (Comprehension & Vocabulary)	Fluency (Rate & Expression)
STRONG	WEAK	STRONG

The dominant characteristic of students in this cluster is their ability to recognize words quickly and accurately. Unfortunately, these students exhibit very poor comprehension. They may be characterized as word callers. Their rate of reading in words per minute (WPM) could be quite high compared to the rates of average students. The majority of students in this cluster qualify for free or reduced lunch, and they are English-language learners who no longer receive special services.

In terms of performance on a reading inventory, a typical student in this cluster may score far above grade level in the graded word lists and passages and below grade level in comprehension. Comprehension difficulties are more complex than individual word meanings.

Instructional Interventions

Students in this cluster should first be helped to understand text. They may also be asked to adjust rate (slow down), focus on meaning, and think about the ideas while reading. Because many of these students are English-language learners, opportunities for language and conceptual development (Antunez, 2002), listening to and discussing classroom read-alouds, and lots of independent reading would help build language and attention to understanding. Other ideas for explicit instruction can be found in *Improving Reading: Strategies, Resources, and Common Core Connections* (Johns & Lenski, 2019) and are listed in the chart below.

Possible Area of Instructional Need	Where to Look in *Improving Reading* (7th ed.)
Understanding the purpose of reading	Section 2.2, Strategy 6
Creating purposes for reading	Section 6.1, Strategies 1, 2, and 3
Self-monitoring and think-alouds	Section 6.5, Strategies 1, 2, and 3
Adjusting rate	Section 4.6 Section 6.11, Strategies 1, 2, and 3
Various areas of comprehension	Chapters 6, 7, and 8, Choose appropriate interventions
Building vocabulary	Section 2.1, Strategy 3 Chapter 5, Choose appropriate interventions
Activating prior knowledge	Section 6.2, Strategies 1, 2, 3, and 4 Section 6.3, Strategies 1, 2, and 3
Understanding fictional text structure	Section 7.1
Understanding informational text structure	Section 8.1
Learning new words and concepts	Chapter 5, Choose appropriate interventions

Struggling Word Callers (15%)

Word Identification (Isolation & Context)	Meaning (Comprehension & Vocabulary)	Fluency (Rate & Expression)
WEAK	WEAK	FAIR

The students in this cluster struggle with both decoding and meaning. Their rather high rate of reading may be deceiving, because they say words quickly whether or not they are correct. Furthermore, these students seldom self-correct or monitor their reading. Expression and phrasing are uneven.

In terms of performance on a reading inventory, students in this cluster may score near grade level on the graded word lists. Word identification difficulties on the graded passages are much more pronounced and contribute to difficulties in comprehension. In addition, these students are often in the lower percentiles of oral assessment of vocabulary knowledge. Because 56 percent of students in this cluster are English-language learners, a lack of oral vocabulary and language may contribute to students' struggles with reading.

Instructional Interventions

Students in this cluster require specific, focused instruction in word identification that is determined through an analysis of reading miscues (see pages 71–80). Instruction should take place at students' instructional levels, which will typically be below grade placement. Exposure to the content and vocabulary of grade-level texts can be achieved through teacher read-alouds, recorded texts, and partner reading so that students' conceptual understandings continue to grow. Lots of reading should be done at the independent level or with texts that take students' background knowledge and interests into account. A good deal of background building by the teacher may be required.

Possible Area of Instructional Need	Where to Look in *Improving Reading* (7th ed.)
Expanding oral language	Section 2.1, Strategies 1, 4, 5, 6, 7, 8, 9, 12, 13, 15, 17, and 18
Strengthening word identification	Chapters 2 and 3, Choose appropriate interventions
Building vocabulary	Sections 5.1, 5.3, 5.4, and 5.7
Self-correcting miscues	Sections 4.4, 4.8, 4.10, and 4.11
Self-monitoring	Section 6.5, Strategies 1, 2, and 3
Unifying word identification strategies	Sections 3.10 and 3.11
Strengthening sight vocabulary	Section 3.5, Strategies 1, 2, 3, and 4 Section 3.6, Strategies 1, 2, and 3 Section 3.7, Strategies 1 and 2
Oral reading opportunities	Page 235
Activating prior knowledge	Section 6.2
Making predictions	Section 6.3

Cluster 3

Word Stumblers (17%)

Word Identification (Isolation & Context)	Meaning (Comprehension & Vocabulary)	Fluency (Rate & Expression)
WEAK	FAIR	WEAK

The students in this cluster have substantial difficulty with word recognition, but they still have surprisingly strong comprehension. Teachers may wonder how students can initially stumble on many words and repeat text, but still be able to comprehend so well.

In terms of performance on an informal reading inventory, word recognition in context may be a couple of years below grade level. When the impact of the students' miscues is taken into account, many of them are self-corrected. In addition, words substituted for those in the passage tend to preserve the meaning. Because of weak word identification strategies, students may over-rely on context. Self-corrections and rereading slow the students' reading rate and expression suffers. When the comprehension questions are asked, the students' comprehension scores may be independent at grade level, even though the word recognition in context score is at the frustration level. Such students generally understand that reading should make sense, self-monitoring strategies are important, and background knowledge is actively used in constructing meaning.

Instructional Interventions

Students in this cluster know that reading should make sense, and they use numerous strategies to compensate for difficulties in word identification. Specific systematic instruction in word identification should be coupled with wide reading at the students' independent and instructional levels to help build fluency and automaticity with words. Meaningful reading to younger students, repeated readings, and reader's theater will help strengthen word identification and fluency.

Possible Area of Instructional Need	Where to Look in *Improving Reading* (7th ed.)
Strengthening word identification	Chapters 2 and 3, Choose appropriate interventions
Building sight vocabulary	Sections 3.5 and 3.6
Effective oral reading behaviors	Chapter 4, Choose appropriate interventions
Developing automaticity	Sections 4.1, 4.2, 4.3, 4.4, 4.5, and 4.6 Oral Reading as Performance, pages 234–235
Learning word meanings	Sections 5.1 and 5.7

Cluster 4

Slow Comprehenders (24%)

Word Identification (Isolation & Context)	Meaning (Comprehension & Vocabulary)	Fluency (Rate & Expression)
FAIR	STRONG	WEAK

Students in this cluster have adequate to good word identification and strong comprehension but an extremely slow rate of reading. The student may experience some difficulty in decoding multisyllabic words efficiently.

In terms of performance on an informal reading inventory, these students may score above grade level on the graded word lists and have generally good word identification on the graded passages. What is readily apparent, however, is a rate of reading that is far below average students.

Instructional Interventions

These students can identify words and construct meaning; however, their slow rate of reading makes it quite unlikely that they will spend much time reading. As the amount of reading increases in the upper grades and middle school, such students are likely to encounter frustration in the amount of time it takes them to complete assigned readings. Instruction should focus on building fluency (see Johns & Berglund, 2010) and helping develop effective strategies for how to attack multisyllabic words. Supply materials of interest that can be completed in a relatively short period of time. Gradually increase the length of the materials. Through such activities, students may begin to choose reading as a leisure-time activity.

Possible Area of Instructional Need	Where to Look in *Improving Reading* (7th ed.)
Strengthening fluency	Section 4.1, Strategies 2, 4, and 10 for emergent readers, page 235 Section 4.1, Strategies 3, 4, and 5 for older readers, page 236 Section 4.1, Strategies 1, 2, and 3 Oral Reading as Performance, pages 234 and 235
Facility with longer words	Section 3.4, Strategies 2, 3, 4, 5, 6, 7, 8, and 9 Section 5.4
Increasing motivation	Section 1.1, Strategies 2, 4, and 5 Section 1.2, Strategies 3, 4, and 5 Section 1.3, Strategies 2 and 3 Section 1.4, Strategies 4 and 5 Section 1.5, Strategies 1 and 4

Cluster 5

Slow Word Callers (17%)

Word Identification (Isolation & Context)	Meaning (Comprehension & Vocabulary)	Fluency (Rate & Expression)
FAIR	WEAK	WEAK

The students in this cluster are a fairly even mix of English-language learners and native English speakers who have difficulty in comprehension and fluency.

In terms of performance on an informal reading inventory, these students generally score above grade level on the word lists and when reading the passages. Comprehension, however, is often significantly below grade level. These students may be experiencing significant difficulties with word meanings and a slow rate of reading in which phrasing and meaningful expression are lacking. To further understand the student's needs, try materials where the student has strong background knowledge so that word meanings and comprehension are unlikely to be a problem. If rate and expression improve with such materials, instruction should probably focus on meaning and building vocabulary. On the other hand, if rate and expression are still concerns under these conditions, instruction should focus on both meaning and fluency. This cluster of readers can have a wide range of needs, so prioritize student needs and select the most appropriate strategies for initial instruction and intervention.

Instructional Interventions

The specific instruction needed for these students will result from a careful appraisal of their reading. Extensive reading at the independent level and listening to teacher read-alouds (with discussion) are critical. Some typical areas for instruction are provided below. Choose specific strategies and interventions from the chapters and sections that are related to students' needs.

Possible Area of Instructional Need	Where to Look in *Improving Reading* (7th ed.)
Strengthening vocabulary	Chapter 5, Choose appropriate interventions
Building and expanding comprehension	Chapter 6, Choose appropriate interventions
Comprehending fictional texts	Chapter 7, Choose appropriate interventions
Comprehending informational texts	Chapter 8, Choose appropriate interventions
Improving fluency	Chapter 4, Choose appropriate interventions Oral Reading as Performance, pages 234–235
Activating prior knowledge	Section 6.2
Making predictions	Section 6.3

Cluster 6

Disabled Readers (9%)

Word Identification (Isolation & Context)	Meaning (Comprehension & Vocabulary)	Fluency (Rate & Expression)
VERY WEAK	VERY WEAK	VERY WEAK

The students in this cluster experience significant difficulties with all areas of reading. The dominant characteristic of students in this cluster is an extremely limited ability in word identification.

In terms of performance on an informal reading inventory, these students typically score far below grade level on all measures. Even high-frequency word knowledge is minimal. These students possess average receptive language, so there is an adequate knowledge base for reading. What is missing is a sufficient level of decoding ability and sight words, so fluency and comprehension are significantly impacted.

Instructional Interventions

These students, regardless of their grade placement, are really at the early stages of reading instruction. A primary need is intensive, systematic instruction in word identification that includes needed elements of phonics along with building sight vocabulary. Reading materials should be easy and provide successful experiences with print. These students are likely to benefit from additional instruction with a reading specialist, interventionist, or coach. A concerted effort with the combined talents of the classroom teacher and a reading specialist, along with support at home, will provide a solid foundation for growth in reading. Major areas for instruction are listed below. Begin interventions in decoding and word identification by selecting strategies most needed by students.

Possible Area of Instructional Need	Where to Look in *Improving Reading* (7th ed.)
Decoding and word recognition	Chapters 2 and 3, Choose appropriate interventions
Building sight vocabulary	Sections 3.5 and 3.6
Expanding vocabulary	Section 5.1, Strategies 2 and 3
Developing fluency	Sections 4.1, 4.2, 4.3, 4.4, and 4.5
Motivating reading	Sections 1.1, 1.2, and 1.4
Comprehension skills and strategies	Chapter 6, Choose appropriate interventions

A Teacher's Administration of the Basic Reading Inventory

Over the years, we have had the privilege of conducting many Basic Reading Inventory training workshops for classroom teachers, reading coaches, special education teachers, reading specialists, and interventionists. During the workshops, live demonstrations with students have been done. These sample administrations have been well received by workshop participants.

In one of these workshops, a local classroom teacher administered the Basic Reading Inventory before the workshop and shared the student's performance with teachers in the workshop. Joelle was the teacher who agreed to administer the Basic Reading Inventory. It was her first administration, and she did an excellent job. The results, which you are about to see, will give you a wonderful opportunity to see the big picture of how the Basic Reading Inventory can be used to determine a student's three reading levels and offer insights for instruction. This example is from the eleventh edition of the Basic Reading Inventory, so you will notice some differences with the current, twelfth edition passages and the performance booklet cover.

About the Student

Logan (not his real name) entered Joelle's school in second grade as a struggling reader. His motivation was low, and he exhibited immaturity. He began receiving Tier II instruction for weak decoding and word identification skills. By the end of second grade, improvement in reading ability increased. The Title I teacher indicated that focused small group instruction and highly structured motivational incentives helped Logan's progress. Near the middle of third grade, Joelle assessed Logan with the Basic Reading Inventory. Her purpose was to evaluate his progress and to determine the type of instruction and interventions that would help Logan strengthen his reading.

Results of the Basic Reading Inventory

Beginning with the performance booklet summary sheet, Logan's results are shown followed by his actual performance on the word lists and passages he read. Refer to these pages as you read the commentary below.

Logan's Word List Performance. Logan read word lists ranging from first grade through sixth grade. He made minimal miscues on all the lists through fifth grade and was able to correct some of the words he initially mispronounced. By sixth grade, however, Logan had great difficulty with the words, but he demonstrated a willingness to try to pronounce a number of the words. Logan also demonstrated a strong ability to pronounce words at and above his grade placement. It would appear that his weak decoding skills in second grade improved significantly because of the Tier II instructional interventions he received that year.

Logan's Passage Reading, Comprehension, and Rate. Logan read passages ranging from first through fifth grade. On the first-grade passage, Logan made two miscues, had excellent comprehension, and demonstrated excellent rate (90th percentile). On the second-grade passage, his miscue count was slightly higher (4), he missed parts of two comprehension questions, and his rate was average (50th percentile). His performance on the third-grade passage demonstrated adequate word identification, excellent comprehension, and a reading rate at the 25th percentile. Except for his rate, Logan demonstrated very good performance at his grade level. On the fourth-grade passage, Logan maintained good word identification but had lower comprehension (he missed three questions) and an oral reading rate at the 10th percentile. On the fifth-grade passage, Logan made many miscues, but he still understood much of the passage. His oral reading rate, however, was below the 10th percentile.

Logan's Reading Strengths and Weaknesses. The area of comprehension appears to be Logan's strength. He did not reach a clear frustration level in comprehension on any passage. Word recognition in isolation was stronger than words in context, but both areas were fully satisfactory at the fourth-grade level. An informal analysis of Logan's miscues revealed a preponderance of substitutions that had little impact on meaning. His overall abilities in word recognition indicate that the earlier interventions in decoding were very successful. Reading rate, however, reveals a consistent decline as increasingly difficult passages are read. Logan's reading rate at grade level is below average in spite of his strong abilities in word identification and comprehension.

Suggestions to Strengthen Logan's Reading. It seems clear that the Tier II instruction Logan received in decoding successfully strengthened his overall ability to recognize words. His current instructional level is fourth grade, a year above his grade placement. It is possible that he is quite focused on using various word attack skills and has not fully achieved automaticity in his passage reading. This focus can influence reading rate as clearly shown.

To help target instruction, it could be helpful to see if Logan's overall reading fits one of the clusters of struggling readers found on pages 92–97. After a careful comparison of his overall performance on the Basic Reading Inventory to the six clusters, it appears that Cluster 4 on page 95 is the best fit for Logan. Logan has adequate to good word recognition, strong comprehension, but an extremely slow rate of reading.

Tier II intervention and small-group instruction needs to focus on building fluency. Because Joelle noted Logan's low motivation, there may also be a need to use motivational incentives to encourage his engagement in reading. The instructional interventions grid on page 89 provides numerous ideas found in *Improving Reading* (Johns & Lenski, 2014). Some specific suggestions are listed below:

- Encourage plenty of easy reading using materials of interest that are at or below Logan's instructional level of fourth grade. Materials that are easy to read will help foster automaticity with words and build Logan's confidence.

- Commend Logan for the strong gains he has made in reading and offer him personal encouragement.

- Support Logan's rereading of favorite books and stories.

- Invite Logan to prepare a story to read orally to younger students. Ensure that the experience will be a positive one by providing plenty of practice prior to the sharing. Videotape and/or digital recordings could provide one basis for monitoring his progress.

- Use structured repeated reading (Johns & Lenski, 2014, p. 238) to increase motivation and use a Reading Progress Chart as a visible means of demonstrating progress.

- Secure scripts for readers theater (www.aaronshep.com), assign an appropriate part for Logan and other students, have students practice over several days, and then perform the script for an appropriate audience.

In Conclusion

Joelle's first administration of the Basic Reading Inventory helped her see Logan's progress and the need for focused instructional interventions in fluency, specifically rate of reading. We hope this example will encourage you to do the same with your students so they can become better readers. Be patient with yourself as you learn how to administer the Basic Reading Inventory and use the results to energize instruction and to provide appropriate, high-quality interventions.

Eleventh Edition

BASIC READING INVENTORY PERFORMANCE BOOKLET
Jerry L. Johns, Ph.D.

Form A

Student __Logan__   Grade __3__   Gender Ⓜ F   Date of Test __April 4__

School _____   Examiner __Joelle__   Date of Birth _____

Address _____   Current Book/Level _____   Age _____

SUMMARY OF STUDENT'S READING PERFORMANCE

| Grade | Word Recognition | | | | | | | Comprehension | | Reading Rate | |
| | Isolation (Word Lists) | | | | Context (Passages) | | Form A | | Words Group Minute (WPM) | Norm Per-centile |
	Sight	Analy-sis	Total	Level	Mis-cues	Level	Ques-tions Missed	per Level		
PP1										
PP2										
P										
1	19	1	20	Ind.	2	Ind./Inst.	0	Ind.	71	90
2	20		20	Ind.	4	Ind./Inst.	1	Ind.	79	50
3	19	1	20	Ind.	3	Ind./Inst.	1	Ind.	53	25
4	17	1	18	Inst.	3	Ind./Inst.	3	Inst./Frust.	52	10
5	18	1	19	Ind.	10	Frust.	4	Inst./Frust.	41	<10
6	10	3	13	Frust.						
7										
8										
9										
10										
11										
12										

ESTIMATE OF READING LEVELS

Independent __3__   Instructional __4__   Frustration __5__

LISTENING LEVEL

Form _____

Grade	Questions Missed	Level
1		
2		
3		
4		
5		
6		
7		
8		

ESTIMATED LEVEL: _____

GENERAL OBSERVATIONS

– Hard-working student
– Improved word recognition skills since second grade
– Strong comprehension skills

INFORMAL ANALYSIS OF ORAL READING

| Oral Reading Behaviors | Frequency of Occurrence | | | General Impact on Meaning | | |
	Seldom	Sometimes	Frequently	No Change	Little Change	Much Change
Substitutions			✔		✔	
Insertions	✔			✔		
Omissions	✔					
Reversals						
Repetitions						

QUALITATIVE ANALYSIS OF BASIC READING INVENTORY INSIGHTS

General Directions: Note the degree to which the student shows behavior or evidence in the following areas. Space is provided for additional items.

Seldom / Weak / Poor .... Always / Strong / Excellent

COMPREHENSION

Seeks to construct meaning
Makes predictions
Activates background knowledge
Possesses appropriate concepts and vocabulary
Monitors reading
Varies reading rate as needed
Understands topic and major ideas
Remembers facts or details
Makes and supports appropriate inferences
Evaluates ideas from passages
Understands vocabulary used
Provides appropriate definitions of words
Engages with passages

WORD IDENTIFICATION

Possesses numerous strategies
Uses strategies flexibly
Uses graphophonic information
Uses semantic information
Uses syntactic information
Knows basic sight words automatically
Possesses sight vocabulary

ORAL AND SILENT READING

Reads fluently
Reads with expression
Attends to punctuation
Keeps place while reading
Reads at appropriate rate
Reads silently without vocalization *NA*

ATTITUDE AND CONFIDENCE

Enjoys reading
Demonstrates willingness to risk
Possesses positive self-concept
Chooses to read
Regards himself/herself as a reader
Exhibits persistence

Form A • Graded Word Lists • Performance Booklet • Student Booklet copy is on page 3.

List A 7141 (Grade 1)	Sight	Analysis	List A 8224 (Grade 2)	Sight	Analysis
1. here*	+		1. ten*	+	
2. down*	+		2. poor	+	
3. then*	+		3. city	+	
4. how*	+		4. teacher	+	
5. saw*	+		5. turn*	+	
6. pocket	*pack*	+	6. fight	+	
7. hello	+		7. because*	+	
8. aunt	+		8. soft	+	
9. never*	+		9. open*	+	
10. puppy	+		10. winter	+	
11. could*	+		11. joke	+	
12. after*	+		12. different	+	
13. hill	+		13. say*	+	
14. men	+		14. quiet	+	
15. gone*	+		15. sister	+	
16. ran*	+		16. above	+	
17. gave*	+		17. seed	+	
18. or*	+		18. thought*	+	
19. way	+		19. such	+	
20. coat	+		20. chase	+	

*denotes basic sight word from Revised Dolch List

*denotes basic sight word from Revised Dolch List

Number Correct ___19___ ___1___   Number Correct ___20___ _____

Total ___20___   Total ___20___

Scoring Guide for Graded Word Lists			
Independent	Instructional	Inst./Frust.	Frustration
20 19	18 17 16	15 14	13 or less

Form A • Graded Word Lists • Performance Booklet • Student Booklet copy is on page 4.

List A 3183 (Grade 3)	Sight	Analysis	List A 5414 (Grade 4)	Sight	Analysis
1. trail	+		1. stove	+	
2. stream	+		2. government	govenment	x
3. beach	+		3. program	+	
4. snake	+		4. grape	+	
5. lift	+		5. favorite	+	
6. cabin	+		6. blizzard	+	
7. bless	+		7. noon	+	
8. rooster	+		8. greet	+	
9. journey	+		9. sport	+	
10. treasure	+		10. rumble	+	
11. hero	+		11. tropical	+	
12. beyond	+		12. language	+	
13. moan	+		13. expert	+	
14. glitter	+		14. nervous	+	
15. impossible	+		15. starve	stārv	x
16. shot	+		16. voyage	+	
17. island	izland	+	17. silence	sĭlence	+
18. manage	+		18. scamper	+	
19. receive	+		19. prairie	+	
20. automobile	+		20. moccasin	+	
Number Correct	19	1	Number Correct	17	1
Total	20		Total	18	

Scoring Guide for Graded Word Lists			
Independent	Instructional	Inst./Frust.	Frustration
20 19	18 17 16	15 14	13 or less

Form A • Graded Word Lists • Performance Booklet • Student Booklet copy is on page 5.

List A 8595 (Grade 5)	Sight	Analysis		List A 6867 (Grade 6)	Sight	Analysis
1. lizard	+			1. bleed	+	
2. double	+			2. accomplishment	pass	pass
3. scarlet	+			3. whimper	+	
4. helmet	+			4. marriage	+	
5. dusk	+			5. frisky	+	
6. bandit	+			6. seam	+	
7. loyal	+			7. backward	pass	+
8. choice	+			8. location	pass	pass
9. furnish	+			9. nightmare	+	
10. century	+			10. gently	+	
11. kindergarten	+			11. employ	employee	employee
12. entrance	+			12. broadcast	+	
13. dentist	+			13. kennel	+	
14. celebration	+			14. pulp	+	
15. blister	+			15. satisfaction	pass	+
16. symbol	+			16. cushion	cŭshion	+
17. drowsy	+			17. graduate	pass	gratitude
18. attach	autŭch	x		18. harmonica	pass	harmon passs
19. rehearse	rěh-	+		19. definite	definĭt	pass
20. terrace	+			20. yacht	pass	yăcht
Number Correct	18	1		Number Correct	10	3
Total		19		Total		13

Scoring Guide for Graded Word Lists			
Independent	Instructional	Inst./Frust.	Frustration
20 19	18 17 16	15 14	13 or less

Student Booklet copy is on page 13.

A 7141 (Grade 1) Activating Background: Read the title to yourself. Then tell me what you think this might be about. *A dog is going to learn how to swim.*

Background: Low ├────┼─*x*──┤ High

Spotty Swims

		Substitution	Insertion	Omission	Reversal	Repetition	Self-Correction of Unacceptable Miscue	Meaning Change (Significant Miscue)
		MISCUES						
One day Spotty went for a walk.	7							
The sun was warm. Spotty walked to	14							
where the pond! There he saw a frog. The	22	1						
frog was on a log. Spotty wanted to	30							
play. Spotty began to bark. The frog	37							
jumped into the water.	41							
Then Spotty jumped into the water.	47							
But poor Spotty did not know what to	55							
do. The water was very deep. The water	63							
went way over his head. Spotty moved	70							
his legs. Soon his head came out of the	79							
water. He kept on moving. He came to	87							
the other side of the pond. That is how	96							
how Spotty learned to swim.	100		1					
TOTAL		1	1					

Word Recognition Scoring Guide		
Total Miscues	Level	Significant Miscues
0–1	Independent	0–1
2–4	Ind./Inst.	2
5	Instructional	3
6–9	Inst./Frust.	4
10 +	Frustration	5 +

Total Miscues **2**   Significant Miscues [ ]

Oral Reading Rate	Norm Group Percentile
71 WPM 84)6000	☒ 90 ☐ 75 ☐ 50 ☐ 25 ☐ 10

A 7141 (Grade 1)
Comprehension Questions

T   1. __+__ What is this story about?
          (Spotty and a frog; how Spotty
    A dog learned to swim)

F   2. __+__ Where did Spotty go?
          (to the pond; for a walk)

F   3. __+__ What did Spotty see?
          (a frog)

F   4. __+__ What happened when Spotty saw
          the frog?
          (he barked; he wanted to play; he
          jumped into the water [any 1])

F   5. __+__ What did the frog do when Spotty
          barked?
          (the frog jumped into the water)

F   6. __+__ What did Spotty do when the water
          went over his head?
          (moved his legs; he didn't know
          what to do)

F   7. __+__ What did Spotty learn in this story?
          (how to swim)

I   8. __+__ Who was Spotty?
          (any logical response; a dog)

E   9. __+__ Why do you think Spotty wanted to
          play with the frog?
          (any logical response; he was
          lonesome) *Dogs like to play.*

V 10. __+__ What is a "pond"?
          (like a lake; water) *but ponds are*
          smaller

Retelling Notes

0	Questions Missed

Comprehension Scoring Guide	
Questions Missed	Level
0–1	Independent
1½–2	Ind./Inst.
2½	Instructional
3–4½	Inst./Frust.
5 +	Frustration

Retelling Rubric for the Three Reading Levels
Independent Level/Excellent
Recalls central or key ideas
Remembers important facts
Retains the general sequence of events
Relates most of the content in an organized manner
Instructional Level/Satisfactory
Recalls most central or key ideas
Remembers some important facts
Retains the general sequence of events
Relates an overall sense of the content
Frustration Level/Unsatisfactory
Recalls bits of information in a haphazard manner
Little apparent organization

Student Booklet copy is on page 14.

A 8224 (Grade 2) Activating Background: Read the title to yourself. Then tell me what you think this might be about. *A guy named Billy who goes to camp.*

Background: Low ├────┼─*x*─┤ High

Bill at Camp

		MISCUES						
		Substitution	Insertion	Omission	Reversal	Repetition	Self-Correction of Unacceptable Miscue	Meaning Change (Significant Miscue)
Billy It was the first time Bill went to	8	1						
camp. He was very happy to be there. Soon	17							
he went for a walk in the woods to look for	28							
many kinds of leaves. He found leaves	35							
from some maple and oak trees. As Bill	43							
walked in the woods, he saw some animal *s*	51		1					
tracks. At that moment, a mouse ran into	59							
the a small hole by a tree. Bill wondered if the	69	1						
tracks were made by the mouse. He looked	77							
around for other animals. He did not see	85							
any. The last thing Bill saw was an old	94							
the bird nest in a pine tree.	100	1						
TOTAL		3	1					

Total Miscues **4**   Significant Miscues ☐

Word Recognition Scoring Guide		
Total Miscues	Level	Significant Miscues
0–1	Independent	0–1
2–4	Ind./Inst.	2
5	Instructional	3
6–9	Inst./Frust.	4
10 +	Frustration	5 +

Oral Reading Rate	Norm Group Percentile
$\dfrac{79}{76\,)\overline{6000}}$ WPM	☐ 90 ☐ 75 ☒ 50 ☐ 25 ☐ 10

A 8224 (Grade 2)
Comprehension Questions

T 1. _+_ What is this story about?
(a boy at camp; Bill's walk in the
woods) *A guy goes to camp and*
then into the words.

F 2. _1/2_ Did Bill enjoy going to camp? How
do you know?
(<u>yes,</u> the story said he was happy
there) *It said so in the story.*

F 3. _+_ Why did Bill go walking in the
woods?
(to look for leaves) *to find leaves*

F 4. _1/2_ What kinds of leaves did Bill find in
the woods?
(maple and oak leaves)
maple and pine

F 5. _+_ What else did Bill see besides the
mouse? *beside a tree*
(<u>a bird nest</u>; animal tracks)

F 6. _+_ Where did the mouse go?
(<u>into a small hole</u> by or in a tree)

F 7. _+_ What other animals did Bill see?
(none; he didn't see any)

I 8. _+_ Do you think Bill went on this walk
by himself? What makes you think
so?
(any logical response)
No other names were mentioned.

E 9. _+_ What other animals might Bill see if
he goes for another walk?
(any logical response)
squirrel in a tree; deer

V 10. _+_ What are "tracks"?
(footprints made in the dirt; something made by animals when they
walk or run)
like footprints you leave somewhere
when you walk

1	Questions Missed

Comprehension Scoring Guide	
Questions Missed	Level
0–1	Independent
1½–2	Ind./Inst.
2½	Instructional
3–4½	Inst./Frust.
5 +	Frustration

Retelling Notes

Retelling Rubric for the Three Reading Levels

Independent Level/Excellent
Recalls central or key ideas
Remembers important facts
Retains the general sequence of events
Relates most of the content in an organized manner

Instructional Level/Satisfactory
Recalls most central or key ideas
Remembers some important facts
Retains the general sequence of events
Relates an overall sense of the content

Frustration Level/Unsatisfactory
Recalls bits of information in a haphazard manner
Little apparent organization

Student Booklet copy is on page 15.

A 3183 (Grade 3) Activating Background: Read the title to yourself. Then tell me what you think this might be about. *A bear goes into the forest to hunt for food.*

Background: Low ├───────┼───x─┤ High

The Hungry Bear

Text		Substitution	Insertion	Omission	Reversal	Repetition	Self-Correction of Unacceptable Miscue	Meaning Change (Significant Miscue)
		MISCUES						
buzzy / The busy bees had been making honey all	8	1						
dump / day. That night it was cool and damp. I had	18	1						
me (sc) / slept well until I heard a loud noise near my	28	1						
window. It sounded as if someone were	35							
a (sc) / trying to break into my cabin. As I moved	44	1						
from my cot, I could see something black	52							
standing near the window. In fright I knocked	60							
on the window. Very slowly and quietly the	68							
great shadow moved back and went away.	75							
The next day we found huge bear tracks.	83		1					
The bear had come for the honey the bees	92							
were making in the attic of the cabin.	100							
TOTAL		4	1					

Total Miscues **3***   Significant Miscues ☐

*did not count self-corrections
(*me* for *my* and *a* for *I*)

Word Recognition Scoring Guide		
Total Miscues	Level	Significant Miscues
0–1	Independent	0–1
2–4	Ind./Inst.	2
5	Instructional	3
6–9	Inst./Frust.	4
10 +	Frustration	5 +

Oral Reading Rate	Norm Group Percentile
53 WPM 114)6000	☐ 90 ☐ 75 ☐ 50 ☒ 25 ☐ 10

A 3183 (Grade 3)
Comprehension Questions

T 1. __+__ What is this story about?
(a bear trying to get honey; being
scared) *A hungry bear*

F 2. __+__ What had the bees been doing?
(making honey)

F 3. __−__ Where were the bees making honey?
(in the attic of the cabin)
in their hive

F 4. __+__ Who or what woke the person in this
story?
(a bear; a loud noise at the
window)

F 5. __+__ What was near the window?
(blackness; a shadow; a bear)

F 6. __+__ What was found the next day?
(bear tracks)

F 7. __+__ What did the bear want?
(honey)

I 8. __+__ Why do you think the bear walked
away?
(any logical response; it heard the
knock) *Because he could tell there
was a person inside*

E 9. __+__ What might you do to keep the bear
away?
(any logical response; remove the
honey) *I'd get a shot gun!*

V 10. __+__ What is an "attic"?
(a place way upstairs in your house
where you put junk and stuff)
*It's upstairs and there's a lot of
old stuff. We have an attic.*

1	Questions Missed

Comprehension Scoring Guide

Questions Missed	Level
0–1	Independent
1½–2	Ind./Inst.
2½	Instructional
3–4½	Inst./Frust.
5 +	Frustration

Retelling Notes

Retelling Rubric for the Three Reading Levels

Independent Level/Excellent
Recalls central or key ideas
Remembers important facts
Retains the general sequence of events
Relates most of the content in an organized manner

Instructional Level/Satisfactory
Recalls most central or key ideas
Remembers some important facts
Retains the general sequence of events
Relates an overall sense of the content

Frustration Level/Unsatisfactory
Recalls bits of information in a haphazard manner
Little apparent organization

Student Booklet copy is on page 16.

A 5414 (Grade 4) Activating Background: Read the title to yourself. Then tell me what you think this might be about. *There might be a fire close to an animal colony.*

Background: Low ├────+─×──┤ High

Fire and Animals

		MISCUES						
	Substitution	Insertion	Omission	Reversal	Repetition	Self-Correction of Unacceptable Miscue	Meaning Change (Significant Miscue)
The summer was a dry one, u̶n̶u̶s̶u̶a̶l̶ **7**			1				
for this area. Trees and bushes in the forest **16**							
wilted and died. One afternoon a storm *strom* (sc) **23**	1						
came to the forest. Thunder was heard and **31**							
lightning was seen. Then it began to **38**							
rain. A spark touched the leaves and a *leaf* **46**	1						
fire began. The fire spread quickly. The *And* **53**	1						
animals warned each other as they hurried **60**							
to escape the flames. As the fire came **68**							
closer, trees fell to the ground. Their **75**							
branches were yellow, orange, and red. **81**							
The smoke was so thick that the animals **89**							
could hardly breathe. Many couldn't **94**							
escape the danger of the flames. **100**							
TOTAL	3		1				

<table>
<tr><td colspan="3">Word Recognition Scoring Guide</td></tr>
<tr><td>Total Miscues</td><td>Level</td><td>Significant Miscues</td></tr>
<tr><td>0–1</td><td>Independent</td><td>0–1</td></tr>
<tr><td>2–4</td><td>Ind./Inst.</td><td>2</td></tr>
<tr><td>5</td><td>Instructional</td><td>3</td></tr>
<tr><td>6–9</td><td>Inst./Frust.</td><td>4</td></tr>
<tr><td>10 +</td><td>Frustration</td><td>5 +</td></tr>
</table>

Total Miscues **3***   Significant Miscues [ ]

*did not count self-correction (*strom* for *storm*)

Oral Reading Rate	Norm Group Percentile
$\frac{52}{116\,)6000}$ **WPM**	☐ 90 ☐ 75 ☐ 50 ☐ 25 ☒ 10

A 5414 (Grade 4)
Comprehension Questions

T 1. _+_ What is this story about?
(a forest fire) *A spark touched a leaf*
          and there was a fire.

F 2. _+_ What did the animals try to do?
(<u>escape</u>; warn each other)

F 3. _−_ What was unusual about this
summer?
(it had been a dry one)
It rained.

F 4. _−_ What was heard and seen in the
woods before the fire began?
(thunder and lightning)
I don't remember.

F 5. _+_ What started the fire?
(<u>a spark</u>; lightning)

F 6. _+_ What colors were the trees in this
story?
(<u>yellow</u>, <u>orange</u>, and <u>red</u> [any 2])

F 7. _+_ Why was it difficult for the
animals to breathe?
(<u>smoke filled the air</u>; the fire)

I 8. _−_ Why do you think the fire spread
quickly?
(any logical response; it had been
a dry summer)
It was thick.

E 9. _+_ What problems do you think the
animals that survived the fire
might have?
(any logical response)
cuts, scars

V 10. _+_ What does "escape" mean?
(<u>get away</u>; any logical response)

Retelling Notes	

Retelling Rubric for the Three Reading Levels

Independent Level/Excellent
Recalls central or key ideas
Remembers important facts
Retains the general sequence of events
Relates most of the content in an organized manner

Instructional Level/Satisfactory
Recalls most central or key ideas
Remembers some important facts
Retains the general sequence of events
Relates an overall sense of the content

Frustration Level/Unsatisfactory
Recalls bits of information in a haphazard manner
Little apparent organization

3	Questions Missed

Comprehension Scoring Guide

Questions Missed	Level
0–1	Independent
1½–2	Ind./Inst.
2½	Instructional
3–4½	Inst./Frust.
5 +	Frustration

Student Booklet copy is on page 17.

A 8595 (Grade 5) Activating Background: Read the title to yourself. Then tell me what you think this might be about. *It might have a surprise ending or a big secret.*

Background: Low |———+——X—| High

The Mystery

		Substitution	Insertion	Omission	Reversal	Repetition	Self-Correction of Unacceptable Miscue	Meaning Change (Significant Miscue)
		MISCUES						
Everyone turned to stare as a black *(back)*	7	1						
(hode) hooded figure whizzed *(wized)* by on a skateboard.	14	2						
It was a mystery because no one knew	22							
who the talented person was. Ken saw	29							
the skateboarder slide *(slid)* down the library	35	1						
railing and disappear *(disappoint)* into the alley. Nita	42	1						
followed the person *(persons)* from school and	48		1					
watched as a curb was jumped and a	56							
three hundred sixty degree *(de/gree)* turn was	62	1						
completed *(complicate)* with ease. One day Ken	68	1						
noticed a skateboard and a black hooded *(hooded)*	75	1						
jacket next to Rose's house. He also saw	83							
a library book called *Skateboarding Tips*	89							
in her desk at school. Ken had solved *(slaved)*	97	1						
the challenging mystery.	100							
TOTAL		9	1					

Total Miscues [10]   Significant Miscues [ ]

Word Recognition Scoring Guide		
Total Miscues	Level	Significant Miscues
0–1	Independent	0–1
2–4	Ind./Inst.	2
5	Instructional	3
6–9	Inst./Frust.	4
10 +	Frustration	5 +

Oral Reading Rate	Norm Group Percentile
41 WPM 147)6000	☐ 90 ☐ 75 ☐ 50 ☐ 25 ☒ 10

A 8595 (Grade 5)
Comprehension Questions

T   1. __+__   What is this story about?
(a skateboarder; finding out who the
skateboarder was) *and a mystery*

F   2. __−__   What did the mystery person look
like?
(wore a black hood; rode a
skateboard)
ordinary

F   3. __−__   Why was this person such a
mystery?
(no one knew who the person was)
He skateboarded so fast.

F   4. __+__   Who saw the skateboarder?
(everyone; Ken and Nita)

F   5. __+__   What kind of stunts did the mystery
person do?
(slide down a railing; three hundred
sixty degree turn; jump a curb
[any 1])

F   6. __+__   Who solved the mystery?
(Ken)

F   7. __+__   What items did Ken see that helped
him solve the mystery?
(hooded jacket; skateboard; book
[any 2])

I   8. __−__   Who was the mystery person?
(Rose) *Someone at Rose's house*

E   9. __−__   If you were Ken, how might you
have solved the mystery differently?
(any logical response)
I'm not sure.

V   10. __+__   What does "talented" mean?
(good at something; gifted)
do stuff real good

Retelling Notes

__4__	Questions Missed

Comprehension Scoring Guide

Questions Missed	Level
0–1	Independent
1½–2	Ind./Inst.
2½	Instructional
3–4½	Inst./Frust.
5 +	Frustration

Retelling Rubric for the Three Reading Levels

Independent Level/Excellent
Recalls central or key ideas
Remembers important facts
Retains the general sequence of events
Relates most of the content in an organized manner

Instructional Level/Satisfactory
Recalls most central or key ideas
Remembers some important facts
Retains the general sequence of events
Relates an overall sense of the content

Frustration Level/Unsatisfactory
Recalls bits of information in a haphazard manner
Little apparent organization

How the Basic Reading Inventory Helps Your Students

The results of the Basic Reading Inventory can be used as a valuable basis for instruction. The insights can be used to inform instruction, prepare strategy lessons, and provide appropriate interventions. The *total* results from the Basic Reading Inventory must be used to help plan effective instruction, taking into account each student's *specific* strengths and needs in word identification, comprehension, and/or fluency.

Assessments like the Basic Reading Inventory play a substantial role in providing data for

- matching students with appropriate instructional materials,
- assessing reading behavior,
- providing helpful and appropriate interventions,
- differentiating instruction,
- developing reading strategy lessons
- helping students strengthen their reading, and
- monitoring progress.

Unless Basic Reading Inventory results are used in conjunction with observation, cumulative records, portfolios, and other evaluative techniques, serious errors may result. One should not underestimate the importance of the Basic Reading Inventory for classroom, resource room, and clinical use; however, the results should be used to *guide* your responses to a student's reading. Results should not be used to dictate your actions, thereby dominating your professional knowledge and experience. Professionals who use the Basic Reading Inventory as suggested in this manual will help ensure that students are placed in appropriate reading materials, taught needed reading strategies, and given appropriate interventions.

The professional who places students in reading materials at their appropriate instructional levels and provides responsive instructional interventions for specific areas of need will help students become better readers. That's the essence of realizing and acting upon "the point that individual differences are a fact of life in schools and classrooms" (Pearson, 2007, p. 155). Using the Basic Reading Inventory to discover students' instructional levels and needs in reading, coupled with responsive teaching and interventions, is an appropriate way to design and implement high-quality reading instruction.

Caution

SECTION

5

Targeted Interventions for Reading Difficulties

Focused instructional interventions help students become better readers.

- Scenario 1: The Student Repeats Words, Phrases, or Sentences   117
- Scenario 2: The Student Waits to Be Told Unknown Words   118
- Scenario 3: The Student Produces a Nonword or Omits Unknown Words   119
- Scenario 4: The Student Substitutes Words That Make Sense   120
- Scenario 5: The Student Substitutes Words That Do Not Make Sense   121
- Scenario 6: The Student Habitually Tries to Sound Out Unknown Words   123

- Scenario 7: The Student Ignores Punctuation, Adds Punctuation, or Uses Inappropriate Intonation   124
- Scenario 8: The Student Overrelies on Context While Reading   125
- Scenario 9: The Student's Oral Reading Lacks Fluency   126
- Scenario 10: The Student Is Overly Concerned with Rate When Reading Is Timed   127
- Scenario 11: The Student Does Not Read for Meaning   128

The Student Repeats Words, Phrases, or Sentences	scenario

Repetitions may help the student understand what he or she has read. You must decide whether the student is anticipating a "hard" word, making a legitimate effort to have the reading make sense, or merely repeating from habit. Consider the following:

- If the student's repetitions are frequent, it is possible that the reading material is too difficult. If this is the case, provide the student with reading materials at his or her instructional level.

- Repetitions that are "stalls" may provide additional time to unlock an unknown word. This behavior may be a normal part of the reading process. Excessive use of the "stall" technique, however, may indicate that the reading material is too difficult and/or that more effective reading strategies are needed. It may also indicate a need to teach how context and language cues can be used to anticipate words (see Johns & Lenski, 2014). Many repetitions can also impact rate of reading, one aspect of fluency.

- Praise the student when a word, phrase, or sentence is corrected to preserve ongoing meaning. Tell the student that such behavior is fully acceptable when reading doesn't make sense. Provide examples from students' reading similar to the following that a student and/or class could discuss and evaluate. Note that the miscues distorted the meaning in the first two examples, and the student went back and corrected them.

1. ⓒ *They grew*
   He knew he must try to save the woods he loved so much.

2. ⓒ *in*
   He jumped on the high wall perfectly.

3. Jack woke up Saturday morning.

4. *saved*
   Ken had solved the mystery.

- If repetitions are merely a habit (as in the third example above), it may be helpful to have the student record his or her reading and then discuss it with you. The student should then be guided to realize that the majority of the repetitions are a habit that generally detract from effective reading. Such repetitions also reduce fluency.

- Sometimes a student repeatedly overcorrects to ensure word-for-word accuracy. Such students should be encouraged not to repeat and break the flow when the miscue does not significantly alter the meaning (such as substituting *the* for *a*). Have the student follow along as you read and model the process.

---

scenario

2 | The Student Waits to Be Told Unknown Words

The reluctance of some students to attempt unknown words may be due to several factors. First, students may not have been taught a functional strategy for word identification, or they do not have a variety of strategies to use when confronted with an unknown word. Although students may have been taught phonics and the use of context, they do not apply these strategies during reading. Second, students may often be told unknown words, thereby reducing their need to acquire or use an internal strategy for word identification. Third, students who struggle in reading may be reluctant to take risks. Instead, they frequently reply on you or other students to tell them unknown words. The following strategies may be helpful:

- Stress that you want the student to attempt unknown words without help.

- Wait 5 or 10 seconds and see whether this will suggest to the student that you expect him or her to attempt to pronounce the word.

- Discuss what the student thinks should be done when confronted with an unknown word. Guide the student toward effective strategies that have been taught to help identify unknown words.

- Have the student continue reading to see whether subsequent textual information will help with the unknown word.

- Ask the student to go back a line and see whether the preceding sentence and the words around the "unknown" word suggest the word. If the student does not suggest a word, ask him or her to reread the sentence until a good guess is made.

- Ask the student to reread the sentence and try to guess a word that begins with the initial sound of the "unknown" word and makes sense.

- Provide oral examples where the student uses the information provided to anticipate the missing word.

> I saw a _____.
>
> I would like to play _____.
>
> It's time to go _____.
>
> I found a _____ in the lawn.

- Use easy cloze exercises where the student is asked to say or write in a word that makes sense. Discuss various choices offered by a group of students. Gradually include some graphic information, as in the third example, about the exact word the author used.

> I like _____.
>
> I like to go to the _____.
>
> I like to go to the s_____.

- If the student encounters several unknown words in a line of print, it is probable that the reading material is too difficult. Provide reading material at the student's instructional level.

- Teach a functional set of strategies for word identification. The approach in the list below can be adapted and taught.

Figuring Out Unknown Words

1. Use the words around the unknown word to help think of a word that makes sense in the sentence.
2. Use the letters, and the sounds associated with the letters, along with the words around the unknown word, to say a word that makes sense in the sentence.
3. Look for root words, prefixes, suffixes, and endings. Try to pronounce the various word parts to see whether you have heard it before. Try various pronunciations, especially for the vowels.
4. Continue reading. Later sentences may help you figure out the unfamiliar word.
5. As a last resort, ask someone or skip the unknown word.

The Student Produces a Nonword or Omits Unknown Words

scenario

3

The student must be helped to realize that reading is a meaningful process and words pronounced should make sense. In short, reading should sound like oral language. Try the following strategies:

- Ask the student what the nonword means. It is possible that the student knows the meaning but has mispronounced the word.

- Share oral and written examples where the student attempts to predict the appropriate word that has been omitted. Discuss the student's choices and the clues that the student used to predict the omitted word.

> I will mail the _____.
>
> The horse _____ over the fence.
>
> Jack and Tom _____ into the kitchen.

- Provide examples that contain a nonword and ask the student to tell what the nonword could mean. Have the student share clues in the sentence that were helpful in predicting the meaning of the unknown word.

> He drank a glass of *fax*.
>
> The *zop* bought some candy.
>
> I went swimming in the *tos*.

- Place opaque white tape over certain words in the student's reading material that can be easily predicted. Encourage the student to supply a real word that makes sense. Then compare the student's word to the word in the reading material. If the words are different, encourage the student to evaluate his or her choice in light of the actual word. Help the student to transfer this prediction strategy to identifying unknown words when reading.

- Many nonwords may indicate that the reading material is too difficult. Provide materials at the student's independent or instructional level.

- If the student omits an unknown word, ask questions such as:

> Does that sound like language to you?
>
> What word do you think could go in this spot?
>
> Why do you think so?
>
> What word do you know that begins like _____ that would make sense?

If the student is unable to produce a word with the same beginning sound, ask the student to try a word that he or she thinks would make sense.

The goal should be to have the student produce a word or nonword rather than omitting the word. Remember that there are times when a word can be omitted without any or much loss in meaning.

---

scenario

4

The Student Substitutes Words That Make Sense

The most important strategy must be enacted by you: remain silent. Try to keep other students from breaking the thought line. You might tell students that readers will sometimes substitute words that make sense. Only substitutions that do not make sense or alter the meaning should be corrected. To help students decide whether substitutions do or do not make sense, try the following strategies:

- Provide sentences that contain a substituted word written above the text. Have students discuss whether or not the substituted word makes sense. You could also read a text and make substitution miscues that students could evaluate.

> *before*
> He tried to make up for it by shocking people with his rude behavior.

> *they*
> They went to the zoo because there were many things to see.

> *big*
> He put the bag down.

- Provide exercises that contain substitutions two different readers made in the same sentence. Discuss which substitution, if either, appears to be closer to the author's intended meaning.

> *the*
> Billy decided to ride along a little road.

> *walk*
> Billy decided to ride along a little road.

- Develop lessons where students can discuss the subtle differences in words even though such differences are unlikely to significantly influence the author's intended meaning. For example, what is the difference between *street* and *road*, *house* and *home*, *tall* and *big*, *little* and *small*?

NOTE: Similar strategies may also be used with omissions. For example:

> He knew that there were ~~so~~ many things to see. He remembered how bare and black it ~~had~~ looked.

> He gave the boy twenty-~~five~~ cents.

> He found leaves from ~~some~~ maple and oak trees.

> Dad went out to get your sleds. First we will eat.

> In the sky I saw a ~~strange~~ object.

| The Student Substitutes Words That Do Not Make Sense | scenario 5 |

Tell the student that reading is a process of constructing meaning. (Did that sound right to you?) The student should be taught to use semantic (contextual) cues. Try the following strategies:

- Remind the student to think while reading so that he or she will stop and reread the material if it is not making sense. This student may view reading primarily as a "word-calling" process. You may need to help the student develop a concept of reading that involves meaning as the crucial element.

- Give the student oral exercises in which he or she identifies words that do not make sense in the context of the sentences or the story. Discuss why the word or words do not make sense. Do similar written exercises. For example:

> I like to drink apples.

> The postman delivered the groceries.

He set his calendar so he would wake up at seven o'clock.

Bill went to the beach to buy some candy for his sister.

She likes to eat books.

- Provide the student with oral and written exercises containing closure tasks in which the student anticipates omitted words that make sense. Use the cloze procedure as a teaching technique. Develop the notion that language dictates that only certain types of words can be placed after certain language structures.

  After playing, the children _____.

  I will see you after _____.

  He was reading a _____.

  "I lost my money," _____ Bill.

  The _____ climbed the tree.

- Use small group activities where certain key words in a story are covered. Elicit responses from the group and have students evaluate the responses. The ultimate criterion is: "Does the word you suggest make sense in the phrase (sentence, paragraph)?" Demonstrate how the flow of the story helps the reader to predict certain words. Think out loud so students can "see" you model the process. Be sure some of your predictions do not match the text and take time to have students explain why they are inappropriate in the context.

- Keep track of the student's substitutions to see whether certain words are habitually associated with other words. Write selections where the grammatical structures make it highly unlikely for the habitual associations to occur. For example:

  was and saw

Once upon a time there was a girl named Ebony. Her hair was long and black. Ebony liked to wear beads in her hair. One day, while she was walking downtown, she saw some beads in a store window. She saw blue, yellow, and pink beads.

  in and on

Jim liked to collect insects. He kept the spiders in a jar on top of his dresser. One Friday, his mother invited some friends to come over for coffee. They were talking in the kitchen. Jim took his jar of spiders into the kitchen and set it on the table. When one lady reached for a cup on the table, she bumped the jar. It landed on the floor. What do you think happened next?

  when and then

José and his mother had some errands to do. His mother said, "I will get my coat; then I will be ready to go. When you find your jacket, come out to the car. First, we will go to the market; then we can go to the pet shop to find out when the puppy will be ready to come home. When we bring the puppy home, you will get the basket out of the closet."

- Provide sentences that contain a substituted word written above the text. Have students discuss whether the substituted word makes sense. Be sure that students give reasons or explain their responses. For example:

  then
  Sam did not see them.

  they
  They went to the zoo because there were many things to see.

  radius
  The key to success was in the radium reaction.

- Provide exercises that contain substitutions two different readers made in the same sentence. Discuss which substitution appears to be closer to the author's intended meaning. For example:

  the
  Billy decided to ride along a little road.

  walk
  Billy decided to ride along a little road.

- Record the student's reading. Have the student listen to the reading and note substitutions that resulted in a partial or significant loss of meaning. Discuss and use some of the appropriate strategies already presented. In addition, encourage the student to monitor his or her reading by asking, "Does that make sense?" Ask this question from time to time when the reading makes sense so students are not automatically cued by the question that there is a significant miscue.

- If there are many substitutions that distort the author's intended meaning, the book may be too difficult. Choose materials at the student's instructional level. Books at this level should contain words that are usually within the student's meaning vocabulary. In other words, the student should have the necessary background, experiences, and concepts to understand the words.

  NOTE: Similar strategies may also be used with omissions that distort the meaning.

The Student Habitually Tries to Sound Out Unknown Words
scenario
6

Some students may have been taught or think that the only appropriate strategy is to sound out words when they are unknown. Other students may not have been taught any strategies that can be applied in such a situation. In either case, help students use their knowledge of language (syntax) and teach the value of context (semantic) cues. The following strategies represent an appropriate beginning:

- Show the student that a word in oral language can often be predicted correctly before it is heard. Model the process. Then, help the student use this same knowledge in reading. The following examples may be useful:

  He gave the kitten some _____.

  Put a stamp on the _____.

  Five pennies make a _____.

  The bird began to _____ to the tree.

- Offer examples where two readers have come across the same unknown word. Discuss the responses of the two readers in an attempt to decide which reader has been most effective and why.

Text:	The car went down the old *street*.
Reader 1:	The car went down the old *road*.
Reader 2:	The car went down the old *stream*.

- Provide words that the student is probably able to pronounce but that are not familiar in meaning. Then provide a sentence that builds meaning for the word. Have students identify and explain which clues in the sentence were helpful. For example:

kingcups	He picked some kingcups for his mother because she likes flowers.
kipper	The kipper is not usually caught by fishermen.

- Provide words in the student's meaning vocabulary that he or she is unable to pronounce. Such words can then be placed in a context that builds meaning for the words. Through such exercises the student should realize that meaning can be achieved without always sounding out words.
- Teach the student a set of strategies for word identification. A chart or bookmark could be adapted from the items listed below.

Figuring Out Unknown Words

1. What makes sense here?
2. What sound does it start with?
3. Chunk the sounds.
4. Are there root words, prefixes, or endings?
5. Keep reading to try to figure it out.
6. Use these last:
   - dictionary
   - someone's help
   - skip it

---

scenario 7

The Student Ignores Punctuation, Adds Punctuation, or Uses Inappropriate Intonation

Try the following strategies to rectify misuses of punctuation and intonation:

- The student should be shown examples where punctuation is ignored or substituted. In some cases meaning may not be disturbed; in other cases a change in meaning may occur. Discuss whether or not meaning is impacted. The following examples may be useful:

. He

He woke up ˄ ~~and~~ got ready for school.

Billy looked ahead. He ~~and~~ saw smoke coming out of a pile of dry brush.

Even as Billy looked at, the flames burst out.

But Blaze scrambled up the bank, and Billy held on somehow, with his arms around the pony's neck.

Down Blaze went to his knees. ~~and~~ Billy slipped out of the saddle.

Model similar oral examples using classroom materials.

- Read plays and help the student see the role of punctuation.

- Teach the basic marks of punctuation, as needed, in a natural writing situation.

- Discuss reading that has been recorded and ask the student to point out areas where it can be improved.

- Remember that some intonation patterns may be the result of the student's dialect. In such cases, no interventions are necessary.

- Use slash marks to indicate appropriate phrasing (for instance, Bill,/my brother,/ has gone away.). Reduce the number of slash marks as the student's phrasing and attention to punctuation improve. Students can also be encouraged to mark appropriate phrases in reproduced copies of selected reading selections.

- Use pattern books. Each time the pattern is repeated, ask the student to read it. Stress that the pattern should sound like speech.

- List phrases on cards and have the student read the phrases as they would sound naturally.

at school	at home	near my house	by the school
on the table	by my house	in the box	near the tree

- Model correct phrasing and punctuation in a passage that is easy for the student. Invite the student to read it like you do. Then have the student read along with you. Finally, have the student read the passage independently.

The Student Overrelies on Context While Reading

Some students read fluently, but they often add a number of words that were not written by the author. These same students may also omit a number of words. The result is often quite different from the one in print. These students seem to rely heavily on their background knowledge to the partial exclusion of graphophonic knowledge. Because effective reading requires the use of context, language cues, and graphophonic cues, the following strategies and interventions may be helpful:

- Tell the student that background knowledge is important to help predict words while reading, but other cues should also be used. Model how initial sounds, along with context clues, can be used to help pronounce words. Possible responses are provided in parentheses.

    The leaves on the tree are g_____. (green)

    To write, you need p_____ and p_____. (pencil/pen/paper)

Jamie is my best f_____. (friend)

The h_____ has a roof and ch_____. (house, chimney)

- Record the student's reading, listen to it, and mark any miscues. Then review selected miscues with the student and discuss how meaning is changed even though the miscue may make sense in the sentence. Model how graphic cues can be used along with the context to determine the actual word used by the author.

  quietly
  She quickly dashed down the hill.

  perplexed
  The soft buzz of the computer relaxed Anthony.

- Present sentences where the student can make initial predictions of a missing word. Then provide a series of graphic cues to help the student correctly identify the word used by the author.

  I must put the _____ away.

  I must put the d_____ away.

  I must put the de_____s away.

  I must put the decor_____s away.

  I must put the decorations away.

- Tell the student that all readers make miscues, but stress the importance of trying to pay attention to the words written by the author. Relate the situation to a piece of the student's writing. The expectation is that the reader will read the words that were written.

---

scenario 9	The Student's Oral Reading Lacks Fluency

Students at the beginning stages of reading are seldom fluent readers (National Reading Panel, 2000). This situation is to be expected and no intervention is required. Such students are beginning to acquire a sight vocabulary and learn strategies such as phonics so they can identify unknown words. Such is the case for most beginning readers, whatever their age. If, however, students remain in a stage where they continue to read word for word, the following strategies may be considered.

- Be sure students are placed in materials at an appropriate instructional level. At the instructional level, the student will generally miss no more than one word in twenty.

- Recognize that reading is a developmental process. Fluency will usually improve as sight vocabularies and word-identification strategies develop.

- Encourage the repeated readings of pattern books and books at the student's independent and instructional levels.

- Use echo reading. Have the student echo your phrasing and expression from a book.

- Promote wide reading and oral reading of plays and jokes.

- Engage students in choral reading and reader's theater.

- Have older students practice "easy" books that can be read orally to younger students. Practice sessions can include tape recording the reading and evaluating the fluency and expression.

- Provide books on tape so students can listen and follow along.

- Remember that a lack of fluency may be symptomatic of limited word-identification strategies, poor sight vocabulary, and/or insufficient meaningful practice. Consider these areas carefully when evaluating the student's fluency.

Johns and Berglund (2010) have prepared a compact book on fluency that answers common questions often asked by teachers and offers over 30 strategies to strengthen fluency. Each strategy contains a brief description followed by an easy-to-use lesson plan.

The Student Is Overly Concerned with Rate When Reading Is Timed

scenario

10

The increased emphasis on fluency has resulted in progress monitoring, usually with timed readings. While the ability to read with appropriate speed, accuracy, and expression are worthwhile instructional goals, some students may focus so much on speed that meaning is forgotten. If instruction in fluency is perceived only as fast reading, there is the real risk of students becoming word-callers, not meaning seekers (Marcell, 2007). The following strategies may help students develop, embrace, and maintain a concept of fluency that embodies much more than "faster is better."

- Help students realize that fluency involves comprehension, accuracy, speed, and expression (prosody). Put a fluency diamond on poster board to remind students of the four components that make up fluency. Model each of these aspects of fluency during read alouds and in the ongoing instructional program.

- Compare and contrast multiple readings of a portion of text where 1) it is read without expression, 2) many errors are made, and 3) it is read quickly without attending to meaning. Stress a broad concept of fluency when oral reading and progress monitoring occurs.

- Create purposes prior to reading and have students read to answer the purpose-setting questions.

- Incorporate retelling or summarizing into fluency assessments so students will realize that comprehension is important. Questions can also be asked.

- If the student reads fast and does not understand what was read, stress that the reason to read is to construct meaning, gain information, and make sense of the reading material. Provide examples of various types of reading materials and have the student explain what the reader would probably like to achieve. Use or adapt the examples below.

a recipe for a favorite treat	the ingredients on a food label
comics in the newspaper	a book about various sports
a sports magazine	the directions inside a model car kit
a joke or riddle book	receiving a postcard from a friend
directions in a new game	the school newspaper

- If the student makes many miscues in an effort to increase rate, stop the reading and remind the student that accuracy is an important part of reading. Have the student practice the selection so it can be read accurately.

- If the student reads without expression or with inappropriate expression in an effort to increase rate, model appropriate expression in a portion of the selection for the student. Then have the student reread the same selection in an effort to emulate the modeled expression.

- Use reader's theater scripts to help students practice appropriate rate and expression to help convey meaning to the audience.

- Remind students that oral reading should sound a lot like conversations that people have with each other. Have students prepare written "conversations" between two classmates. Then have partners practice the "conversations" using appropriate phrasing, rate, and expression.

- Strive to have progress monitoring in the classroom "reflect a more comprehensive model of fluency in which comprehension and expression join speed and accuracy" (Johns, 2007, p. 18).

scenario	The Student Does Not Read for Meaning

11

Some students are so focused on decoding words accurately that they do not focus on comprehending what they read. Many younger readers and struggling readers may believe that the purpose of reading is to identify the words rather than to construct meaning from those words. Because the purpose of all reading is comprehension, it is essential that students be taught to read for meaning at all times. The following strategies may help students understand that the purpose of reading is to construct meaning.

- Explain to the student that there are many purposes for reading. These include learning, enjoyment, and to solve problems. Explain that all of these purposes require the student to understand what has been read.

- Model the importance of reading for meaning by reading a short set of instructions aloud. Complete some of the steps correctly and some incorrectly. Ask the student why it is important to read for meaning in this situation.

- Explain that sometimes the purpose for reading is enjoyment. Read a short text aloud to the student. Do a brief think-aloud to demonstrate your understanding and enjoyment of the text. Ask the student to think of a text he or she enjoyed reading. Discuss the importance of reading for meaning to promote enjoyment.

- Tell the student that the purpose of many school reading assignments is to read for information. Using a science or social studies textbook, show the student the questions that appear at the end of each section. Read these questions together and explain that they can set a purpose for reading that section. In other words, clarify that the student should be thinking about these questions while reading, and that after reading, he or she should be able to answer them.

- Prior to reading, help the student set a specific purpose for reading to focus attention on understanding the text. These purposes may include answering specific questions, stating the main idea, checking to see if predictions were accurate, or enjoying the text. When the student has read the text, have him or her reflect and discuss whether the purpose was met.

- Teach the student to use the Read-Cover-Remember-Retell strategy. First, the student will read a piece of text that is no larger than can be covered by his or her hand. Next, the student covers the text and consciously remembers what was read. Finally, the student retells what was just read to a partner. If he or she can't retell accurately, he or she can go back and read the text again. Once the student understands the Read-Cover-Remember-Retell strategy, ask him or her to apply it while reading independently or with a partner.

Access to a wide range of interesting books is important to promote reading for all.

Development, Reliability, and Validity Data for the Basic Reading Inventory

The authors debrief after a day of field testing.

Basis for the Graded Word Lists

The word lists were selected from two sources: *EDL Core Vocabularies in Reading, Mathematics, Science, and Social Studies* (Taylor et al., 1979) and *Basic Skills Word List: Grades 1–12* (IOX, 1980). These two word lists and their development are described here.

The first source was the Reading Core Vocabulary portion from the *EDL Core Vocabularies*. Fourteen graded word lists, from pre-primer through grade thirteen, are included. The lists are composed of words "introduced in the more widely used basal reading series and/or found on frequency lists" (p. 1). Originally published in 1949, the EDL Reading Core Vocabulary was revised in 1951, 1955, 1969, and 1979. In the 1979 revision, several procedures were used to select words for the 14 graded word lists for each of the three forms.

The lists through grade three were developed by determining the level at which words were introduced in nine different basal reader series. A word was included if it was introduced at the same level in at least three of the nine basal series.

In selecting words for the fourth-, fifth-, and sixth-grade lists, words occurring in at least three basals on the same level or below were judged to be suitable for that level. In addition, words occurring in two readers at the same level were checked against the Rinsland (1945) list and the Thorndike and Lorge (1944) list. The Rinsland list was used to confirm student knowledge of the word at that particular level. The Thorndike-Lorge list was used to determine whether a word occurred with sufficient frequency to justify its inclusion.

For grades seven and eight, words used in basal readers in grades four through six that did not occur with sufficient frequency to be included in earlier lists were checked against the

Rinsland and Thorndike-Lorge lists for frequency. If warranted, these words were included in the Reading Core Vocabulary. The remaining words for grades seven and eight were derived, for the most part, from frequency on these same two word lists.

Nine of the Reading Core Vocabulary graded lists were used for the graded word lists on the Basic Reading Inventory: pre-primer through grade eight. The pre-primer list contained 68 different words; the eighth-grade word list contained over 700 different words.

The second source, *Basic Skills Word List: Grades 1–12* (IOX, 1980), contains lists of words for grades one through twelve. The graded word lists contain key words that students need to master in each grade and were designed as a resource for reading teachers and for the development of tests.

To select the words for the Basic Skills Word List, three criteria were used:

1. the frequency of words in basal readers
2. the frequency of words in general reading materials
3. students' demonstrated familiarity with particular words.

The initial source of words, the *EDL Core Vocabularies*, was described earlier. All the words on the *EDL Core Vocabularies* were checked for their familiarity to children by using *The Living Word Vocabulary: The Words We Know* (Dale & O'Rourke, 1976). To determine students' knowledge of commonly encountered words, Dale and O'Rourke administered three-option, multiple-choice test items to students. Students were given a word and asked to choose the correct definition for it. *The Living Word Vocabulary* provides a "familiarity percentage" for each word listed. This index reflects the percentage of students who answered that word's multiple-choice test item correctly. In order to assign a word to a particular grade level, Dale and O'Rourke aimed for each tested word to have a familiarity percentage for a given grade level that was within the range of 67 percent to 84 percent. Therefore, if a word was tested at the sixth grade and only 66 percent of the students at that grade were familiar with it, then the word was retested at the eighth grade. Conversely, if a word tested at the eighth grade received a familiarity score higher than 84 percent, it was retested at the sixth grade. The familiarity percentage supplied with each word in *The Living Word Vocabulary* reflects the percentage of correct student responses at the grade level to which the word was ultimately assigned.

The authors of *The Living Word Vocabulary* did not begin testing words until the fourth grade; after that, they tested words only at alternate grades. Thus, familiarity percentages appear only for grades four, six, eight, and so on. Therefore, EDL words through grade four were checked for their familiarity to students according to the fourth-grade Dale-O'Rourke familiarity percentages. Fifth-grade EDL words were checked against both fourth- and sixth-grade familiarity percentages. Words in all subsequent grade lists were checked for familiarity ratings at either the grade level at which they appeared in EDL or at a lower grade.

Words that were not familiar to at least 65 percent of students at a given grade on the basis of the Dale-O'Rourke study were moved to a higher grade level in the Basic Skills Word List. The exact familiarity percentages necessary for an EDL word to be retained at the same grade level on the Basic Skills Word List varied slightly from grade to grade. These percentages were adjusted in order to meet the requirements of a predetermined word load for each grade. (This word load factor will be described subsequently.) Table 6.1 contains the minimum familiarity percentages used through grade twelve.

The rationale for employing a stringent familiarity criterion was straightforward: even if a word is found in several reading series at a given grade level, it may still be unfamiliar to many students and therefore should not be assigned to that grade level. The effect of this student familiarity screen was to move some words from each of the graded EDL word lists to higher grade levels.

Table 6.1

Minimum Familiarity Percentages: Pre-Primer through Twelfth Grade

Grade at Which Word Appeared in EDL	Grade to Which Word Was Assigned in Dale-O'Rourke Study*	Minimum Familiarity Percentage Required for Retention in Same Grade Level as EDL on Basic Skills Word List
Pre-Primer and First	Fourth	80%
Second	Fourth	83%
Third	Fourth	76%
Fourth	Fourth	65%
	Sixth	75%
Fifth	Fourth	65%
	Sixth	75%
Sixth	Fourth	65%
	Sixth	84%
Seventh	Fourth and Sixth	65%
Eighth	Fourth and Sixth	65%
	Eighth	80%
Ninth	Sixth and Eighth	65%
Tenth	Sixth and Eighth	65%
	Tenth	75%
Eleventh	Eighth and Tenth	65%
Twelfth	Eighth and Tenth	65%
	Twelfth	75%

*This study did not include words from the pre-primer through third grade.

For instructional purposes, it is desirable to allocate words to grade levels on a proportional basis. It would make little sense to assign 200 words to one grade level and 2,000 words to another. One of the best guides to the determination of an appropriate word load per grade level is the average number of words introduced per grade level by publishers of reading textbook series. These commercially published textbooks, many of them revised more than once, provide an experience-based estimate of how many new words can be reasonably introduced at each grade level. In the process of researching the background for their core vocabularies, developers of the EDL word lists calculated the average number of words introduced at grades one through six for nine different textbook series. These textbook-derived word loads were the following:

Grade	1	2	3	4	5	6
Word Load	341	440	708	787	1,063	1,077

The word loads for the Basic Skills Word List at grades one through four were designed to coincide as closely as possible with these textbook-derived word loads. The word loads for the Basic Skills Word List at grades one through four are as follows:

Grade	1	2	3	4
Word Load	341	439	708	785

In grades five through twelve, students' familiarity with words, as reflected by the Dale-O'Rourke study, became a major determinant of grade level word load for the Basic Skills Word List. Students at these grade levels displayed insufficient familiarity with many potentially includable words, thus reducing the word loads—particularly in grades nine through twelve. The word loads for the Basic Skills Word List in grades five through twelve are as follows:

Grade	5	6	7	8	9	10	11	12
Word Load	971	846	884	874	325	407	393	345

The final step in the selection of words for the Basic Skills Word List was based on a massive study by Carroll, Davies, and Richman (1971). This study analyzed 5,000,000 running words of text. These 5,000,000 words were taken from approximately 10,000 samples of 500 words excerpted from textbooks in 17 different curriculum areas in grades three through nine, plus magazines, books, newspapers, and poetry. The result of the study is a list of 87,000 words, accompanied by the frequency with which each of those words appears in print. Unfortunately, this enormous set of words is listed alphabetically rather than in the order of each word's frequency of usage. Hence, one cannot readily determine the most frequently encountered words. Sakiey and Fry (1979), however, have drawn on the 87,000 words to provide a list of the 3,000 most frequently occurring words ranked according to their frequency of usage in print. These words, in order of decreasing frequency of appearance, were added at each grade level of the Basic Skills Word List if they were not already listed. This ensured that words appearing very frequently in general reading materials were not overlooked because they did not have a high enough familiarity percentage.

Selection of the Graded Word Lists

Thirteen graded word lists accompany Forms A, B, and C of the Basic Reading Inventory. Each list, with the exception of kindergarten, contains 20 words. The original lists ranged in difficulty from pre-primer through the twelfth-grade level.

The general rule for selecting words for inclusion in the graded word lists for grades one through eight was that the word had to be assigned to the same grade on both the Reading Core Vocabulary and the Basic Skills Word List. Words from an earlier edition of the Basic Reading Inventory were used when they met the criterion. The remaining words to complete each list were selected at random within each grade level designation of the published word lists. Once a word was selected, it was checked for inclusion on the other list. If the word appeared on both lists it was included; otherwise, another word was randomly selected and the checking procedure was repeated until 20 words were secured for each word list.

A slight modification was used to select words for the original pre-primer and primer graded word lists because neither published word list used the term *primer*. Words selected at the pre-primer and primer levels had to appear on either the pre-primer or first-grade list of the Reading Core Vocabulary *and* on the first-grade level of the Basic Skills Word List. After the words were selected, they were assigned to one of the three forms of the Basic Reading Inventory.

Field testing the pre-primer through grade eight word lists involved 309 students in grades one through eight from the United States and Canada. The vast majority of the students were identified as average readers by their teachers. As the students pronounced the words on the graded word lists, examiners marked the words that were mispronounced. The major change resulting from field testing the graded word lists was moving some of the words from one form to another form. Equivalence of forms was accomplished by the initial selection of words from large scale vocabulary studies and field testing to help ensure that the more difficult words were evenly distributed among the three forms of word lists at each grade level. In addition, the words on each list are arranged from easier to more difficult based on field test results.

The kindergarten word lists for the twelfth edition were derived from the pre-primer and primer word lists because these words had already undergone a rigorous review process. Three reading specialists reviewed various high-frequency word lists and made selections from the existing pre-primer and primer word lists for each form. In addition, the 25 most frequent words in the English language were also considered for inclusion (Zeno, Ivens, Millard, & Duvvuri, 1995). All these words were distributed in the new forms of the kindergarten word lists except *with* and *or* which are found in the first-grade word lists. Field tests were done with 32 kindergarten students in three different elementary schools. As expected, most students could identify a few of the words in the beginning and mid-year lists, depending in large part, on the particular words being taught in the various schools. There were also a few kindergarten students who knew practically all the words on the three kindergarten lists; these students could already read and were successful in reading some first- and second-grade passages. Such students were the exception rather than the rule.

A three-phase process was used to develop the graded word lists for grades nine through twelve. First, all words common to both the Reading Core Vocabulary and the Basic Skills Word List for grades nine through twelve were listed. A total of 66 words was randomly selected from each graded list.

Next, the 66 words were randomly divided into three forms and field tested with 334 students in ninth grade, 544 students in tenth grade, 301 students in eleventh grade, and 207 students in twelfth grade. The students attended schools in Washington, South Carolina, and Illinois. The students marked each word they could read with a plus sign (+) and used a minus sign (–) for each word they thought they couldn't read. Students were instructed not to mark a word if they were in doubt. All words marked with a minus sign were tallied across forms for each grade level. Then, using the student responses, three new forms were devised. Words were ranked and distributed among the three forms. Six words were deleted from each grade level because students' responses indicated that the words were either very easy or very difficult.

Finally, the revised forms were given to 330 students in grade nine, 276 students in grade ten, 231 students in grade eleven, and 263 students in grade twelve who crossed out any words they were unable to pronounce. The students attended high schools in New York or Illinois. Research assistants then asked 65 students in grade nine, 61 students in grade ten, 75 students in grade eleven, and 157 students in grade twelve to respond individually to the words that were not crossed out. Based on an analysis of student responses, several words were rearranged so the words at the end of each list were the most difficult.

Reliability Studies of the Word Lists

In the late spring of the 2003 school year, the author and five assistants who had classroom teaching experience undertook two studies with the word lists. All the assistants had advanced degrees, and two assistants were working on doctoral degrees. Training sessions were conducted by the author to familiarize the assistants with the word lists and how the data would be gathered. The training session lasted about an hour, and debriefing sessions were held at the end of each school day to address any additional questions or concerns. The data were collected during one school week near the end of the school year.

The students in this Midwest K–5 elementary school, according to the school's 2003 state report card, represented various racial/ethnic backgrounds: White, 85%; Black; 9%; Hispanic, 5%; and Asian/Pacific Islander, 1%. The mobility rate was 26%, and 25% of the students were from low-income families. Overall, approximately 77% of the students in grade three met or exceeded state standards in reading. Approximately 73% of the students in grade five met or exceeded state standards in reading.

The first study undertaken was an alternate-form reliability study for the three forms of the graded word lists in the Basic Reading Inventory. A total of 115 students participated in the study: African American, 6; Asian, 2; Hispanic, 6; and White, 101. Table 6.2 contains a breakdown of number and sex of students in the study. Boys represented 56% of the sample; girls represented 44% of the sample. Teachers in grades one through five who agreed to participate in the study had all their students assessed, except those who were absent. For kindergarten, the teacher recommended students for assessment who were most likely to be able to read some of the words on the lists.

Table 6.2

Number and Sex of Students in Basic Reading Inventory Alternate-Form Reliability Study

Grade	Boys	Girls	Total
K	6	7	13
1	9	5	14
2	10	7	17
3	8	10	18
4	9	9	18
5	22	13	35
Totals	64	51	115

African American, 6; Asian, 2; Hispanic, 6; White, 101

Students were tested in an area reasonably free of distractions. Usually, an empty classroom was used, but some students were also assessed in the hall. The first word list used was at grade level. The form initially presented was determined randomly. The same procedure was used with the two remaining forms at the same level. Students read lists until they reached a frustration level or the grade eight word list. If the initial list was too difficult, easier lists were used. The raw scores (number of words correct) were entered into a database and analyzed by an SPSS program to determine the reliability of Forms A and B, Forms A and C, and Forms B and C. Two analyses were completed. Table 6.3 shows the alternate-form reliability for the ten different word lists (pre-primer through grade eight). The constant was the graded list, but students who read the lists were from different grades. In this analysis, the N indicates that students from various grades read lists at several levels, especially students in the upper grades. The overall reliability coefficient for each of the comparisons was .84 or higher. The lower reliability coefficients were .42 for Forms B and C in grade five and .47 for Forms A and B in grade five. All the remaining reliability coefficients were .61 or higher. In addition, all the Pearson r coefficients in Table 6.3 are statistically significant ($p<.0001$).

Table 6.3

Basic Reading Inventory Word List Alternate-Form Reliability by Level

Level	N	Form		
		A & B	A & C	B & C
PP	17	.95	.95	.95
P	8	.79	.90	.79
1	17	.87	.79	.95
2	32	.93	.89	.94
3	37	.86	.80	.91
4	59	.87	.78	.76
5	67	.47	.65	.42
6	67	.81	.78	.74
7	47	.76	.73	.79
8	37	.84	.63	.61
Overall r		.85	.84	.85

All paired correlations are statistically significant ($p<.0001$).

Another analysis of the data was done to determine the alternate-form reliability for the students' grade placements. The constant was the grade in which the student was enrolled. The actual administration of the Basic Reading Inventory often involves a student reading various word lists until his or her frustration level is reached. This analysis may be a more realistic indication of the alternate-form reliability of the word lists. The results of this analysis are presented in Table 6.4. The alternate-form reliability coefficients ranged from .52 to .97, with a majority of the coefficients .80 or higher. Overall, the results demonstrate moderate to high alternate-form reliability for almost all of the comparisons.

Table 6.4

Basic Reading Inventory Word List Alternate-Form Reliability by Grade

Grade	N*	Form		
		A & B	A & C	B & C
K	19	.97	.98	.97
1	52	.80	.71	.88
2	72	.82	.82	.87
3	55	.88	.83	.84
4	75	.73	.68	.67
5	117	.53	.71	.52

*Refers to number of word lists read by students. Range of Word Lists Read: K (PP–1), 1 (PP–7), 2 (PP–8), 3 (1–6), 4 (3–8), 5 (2–8).
All paired correlations are statistically significant ($p<.0001$).

The second study examined test-retest differences by using a random sample of 30 students from the first study. Table 6.5 reports the number of students at each grade in this study. Each student selected was asked to read some of the same word lists read the day before. Lists where students got all the words correct in each form were not used. The order in which each list was presented was random. The student rolled a die, and each specific number corresponded to a particular form of the graded word lists. The student's raw scores (number of words correct) for each of the lists read on day one and day two were entered into a database and analyzed using dependent t-tests with an SPSS program. The analysis compared the day one scores to the day two scores to find any differences and to determine whether any of the differences were statistically significant at the .05 level. Table 6.6 contains the results of this analysis. In all the comparisons, there were no significant test-retest differences for these 30 students a day after the initial lists were read. Although the sample size is small, the results indicate that K–5 students will perform very similarly on the same word lists if they are re-administered within a day.

Table 6.5

Number of Students in Basic Reading Inventory Test-Retest Study

Grade	Total
K	4
1	4
2	5
3	7
4	6
5	4
Totals	30

African American, 3; Asian, 1; Hispanic, 2; White, 24
Females, 12; Males, 18

Table 6.6

Basic Reading Inventory Word List Mean Test-Retest Differences in Alternate Forms

Grade	N*	Form		
		A & B	A & C	B & C
K	8	1.25	.25	1.00
1	8	.88	1.38	.50
2	10	.20	.10	.30
3	14	.43	.29	.71
4	12	.00	.67	.67
5	8	1.13	.75	.37

*Refers to the pairs of word lists read by students. There were no significant differences in any of the forms for the various grades.

Validity of Graded Word List Criteria

Ferroli (2008) conducted a series of studies over five consecutive summers to help establish and validate criteria for the reading levels associated with untimed scores on the graded word lists. Ninety-six students were involved in the studies. The students were struggling in reading and represented a variety of grade levels. Graduate students who had completed two diagnostic and clinical reading courses used the Basic Reading Inventory and other data (developmental spelling tests, phonics inventories, standardized measures, interest inventories, and students' responses to several hours of tutoring) to determine each student's instructional reading level. After the student's instructional reading level was determined, the word list scores were examined and analyzed for the level identified as instructional and the next higher word list. After combining and analyzing the data for all the students, Ferroli concluded that untimed scores of 16, 17, and 18 were closely associated with students' overall instructional levels. Scores of 14 and 15 could be thought of as being in a gray area between instructional and frustration levels. Scoring guides reflecting these findings were included in the tenth edition of the Basic Reading Inventory.

The revised graded word list criteria should be especially helpful with students who struggle in reading. The inclusion of a gray area for scores of 14 and 15 provide additional flexibility for teachers as they assess so-called average students. These criteria, along with the results of the student's word recognition in context score, comprehension score, and overall fluency should help in determining an appropriate instructional level for initial instruction.

Reliability of Graded Passages

A recent study of the Basic Reading Inventory was conducted to determine technical adequacy for use of the BRI as a universal screening and progress monitoring assessment for oral reading fluency and comprehension (Bieber, 2011a). A total of 149 students (i.e., 55 third-grade students, 50 fourth-grade students, and 44 fifth-grade students) participated in the study which examined the third-, fourth-, and fifth-grade passages from Forms A–E.

Alternate forms reliability analyses were conducted for accuracy on Forms A–E of the third-, fourth-, and fifth-grade passages. These analyses provided results regarding the equivalence or interchangeability of the various forms of the third-, fourth-, and fifth-grade passages. Adequate alternate forms reliability requires a coefficient of .80 or higher (Sattler, 2001).

For the third-grade passages, reliability coefficients ranged from .82 to .92 with a median of .90. Results for each of the forms are provided in Table 6.7 below.

Table 6.7

Third Grade Accuracy Alternate Forms Reliability (N=55) for the Basic Reading Inventory

	Pearson Correlations for Passages			
Form	B	C	D	E
A	.91	.89	.86	.92
B		.92	.87	.90
C			.82	.91
D				.90

Note: All correlations $p<.001$; Pearson $r=.82–.92$ (Median=.90)
[Bieber, G. A. (2011b). *Basic Reading Inventory: Accuracy data tables*. Unpublished manuscript.]
Copyright © by Gregg Bieber. Reprinted by permission of the author.

For the fourth-grade passages, reliability coefficients ranged from .88 to .95 with a median of .93. Results for each of the forms included in the analysis for the fourth-grade passages are provided in Table 6.8.

Table 6.8

Fourth Grade Accuracy Alternate Forms Reliability (*N*=50) for the Basic Reading Inventory

Form	Pearson Correlations for Passages			
	B	C	D	E
A	.94	.92	.91	.93
B		.95	.90	.92
C			.92	.93
D				.88

Note: All correlations *p*<.001; Pearson *r*=.88–.95 (Median=.93)
[Bieber, G. A. (2011b). *Basic Reading Inventory: Accuracy data tables.* Unpublished manuscript.]
Copyright © by Gregg Bieber. Reprinted by permission of the author.

For the fifth-grade passages, reliability coefficients ranged from .62 to .82 with a median of .77. Results for the fifth-grade passages are provided in Table 6.9.

Table 6.9

Fifth Grade Accuracy Alternate Forms Reliability (*N*=44) for the Basic Reading Inventory

Form	Pearson Correlations for Passages			
	B	C	D	E
A	.75	.62	.82	.82
B		.80	.69	.79
C			.73	.74
D				.81

Note: All correlations *p*<.001; Pearson *r*=.62–.82 (Median=.77)
[Bieber, G. A. (2011b). *Basic Reading Inventory: Accuracy data tables.* Unpublished manuscript.]
Copyright © by Gregg Bieber. Reprinted by permission of the author.

Test-retest reliability was calculated in relation to oral reading accuracy on the third-, fourth-, and fifth-grade passages. Pearson correlations ranged from .75 to .84 for the third-grade passages; from .77 to .89 for the fourth-grade passages; and from .71 to .90 for the fifth-grade passages. The median across all passages in the study was calculated at .80. Results for test-retest reliability are provided in Table 6.10.

Table 6.10

Accuracy Test-Retest Reliability Pearson Correlations (*N*=35) for the Basic Reading Inventory

Passage	Third Grade Retest	Fourth Grade Retest	Fifth Grade Retest
A	.80	.77	.76
B	.80	.86	.71
C	.75	.81	.72
D	.81	.80	.90
E	.84	.89	.86

Note: All correlations *p*<.001; Pearson *r*=.71–.90 (Median=.80)
[Bieber, G. A. (2011b). *Basic Reading Inventory: Accuracy data tables*. Unpublished manuscript.]
Copyright © by Gregg Bieber. Reprinted by permission of the author.

Accuracy and fluency correlations were also calculated for Forms A–E. Results are provided in Table 6.11.

Table 6.11

Accuracy and Fluency Pearson Correlations for the Basic Reading Inventory

Passages		Third Grade (*N*=55)	Fourth Grade (*N*=50)	Fifth Grade (*N*=44)
Accuracy	Fluency			
A	A	.73	.76	.62
B	B	.70	.75	.73
C	C	.74	.76	.69
D	D	.68	.76	.66
E	E	.75	.78	.72

Note: All correlations *p*<.001
[Bieber, G. A. (2011b). *Basic Reading Inventory: Accuracy data tables*. Unpublished manuscript.]
Copyright © by Gregg Bieber. Reprinted by permission of the author.

Bieber (2011a) also calculated the correlations for fluency rates on the Basic Reading Inventory and the Dynamic Indicators of Basic Early Literacy (DIBELS) Oral Reading Fluency (ORF). This analysis was undertaken to determine if adequate criterion-related concurrent validity was present when comparing the Basic Reading Inventory fluency rates to the DIBELS-ORF. All correlations were above .80 indicating a high level of criterion-related concurrent validity. The results are provided in Table 6.12.

Table 6.12

DIBELS-ORF Pearson Correlations with the Basic Reading Inventory

Passage	Third Grade (*N*=53)	Fourth Grade (*N*=49)	Fifth Grade (*N*=42)
A	.96	.93	.88
B	.97	.89	.85
C	.95	.93	.87
D	.96	.92	.90
E	.93	.92	.86

Note: All correlations *p*<.001
[Bieber, G. A. (2011b). *Basic Reading Inventory: Accuracy data tables*. Unpublished manuscript.]
Copyright © by Gregg Bieber. Reprinted by permission of the author.

Strengthening the Manual, Graded Passages, and Comprehension Questions

The passages in the Basic Reading Inventory were evaluated by one or more readability formulas (Spache, Fry, and Dale-Chall). A readability computer program (Hardy & Jerman, 1985; Micro Power & Light Co., 1995) was used to help assess the appropriateness of passages for assigned grade levels. The passages were also analyzed to determine placement on the Lexile scale. The results are shown in Table 6.13. Remember that Lexile measures do not translate specifically to grade levels. Guided Reading Levels for the elementary grades (K–5) are listed in Table 6.14.

Table 6.13

Lexile Measures for the Seven Forms of the Basic Reading Inventory Passages for Grades Two through Twelve

Grade Level	Form of the Basic Reading Inventory						
	A	B	C	D	E	LL	LI
2	570	570	650	620	590	—	—
3	840	580	640	740	580	700	650
4	720	690	880	830	860	760	760
5	850	730	1000	900	910	850	870
6	1030	920	1030	1020	1050	990	980
7	1030	1060	1130	1050	1100	1000	1000
8	1030	1060	1130	1090	1150	1090	1100
9	—	—	—	—	—	1150	1100
10	—	—	—	—	—	1170	1110
11	—	—	—	—	—	1200	1130
12	—	—	—	—	—	1320	1240

Table 6.14

Guided Reading Levels for Grades K–5 Passages

Grade Level	Form of the Basic Reading Inventory						
	A	B	C	D	E	LL	LI
Kb	A	A	A	A	A	A	A
Km	B	B	B	B	B	B	B
Ke	D	D	D	D	D	D	D
1b	E	E	E	E	E	E	E
1m	G	G	G	G	G	G	G
1e	J	J	J	J	J	J	J
2	L	L	L	L	L	L	L
3	O	O	O	O	O	O	O
4	R	R	R	R	R	R	R
5	V	V	V	U	U	U	U

To revise the graded passages for the Basic Reading Inventory, data and input were gathered from a wide variety of sources. First, users of the inventory in the United States and Canada were invited to share reactions based on use of the inventory in their particular educational setting. Second, undergraduate and graduate students at Northern Illinois University who used the inventory in classroom and clinical situations critiqued the passages and questions. Third, letters and emails sent to the authors that contained suggestions for improving the passages and questions were given careful consideration. Fourth, relevant articles and research studies pertaining to informal reading

Field test results are discusssed.

inventories were critically reviewed. Fifth, several reading professionals who used the Basic Reading Inventory provided input for revision of the manual, word lists, passages, questions, and related features. Finally, our use of the Basic Reading Inventory with students and in numerous workshops provided still more input. Based on findings from Bieber (2011a), the third-grade passage in Form E was replaced. The topic, Necco Wafers, was unfamiliar to many students in the study, and their oral fluency rate was slower than on any of the other third-grade passages. In addition, the students scored significantly lower on the comprehension questions on this passage than any of the other forms at the third-grade level. For these reasons, the third-grade passage in Form D was substituted for Necco Wafers and a new passage, Big Star, for third-grade Form D was added to the eleventh edition after field testing with 73 students of diverse backgrounds in public and private schools in Illinois and Florida.

From 2013–2016, a number of new passages were developed for many of the forms of the Basic Reading Inventory, and a number of existing passages and questions were also revised. Because of the large number of changes, field testing was undertaken. The field testing involved 727 K–12 students in eight different schools in the South, Midwest, and far West of the United States. All except 73 students were from the five schools characterized by the data shown in Table 6.15 below. These 73 students attended schools in the city and suburbs, and several colleagues agreed to try out the kindergarten word lists and a range of reading passages. Most of the 727 students were from elementary and middle schools and represented a range of racial groups. Based on the available data, a majority of students in two of the schools participated in free or reduced price lunch. Additional demographics are in Table 6.15.

Table 6.15

Student Demographics in Schools Used for Field Testing

Student Characteristics	School A	School B	School C	School D	School E
% Male	47	46	50	54	51
% Female	53	54	50	46	49
% White	2	77	87	76	84
% Hispanic	74	4	4	18	3
% Black	23	4	2	2	7
% American Indian/Alaska Native	1	1	0	0	0
% Asian	0	1	3	2	1
% Two or more races	1	12	3	2	6
% English Language Learners	51	6	0	3	*
% Participating in free or reduced price lunch	97	53	*	29	*
Number participating in field tests	117	96	123	162	163

*Not available/not offered

Most of the students read two to four passages and answered comprehension questions; over 2,000 passages were read. The author team, along with a small group of trained assistants (mostly reading teachers and the assistant director of the Jerry L. Johns Literacy Clinic) did the field testing. Debriefing sessions were held and a dynamic process was used to refine the passages and questions throughout the field testing. That meant that suggested changes could be tried out with new students and evaluated. Ultimately, the data gleaned from the field tests were used in the creation of the current edition of the Basic Reading Inventory.

Development of Forms LL and LI

In late 1987, the development of two new forms for grades three through eight was begun. In 1990, the development of longer passages for grades nine and ten was undertaken. The longer passages for grades eleven and twelve used in the seventh edition were adapted from an inventory developed by Johns (1990b). The forms were developed to (1) provide additional passages for initial assessment, (2) provide for assessment of the student's ability to read longer narrative and expository passages, (3) allow posttesting with different passages, and (4) give teachers greater flexibility in using the Basic Reading Inventory.

Written or adapted drafts of the initial passages were based on topics that would be interesting and appropriate for average readers in grades three through eight. The initial passages were analyzed by a readability program (Hardy & Jerman, 1985) to help assess their appropriateness for a particular grade level. Comprehension questions were prepared for each passage. Numerous changes in the passages and questions were made based on an initial limited field testing and critical reviews of the passages and questions by 26 teachers and graduate students enrolled in an advanced reading course.

Field testing for grade three through grade eight passages began in 1989 and continued into 1990. Classroom teachers, reading teachers, and research assistants participated in the field tests. The field tests took place in Illinois, Missouri, and Michigan. Average, above-average, and below-average students in grades three through eight participated in the field testing. A total of 537 students read Form LN and LE passages, now referred to as LL and LI respectively.

In 1990, two new grade levels (nine and ten) were developed for forms LL and LI using the general procedures just described. Both comprehension questions and passages underwent numerous revisions based on limited field testing and the critical analysis by several reading professionals.

Actual field testing was carried out early in 1993 with the cooperation of a local high school and two research assistants. Table 6.16 contains the number of students who read each passage in grades three through ten. As mentioned earlier, the passages for grades eleven and twelve were adapted from Johns (1990b).

Table 6.16

Number of Students Involved in Field testing Forms LL and LI

Passage	Form	
	LL	LI
3	51	47
4	47	50
5	48	55
6	41	48
7	36	40
8	34	40
9	48	50
10	51	49
Totals	356	379

During the process of field testing, a number of changes were suggested. These changes were incorporated into subsequent field tests. The nature of the changes involved some changes in the vocabulary used in the passages and, in one instance, modification in the organization of the passage. Other changes included revisions in the wording of comprehension questions. Students initially responded to more than 10 questions, and their answers were very useful in the selection of the final comprehension questions.

Development of Form E and New Pre-Primer Levels

The development of Form E began in 1992. The passages were used in the Reading Clinic at Northern Illinois University for two years and then revised. These revised passages were then shared with teachers in two states for use with students. Feedback for the passages and questions were used to finalize the passages and questions. The passages were also evaluated with two readability formulas. The Fry formula was used for all the passages. The Spache formula was appropriate to use with the passages through grade three. The grade levels of the passages in Form E are presented in Table 6.17. Readability formulas and field test results were used to assign passages to grade levels. Teachers should also remember that expository passages could be more difficult for students to read, because of a heavier vocabulary load and text structure that may be less familiar to students.

Table 6.17

Readability Ratings for Form E

Readability Formula	Graded Passage									
	PP	P	1	2	3	4	5	6	7	8
Fry	P	1	1	3	3	4	4	6	7	8
Spache	1.2	1.5	1.5	2.2	2.8	—	—	—	—	—

New Pre-Primer Passages

Reports from teachers indicated that the pre-primer passages in the eighth edition were quite challenging for students at the beginning of first grade. Many students are in the emergent stage of learning to read, so this finding is not surprising. The length of the passages (approximately 50 words) was also thought to contribute to the challenge. To help teachers more accurately assess students who are beginning to process text, five new passages were developed for Forms A, B, C, D, and E. An experienced first-grade teacher was invited to draft some initial passages that could be read by students in the early stages of formal reading instruction.

The passages were designed with simple, helpful illustrations to help convey the story or information. After initial tryouts with a small sample of first graders, the revised passages were field tested by teachers in two states. Their feedback was used to create the final passages. The Fry readability formula was applied to each of the passages, and the results were all in the pre-primer or primer area with the exception of a passage about apples (a two-syllable word). Because of the helpful illustrations and the positive results from the field trials, the passage was judged to be appropriate for the pre-primer level.

Reliability Studies

Several studies have been reported which involve the Basic Reading Inventory. Bristow, Pikulski, and Pelosi (1983) conducted a study involving 72 students, 24 each from grades two, four, and six. One part of the study compared the results of the Basic Reading Inventory to the students' actual placement in books. The comparison revealed the Basic Reading Inventory and book placement were identical 35% of the time, within one level 76% of the time, and within two levels 92% of the time.

An alternate-form reliability study reported by Helgren-Lempesis and Mangrum (1986) involved 75 fourth-grade students who were randomly assigned to one of three commercially-prepared reading inventories, one of which was the Basic Reading Inventory. Pearson *r* coefficients were .64 for the independent level, .72 for the instructional level, and .73 for the frustration level. According to estimated variance components from the generalizability analysis, little error could be directly attributed to the forms, as the students were the source of the greatest variance.

Pikulski and Shanahan (1982) studied 33 students who were evaluated at the Reading Center at the University of Delaware. The students represented a wide range in terms of chronological age (7 yrs., 2 mos. to 15 yrs., 11 mos.) and reading ability (pre-primer through sixth grade). Comparisons of the Basic Reading Inventory with a clinician constructed informal reading inventory resulted in "an outstanding amount of agreement between the two forms of the IRI" (p. 110). The two reading inventories were remarkably similar: 22 or 66% of the students were placed at the same instructional level; the remaining 11 students (33%) were within one grade level of each other.

Three recent studies examined how reliably participants scored the Basic Reading Inventory. In the first study, Johns and L'Allier (2003) investigated how reliably 31 practicing teachers completed summary sheets and interpreted data regarding three students' performances on the Basic Reading Inventory. After basic instruction in the administration, scoring, and interpretation of the Basic Reading Inventory, teachers completed summary sheets and interpreted those results to determine the independent, instructional, and frustration reading levels for each student. The teachers were able to reliably complete the summary sheet, showing 98% agreement with the experts. With respect to determining the students' three reading levels (independent, instructional, and frustration), there was an 89% average agreement rate.

In the second study, Johns and L'Allier (2004) examined how reliably preservice teachers scored and interpreted the Basic Reading Inventory with respect to word recognition, oral miscues, and comprehension. The 49 preservice teachers were enrolled in their second undergraduate reading course. After instruction in the Basic Reading Inventory, they completed four scoring and interpretation tasks. Results indicated that the preservice teachers were highly reliable with the scoring related to word lists (92% agreement) and total miscues (86% and 90% agreement on the two passages). They had some difficulty with the scoring of comprehension (79% and 81% agreement on the two sets of comprehension questions), and they had the most difficulty in identifying significant miscues (68% and 72% on the two passages). The researchers recommended that preservice teachers who use reading inventories in early clinical experiences rely on total miscues to help them determine the three reading levels and that they receive additional instruction in scoring significant miscues.

The third study (Johns & L'Allier, 2007) examined whether additional targeted instruction enabled preservice teachers to more reliably score a student's oral miscues on an informal reading inventory. Participants (N=94) enrolled in their second undergraduate reading course were randomly divided into an experimental group (N=43) and a control group (N=51). All participants received instruction in the administration, scoring, and interpretation of the Basic Reading Inventory. One week after the initial instruction, all participants scored the oral miscues on a reading passage. Errors in scoring were analyzed and additional instruction, based on common errors, was planned for the experimental group. Teacher think alouds, explicit explanation regarding significant miscues, and additional guided practice in the scoring of oral miscues were included in the forty-minute instructional session. One week later, all participants scored the oral reading miscues on a second reading passage.

Results after initial instruction indicated that the two groups were similar in their accuracy in scoring total miscues and significant miscues, but they had particular difficulty identifying significant miscues. On average, they had 77% agreement with the consensus responses of three experts. Results from the scored passages after the experimental group had received additional instruction indicated that both groups had improved in their ability to score total and significant miscues; they had 87% agreement with the experts. No significant differences between the two groups were found. The fact that both groups had access to a concise set of guidelines while scoring the passages and the relatively short amount of additional instruction and practice for the experimental group may have influenced the results. The results suggest that preservice and beginning teachers should frequently refer to the scoring guidelines when scoring informal reading inventories, use total miscues, rather than significant miscues, when determining reading levels, and review their scoring of significant miscues with a more experienced user of informal reading inventories in order to gain more skill in this area.

Validity Considerations

Validity can be considered in a variety of ways. Face and content validity are two ways to consider whether the Basic Reading Inventory looks like it is measuring what it purports to measure and that those factors are important components of reading. Numerous professionals have reported that the Basic Reading Inventory contains a representative sample of word lists, passages, and comprehension questions that are helpful in assessing students' reading behavior. Bieber's (2011a) study of the Basic Reading Inventory concluded that it did measure what it purported to measure—word identification (accuracy), fluency, and comprehension. These areas are generally regarded as core components of reading and appropriate and important areas for assessment. Concurrent validity data were reported by Bieber (2011a) by correlating the percentages of comprehension in the Basic Reading Inventory with the Scholastic Reading Inventory (SRI) Lexiles which provide an overall achievement level. Most of the correlations for students in grades three, four, and five were significant but below the level required for technical adequacy. The SRI is a computer test that uses a branching program to determine a student's achievement level in Lexiles. It may be inappropriate to compare an overall reading achievement score from the SRI to a single passage of the Basic Reading Inventory that may or may not accurately represent the student's instructional level. A more helpful approach could be determining a student's three reading levels with the Basic Reading Inventory and then making comparisons to an assessment that provides grade levels.

Conclusion

A recent study by Bieber, Hulac, and Schweinle (2015) was part of a larger program evaluation to understand the use of reading instruments with 149 students in grades three (n=55), four (n=50), and five (n=44). One of the instruments was the Basic Reading Inventory. The investigators found that the passages displayed high levels of inter-rater reliability and alternate-forms reliability. Test-retest reliability was also strong. The investigators concluded that the Basic Reading Inventory can be used for making relative decisions about students' reading, but not for monitoring students' reading on a weekly basis.

Based upon numerous studies of the Basic Reading Inventory (Bieber, 2011a; Bristow, Pikulski, & Pelosi, 1983; Cunningham, Hall, & Defee, 1991; Helgren-Lempesis, & Mangrum, 1986; Nilsson, 2008; Pikulski & Shanahan, 1982), it can be concluded that the BRI exhibits reasonable reliability and validity to informally assess students' reading.

PART TWO

Basic Reading Inventory Performance Booklets

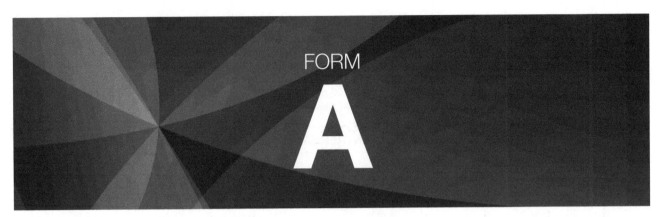

FORM

A

Performance Booklet

Teacher Copy

Form A

Primary Uses:

- Oral Reading
- Initial Assessment

Other Uses:

- Silent Reading
- Listening Level

Note: This Performance Booklet is on the Basic Reading Inventory website.

Twelfth Edition

BASIC READING INVENTORY PERFORMANCE BOOKLET

Form A

Jerry L. Johns, Laurie Elish-Piper, and Beth Johns

Student _____ Grade _____ Gender M F Date of Test _____

School _____ Examiner _____ Date of Birth _____

Address _____ Current Book/Level _____ Age _____

SUMMARY OF STUDENT'S READING PERFORMANCE

| Grade | Word Recognition | | | | | | Comprehension | | Reading Rate | |
| | Isolation (Word Lists) | | | | Context (Passages) | | Form A | | | |
	Sight	Analysis	Total	Level	Miscues	Level	Questions Missed	Level	Words per Minute (WPM)	Norm Group Percentile
Kb			/ 6							
Km			/ 9							
Ke			/12							
1b			/20							
1m										
1e										
2			/20							
3			/20							
4			/20							
5			/20							
6			/20							
7			/20							
8			/20							
9			/20							
10			/20			ESTIMATE OF READING LEVELS				
11			/20							
12			/20			Independent _____ Instructional _____ Frustration _____				

INFORMAL ANALYSIS OF ORAL READING

| Oral Reading Behaviors | Frequency of Occurrence | | | General Impact on Meaning | | |
	Seldom	Sometimes	Frequently	No Change	Little Change	Much Change
Substitutions						
Insertions						
Omissions						
Reversals						
Repetitions						

LISTENING LEVEL, FORM _____

Grade	1	2	3	4	5	6	7	8
Questions Missed								
Level								

ESTIMATED LISTENING LEVEL: _____

QUALITATIVE ANALYSIS OF BASIC READING INVENTORY INSIGHTS

General Directions: Note the degree to which the student shows behavior or evidence in the following areas. Space is provided for additional items.

Seldom   Always
Weak   Strong
Poor   Excellent

COMPREHENSION

Seeks to construct meaning

Makes predictions

Activates background knowledge

Possesses appropriate concepts and vocabulary

Monitors reading

Varies reading rate as needed

Understands topic and major ideas

Remembers facts or details

Makes and supports appropriate inferences

Evaluates ideas from passages

Understands vocabulary used

Provides appropriate definitions of words

Engages with passages

WORD IDENTIFICATION

Possesses numerous strategies

Uses strategies flexibly

Uses graphophonic information

Uses semantic information

Uses syntactic information

Knows high-frequency words automatically

Possesses sight vocabulary

ORAL AND SILENT READING

Reads fluently

Reads with expression

Attends to punctuation

Keeps place while reading

Reads at appropriate rate

Reads silently without vocalization

ATTITUDE AND CONFIDENCE

Enjoys reading

Demonstrates willingness to risk

Possesses positive self-concept

Chooses to read

Regards himself/herself as a reader

Exhibits persistence

151

Form A • Graded Word Lists • Performance Booklet • Student Book copy is on page 2.

List A Kb (Beginning Kindergarten)	**Sight**	**Analysis**
1. go*	_____	_____
2. I*	_____	_____
3. is*	_____	_____
4. he*	_____	_____
5. dog	_____	_____
6. run*	_____	_____

*denotes high-frequency word from Revised Dolch List

Number Correct _____ _____

Total _____

List A Km (Middle Kindergarten)	**Sight**	**Analysis**
1. on*	_____	_____
2. be*	_____	_____
3. had*	_____	_____
4. did*	_____	_____
5. went*	_____	_____
6. all*	_____	_____
7. like*	_____	_____
8. get*	_____	_____
9. him*	_____	_____

*denotes high-frequency word from Revised Dolch List

Number Correct _____ _____

Total _____

List A Ke (End Kindergarten)	**Sight**	**Analysis**
1. me*	_____	_____
2. not*	_____	_____
3. book	_____	_____
4. this*	_____	_____
5. home	_____	_____
6. girl	_____	_____
7. brown	_____	_____
8. tree	_____	_____
9. what*	_____	_____
10. but*	_____	_____
11. take*	_____	_____
12. eat*	_____	_____

*denotes high-frequency word from Revised Dolch List

Number Correct _____ _____

Total _____

IMPORTANT NOTE: In kindergarten, the average student's experience with words in isolation is very limited, especially at the beginning of the school year. The number of words correct may depend more on the school's curriculum rather than the student's emerging skills. The number correct is not as important as the word attack strategies the student exhibits. The chart below is one way that teacher judgment can be used to quickly analyze a student's performance to better understand his or her strengths and weaknesses as an emergent reader.

Qualitative Analysis of Word List Responses			
(0 = not evident 1 = emerging 2 = evident)			
Uses initial sounds	0	1	2
Blends sounds	0	1	2
Recognizes vowels/vowel patterns	0	1	2
Knows high-frequency words by sight	0	1	2

Form A • Graded Word Lists • Performance Booklet • Student Book copy is on page 3.

List A 7141 (Grade 1)	Sight	Analysis	List A 8224 (Grade 2)	Sight	Analysis
1. here*	_____	_____	1. ten*	_____	_____
2. down*	_____	_____	2. poor	_____	_____
3. then*	_____	_____	3. city	_____	_____
4. how*	_____	_____	4. teacher	_____	_____
5. saw*	_____	_____	5. turn*	_____	_____
6. pocket	_____	_____	6. fight	_____	_____
7. hello	_____	_____	7. because*	_____	_____
8. aunt	_____	_____	8. soft	_____	_____
9. never*	_____	_____	9. open*	_____	_____
10. puppy	_____	_____	10. winter	_____	_____
11. could*	_____	_____	11. joke	_____	_____
12. after*	_____	_____	12. different	_____	_____
13. hill	_____	_____	13. say*	_____	_____
14. men	_____	_____	14. quiet	_____	_____
15. gone*	_____	_____	15. sister	_____	_____
16. ran*	_____	_____	16. above	_____	_____
17. gave*	_____	_____	17. seed	_____	_____
18. or*	_____	_____	18. thought*	_____	_____
19. way	_____	_____	19. such	_____	_____
20. coat	_____	_____	20. chase	_____	_____

*denotes high-frequency word from Revised Dolch List

*denotes high-frequency word from Revised Dolch List

Number Correct _____ _____

Number Correct _____ _____

Total _____

Total _____

Scoring Guide for Graded Word Lists			
Independent	Instructional	Inst./Frust.	Frustration
20 19	18 17 16	15 14	13 or less

Form A • Graded Word Lists • Performance Booklet • Student Book copy is on page 4.

List A 3183 (Grade 3)	**Sight**	**Analysis**	**List A 5414** (Grade 4)	**Sight**	**Analysis**
1. trail			1. stove		
2. stream			2. government		
3. beach			3. program		
4. snake			4. grape		
5. lift			5. favorite		
6. cabin			6. blizzard		
7. bless			7. noon		
8. rooster			8. greet		
9. journey			9. sport		
10. treasure			10. rumble		
11. hero			11. tropical		
12. beyond			12. language		
13. moan			13. expert		
14. glitter			14. nervous		
15. impossible			15. starve		
16. shot			16. voyage		
17. island			17. silence		
18. manage			18. scamper		
19. receive			19. prairie		
20. automobile			20. moccasin		
Number Correct			Number Correct		
Total			Total		

Scoring Guide for Graded Word Lists			
Independent	Instructional	Inst./Frust.	Frustration
20 19	18 17 16	15 14	13 or less

Form A • Graded Word Lists • Performance Booklet • Student Book copy is on page 5.

List A 8595 (Grade 5)	**Sight**	**Analysis**	**List A 6867** (Grade 6)	**Sight**	**Analysis**
1. lizard	_____	_____	1. bleed	_____	_____
2. double	_____	_____	2. accomplishment	_____	_____
3. scarlet	_____	_____	3. whimper	_____	_____
4. helmet	_____	_____	4. marriage	_____	_____
5. dusk	_____	_____	5. frisky	_____	_____
6. bandit	_____	_____	6. seam	_____	_____
7. loyal	_____	_____	7. backward	_____	_____
8. choice	_____	_____	8. location	_____	_____
9. furnish	_____	_____	9. nightmare	_____	_____
10. century	_____	_____	10. gently	_____	_____
11. kindergarten	_____	_____	11. employ	_____	_____
12. entrance	_____	_____	12. broadcast	_____	_____
13. dentist	_____	_____	13. kennel	_____	_____
14. celebration	_____	_____	14. pulp	_____	_____
15. blister	_____	_____	15. satisfaction	_____	_____
16. symbol	_____	_____	16. cushion	_____	_____
17. drowsy	_____	_____	17. graduate	_____	_____
18. attach	_____	_____	18. harmonica	_____	_____
19. rehearse	_____	_____	19. definite	_____	_____
20. terrace	_____	_____	20. yacht	_____	_____
Number Correct	_____	_____	Number Correct	_____	_____
Total		_____	Total		_____

Scoring Guide for Graded Word Lists			
Independent	Instructional	Inst./Frust.	Frustration
20 19	18 17 16	15 14	13 or less

155

Form A • Graded Word Lists • Performance Booklet • Student Book copy is on page 6.

List A 3717 (Grade 7)	Sight	Analysis	List A 8183 (Grade 8)	Sight	Analysis
1. dwell			1. quote		
2. slogan			2. ventilate		
3. knapsack			3. surgeon		
4. administration			4. analyze		
5. gangster			5. masterpiece		
6. flatter			6. disinfectant		
7. incredible			7. extraordinary		
8. algebra			8. camouflage		
9. bachelor			9. ruthless		
10. vocabulary			10. perpendicular		
11. longitude			11. juvenile		
12. saliva			12. vacancy		
13. peninsula			13. dictator		
14. monarch			14. negative		
15. feminine			15. honorary		
16. quench			16. custody		
17. competition			17. maneuver		
18. pollute			18. faculty		
19. ambitious			19. pneumonia		
20. orchid			20. embassy		
Number Correct			Number Correct		
Total			Total		

Scoring Guide for Graded Word Lists			
Independent	Instructional	Inst./Frust.	Frustration
20 19	18 17 16	15 14	13 or less

Form A • Graded Word Lists • Performance Booklet • Student Book copy is on page 7.

List A 4959 (Grade 9)	**Sight**	**Analysis**	**List A 1047** (Grade 10)	**Sight**	**Analysis**
1. random	_____	_____	1. displacement	_____	_____
2. disrupt	_____	_____	2. heritage	_____	_____
3. autobiography	_____	_____	3. exponent	_____	_____
4. expire	_____	_____	4. variable	_____	_____
5. contestant	_____	_____	5. preliminary	_____	_____
6. strategy	_____	_____	6. embryo	_____	_____
7. crave	_____	_____	7. sterile	_____	_____
8. detach	_____	_____	8. gratify	_____	_____
9. apprehend	_____	_____	9. maternity	_____	_____
10. idolize	_____	_____	10. incorporate	_____	_____
11. consecutive	_____	_____	11. gore	_____	_____
12. vacate	_____	_____	12. illogical	_____	_____
13. debatable	_____	_____	13. radiate	_____	_____
14. combustion	_____	_____	14. forum	_____	_____
15. famished	_____	_____	15. predominant	_____	_____
16. detract	_____	_____	16. fictitious	_____	_____
17. crochet	_____	_____	17. cuticle	_____	_____
18. insomnia	_____	_____	18. panorama	_____	_____
19. siesta	_____	_____	19. inquisitive	_____	_____
20. bayonet	_____	_____	20. artisan	_____	_____
Number Correct	_____	_____	Number Correct	_____	_____
Total		_____	Total		_____

Scoring Guide for Graded Word Lists			
Independent	Instructional	Inst./Frust.	Frustration
20 19	18 17 16	15 14	13 or less

157

Form A • Graded Word Lists • Performance Booklet • Student Book copy is on page 8.

List A 1187 (Grade 11)	Sight	Analysis	List A 1296 (Grade 12)	Sight	Analysis
1. insensible			1. denote		
2. beneficiary			2. hallowed		
3. spectrum			3. transcend		
4. idealism			4. affiliate		
5. epic			5. obtuse		
6. composite			6. recipient		
7. informant			7. consensus		
8. ransack			8. concentric		
9. interlude			9. postulate		
10. suede			10. impel		
11. renaissance			11. collateral		
12. dissociate			12. repugnant		
13. commemorate			13. promissory		
14. populous			14. meticulous		
15. fraudulent			15. flippant		
16. inquisition			16. sardonic		
17. dexterity			17. indemnity		
18. lenient			18. adamant		
19. dilapidated			19. effigy		
20. disheveled			20. tithe		
Number Correct			Number Correct		
Total			Total		

Scoring Guide for Graded Word Lists			
Independent	Instructional	Inst./Frust.	Frustration
20 19	18 17 16	15 14	13 or less

Student Book copy is on page 10.

A Kb (Beginning K) Point to each word in the title as you read it. Then say: "Read this story about the cat. I'll ask you some questions about it when you're done."

Guided Reading Level: A

The Cat

		MISCUES					
	Substitution	Insertion	Omission	Reversal	Repetition	Self-Correction of Unacceptable Miscue	Meaning Change (Significant Miscue)
The cat sits. 3							
The cat walks. 6							
The cat eats. 9							
The cat sleeps. 12							
TOTAL							

Total Miscues ☐   Significant Miscues ☐

Word Recognition Scoring Guide		
Total Miscues	Level	Significant Miscues
0	Independent	0
—	Ind./Inst.	—
—	Instructional	—
1	Inst./Frust.	1
2 +	Frustration	2 +

Qualitative Analysis of Word Identification		
(0 = not evident 1 = emerging 2 = evident)		
Uses letter-sound relationships		0 1 2
Points to words while reading		0 1 2
Uses monitoring (rereads; corrects)		0 1 2
Knows high-frequency words		0 1 2
Possesses sight vocabulary		0 1 2
Exhibits persistence		0 1 2
Seems confident		0 1 2

Important Note: If the scoring guides are used, teacher judgment is especially important because of the length of the passage and the limited number of questions.

A Kb (Beginning K)

The Cat

T 1. _____ What is this story about? [If student says "a cat," say "tell me more."]
(what a cat does; that a cat sits, walks, eats, and sleeps)

F 2. _____ What's something else the cat does in the story?
(any one of the following: sits, walks, eats, sleeps)

I 3. _____ If you wanted to add more to the story, tell me what else the cat might do.
(any logical response; jump; play; purr; meow)

E 4. _____ Where do you think you would probably need to go to see the cat?
(any logical response; a house; a pet store; an animal shelter)

V 5. _____ What does the word "sleeps" mean?
(any logical response; to take a nap; to go to bed)

Retelling Notes

Retelling Rubric

Independent Level/Excellent
States central or key ideas
Identifies important facts
Retains the general sequence of events
Relates most of the content in an organized manner

Instructional Level/Satisfactory
States most central or key ideas
Identifies some important facts
Retains the general sequence of events
Relates an overall sense of the content

Frustration Level/Unsatisfactory
Provides bits of information in a haphazard manner
Little apparent organization

Questions Missed

Comprehension Scoring Guide	
Questions Missed	Level
0	Independent
1	Ind./Inst.
1½	Instructional
2	Inst./Frust.
2½ +	Frustration

Qualitative Analysis of Comprehension			
(0 = not evident 1 = emerging 2 = evident)			
Seeks to construct meaning	0	1	2
Understands topic and major ideas	0	1	2
Identifies facts or details	0	1	2
Evaluates ideas from story	0	1	2
Makes and supports appropriate inferences	0	1	2
Seems engaged with story	0	1	2

Writing Prompt: Write about what you would name a cat and why.

Rubric for Writing Response	
3	• Response is very closely related to prompt. • Response makes complete sense. • Response is well organized. • Response meets all age-appropriate spelling expectations and writing conventions.
2	• Response is related to prompt. • Response makes sense. • Response is organized in an acceptable manner. • Response meets most age-appropriate spelling expectations and writing conventions.
1	• Response is loosely related to prompt. • Some aspects of response make sense. • Response is not well organized. • Response lacks some age-appropriate spelling expectations and writing conventions.
0	• Response is unrelated to prompt. • Response does not make sense. • Response is poorly organized. • Response lacks most age-appropriate spelling expectations and writing conventions.

Important Note: If the scoring guides are used, teacher judgment is especially important because of the length of the passage and the limited number of questions.

Student Book copy is on page 11.

A Km (Middle K) Point to each word in the title as you read it. Then say: "Read this story about getting dressed. I'll ask you some questions about it when you're done."

Guided Reading Level: B

Getting Dressed		Substitution	Insertion	Omission	Reversal	Repetition	Self-Correction of Unacceptable Miscue	Meaning Change (Significant Miscue)
		MISCUES						
I put on my top.	5							
I put on my pants.	10							
I put on my socks.	15							
I put on my shoes.	20							
TOTAL								

Total Miscues [ ]   Significant Miscues [ ]

Word Recognition Scoring Guide		
Total Miscues	Level	Significant Miscues
0	Independent	0
—	Ind./Inst.	—
1	Instructional	1
2	Inst./Frust.	2
3 +	Frustration	3 +

Qualitative Analysis of Word Identification		
(0 = not evident 1 = emerging 2 = evident)		
Uses letter-sound relationships		0 1 2
Points to words while reading		0 1 2
Uses monitoring (rereads; corrects)		0 1 2
Knows high-frequency words		0 1 2
Possesses sight vocabulary		0 1 2
Exhibits persistence		0 1 2
Seems confident		0 1 2

Important Note: If the scoring guides are used, teacher judgment is especially important because of the length of the passage and the limited number of questions.

A Km (Middle K)

Getting Dressed

T 1. _____ What is this story about? [If student says "getting dressed," say "tell me more."]
(how the girl gets dressed; how the girl puts on her clothes)

F 2. _____ What's something else the girl does in the story?
(any one of the following: put on her top; put on her pants; put on her socks; put on her shoes)

I 3. _____ If you wanted to add more to the story, tell me what else the girl might do.
(any logical response; put on her coat; go to school; go outside; eat breakfast)

E 4. _____ Where do you think you would probably need to go to see the girl?
(any logical response; her house; her bedroom)

V 5. _____ What does the word "top" mean?
(any logical response; a shirt; a blouse; a t-shirt)

Questions Missed

Retelling Notes

Retelling Rubric

Independent Level/Excellent
States central or key ideas
Identifies important facts
Retains the general sequence of events
Relates most of the content in an organized manner

Instructional Level/Satisfactory
States most central or key ideas
Identifies some important facts
Retains the general sequence of events
Relates an overall sense of the content

Frustration Level/Unsatisfactory
Provides bits of information in a haphazard manner
Little apparent organization

Comprehension Scoring Guide

Questions Missed	Level
0	Independent
1	Ind./Inst.
1½	Instructional
2	Inst./Frust.
2½ +	Frustration

Qualitative Analysis of Comprehension
(0 = not evident   1 = emerging   2 = evident)

Seeks to construct meaning	0	1	2
Understands topic and major ideas	0	1	2
Identifies facts or details	0	1	2
Evaluates ideas from story	0	1	2
Makes and supports appropriate inferences	0	1	2
Seems engaged with story	0	1	2

Writing Prompt: Write about something you like to wear.

Rubric for Writing Response

3	• Response is very closely related to prompt. • Response makes complete sense. • Response is well organized. • Response meets all age-appropriate spelling expectations and writing conventions.
2	• Response is related to prompt. • Response makes sense. • Response is organized in an acceptable manner. • Response meets most age-appropriate spelling expectations and writing conventions.
1	• Response is loosely related to prompt. • Some aspects of response make sense. • Response is not well organized. • Response lacks some age-appropriate spelling expectations and writing conventions.
0	• Response is unrelated to prompt. • Response does not make sense. • Response is poorly organized. • Response lacks most age-appropriate spelling expectations and writing conventions.

Important Note: If the scoring guides are used, teacher judgment is especially important because of the length of the passage and the limited number of questions.

162

Student Book copy is on page 12.

A Ke (End K) Point to each word in the title as you read it. Then say: "Read this story about apples. I'll ask you some questions about it when you're done."

Guided Reading Level: D

Apples

		Substitution	Insertion	Omission	Reversal	Repetition	Self-Correction of Unacceptable Miscue	Meaning Change (Significant Miscue)
		MISCUES						
I like apples!	3							
I like red and yellow apples.	9							
Apples can be green.	13							
I like to eat big apples.	19							
An apple is fun to eat.	25							
TOTAL								

Total Miscues ☐   Significant Miscues ☐

Word Recognition Scoring Guide		
Total Miscues	Level	Significant Miscues
0	Independent	0
1	Ind./Inst.	—
2	Instructional	1
3	Inst./Frust.	2
4 +	Frustration	3 +

Qualitative Analysis of Word Identification			
(0 = not evident 1 = emerging 2 = evident)			
Uses letter-sound relationships	0	1	2
Points to words while reading	0	1	2
Uses monitoring (rereads; corrects)	0	1	2
Knows high-frequency words	0	1	2
Possesses sight vocabulary	0	1	2
Exhibits persistence	0	1	2
Seems confident	0	1	2

Important Note: If the scoring guides are used, teacher judgment is especially important because of the length of the passage and the limited number of questions.

A Ke (End K)

Apples

T 1. _____ What is this story about? [If student says "apples," say "tell me more."] (how the girl likes apples; eating many kinds of apples)

F 2. _____ What's something else the girl does in the story? (any one of the following: she likes apples; she likes to eat big apples; she thinks eating apples is fun)

I 3. _____ If you wanted to add more to the story, tell me what else the girl might do. (any logical response; share an apple with a friend; go outside and play)

E 4. _____ Where do you think you would probably need to go to see the girl? (any logical response; her house; the kitchen; the cafeteria)

V 5. _____ What does the word "yellow" mean? (any logical response; a color; the color of the sun; child points to something yellow)

	Questions Missed

Comprehension Scoring Guide

Questions Missed	Level
0	Independent
1	Ind./Inst.
1½	Instructional
2	Inst./Frust.
2½ +	Frustration

Qualitative Analysis of Comprehension
(0 = not evident   1 = emerging   2 = evident)

Seeks to construct meaning	0	1	2
Understands topic and major ideas	0	1	2
Identifies facts or details	0	1	2
Evaluates ideas from story	0	1	2
Makes and supports appropriate inferences	0	1	2
Seems engaged with story	0	1	2

Retelling Notes

Retelling Rubric

Independent Level/Excellent

States central or key ideas
Identifies important facts
Retains the general sequence of events
Relates most of the content in an organized manner

Instructional Level/Satisfactory

States most central or key ideas
Identifies some important facts
Retains the general sequence of events
Relates an overall sense of the content

Frustration Level/Unsatisfactory

Provides bits of information in a haphazard manner
Little apparent organization

Writing Prompt: Write about your favorite snack food.

Rubric for Writing Response

3	• Response is very closely related to prompt. • Response makes complete sense. • Response is well organized. • Response meets all age-appropriate spelling expectations and writing conventions.
2	• Response is related to prompt. • Response makes sense. • Response is organized in an acceptable manner. • Response meets most age-appropriate spelling expectations and writing conventions.
1	• Response is loosely related to prompt. • Some aspects of response make sense. • Response is not well organized. • Response lacks some age-appropriate spelling expectations and writing conventions.
0	• Response is unrelated to prompt. • Response does not make sense. • Response is poorly organized. • Response lacks most age-appropriate spelling expectations and writing conventions.

Important Note: If the scoring guides are used, teacher judgment is especially important because of the length of the passage and the limited number of questions.

Student Book copy is on page 13.

A 7141b (Beginning Grade 1) Point to each word in the title as you read it. Then say: "Read this story about birds. I'll ask you some questions about it when you're done."

Guided Reading Level: E

I Like Birds		MISCUES						
		Substitution	Insertion	Omission	Reversal	Repetition	Self-Correction of Unacceptable Miscue	Meaning Change (Significant Miscue)
I can look for birds. I look up in	9							
a tree. I see a big bird. It is brown.	19							
I see a baby bird. It is little. It is	29							
brown too.	31							
The big bird can fly. The baby	38							
bird can not fly. It is little. I like to	48							
see birds.	50							
TOTAL								

Total Miscues [ ]   Significant Miscues [ ]

Word Recognition Scoring Guide		
Total Miscues	Level	Significant Miscues
0	Independent	0
1–2	Ind./Inst.	1
3	Instructional	2
4	Inst./Frust.	3
5 +	Frustration	4 +

Qualitative Analysis of Word Identification (0 = not evident 1 = emerging 2 = evident)			
Uses letter-sound relationships	0	1	2
Points to words while reading	0	1	2
Uses monitoring (rereads; corrects)	0	1	2
Knows high-frequency words	0	1	2
Possesses sight vocabulary	0	1	2
Exhibits persistence	0	1	2
Seems confident	0	1	2

Important Note: If the scoring guides are used, teacher judgment is especially important because of the length of the passage and the limited number of questions.

A 7141b (Beginning Grade 1)

I Like Birds

T 1. _____ What is this story about? [If student
              says "birds," say "tell me more."]
              (a girl that likes birds; the kinds of birds
              the girl can see)

F 2. _____ What kinds of birds did the girl see?
              (big bird; baby bird; brown bird; little
              bird [any 2])

I 3. _____ Besides being too little, why do you
              think the baby bird could not fly?
              (any logical response; it was scared;
              it wasn't strong enough)

E 4. _____ Why do you think the person looked up
              in a tree to find birds?
              (any logical response; birds live there)

V 5. _____ What does "little" mean?
              (small; tiny; baby)

☐	Questions Missed

Comprehension Scoring Guide

Questions Missed	Level
0	Independent
1	Ind./Inst.
1½	Instructional
2	Inst./Frust.
2½ +	Frustration

Qualitative Analysis of Comprehension
(0 = not evident   1 = emerging   2 = evident)

Seeks to construct meaning	0	1	2
Understands topic and major ideas	0	1	2
Identifies facts or details	0	1	2
Evaluates ideas from story	0	1	2
Makes and supports appropriate inferences	0	1	2
Seems engaged with story	0	1	2

Retelling Notes

Retelling Rubric

Independent Level/Excellent
States central or key ideas
Identifies important facts
Retains the general sequence of events
Relates most of the content in an organized manner

Instructional Level/Satisfactory
States most central or key ideas
Identifies some important facts
Retains the general sequence of events
Relates an overall sense of the content

Frustration Level/Unsatisfactory
Provides bits of information in a haphazard manner
Little apparent organization

Writing Prompt: Write about different kinds of birds.

Rubric for Writing Response

3	• Response is very closely related to prompt. • Response makes complete sense. • Response is well organized. • Response meets all age-appropriate spelling expectations and writing conventions.
2	• Response is related to prompt. • Response makes sense. • Response is organized in an acceptable manner. • Response meets most age-appropriate spelling expectations and writing conventions.
1	• Response is loosely related to prompt. • Some aspects of response make sense. • Response is not well organized. • Response lacks some age-appropriate spelling expectations and writing conventions.
0	• Response is unrelated to prompt. • Response does not make sense. • Response is poorly organized. • Response lacks most age-appropriate spelling expectations and writing conventions.

Important Note: If the scoring guides are used, teacher judgment is especially important because of the length of the passage and the limited number of questions.

Student Book copy is on page 14.

A 7141m (Middle Grade 1) Point to each word in the title as you read it. Then say: "Read this story about Spotty. I'll ask you some questions about it when you're done."

Guided Reading Level: G

Spotty		Substitution	Insertion	Omission	Reversal	Repetition	Self-Correction of Unacceptable Miscue	Meaning Change (Significant Miscue)
		MISCUES						
One day Spotty went for a walk.	7							
The sun was warm. Spotty walked to	14							
the pond. There he saw a frog. The	22							
frog was on a log. Spotty wanted to	30							
play. Spotty began to bark. The frog	37							
jumped into the water.	41							
Then Spotty jumped into the water.	47							
But poor Spotty did not know what to	55							
do. The water was very deep. The water	63							
went way over his head. Spotty moved	70							
his legs. Soon his head came out of the	79							
water. He kept on moving. He came to	87							
the other side of the pond. That is how	96							
Spotty learned to swim.	100							
TOTAL								

Word Recognition Scoring Guide		
Total Miscues	Level	Significant Miscues
0–1	Independent	0–1
2–4	Ind./Inst.	2
5	Instructional	3
6–9	Inst./Frust.	4
10 +	Frustration	5 +

Total Miscues [ ]   Significant Miscues [ ]

Oral Reading Rate	Norm Group Percentile
___ WPM)6000	☐ 90 ☐ 75 ☐ 50 ☐ 25 ☐ 10

A 7141m (Middle Grade 1)

Spotty

T 1. _____ What is this story about?
(Spotty and a frog; how Spotty learned to swim)

F 2. _____ Where did Spotty go?
(to the pond; for a walk)

F 3. _____ What did Spotty see?
(a frog)

F 4. _____ Where was the frog?
(on a log)

F 5. _____ What did the frog do when Spotty barked?
(jumped into the water)

F 6. _____ What did Spotty do when the water went over his head?
(moved his legs; he didn't know what to do)

F 7. _____ What did Spotty learn in this story?
(how to swim)

I 8. _____ Who was Spotty?
(a dog)

E 9. _____ Why do you think Spotty wanted to play with the frog?
(any logical response; he was lonesome)

V 10. _____ What is a "pond"?
(like a lake; water)

[ ] Questions Missed

Comprehension Scoring Guide	
Questions Missed	Level
0–1	Independent
1½–2	Ind./Inst.
2½	Instructional
3–4½	Inst./Frust.
5 +	Frustration

Retelling Notes

Retelling Rubric

Independent Level/Excellent
States central or key ideas
Identifies important facts
Retains the general sequence of events
Relates most of the content in an organized manner

Instructional Level/Satisfactory
States most central or key ideas
Identifies some important facts
Retains the general sequence of events
Relates an overall sense of the content

Frustration Level/Unsatisfactory
Provides bits of information in a haphazard manner
Little apparent organization

Writing Prompt: Write about something that you learned how to do.

Rubric for Writing Response

3	• Response is very closely related to prompt. • Response makes complete sense. • Response is well organized. • Response meets all age-appropriate spelling expectations and writing conventions.
2	• Response is related to prompt. • Response makes sense. • Response is organized in an acceptable manner. • Response meets most age-appropriate spelling expectations and writing conventions.
1	• Response is loosely related to prompt. • Some aspects of response make sense. • Response is not well organized. • Response lacks some age-appropriate spelling expectations and writing conventions.
0	• Response is unrelated to prompt. • Response does not make sense. • Response is poorly organized. • Response lacks most age-appropriate spelling expectations and writing conventions.

Student Book copy is on page 15.

A 7141e (End Grade 1) Point to each word in the title as you read it. Then say: "Read this story about a tree. I'll ask you some questions about it when you're done."

Guided Reading Level: J

Up a Tree		Substitution	Insertion	Omission	Reversal	Repetition	Self-Correction of Unacceptable Miscue	Meaning Change (Significant Miscue)
		MISCUES						
Jeff likes to play with his cat Boots.	8							
One day a dog walked by, and Boots ran	17							
up a big tree.	21							
Jeff said, "Come down Boots." The	27							
cat did not come down. Jeff did not know	36							
what to do, so he called his mom.	44							
His mom said, "Come here, Boots."	50							
The cat did not come.	55							
Jeff went home. He came back with	62							
a bag. He put the bag down and took	71							
out some milk. He walked to the tree with	80							
the milk. He said, "Here Boots. Come	87							
get some milk." Boots came down and	94							
had some milk. Jeff was happy.	100							
TOTAL								

Total Miscues ☐   Significant Miscues ☐

Word Recognition Scoring Guide		
Total Miscues	Level	Significant Miscues
0–1	Independent	0–1
2–4	Ind./Inst.	2
5	Instructional	3
6–9	Inst./Frust.	4
10 +	Frustration	5 +

Oral Reading Rate	Norm Group Percentile
WPM ⟌6000	☐ 90 ☐ 75 ☐ 50 ☐ 25 ☐ 10

A 7141e (End Grade 1)

Up a Tree

T   1. _____   What is this story about?
                 (Boots; getting Boots down from a tree;
                 a cat)

F   2. _____   Why did Boots run up the tree?
                 (a dog walked by; the dog scared the
                 cat)

F   3. _____   At first, how did Jeff try to get Boots
                 down?
                 (called the cat; called mom)

F   4. _____   Where did Jeff go after mom came?
                 (home)

F   5. _____   What did he bring from home?
                 (a bag; milk)

F   6. _____   How did Jeff finally get Boots down?
                 (he brought milk; told Boots to get
                 the milk)

F   7. _____   How did Jeff feel at the end of the
                 story?
                 (happy)

I   8. _____   Why do you think Boots didn't come
                 down when Jeff and his mom called?
                 (any logical response; it was scared of
                 the dog; it didn't want to)

E   9. _____   How would you feel if your cat ran up
                 a tree? Why?
                 (any logical response; sad; scared)

V   10. _____ What is a "bag"?
                 (a sack; something to put things in)

☐ Questions Missed

Comprehension Scoring Guide	
Questions Missed	Level
0–1	Independent
1½–2	Ind./Inst.
2½	Instructional
3–4½	Inst./Frust.
5 +	Frustration

Retelling Notes

Retelling Rubric

Independent Level/Excellent
States central or key ideas
Identifies important facts
Retains the general sequence of events
Relates most of the content in an organized manner

Instructional Level/Satisfactory
States most central or key ideas
Identifies some important facts
Retains the general sequence of events
Relates an overall sense of the content

Frustration Level/Unsatisfactory
Provides bits of information in a haphazard manner
Little apparent organization

Writing Prompt: Write about how you solved a problem.

Rubric for Writing Response

3	• Response is very closely related to prompt. • Response makes complete sense. • Response is well organized. • Response meets all age-appropriate spelling expectations and writing conventions.
2	• Response is related to prompt. • Response makes sense. • Response is organized in an acceptable manner. • Response meets most age-appropriate spelling expectations and writing conventions.
1	• Response is loosely related to prompt. • Some aspects of response make sense. • Response is not well organized. • Response lacks some age-appropriate spelling expectations and writing conventions.
0	• Response is unrelated to prompt. • Response does not make sense. • Response is poorly organized. • Response lacks most age-appropriate spelling expectations and writing conventions.

Student Book copy is on page 16.

A 8224 (Grade 2) Say: "I'd like you to read out loud [silently]. Think about what you're reading because I'll ask you some questions about it when you're done. Please begin here." [Point to title.]

Guided Reading Level: L; Lexile: 570

Dodge Ball

			MISCUES			Repetition	Self-Correction of Unacceptable Miscue	Meaning Change (Significant Miscue)
		Substitution	Insertion	Omission	Reversal			
David did not really enjoy gym. He	7							
actually wished he could avoid ever	13							
attending gym class. Because David was	19							
somewhat shy and quiet, he had trouble	26							
making friends. Whenever teams were	31							
chosen, he feared he would be picked last.	39							
One day, however, David had a great	46							
experience. Coach Kris brought out a dodge	53							
ball. David had never played this game.	60							
As Coach Kris explained the rules,	66							
David's hopes began to rise. He knew he	74							
could run fast and jump high. He was not	83							
disappointed. The ball never did tag him.	90							
For the first time, he felt like a real winner!	100							
TOTAL								

Total Miscues [ ]   Significant Miscues [ ]

Word Recognition Scoring Guide		
Total Miscues	Level	Significant Miscues
0–1	Independent	0–1
2–4	Ind./Inst.	2
5	Instructional	3
6–9	Inst./Frust.	4
10 +	Frustration	5 +

Oral Reading Rate	Norm Group Percentile
_____ WPM ⟌6000	☐ 90 ☐ 75 ☐ 50 ☐ 25 ☐ 10

A 8224 (Grade 2)

Dodge Ball

T   1. _____   What is this story about?
(playing dodge ball; David in gym class)

F   2. _____   How did David feel about gym class?
(he didn't like it; he wished he could avoid it)

F   3. _____   Why did David have trouble making friends?
(he was shy; quiet)

F   4. _____   What did David fear?
(being picked last for a team)

F   5. _____   What is the name of the coach?
(Kris)

F   6. _____   How many times had David played dodge ball before?
(zero; it was his first time)

F   7. _____   What did David know he could do?
(run fast and jump high)

I   8. _____   How did David feel at the end of the story?
(like a winner; happy)

E   9. _____   Would you want David on your dodge ball team? Why?
(any logical response)

V 10. _____   What does "dodge" mean?
(avoid or move away from something)

☐ Questions Missed

Comprehension Scoring Guide	
Questions Missed	Level
0–1	Independent
1½–2	Ind./Inst.
2½	Instructional
3–4½	Inst./Frust.
5 +	Frustration

Retelling Notes

Retelling Rubric

Independent Level/Excellent
States central or key ideas
Identifies important facts
Retains the general sequence of events
Relates most of the content in an organized manner

Instructional Level/Satisfactory
States most central or key ideas
Identifies some important facts
Retains the general sequence of events
Relates an overall sense of the content

Frustration Level/Unsatisfactory
Provides bits of information in a haphazard manner
Little apparent organization

Writing Prompt: Write about a time when you felt like a winner.

Rubric for Writing Response

3	• Response is very closely related to prompt. • Response makes complete sense. • Response is well organized. • Response meets all age-appropriate spelling expectations and writing conventions.
2	• Response is related to prompt. • Response makes sense. • Response is organized in an acceptable manner. • Response meets most age-appropriate spelling expectations and writing conventions.
1	• Response is loosely related to prompt. • Some aspects of response make sense. • Response is not well organized. • Response lacks some age-appropriate spelling expectations and writing conventions.
0	• Response is unrelated to prompt. • Response does not make sense. • Response is poorly organized. • Response lacks most age-appropriate spelling expectations and writing conventions.

Student Book copy is on page 17.

A 3183 (Grade 3) Say: "I'd like you to read out loud [silently]. Think about what you're reading because I'll ask you some questions about it when you're done. Please begin here." [Point to title.]

Guided Reading Level: O; Lexile: 840

Joe Goes Fishing

		Substitution	Insertion	Omission	Reversal	Repetition	Self-Correction of Unacceptable Miscue	Meaning Change (Significant Miscue)
		MISCUES						
One summer day, Joe wished he could go	8							
fishing, but he didn't have a fishing pole. Then	17							
he got a creative idea. He decided to make a	27							
fishing pole out of a stick, string, and a paper	37							
clip for a hook. He dug a hole in the dirt beside	49							
the pond and found some worms to use as bait.	59							
After baiting the hook, Joe tossed the string	67							
into the pond and waited. Suddenly he felt a tug	77							
on the string. He quickly jerked the string out	86							
of the water and was delighted to find he had	96							
caught a little fish.	100							
TOTAL								

Total Miscues [ ]   Significant Miscues [ ]

Word Recognition Scoring Guide		
Total Miscues	Level	Significant Miscues
0–1	Independent	0–1
2–4	Ind./Inst.	2
5	Instructional	3
6–9	Inst./Frust.	4
10 +	Frustration	5 +

Oral Reading Rate	Norm Group Percentile
_____ WPM /)6000	☐ 90 ☐ 75 ☐ 50 ☐ 25 ☐ 10

A 3183 (Grade 3)

Joe Goes Fishing

T   1. _____   What is this story about?
                (Joe wanting to go fishing; Joe making
                his own fishing pole)

F   2. _____   What time of year was it?
                (summer)

F   3. _____   What did Joe use for a hook?
                (a paper clip)

F   4. _____   What did Joe use for a fishing pole?
                (a stick)

F   5. _____   How did Joe get bait for fishing?
                (dug for worms)

F   6. _____   Why did Joe make his own fishing pole?
                (he didn't have one)

F   7. _____   How did Joe feel when he caught a fish?
                (happy; delighted)

I   8. _____   What did the tug on his string mean?
                (He had a fish on his hook.)

E   9. _____   What do you think Joe will do with
                his fish?
                (any logical response; take it home to
                eat; throw it back into the pond)

V 10. _____   What is "bait"?
                (something you use to catch fish)

[ ] Questions Missed

Comprehension Scoring Guide	
Questions Missed	Level
0–1	Independent
1½–2	Ind./Inst.
2½	Instructional
3–4½	Inst./Frust.
5 +	Frustration

Retelling Notes

Retelling Rubric

Independent Level/Excellent
States central or key ideas
Identifies important facts
Retains the general sequence of events
Relates most of the content in an organized manner

Instructional Level/Satisfactory
States most central or key ideas
Identifies some important facts
Retains the general sequence of events
Relates an overall sense of the content

Frustration Level/Unsatisfactory
Provides bits of information in a haphazard manner
Little apparent organization

Writing Prompt: Write about a time you had a creative idea.

Rubric for Writing Response

3	• Response is very closely related to prompt. • Response makes complete sense. • Response is well organized. • Response meets all age-appropriate spelling expectations and writing conventions.
2	• Response is related to prompt. • Response makes sense. • Response is organized in an acceptable manner. • Response meets most age-appropriate spelling expectations and writing conventions.
1	• Response is loosely related to prompt. • Some aspects of response make sense. • Response is not well organized. • Response lacks some age-appropriate spelling expectations and writing conventions.
0	• Response is unrelated to prompt. • Response does not make sense. • Response is poorly organized. • Response lacks most age-appropriate spelling expectations and writing conventions.

Student Book copy is on page 18.

A 5414 (Grade 4) Say: "I'd like you to read out loud [silently]. Think about what you're reading because I'll ask you some questions about it when you're done. Please begin here." [Point to title.]

Guided Reading Level: R; Lexile: 720

My Wish

		Substitution	Insertion	Omission	Reversal	Repetition	Self-Correction of Unacceptable Miscue	Meaning Change (Significant Miscue)
		MISCUES						
At my school, I read about a belief from	9							
Japan—if you fold a thousand paper birds	17							
called cranes, you earn one wish. I knew my	26							
wish, but I didn't know how to fold a crane.	36							
I learned from a book and became an expert.	45							
I started to turn paper scraps into cranes.	53							
Classmates asked me how to fold a crane, and	62							
eventually a group of us folded cranes daily at	71							
recess. I counted the cranes; we needed eight	79							
more. There were eight of us in our group, so	89							
we each made one. My wish to make friends	98							
came true.	100							
TOTAL								

Total Miscues ☐   Significant Miscues ☐

Word Recognition Scoring Guide

Total Miscues	Level	Significant Miscues
0–1	Independent	0–1
2–4	Ind./Inst.	2
5	Instructional	3
6–9	Inst./Frust.	4
10 +	Frustration	5 +

Oral Reading Rate	Norm Group Percentile				
_____ WPM)6000	☐ 90	☐ 75	☐ 50	☐ 25	☐ 10

A 5414 (Grade 4)

My Wish

T   1. _____   What is this passage about?
(learning to fold paper cranes; wishing
for friends; a belief from Japan)

F   2. _____   Where did the belief about folding
cranes come from?
(Japan; a book)

F   3. _____   How many cranes does a person have to
fold to earn one wish?
(a thousand)

F   4. _____   How did the author learn how to fold
cranes?
(from a book)

F   5. _____   When did the author fold cranes with
other students?
(at recess; during school)

F   6. _____   How many students were in the group?
(eight)

F   7. _____   What was the author's wish?
(to make friends)

I   8. _____   Why do you think the other students
wanted to learn how to make cranes?
(any logical response; they wanted a
wish too; they wanted to be friends with
the new student)

E   9. _____   Do you think it would be hard to fold
paper into cranes? Why?
(any logical response)

V 10. _____   What is a "scrap" of paper?
(a small bit of paper; paper that would
usually be thrown away)

Retelling Rubric

Independent Level/Excellent
States central or key ideas
Identifies important facts
Retains the general sequence of events
Relates most of the content in an organized manner

Instructional Level/Satisfactory
States most central or key ideas
Identifies some important facts
Retains the general sequence of events
Relates an overall sense of the content

Frustration Level/Unsatisfactory
Provides bits of information in a haphazard manner
Little apparent organization

Writing Prompt: Write about how you could help a new student at your school.

	Rubric for Writing Response
3	• Response is very closely related to prompt. • Response makes complete sense. • Response is well organized. • Response meets all age-appropriate spelling expectations and writing conventions.
2	• Response is related to prompt. • Response makes sense. • Response is organized in an acceptable manner. • Response meets most age-appropriate spelling expectations and writing conventions.
1	• Response is loosely related to prompt. • Some aspects of response make sense. • Response is not well organized. • Response lacks some age-appropriate spelling expectations and writing conventions.
0	• Response is unrelated to prompt. • Response does not make sense. • Response is poorly organized. • Response lacks most age-appropriate spelling expectations and writing conventions.

[ ] Questions
Missed

Comprehension Scoring Guide	
Questions Missed	Level
0–1	Independent
1½–2	Ind./Inst.
2½	Instructional
3–4½	Inst./Frust.
5 +	Frustration

Student Book copy is on page 19.

A 8595 (Grade 5) Say: "I'd like you to read out loud [silently]. Think about what you're reading because I'll ask you some questions about it when you're done. Please begin here." [Point to title.]

Guided Reading Level: V; Lexile: 850

Pioneer House Building

		Substitution	Insertion	Omission	Reversal	Repetition	Self-Correction of Unacceptable Miscue	Meaning Change (Significant Miscue)
		MISCUES						
We learned about pioneer life in class.	7							
There were no experts like architects to build	15							
or design houses, so pioneers all worked	22							
together. Everyone in the area would come	29							
and share their skills. Some people would cut	37							
trees while others would start forming the	44							
frame of the house. The older children helped	52							
by cutting the lower tree limbs or carting	60							
wood, and younger children just played.	66							
The work was difficult and gave the people	74							
enormous appetites. Some of the women	80							
prepared large quantities of food and set it	88							
outside on long wooden tables. At night,	95							
everyone gathered and feasted joyfully.	100							
TOTAL								

Total Miscues ☐   Significant Miscues ☐

Word Recognition Scoring Guide		
Total Miscues	Level	Significant Miscues
0–1	Independent	0–1
2–4	Ind./Inst.	2
5	Instructional	3
6–9	Inst./Frust.	4
10 +	Frustration	5 +

Oral Reading Rate	Norm Group Percentile
⎯⎯⎯ WPM)6000	☐ 90 ☐ 75 ☐ 50 ☐ 25 ☐ 10

A 8595 (Grade 5)

Pioneer House Building

T 1. _____ What is this passage about?
(pioneers working on building houses)

F 2. _____ Why did the pioneers have to build their own houses?
(there were no experts to do it; no architects)

F 3. _____ In the passage, who came to help?
(all the people in the area)

F 4. _____ What did the younger children do?
(play)

F 5. _____ What did the older children do?
(cut the limbs; carted bits of wood)

F 6. _____ What other jobs did the people do?
(cut trees; form frames; prepare food)

F 7. _____ Where was the food placed and eaten?
(on wooden tables)

I 8. _____ What do you think was probably the hardest job? Why?
(any logical response)

E 9. _____ Which job would you pick? Why?
(any logical response)

V 10. _____ What does "enormous" mean?
(large; big)

	Questions Missed

Comprehension Scoring Guide

Questions Missed	Level
0–1	Independent
1½–2	Ind./Inst.
2½	Instructional
3–4½	Inst./Frust.
5 +	Frustration

Retelling Notes

Retelling Rubric

Independent Level/Excellent
States central or key ideas
Identifies important facts
Retains the general sequence of events
Relates most of the content in an organized manner

Instructional Level/Satisfactory
States most central or key ideas
Identifies some important facts
Retains the general sequence of events
Relates an overall sense of the content

Frustration Level/Unsatisfactory
Provides bits of information in a haphazard manner
Little apparent organization

Writing Prompt: Write about a way you help your family.

Rubric for Writing Response

3	• Response is very closely related to prompt. • Response makes complete sense. • Response is well organized. • Response meets all age-appropriate spelling expectations and writing conventions.
2	• Response is related to prompt. • Response makes sense. • Response is organized in an acceptable manner. • Response meets most age-appropriate spelling expectations and writing conventions.
1	• Response is loosely related to prompt. • Some aspects of response make sense. • Response is not well organized. • Response lacks some age-appropriate spelling expectations and writing conventions.
0	• Response is unrelated to prompt. • Response does not make sense. • Response is poorly organized. • Response lacks most age-appropriate spelling expectations and writing conventions.

Student Book copy is on page 20.

A 6867 (Grade 6) Say: "I'd like you to read out loud [silently]. Think about what you're reading because I'll ask you some questions about it when you're done. Please begin here." [Point to title.]

Lexile: 1030

Volunteer

		MISCUES					Self-Correction of Unacceptable Miscue	Meaning Change (Significant Miscue)
	Substitution	Insertion	Omission	Reversal	Repetition		
I've always wanted a pet, but my younger	8							
stepbrother is extremely allergic to animal dander.	15							
Instead, I volunteer at our community animal	22							
shelter—it's the perfect solution for my pet	30							
dilemma. Numerous training classes and written	36							
and practical examinations were required to	42							
become a qualified volunteer, but I was dedicated	50							
and succeeded. I originally wanted to exercise	57							
animals, but I had to complete thirty hours of	66							
cleaning beforehand. Once I completed my	72							
responsibilities, I was immediately promoted.	77							
Now I exercise energetic dogs by playing fetch	85							
and exercise cats by playing keep-away with	93							
string. It's like having a hundred pets!	100							
TOTAL								

Total Miscues [ ]   Significant Miscues [ ]

Word Recognition Scoring Guide		
Total Miscues	Level	Significant Miscues
0–1	Independent	0–1
2–4	Ind./Inst.	2
5	Instructional	3
6–9	Inst./Frust.	4
10 +	Frustration	5 +

Oral Reading Rate	Norm Group Percentile
___ WPM)6000	☐ 90 ☐ 75 ☐ 50 ☐ 25 ☐ 10

A 6867 (Grade 6)

Volunteer

T 1. _____ What is this passage about?
(volunteering at an animal shelter)

F 2. _____ What has the author always wanted?
(a pet)

F 3. _____ What does the author do at the animal shelter?
(exercise dogs and cats; clean)

F 4. _____ What did the author do to become a volunteer?
(took a training class; passed written and practical exams)

F 5. _____ How many hours of cleaning were required before the author could exercise the animals?
(thirty)

F 6. _____ How do the dogs get exercise?
(by playing fetch)

F 7. _____ How do the cats get exercise?
(by playing keep away with string)

I 8. _____ Why can't the author have a pet?
(any logical response; the author's stepbrother is allergic to animals)

E 9. _____ Would you like being a volunteer at an animal shelter? Why?
(any logical response; yes, playing with the animals would be fun)

V 10. _____ What is a "dilemma"?
(a problem)

☐ Questions Missed

Comprehension Scoring Guide	
Questions Missed	Level
0–1	Independent
1½–2	Ind./Inst.
2½	Instructional
3–4½	Inst./Frust.
5 +	Frustration

Writing Prompt: Write about what activities you might like to do with a dog or cat.

	Rubric for Writing Response
3	• Response is very closely related to prompt. • Response makes complete sense. • Response is well organized. • Response meets all age-appropriate spelling expectations and writing conventions.
2	• Response is related to prompt. • Response makes sense. • Response is organized in an acceptable manner. • Response meets most age-appropriate spelling expectations and writing conventions.
1	• Response is loosely related to prompt. • Some aspects of response make sense. • Response is not well organized. • Response lacks some age-appropriate spelling expectations and writing conventions.
0	• Response is unrelated to prompt. • Response does not make sense. • Response is poorly organized. • Response lacks most age-appropriate spelling expectations and writing conventions.

Student Book copy is on page 21.

A 3717 (Grade 7) Say: "I'd like you to read out loud [silently]. Think about what you're reading because I'll ask you some questions about it when you're done. Please begin here." [Point to title.]

Lexile: 1030

Blackout		MISCUES				Repetition	Self-Correction of Unacceptable Miscue	Meaning Change (Significant Miscue)
		Substitution	Insertion	Omission	Reversal			
The soft buzzing of the computer relaxed	7							
Anthony as he worked on the quarterly report	15							
for his demanding employer. He typed the final	23							
sentence, sighed in relief, and saved the file.	31							
Suddenly, the office lights flickered, the	37							
computer screen went black, and Salt Lake	44							
City was eerily silent until sirens began blaring.	52							
Emergency personnel guided employees from	57							
several departments down the stairwells.	62							
An hour later, the police chief announced	69							
through his loud speaker, "All is clear." The	77							
workers filed into the elevators like clockwork,	84							
returning to their projects. One observer	90							
commented, "All in a day's work in Salt Lake	99							
City."	100							
TOTAL								

Total Miscues ☐   Significant Miscues ☐

Word Recognition Scoring Guide		
Total Miscues	Level	Significant Miscues
0–1	Independent	0–1
2–4	Ind./Inst.	2
5	Instructional	3
6–9	Inst./Frust.	4
10 +	Frustration	5 +

Oral Reading Rate	Norm Group Percentile
⟌6000 WPM	☐ 90 ☐ 75 ☐ 50 ☐ 25 ☐ 10

A 3717 (Grade 7)

Blackout

T 1. _____ What is this passage about?
(the electricity going off in a building;
people leaving a building after the
power went off)

F 2. _____ What relaxed Anthony?
(the soft buzz of the computer; the
computer noises; having finished his
report)

F 3. _____ What was Anthony working on for his
employer?
(a quarterly report; paper; report)

F 4. _____ Where did the story take place?
(Salt Lake City; office building)

F 5. _____ Who guided the employees down the
stairs?
(emergency personnel)

F 6. _____ Who announced that it was safe to enter
the building?
(the police chief; police)

F 7. _____ How long did the workers wait before
they heard the all clear announcement?
(an hour)

I 8. _____ What time of day do you think the
story probably took place? Why?
(any logical response; morning or early
afternoon because everyone went back
to work)

E 9. _____ How do you think you would feel if
you were in a large building when the
electricity went off? Why?
(any logical response)

V 10. _____ What is an "observer"?
(someone who watches or notices
something)

☐ Questions
Missed

Comprehension Scoring Guide	
Questions Missed	Level
0–1	Independent
1½–2	Ind./Inst.
2½	Instructional
3–4½	Inst./Frust.
5 +	Frustration

Retelling Notes

Retelling Rubric

Independent Level/Excellent
States central or key ideas
Identifies important facts
Retains the general sequence of events
Relates most of the content in an organized manner

Instructional Level/Satisfactory
States most central or key ideas
Identifies some important facts
Retains the general sequence of events
Relates an overall sense of the content

Frustration Level/Unsatisfactory
Provides bits of information in a haphazard manner
Little apparent organization

Writing Prompt: Write about some things you
would do if all the lights went off right now.

Rubric for Writing Response

3	• Response is very closely related to prompt. • Response makes complete sense. • Response is well organized. • Response meets all age-appropriate spelling expectations and writing conventions.
2	• Response is related to prompt. • Response makes sense. • Response is organized in an acceptable manner. • Response meets most age-appropriate spelling expectations and writing conventions.
1	• Response is loosely related to prompt. • Some aspects of response make sense. • Response is not well organized. • Response lacks some age-appropriate spelling expectations and writing conventions.
0	• Response is unrelated to prompt. • Response does not make sense. • Response is poorly organized. • Response lacks most age-appropriate spelling expectations and writing conventions.

Student Book copy is on page 22.

A 8183 (Grade 8) Say: "I'd like you to read out loud [silently]. Think about what you're reading because I'll ask you some questions about it when you're done. Please begin here." [Point to title.]

Lexile: 1030

Sunset Surprise

		MISCUES					
	Substitution	Insertion	Omission	Reversal	Repetition	Self-Correction of Unacceptable Miscue	Meaning Change (Significant Miscue)
Alexandra was captivated by the Magnolia 6							
Hill sunset. The magnificent display of bright 13							
vermilion, magenta, and yellow appeared to be 20							
a scrumptious, ripe mango slowly sinking into 27							
the horizon. Still surrounded by the beautiful 34							
landscape of falling leaves, Alexandra 39							
reluctantly journeyed home for dinner. Turning 45							
east toward her childhood home, she witnessed 52							
a horrible sight: her beloved greenhouse was 59							
enveloped in flames! She quickly dashed down 66							
the hill and transversed a familiar field of 74							
drying corn stalks. Shortly before she arrived, 81							
she realized the unexpected fire was only a 89							
reflection of the sunset on the sparkling glass 97							
of the greenhouse. 100							
TOTAL							

Total Miscues [ ]   Significant Miscues [ ]

Word Recognition Scoring Guide		
Total Miscues	Level	Significant Miscues
0–1	Independent	0–1
2–4	Ind./Inst.	2
5	Instructional	3
6–9	Inst./Frust.	4
10 +	Frustration	5 +

Oral Reading Rate	Norm Group Percentile
____ WPM)6000	☐ 90 ☐ 75 ☐ 50 ☐ 25 ☐ 10

A 8183 (Grade 8)

Sunset Surprise

T 1. _____ What is this passage about?
(an exciting sunset; Alexandra being fooled by a sunset; a greenhouse that appears to be on fire)

F 2. _____ Where was Alexandra enjoying the sunset?
(Magnolia Hill)

F 3. _____ What did the sun resemble as it was setting?
(a mango)

F 4. _____ Why did Alexandra first decide to go home?
(to eat dinner)

F 5. _____ Which direction did she head to go home?
(East)

F 6. _____ How was the greenhouse described when Alexandra first saw it?
(enveloped in flames)

F 7. _____ Why did the greenhouse appear to be on fire?
(the glass reflected the sunset, which is the color of fire)

I 8. _____ Why do you think Alexandra didn't notice the greenhouse sooner?
(any logical response; she was facing West; the sun sets in the West)

E 9. _____ How do you think Alexandra felt when she realized her error? Why?
(any logical response; relieved; embarrassed)

V 10. _____ What does "reluctantly" mean?
(hesitated; not sure at first; didn't want to do it; cautiously)

☐ Questions Missed

Comprehension Scoring Guide	
Questions Missed	Level
0–1	Independent
1½–2	Ind./Inst.
2½	Instructional
3–4½	Inst./Frust.
5 +	Frustration

Retelling Notes

Writing Prompt: Write about a place you would like to explore and what you would see.

	Rubric for Writing Response
3	• Response is very closely related to prompt. • Response makes complete sense. • Response is well organized. • Response meets all age-appropriate spelling expectations and writing conventions.
2	• Response is related to prompt. • Response makes sense. • Response is organized in an acceptable manner. • Response meets most age-appropriate spelling expectations and writing conventions.
1	• Response is loosely related to prompt. • Some aspects of response make sense. • Response is not well organized. • Response lacks some age-appropriate spelling expectations and writing conventions.
0	• Response is unrelated to prompt. • Response does not make sense. • Response is poorly organized. • Response lacks most age-appropriate spelling expectations and writing conventions.

Performance Booklet

Teacher Copy

Form B

Primary Uses:

- Oral Reading
- Later Assessment

Other Uses:

- Silent Reading
- Listening Level
- Progress Monitoring

Note: This Performance Booklet is on the Basic Reading Inventory website.

Twelfth Edition

BASIC READING INVENTORY PERFORMANCE BOOKLET

Form B

Jerry L. Johns, Laurie Elish-Piper, and Beth Johns

Student _____ Grade _____ Gender M F Date of Test _____

School _____ Examiner _____ Date of Birth _____

Address _____ Current Book/Level _____ Age _____

SUMMARY OF STUDENT'S READING PERFORMANCE

Grade	Word Recognition						Comprehension		Reading Rate	
	Isolation (Word Lists)				Context (Passages)		Form B		Words per Minute (WPM)	Norm Group Percentile
	Sight	Analysis	Total	Level	Miscues	Level	Questions Missed	Level		
Kb			/ 6							
Km			/ 9							
Ke			/12							
1b			/20							
1m										
1e										
2			/20							
3			/20							
4			/20							
5			/20							
6			/20							
7			/20							
8			/20							
9			/20							
10			/20							
11			/20							
12			/20							

ESTIMATE OF READING LEVELS

Independent _____   Instructional _____   Frustration _____

INFORMAL ANALYSIS OF ORAL READING

Oral Reading Behaviors	Frequency of Occurrence			General Impact on Meaning		
	Seldom	Sometimes	Frequently	No Change	Little Change	Much Change
Substitutions						
Insertions						
Omissions						
Reversals						
Repetitions						

LISTENING LEVEL, FORM _____

Grade	1	2	3	4	5	6	7	8
Questions Missed								
Level								

ESTIMATED LISTENING LEVEL: _____

QUALITATIVE ANALYSIS OF BASIC READING INVENTORY INSIGHTS

General Directions: Note the degree to which the student shows behavior or evidence in the following areas. Space is provided for additional items.

Seldom / Weak / Poor ———————— Always / Strong / Excellent

COMPREHENSION

Seeks to construct meaning

Makes predictions

Activates background knowledge

Possesses appropriate concepts and vocabulary

Monitors reading

Varies reading rate as needed

Understands topic and major ideas

Remembers facts or details

Makes and supports appropriate inferences

Evaluates ideas from passages

Understands vocabulary used

Provides appropriate definitions of words

Engages with passages

_____

_____

WORD IDENTIFICATION

Possesses numerous strategies

Uses strategies flexibly

Uses graphophonic information

Uses semantic information

Uses syntactic information

Knows high-frequency words automatically

Possesses sight vocabulary

_____

_____

ORAL AND SILENT READING

Reads fluently

Reads with expression

Attends to punctuation

Keeps place while reading

Reads at appropriate rate

Reads silently without vocalization

_____

_____

ATTITUDE AND CONFIDENCE

Enjoys reading

Demonstrates willingness to risk

Possesses positive self-concept

Chooses to read

Regards himself/herself as a reader

Exhibits persistence

_____

_____

Form B • Graded Word Lists • Performance Booklet • Student Book copy is on page 24.

List B Kb (Beginning Kindergarten)	Sight	Analysis
1. the*	_____	_____
2. and*	_____	_____
3. it*	_____	_____
4. at*	_____	_____
5. do*	_____	_____
6. we*	_____	_____

*denotes high-frequency word from Revised Dolch List

Number Correct _____ _____

Total _____

List B Km (Middle Kindergarten)	Sight	Analysis
1. his*	_____	_____
2. back	_____	_____
3. will*	_____	_____
4. blue*	_____	_____
5. was*	_____	_____
6. of*	_____	_____
7. she*	_____	_____
8. one*	_____	_____
9. green*	_____	_____

*denotes high-frequency word from Revised Dolch List

Number Correct _____ _____

Total _____

List B Ke (End Kindergarten)	Sight	Analysis
1. if*	_____	_____
2. duck	_____	_____
3. wish	_____	_____
4. from*	_____	_____
5. out*	_____	_____
6. are*	_____	_____
7. lost	_____	_____
8. they*	_____	_____
9. as*	_____	_____
10. time	_____	_____
11. happy	_____	_____
12. now*	_____	_____

*denotes high-frequency word from Revised Dolch List

Number Correct _____ _____

Total _____

IMPORTANT NOTE: In kindergarten, the average student's experience with words in isolation is very limited, especially at the beginning of the school year. The number of words correct may depend more on the school's curriculum rather than the student's emerging skills. The number correct is not as important as the word attack strategies the student exhibits. The chart below is one way that teacher judgment can be used to quickly analyze a student's performance to better understand his or her strengths and weaknesses as an emergent reader.

Qualitative Analysis of Word List Responses			
(0 = not evident 1 = emerging 2 = evident)			
Uses initial sounds	0	1	2
Blends sounds	0	1	2
Recognizes vowels/vowel patterns	0	1	2
Knows high-frequency words by sight	0	1	2

Form B • Graded Word Lists • Performance Booklet • Student Book copy is on page 25.

List B 7141 (Grade 1)	Sight	Analysis	List B 8224 (Grade 2)	Sight	Analysis
1. little*	_____	_____	1. feel	_____	_____
2. next*	_____	_____	2. drink	_____	_____
3. reads	_____	_____	3. wave	_____	_____
4. my*	_____	_____	4. gray	_____	_____
5. make*	_____	_____	5. start*	_____	_____
6. old*	_____	_____	6. horn	_____	_____
7. mother	_____	_____	7. across*	_____	_____
8. bed	_____	_____	8. warm*	_____	_____
9. grow*	_____	_____	9. bad	_____	_____
10. laugh	_____	_____	10. even*	_____	_____
11. near*	_____	_____	11. feed	_____	_____
12. before*	_____	_____	12. always*	_____	_____
13. lamb	_____	_____	13. round*	_____	_____
14. ride	_____	_____	14. country	_____	_____
15. store	_____	_____	15. enough*	_____	_____
16. high*	_____	_____	16. able	_____	_____
17. began*	_____	_____	17. should*	_____	_____
18. made*	_____	_____	18. bottom	_____	_____
19. cry	_____	_____	19. crawl	_____	_____
20. her*	_____	_____	20. machine	_____	_____

*denotes high-frequency word from Revised Dolch List

*denotes high-frequency word from Revised Dolch List

Number Correct _____ _____

Number Correct _____ _____

Total _____

Total _____

Scoring Guide for Graded Word Lists			
Independent	Instructional	Inst./Frust.	Frustration
20 19	18 17 16	15 14	13 or less

Form B • Graded Word Lists • Performance Booklet • Student Book copy is on page 26.

List B 3183 (Grade 3)	Sight	Analysis	List B 5414 (Grade 4)	Sight	Analysis
1. star	_____	_____	1. bike	_____	_____
2. net	_____	_____	2. castle	_____	_____
3. doctor	_____	_____	3. jungle	_____	_____
4. spoon	_____	_____	4. bullet	_____	_____
5. trap	_____	_____	5. factory	_____	_____
6. valley	_____	_____	6. stripe	_____	_____
7. shirt	_____	_____	7. problem	_____	_____
8. meet	_____	_____	8. target	_____	_____
9. chuckle	_____	_____	9. capture	_____	_____
10. gaze	_____	_____	10. sleeve	_____	_____
11. rib	_____	_____	11. pump	_____	_____
12. discover	_____	_____	12. sausage	_____	_____
13. hundred	_____	_____	13. electric	_____	_____
14. reason	_____	_____	14. business	_____	_____
15. conductor	_____	_____	15. instant	_____	_____
16. coast	_____	_____	16. balance	_____	_____
17. escape	_____	_____	17. surround	_____	_____
18. thirty	_____	_____	18. invention	_____	_____
19. prepare	_____	_____	19. accident	_____	_____
20. nation	_____	_____	20. rifle	_____	_____
Number Correct	_____	_____	Number Correct	_____	_____
Total	_____		Total	_____	

Scoring Guide for Graded Word Lists			
Independent	Instructional	Inst./Frust.	Frustration
20 19	18 17 16	15 14	13 or less

Form B • Graded Word Lists • Performance Booklet • Student Book copy is on page 27.

List B 8595 (Grade 5)	Sight	Analysis
1. science	_____	_____
2. blush	_____	_____
3. marvelous	_____	_____
4. index	_____	_____
5. panther	_____	_____
6. grace	_____	_____
7. boss	_____	_____
8. emergency	_____	_____
9. blond	_____	_____
10. nugget	_____	_____
11. terrific	_____	_____
12. effort	_____	_____
13. observe	_____	_____
14. mammoth	_____	_____
15. transportation	_____	_____
16. liberty	_____	_____
17. balcony	_____	_____
18. scar	_____	_____
19. confidence	_____	_____
20. admiral	_____	_____
Number Correct	_____	_____
Total		_____

List B 6867 (Grade 6)	Sight	Analysis
1. painful	_____	_____
2. raspberry	_____	_____
3. medical	_____	_____
4. label	_____	_____
5. household	_____	_____
6. foreman	_____	_____
7. catalog	_____	_____
8. solar	_____	_____
9. unexpected	_____	_____
10. beggar	_____	_____
11. thermometer	_____	_____
12. portable	_____	_____
13. distrust	_____	_____
14. dandelion	_____	_____
15. charity	_____	_____
16. graduation	_____	_____
17. species	_____	_____
18. variety	_____	_____
19. contribute	_____	_____
20. jagged	_____	_____
Number Correct	_____	_____
Total		_____

Scoring Guide for Graded Word Lists			
Independent	Instructional	Inst./Frust.	Frustration
20 19	18 17 16	15 14	13 or less

List B 3717 (Grade 7)	Sight	Analysis		List B 8183 (Grade 8)	Sight	Analysis
1. focus	_____	_____		1. skyscraper	_____	_____
2. turnpike	_____	_____		2. reaction	_____	_____
3. harmony	_____	_____		3. horsepower	_____	_____
4. uranium	_____	_____		4. justify	_____	_____
5. merchandise	_____	_____		5. garlic	_____	_____
6. irregular	_____	_____		6. omit	_____	_____
7. humidity	_____	_____		7. divorce	_____	_____
8. enlarge	_____	_____		8. exception	_____	_____
9. expel	_____	_____		9. flounder	_____	_____
10. remainder	_____	_____		10. comedian	_____	_____
11. industrious	_____	_____		11. nomination	_____	_____
12. pamphlet	_____	_____		12. barbarian	_____	_____
13. geologist	_____	_____		13. molecule	_____	_____
14. rayon	_____	_____		14. recruit	_____	_____
15. novel	_____	_____		15. imperfect	_____	_____
16. survival	_____	_____		16. upholster	_____	_____
17. meteorite	_____	_____		17. authentic	_____	_____
18. dormitory	_____	_____		18. variation	_____	_____
19. mahogany	_____	_____		19. mortgage	_____	_____
20. chauffeur	_____	_____		20. brigade	_____	_____
Number Correct	_____	_____		Number Correct	_____	_____
Total		_____		Total		_____

Scoring Guide for Graded Word Lists			
Independent	Instructional	Inst./Frust.	Frustration
20 19	18 17 16	15 14	13 or less

Form B • Graded Word Lists • Performance Booklet • Student Book copy is on page 29.

List B 4959 (Grade 9)	Sight	Analysis	List B 1047 (Grade 10)	Sight	Analysis
1. disapprove	_____	_____	1. immature	_____	_____
2. data	_____	_____	2. reorganize	_____	_____
3. texture	_____	_____	3. evaluate	_____	_____
4. disqualify	_____	_____	4. visualize	_____	_____
5. compress	_____	_____	5. grim	_____	_____
6. slur	_____	_____	6. patronize	_____	_____
7. gruesome	_____	_____	7. rupture	_____	_____
8. deceased	_____	_____	8. chronic	_____	_____
9. transaction	_____	_____	9. exploit	_____	_____
10. misconduct	_____	_____	10. obituary	_____	_____
11. sarcasm	_____	_____	11. saturate	_____	_____
12. momentary	_____	_____	12. induce	_____	_____
13. ingenious	_____	_____	13. recuperate	_____	_____
14. mechanism	_____	_____	14. pictorial	_____	_____
15. audible	_____	_____	15. phenomenal	_____	_____
16. embezzle	_____	_____	16. portal	_____	_____
17. robust	_____	_____	17. centennial	_____	_____
18. luminous	_____	_____	18. silhouette	_____	_____
19. heathen	_____	_____	19. boisterous	_____	_____
20. ecstasy	_____	_____	20. impertinent	_____	_____
Number Correct	_____	_____	Number Correct	_____	_____
Total		_____	Total		_____

Scoring Guide for Graded Word Lists			
Independent	Instructional	Inst./Frust.	Frustration
20 19	18 17 16	15 14	13 or less

List B 1187 (Grade 11)	Sight	Analysis	List B 1296 (Grade 12)	Sight	Analysis
1. discredit	_____	_____	1. invalidate	_____	_____
2. habitat	_____	_____	2. metabolism	_____	_____
3. profane	_____	_____	3. metamorphosis	_____	_____
4. intern	_____	_____	4. advert	_____	_____
5. intimidate	_____	_____	5. impotent	_____	_____
6. inseparable	_____	_____	6. predatory	_____	_____
7. binder	_____	_____	7. protocol	_____	_____
8. bilingual	_____	_____	8. prodigy	_____	_____
9. jurisdiction	_____	_____	9. derivative	_____	_____
10. stilt	_____	_____	10. zealous	_____	_____
11. metropolis	_____	_____	11. debase	_____	_____
12. preposterous	_____	_____	12. pretentious	_____	_____
13. pollinate	_____	_____	13. regurgitate	_____	_____
14. patronage	_____	_____	14. herbivorous	_____	_____
15. reminiscent	_____	_____	15. maritime	_____	_____
16. secede	_____	_____	16. aesthetic	_____	_____
17. knoll	_____	_____	17. blasphemy	_____	_____
18. promenade	_____	_____	18. extemporaneous	_____	_____
19. catechism	_____	_____	19. agrarian	_____	_____
20. cavalcade	_____	_____	20. colloquial	_____	_____
Number Correct	_____	_____	Number Correct	_____	_____
Total	_____		Total	_____	

Scoring Guide for Graded Word Lists			
Independent	Instructional	Inst./Frust.	Frustration
20 19	18 17 16	15 14	13 or less

Student Book copy is on page 32.

B Kb (Beginning K) Point to each word in the title as you read it. Then say: "Read this story about the frog. I'll ask you some questions about it when you're done."

Guided Reading Level: A

Frog		MISCUES							
		Substitution	Insertion	Omission	Reversal	Repetition	Self-Correction of Unacceptable Miscue	Meaning Change (Significant Miscue)	
The frog sits.	3								
The frog eats.	6								
The frog jumps.	9								
The frog swims.	12								
TOTAL									

Total Miscues [　]   Significant Miscues [　]

Word Recognition Scoring Guide		
Total Miscues	Level	Significant Miscues
0	Independent	0
—	Ind./Inst.	—
—	Instructional	—
1	Inst./Frust.	1
2 +	Frustration	2 +

Qualitative Analysis of Word Identification (0 = not evident 1 = emerging 2 = evident)		
Uses letter-sound relationships	0 1 2	
Points to words while reading	0 1 2	
Uses monitoring (rereads; corrects)	0 1 2	
Knows high-frequency words	0 1 2	
Possesses sight vocabulary	0 1 2	
Exhibits persistence	0 1 2	
Seems confident	0 1 2	

Important Note: If the scoring guides are used, teacher judgment is especially important because of the length of the passage and the limited number of questions.

B Kb (Beginning K)

Frog

T 1. _____ What is this story about? [If student says "a frog," say "tell me more."]
(what a frog does; how a frog sits, eats, jumps, swims)

F 2. _____ What's something else the frog does in the story?
(any one of the following: sits, eats, jumps, swims)

I 3. _____ If you wanted to add more to the story, tell me what else the frog might do.
(any logical response; sleep; play; catch insects)

E 4. _____ Where do you think you would probably need to go to see a frog?
(any logical response; a pond, a lake, the water)

V 5. _____ What does the word "jumps" mean?
(any logical response; hop; student demonstrates how to jump)

Retelling Notes

Retelling Rubric

Independent Level/Excellent
States central or key ideas
Identifies important facts
Retains the general sequence of events
Relates most of the content in an organized manner

Instructional Level/Satisfactory
States most central or key ideas
Identifies some important facts
Retains the general sequence of events
Relates an overall sense of the content

Frustration Level/Unsatisfactory
Provides bits of information in a haphazard manner
Little apparent organization

Writing Prompt: Write about what you would do for fun if you were a frog.

Rubric for Writing Response

3	• Response is very closely related to prompt. • Response makes complete sense. • Response is well organized. • Response meets all age-appropriate spelling expectations and writing conventions.
2	• Response is related to prompt. • Response makes sense. • Response is organized in an acceptable manner. • Response meets most age-appropriate spelling expectations and writing conventions.
1	• Response is loosely related to prompt. • Some aspects of response make sense. • Response is not well organized. • Response lacks some age-appropriate spelling expectations and writing conventions.
0	• Response is unrelated to prompt. • Response does not make sense. • Response is poorly organized. • Response lacks most age-appropriate spelling expectations and writing conventions.

☐ Questions Missed

Comprehension Scoring Guide

Questions Missed	Level
0	Independent
1	Ind./Inst.
1½	Instructional
2	Inst./Frust.
2½ +	Frustration

Qualitative Analysis of Comprehension
(0 = not evident   1 = emerging   2 = evident)

Seeks to construct meaning	0	1	2
Understands topic and major ideas	0	1	2
Identifies facts or details	0	1	2
Evaluates ideas from story	0	1	2
Makes and supports appropriate inferences	0	1	2
Seems engaged with story	0	1	2

Important Note: If the scoring guides are used, teacher judgment is especially important because of the length of the passage and the limited number of questions.

Student Book copy is on page 33.

B Km (Middle K) Point to each word in the title as you read it. Then say: "Read this story about my home. I'll ask you some questions about it when you're done."

Guided Reading Level: B

My Home		MISCUES						Self-Correction of Unacceptable Miscue	Meaning Change (Significant Miscue)
---	---	Substitution	Insertion	Omission	Reversal	Repetition			
This is my mom.	4								
This is my dad.	8								
This is my dog.	12								
This is my cat.	16								
This is my home.	20								
TOTAL									

Total Miscues [ ]   Significant Miscues [ ]

Word Recognition Scoring Guide		
Total Miscues	Level	Significant Miscues
0	Independent	0
—	Ind./Inst.	—
1	Instructional	1
2	Inst./Frust.	2
3 +	Frustration	3 +

Qualitative Analysis of Word Identification		
(0 = not evident 1 = emerging 2 = evident)		
Uses letter-sound relationships		0 1 2
Points to words while reading		0 1 2
Uses monitoring (rereads; corrects)		0 1 2
Knows high-frequency words		0 1 2
Possesses sight vocabulary		0 1 2
Exhibits persistence		0 1 2
Seems confident		0 1 2

Important Note: If the scoring guides are used, teacher judgment is especially important because of the length of the passage and the limited number of questions.

B Km (Middle K)

My Home

T 1. _____ What is this story about? [If student says "my home," say "tell me more."] (the people and animals in my home)

F 2. _____ What's something else in the home? (any one of the following: mom, dad, dog, cat)

I 3. _____ If you wanted to add more to the story, tell me what else might be in the home. (any logical response; toys; brother; sister)

E 4. _____ Where do you think you would probably need to go to see a home? (any logical response; a neighborhood; down the street; across the street; next door)

V 5. _____ What does the word "home" mean? (any logical response; a house; a place where you live)

□ Questions Missed

Comprehension Scoring Guide	
Questions Missed	Level
0	Independent
1	Ind./Inst.
1½	Instructional
2	Inst./Frust.
2½ +	Frustration

Qualitative Analysis of Comprehension			
(0 = not evident 1 = emerging 2 = evident)			
Seeks to construct meaning	0	1	2
Understands topic and major ideas	0	1	2
Identifies facts or details	0	1	2
Evaluates ideas from story	0	1	2
Makes and supports appropriate inferences	0	1	2
Seems engaged with story	0	1	2

Writing Prompt: Write about the people and things in your home.

Rubric for Writing Response	
3	• Response is very closely related to prompt. • Response makes complete sense. • Response is well organized. • Response meets all age-appropriate spelling expectations and writing conventions.
2	• Response is related to prompt. • Response makes sense. • Response is organized in an acceptable manner. • Response meets most age-appropriate spelling expectations and writing conventions.
1	• Response is loosely related to prompt. • Some aspects of response make sense. • Response is not well organized. • Response lacks some age-appropriate spelling expectations and writing conventions.
0	• Response is unrelated to prompt. • Response does not make sense. • Response is poorly organized. • Response lacks most age-appropriate spelling expectations and writing conventions.

Important Note: If the scoring guides are used, teacher judgment is especially important because of the length of the passage and the limited number of questions.

Student Book copy is on page 34.

B Ke (End K) Point to each word in the title as you read it. Then say: "Read this story about my dog. I'll ask you some questions about it when you're done."

Guided Reading Level: D

My Dog		MISCUES							
		Substitution	Insertion	Omission	Reversal	Repetition	Self-Correction of Unacceptable Miscue	Meaning Change (Significant Miscue)	
I have a dog.	4								
My dog is Spot.	8								
Spot is a big dog.	13								
He plays ball.	16								
I play with Spot.	20								
Spot is a fun dog.	25								
TOTAL									

Total Miscues [ ]   Significant Miscues [ ]

Word Recognition Scoring Guide		
Total Miscues	Level	Significant Miscues
0	Independent	0
1	Ind./Inst.	—
2	Instructional	1
3	Inst./Frust.	2
4 +	Frustration	3 +

Qualitative Analysis of Word Identification			
(0 = not evident 1 = emerging 2 = evident)			
Uses letter-sound relationships	0	1	2
Points to words while reading	0	1	2
Uses monitoring (rereads; corrects)	0	1	2
Knows high-frequency words	0	1	2
Possesses sight vocabulary	0	1	2
Exhibits persistence	0	1	2
Seems confident	0	1	2

Important Note: If the scoring guides are used, teacher judgment is especially important because of the length of the passage and the limited number of questions.

B Ke (End K)

My Dog

T 1. _____ What is this story about? [If student says "a dog," say "tell me more."] (a dog named Spot; a dog and what he does)

F 2. _____ What else do we learn about the dog in the story? (any one of the following: he is a big dog; he plays ball; he is a fun dog)

I 3. _____ If you wanted to add more to the story, tell me what else the girl might do with Spot. (any logical response; go for a walk; feed him; give him a treat)

E 4. _____ Where do you think you would probably need to go to see Spot? (any logical response; the park; the yard; outside)

V 5. _____ What does the word "big" mean? (any logical response; large)

	Questions Missed

Comprehension Scoring Guide	
Questions Missed	Level
0	Independent
1	Ind./Inst.
1½	Instructional
2	Inst./Frust.
2½ +	Frustration

Qualitative Analysis of Comprehension			
(0 = not evident 1 = emerging 2 = evident)			
Seeks to construct meaning	0	1	2
Understands topic and major ideas	0	1	2
Identifies facts or details	0	1	2
Evaluates ideas from story	0	1	2
Makes and supports appropriate inferences	0	1	2
Seems engaged with story	0	1	2

Retelling Notes

Retelling Rubric

Independent Level/Excellent

States central or key ideas
Identifies important facts
Retains the general sequence of events
Relates most of the content in an organized manner

Instructional Level/Satisfactory

States most central or key ideas
Identifies some important facts
Retains the general sequence of events
Relates an overall sense of the content

Frustration Level/Unsatisfactory

Provides bits of information in a haphazard manner
Little apparent organization

Writing Prompt: Write about an activity you would like to do with a dog.

Rubric for Writing Response	
3	• Response is very closely related to prompt. • Response makes complete sense. • Response is well organized. • Response meets all age-appropriate spelling expectations and writing conventions.
2	• Response is related to prompt. • Response makes sense. • Response is organized in an acceptable manner. • Response meets most age-appropriate spelling expectations and writing conventions.
1	• Response is loosely related to prompt. • Some aspects of response make sense. • Response is not well organized. • Response lacks some age-appropriate spelling expectations and writing conventions.
0	• Response is unrelated to prompt. • Response does not make sense. • Response is poorly organized. • Response lacks most age-appropriate spelling expectations and writing conventions.

Important Note: If the scoring guides are used, teacher judgment is especially important because of the length of the passage and the limited number of questions.

Student Book copy is on page 35.

B 7141b (Beginning Grade 1) Point to each word in the title as you read it. Then say: "Read this story about a walk in the fall. I'll ask you some questions about it when you're done."

Guided Reading Level: E

A Walk in the Fall

		MISCUES						
	Substitution	Insertion	Omission	Reversal	Repetition	Self-Correction of Unacceptable Miscue	Meaning Change (Significant Miscue)	
It was fall. Pat went for a walk. She	9							
took her dog Sam. They liked to walk.	17							
They walked for a long time. They saw	25							
trees. Some were red. Some were	31							
green. They were pretty. Pat and Sam	38							
saw birds too. Sam did not run after	46							
them. He was good.	50							
TOTAL								

Total Miscues ☐   Significant Miscues ☐

Word Recognition Scoring Guide		
Total Miscues	Level	Significant Miscues
0	Independent	0
1–2	Ind./Inst.	1
3	Instructional	2
4	Inst./Frust.	3
5 +	Frustration	4 +

Qualitative Analysis of Word Identification			
(0 = not evident 1 = emerging 2 = evident)			
Uses letter-sound relationships	0	1	2
Points to words while reading	0	1	2
Uses monitoring (rereads; corrects)	0	1	2
Knows high-frequency words	0	1	2
Possesses sight vocabulary	0	1	2
Exhibits persistence	0	1	2
Seems confident	0	1	2

Important Note: If the scoring guides are used, teacher judgment is especially important because of the length of the passage and the limited number of questions.

B 7141b (Beginning Grade 1)

A Walk in the Fall

F 1. _____ What is this story about? [If student
says "fall," say "tell me more."]
(taking a walk with a dog)

F 2. _____ What did Pat do?
(went for a walk; took her dog for a
walk)

E 3. _____ Why do you think Pat took her dog on
the walk?
(any logical response; for company;
she liked him)

I 4. _____ Why do you think Sam didn't run after
the birds?
(any logical response)

V 5. _____ What does "pretty" mean?
(nice; any logical response)

| Questions |
| Missed |

Comprehension Scoring Guide	
Questions Missed	Level
0	Independent
1	Ind./Inst.
1½	Instructional
2	Inst./Frust.
2½ +	Frustration

Qualitative Analysis of Comprehension			
(0 = not evident 1 = emerging 2 = evident)			
Seeks to construct meaning	0	1	2
Understands topic and major ideas	0	1	2
Identifies facts or details	0	1	2
Evaluates ideas from story	0	1	2
Makes and supports appropriate inferences	0	1	2
Seems engaged with story	0	1	2

Retelling Notes

Retelling Rubric

Independent Level/Excellent
States central or key ideas
Identifies important facts
Retains the general sequence of events
Relates most of the content in an organized manner

Instructional Level/Satisfactory
States most central or key ideas
Identifies some important facts
Retains the general sequence of events
Relates an overall sense of the content

Frustration Level/Unsatisfactory
Provides bits of information in a haphazard manner
Little apparent organization

Writing Prompt: Write about your favorite season.

	Rubric for Writing Response
3	• Response is very closely related to prompt. • Response makes complete sense. • Response is well organized. • Response meets all age-appropriate spelling expectations and writing conventions.
2	• Response is related to prompt. • Response makes sense. • Response is organized in an acceptable manner. • Response meets most age-appropriate spelling expectations and writing conventions.
1	• Response is loosely related to prompt. • Some aspects of response make sense. • Response is not well organized. • Response lacks some age-appropriate spelling expectations and writing conventions.
0	• Response is unrelated to prompt. • Response does not make sense. • Response is poorly organized. • Response lacks most age-appropriate spelling expectations and writing conventions.

Important Note: If the scoring guides are used, teacher judgment is especially important because of the length of the passage and the limited number of questions.

Student Book copy is on page 36.

B 7141m (Middle Grade 1) Point to each word in the title as you read it. Then say: "Read this story about food for birds. I'll ask you some questions about it when you're done."

Guided Reading Level: G

Food for Birds		MISCUES						
		Substitution	Insertion	Omission	Reversal	Repetition	Self-Correction of Unacceptable Miscue	Meaning Change (Significant Miscue)
"See the small birds," said Jim.	6							
"They are looking in the snow because	13							
they want food."	16							
"The snow is deep, and they cannot	23							
find food," replied Beth.	27							
Jim said, "Let's help them."	32							
"Yes," said Beth. "We can get bread	39							
for them."	41							
Jim and Beth ran home. They asked	48							
Mother for bread, and she gave it to them.	57							
Then they ran back to find the birds.	65							
"There are the birds!" shouted Beth.	71							
"Give them the bread."	75							
Jim put the bread on the snow.	82							
Beth said, "Look at the birds! They are	90							
eating the bread."	93							
"They are very happy now," said Jim.	100							
TOTAL								

Total Miscues ☐   Significant Miscues ☐

Word Recognition Scoring Guide		
Total Miscues	Level	Significant Miscues
0–1	Independent	0–1
2–4	Ind./Inst.	2
5	Instructional	3
6–9	Inst./Frust.	4
10 +	Frustration	5 +

Oral Reading Rate	Norm Group Percentile				
)6000 WPM	☐90	☐75	☐50	☐25	☐10

B 7141m (Middle Grade 1)

Food for Birds

T   1. _____   What is this story about?
                   (feeding the hungry birds)

F   2. _____   Who was in this story?
                   (Jim and Beth; two children; mother)

F   3. _____   What did the children see in the snow?
                   (birds)

F   4. _____   What did the birds want?
                   (food)

F   5. _____   Why couldn't the birds find any food?
                   (the snow was deep)

F   6. _____   Where did the children get bread for
                   the birds?
                   (from their mother)

F   7. _____   Where did Jim put the bread?
                   (on the snow)

I   8. _____   What season of the year is it?
                   (winter)

E   9. _____   How do you think the children felt
                   about the hungry birds? Why?
                   (any logical response)

V   10. _____   What does "deep" mean?
                   (there is a lot; far down; at the bottom)

[ ] Questions
    Missed

Comprehension Scoring Guide

Questions Missed	Level
0–1	Independent
1½–2	Ind./Inst.
2½	Instructional
3–4½	Inst./Frust.
5 +	Frustration

Retelling Notes

Retelling Rubric

Independent Level/Excellent
States central or key ideas
Identifies important facts
Retains the general sequence of events
Relates most of the content in an organized manner

Instructional Level/Satisfactory
States most central or key ideas
Identifies some important facts
Retains the general sequence of events
Relates an overall sense of the content

Frustration Level/Unsatisfactory
Provides bits of information in a haphazard manner
Little apparent organization

Writing Prompt: Write about a time when you helped someone.

Rubric for Writing Response

3	• Response is very closely related to prompt. • Response makes complete sense. • Response is well organized. • Response meets all age-appropriate spelling expectations and writing conventions.
2	• Response is related to prompt. • Response makes sense. • Response is organized in an acceptable manner. • Response meets most age-appropriate spelling expectations and writing conventions.
1	• Response is loosely related to prompt. • Some aspects of response make sense. • Response is not well organized. • Response lacks some age-appropriate spelling expectations and writing conventions.
0	• Response is unrelated to prompt. • Response does not make sense. • Response is poorly organized. • Response lacks most age-appropriate spelling expectations and writing conventions.

Student Book copy is on page 37.

B 7141e (End Grade 1) Point to each word in the title as you read it. Then say: "Read this story about the first snow. I'll ask you some questions about it when you're done."

Guided Reading Level: J

The First Snow		Substitution	Insertion	Omission	Reversal	Repetition	Self-Correction of Unacceptable Miscue	Meaning Change (Significant Miscue)
		MISCUES						
Jack woke up Saturday morning. He	6							
looked out of the window. The ground was	14							
white. The trees were white.	19							
"Oh boy," said Jack, "snow."	24							
"What did you say?" asked Tom, opening	31							
his eyes.	33							
"It snowed last night. Get up and see,"	41							
said Jack.	43							
Both boys ran to the window.	49							
"Look at that!" said Tom. "Come on. Let's	57							
get dressed."	59							
Jack and Tom ran into the kitchen.	66							
"Mom!" they said. "It snowed last night."	73							
"Yes," said Mom. "Dad went out to get	81							
your sleds. First we will eat breakfast. Then we	90							
can have some fun. The first snow is the best!"	100							
TOTAL								

Word Recognition Scoring Guide		
Total Miscues	Level	Significant Miscues
0–1	Independent	0–1
2–4	Ind./Inst.	2
5	Instructional	3
6–9	Inst./Frust.	4
10 +	Frustration	5 +

Total Miscues ☐   Significant Miscues ☐

Oral Reading Rate	Norm Group Percentile
⎽⎽⎽⎽ WPM)6000	☐ 90 ☐ 75 ☐ 50 ☐ 25 ☐ 10

B 7141e (End Grade 1)

The First Snow

T   1. _____   What is this story about?
(boys getting ready to play in the snow)

F   2. _____   On what day of the week does the story
take place?
(Saturday)

F   3. _____   What happened when the boys woke up?
(they ran to the window; they saw
snow)

F   4. _____   Who woke up first?
(Jack)

F   5. _____   What was Dad doing?
(getting the sleds)

F   6. _____   How did the trees look in this story?
(white)

F   7. _____   What did the boys have to do before
playing in the snow?
(eat breakfast)

I   8. _____   Why do you think the boys were so
excited?
(any logical response; they will play in
the snow)

E   9. _____   What things do you think the family
will do outside?
(any logical response; make snowballs;
go sledding)

V   10. _____   What is "ground"?
(dirt; something you walk on; any
logical response)

[ ] Questions
Missed

Comprehension Scoring Guide	
Questions Missed	Level
0–1	Independent
1½–2	Ind./Inst.
2½	Instructional
3–4½	Inst./Frust.
5 +	Frustration

Retelling Notes

Retelling Rubric

Independent Level/Excellent
States central or key ideas
Identifies important facts
Retains the general sequence of events
Relates most of the content in an organized manner

Instructional Level/Satisfactory
States most central or key ideas
Identifies some important facts
Retains the general sequence of events
Relates an overall sense of the content

Frustration Level/Unsatisfactory
Provides bits of information in a haphazard manner
Little apparent organization

Writing Prompt: Write about something people can do in the snow.

	Rubric for Writing Response
3	• Response is very closely related to prompt. • Response makes complete sense. • Response is well organized. • Response meets all age-appropriate spelling expectations and writing conventions.
2	• Response is related to prompt. • Response makes sense. • Response is organized in an acceptable manner. • Response meets most age-appropriate spelling expectations and writing conventions.
1	• Response is loosely related to prompt. • Some aspects of response make sense. • Response is not well organized. • Response lacks some age-appropriate spelling expectations and writing conventions.
0	• Response is unrelated to prompt. • Response does not make sense. • Response is poorly organized. • Response lacks most age-appropriate spelling expectations and writing conventions.

Student Book copy is on page 38.

B 8224 (Grade 2) Say: "I'd like you to read out loud [silently]. Think about what you're reading because I'll ask you some questions about it when you're done. Please begin here." [Point to title.]

Guided Reading Level: L; Lexile: 570

Bill at Camp

		MISCUES						
		Substitution	Insertion	Omission	Reversal	Repetition	Self-Correction of Unacceptable Miscue	Meaning Change (Significant Miscue)
It was the first time Bill went to camp.	9							
He was very happy to be there. Soon he	18							
went for a walk in the woods to look for	28							
many kinds of leaves. He found leaves from	36							
some maple and oak trees. As Bill walked	44							
in the woods, he saw some animal tracks.	52							
At that moment, a mouse ran into a small	61							
hole by a tree. Bill wondered if the tracks	70							
were made by the mouse. He looked around	78							
for other animals. He did not see any. The	87							
last thing Bill saw was an old bird nest in a	98							
pine tree.	100							
TOTAL								

Total Miscues [ ]   Significant Miscues [ ]

Word Recognition Scoring Guide		
Total Miscues	Level	Significant Miscues
0–1	Independent	0–1
2–4	Ind./Inst.	2
5	Instructional	3
6–9	Inst./Frust.	4
10 +	Frustration	5 +

Oral Reading Rate	Norm Group Percentile
_____ WPM $\overline{)6000}$	☐ 90 ☐ 75 ☐ 50 ☐ 25 ☐ 10

B 8224 (Grade 2)

Bill at Camp

T   1. _____   What is this story about?
(a boy at camp; Bill's walk in the woods)

F   2. _____   Did Bill enjoy going to camp? How do you know?
(yes; the story said he was happy there)

F   3. _____   Why did Bill go walking in the woods?
(to look for leaves)

F   4. _____   What kinds of leaves did Bill find in the woods?
(maple and oak leaves)

F   5. _____   What else did Bill see besides the mouse?
(a bird nest; animal tracks)

F   6. _____   Where did the mouse go?
(into a small hole by a tree)

F   7. _____   Had Bill been to camp before? How do you know?
(no; the story said it was his first time)

I   8. _____   Do you think Bill went on this walk by himself? What makes you think so?
(any logical response)

E   9. _____   What other animals might Bill see if he goes for another walk?
(any logical response)

V   10. _____   What are "tracks"?
(footprints made in the dirt; something made by animals when they walk or run)

☐ Questions Missed

Comprehension Scoring Guide	
Questions Missed	Level
0–1	Independent
1½–2	Ind./Inst.
2½	Instructional
3–4½	Inst./Frust.
5 +	Frustration

Retelling Notes

Retelling Rubric

Independent Level/Excellent
States central or key ideas
Identifies important facts
Retains the general sequence of events
Relates most of the content in an organized manner

Instructional Level/Satisfactory
States most central or key ideas
Identifies some important facts
Retains the general sequence of events
Relates an overall sense of the content

Frustration Level/Unsatisfactory
Provides bits of information in a haphazard manner
Little apparent organization

Writing Prompt: Write about what you would like to do in the woods.

	Rubric for Writing Response
3	• Response is very closely related to prompt. • Response makes complete sense. • Response is well organized. • Response meets all age-appropriate spelling expectations and writing conventions.
2	• Response is related to prompt. • Response makes sense. • Response is organized in an acceptable manner. • Response meets most age-appropriate spelling expectations and writing conventions.
1	• Response is loosely related to prompt. • Some aspects of response make sense. • Response is not well organized. • Response lacks some age-appropriate spelling expectations and writing conventions.
0	• Response is unrelated to prompt. • Response does not make sense. • Response is poorly organized. • Response lacks most age-appropriate spelling expectations and writing conventions.

Student Book copy is on page 39.

B 3183 (Grade 3) Say: "I'd like you to read out loud [silently]. Think about what you're reading because I'll ask you some questions about it when you're done. Please begin here." [Point to title.]

Guided Reading Level: O; Lexile: 580

The Pet Shop

		MISCUES						
	Substitution	Insertion	Omission	Reversal	Repetition	Self-Correction of Unacceptable Miscue	Meaning Change (Significant Miscue)	
Mary really wanted a little dog. One — 7								
day she went with her parents to the pet — 16								
shop. They looked at the fish, turtles, — 23								
parrots, and many kinds of dogs. Mary — 30								
and her parents saw one nice puppy that — 38								
acted very lively. It looked like a small, — 46								
bouncing, black ball of fur. The puppy was — 54								
a fluffy black poodle. It jumped around in — 62								
its cage. When Mary petted the puppy, it — 70								
sat up and begged. Mary and her parents — 78								
laughed because the poodle looked so cute. — 85								
They decided to buy the poodle. After all, — 93								
who could resist such a cute dog? — 100								
TOTAL								

Total Miscues ☐   Significant Miscues ☐

Word Recognition Scoring Guide		
Total Miscues	Level	Significant Miscues
0–1	Independent	0–1
2–4	Ind./Inst.	2
5	Instructional	3
6–9	Inst./Frust.	4
10 +	Frustration	5 +

Oral Reading Rate	Norm Group Percentile
___ WPM)6000	☐ 90 ☐ 75 ☐ 50 ☐ 25 ☐ 10

B 3183 (Grade 3)

The Pet Shop

T 1. _____ What is this story about?
(Mary and her parents buying a poodle;
a trip to the pet shop)

F 2. _____ Where did Mary and her parents go?
(to the pet shop)

F 3. _____ What did Mary and her parents see?
(fish; turtles; parrots; dogs [any 2])

F 4. _____ What did the poodle look like?
(small; furry; black; fluffy; bouncing
ball of fur; cute [any 2])

F 5. _____ What did the poodle do when Mary
petted it?
(it sat up; it begged)

F 6. _____ Why did Mary and her parents laugh?
(the poodle looked so cute)

F 7. _____ What happened to the poodle?
(Mary and her parents bought it)

I 8. _____ Why do you think Mary wanted a dog?
(any logical response; she liked dogs;
she didn't have anyone to play with)

E 9. _____ What do you think they will do with the
dog once they get it home?
(any logical response; play with it;
feed it)

V 10. _____ What does "bouncing" mean?
(hopping up and down)

	Questions Missed

Comprehension Scoring Guide	
Questions Missed	Level
0–1	Independent
1½–2	Ind./Inst.
2½	Instructional
3–4½	Inst./Frust.
5 +	Frustration

Retelling Notes

Retelling Rubric

Independent Level/Excellent
States central or key ideas
Identifies important facts
Retains the general sequence of events
Relates most of the content in an organized manner

Instructional Level/Satisfactory
States most central or key ideas
Identifies some important facts
Retains the general sequence of events
Relates an overall sense of the content

Frustration Level/Unsatisfactory
Provides bits of information in a haphazard manner
Little apparent organization

Writing Prompt: Write about a pet you would like to have and why.

	Rubric for Writing Response
3	• Response is very closely related to prompt. • Response makes complete sense. • Response is well organized. • Response meets all age-appropriate spelling expectations and writing conventions.
2	• Response is related to prompt. • Response makes sense. • Response is organized in an acceptable manner. • Response meets most age-appropriate spelling expectations and writing conventions.
1	• Response is loosely related to prompt. • Some aspects of response make sense. • Response is not well organized. • Response lacks some age-appropriate spelling expectations and writing conventions.
0	• Response is unrelated to prompt. • Response does not make sense. • Response is poorly organized. • Response lacks most age-appropriate spelling expectations and writing conventions.

Student Book copy is on page 40.

B 5414 (Grade 4) Say: "I'd like you to read out loud [silently]. Think about what you're reading because I'll ask you some questions about it when you're done. Please begin here." [Point to title.]

Guided Reading Level: R; Lexile: 690

The Purse Detectives

	MISCUES				Repetition	Self-Correction of Unacceptable Miscue	Meaning Change (Significant Miscue)
	Substitution	Insertion	Omission	Reversal			
It had been raining. Kate and her brother 8							
Michael were looking for something entertaining 14							
to do. Aunt Sue came into the living room and 24							
announced, "I can't find my purse." 30							
The children looked for the missing purse in 38							
various parts of the house. Michael looked in the 47							
den where his aunt wrote checks, but no purse. 56							
Kate searched the bedroom carefully because the 63							
purse was last seen there. It wasn't there, but 72							
Kate recalled that her aunt had been shopping 80							
earlier that day. She ran outside. Just as she 89							
arrived, Michael was opening the trunk and Kate 97							
saw the purse. 100							
TOTAL							

Total Miscues [ ]   Significant Miscues [ ]

Word Recognition Scoring Guide		
Total Miscues	Level	Significant Miscues
0–1	Independent	0–1
2–4	Ind./Inst.	2
5	Instructional	3
6–9	Inst./Frust.	4
10 +	Frustration	5 +

Oral Reading Rate	Norm Group Percentile
____ WPM)6000	☐ 90 ☐ 75 ☐ 50 ☐ 25 ☐ 10

B 5414 (Grade 4)

The Purse Detectives

T 1. _____ What is this passage about?
(looking for Aunt Sue's purse)

F 2. _____ What were Kate and Michael doing at
the beginning of the story?
(looking for something entertaining to
do)

F 3. _____ Why were Kate and Michael inside?
(it had been raining)

F 4. _____ Where did Kate and Michael look for
the purse?
(den; bedroom; various places)

F 5. _____ Why did Michael go into the den to
look for the purse?
(that is where his aunt wrote checks)

F 6. _____ Besides the house, where had Aunt Sue
been that day?
(shopping)

F 7. _____ Where was the purse found?
(in Aunt Sue's trunk)

I 8. _____ Why do you think this story is called
"The Purse Detectives"?
(any logical response)

E 9. _____ What qualities made Kate and Michael
good detectives?
(any logical response)

V 10. _____ What does "various" mean?
(several; different; many)

<table>
<tr><td>□</td><td>Questions
Missed</td></tr>
</table>

Comprehension Scoring Guide	
Questions Missed	Level
0–1	Independent
1½–2	Ind./Inst.
2½	Instructional
3–4½	Inst./Frust.
5 +	Frustration

Retelling Notes

Retelling Rubric

Independent Level/Excellent
States central or key ideas
Identifies important facts
Retains the general sequence of events
Relates most of the content in an organized manner

Instructional Level/Satisfactory
States most central or key ideas
Identifies some important facts
Retains the general sequence of events
Relates an overall sense of the content

Frustration Level/Unsatisfactory
Provides bits of information in a haphazard manner
Little apparent organization

Writing Prompt: Write about rainy day activities.

	Rubric for Writing Response
3	• Response is very closely related to prompt. • Response makes complete sense. • Response is well organized. • Response meets all age-appropriate spelling expectations and writing conventions.
2	• Response is related to prompt. • Response makes sense. • Response is organized in an acceptable manner. • Response meets most age-appropriate spelling expectations and writing conventions.
1	• Response is loosely related to prompt. • Some aspects of response make sense. • Response is not well organized. • Response lacks some age-appropriate spelling expectations and writing conventions.
0	• Response is unrelated to prompt. • Response does not make sense. • Response is poorly organized. • Response lacks most age-appropriate spelling expectations and writing conventions.

Student Book copy is on page 41.

B 8595 (Grade 5) Say: "I'd like you to read out loud [silently]. Think about what you're reading because I'll ask you some questions about it when you're done. Please begin here." [Point to title.]

Guided Reading Level: V; Lexile: 730

Imagination Girl

		Substitution	Insertion	Omission	Reversal	Repetition	Self-Correction of Unacceptable Miscue	Meaning Change (Significant Miscue)
		MISCUES						
There once was a girl who could imagine	8							
anything, and it would happen immediately. Her	15							
friends wanted to play ninja. She imagined a	23							
bamboo forest with golden monkeys and pandas.	30							
Suddenly, the forest caught fire! The ninjas	37							
swung from branch to branch, taking the animals	45							
to safety. They rescued the frightened animals	52							
and made it back from recess in record time.	61							
Her teacher wished students could understand	67							
how it feels to walk on the moon. The girl	77							
imagined that the classroom floor was the moon's	85							
pitted surface. In an instant, her classmates were	93							
weightlessly bounding across the room with ease.	100							
TOTAL								

Total Miscues ☐   Significant Miscues ☐

Word Recognition Scoring Guide		
Total Miscues	Level	Significant Miscues
0–1	Independent	0–1
2–4	Ind./Inst.	2
5	Instructional	3
6–9	Inst./Frust.	4
10 +	Frustration	5 +

Oral Reading Rate	Norm Group Percentile
____ WPM)6000	☐ 90 ☐ 75 ☐ 50 ☐ 25 ☐ 10

B 8595 (Grade 5)

Imagination Girl

T 1. _____ What is this passage about?
(a girl who can imagine anything and make it happen immediately)

F 2. _____ Who wanted to play ninja?
(her friends)

F 3. _____ What did she imagine for her friends?
(bamboo forest; golden monkeys; pandas [any 1])

F 4. _____ Who rescued the golden monkeys and pandas?
(her friends; students; ninjas)

F 5. _____ What did the girl's teacher want students to understand?
(how it felt to walk on the moon)

F 6. _____ What did the girl imagine to help the teacher?
(the classroom floor as the surface of the moon)

F 7. _____ What did her classmates do after she imagined the floor is the moon's surface?
(they go bounding weightlessly; move across the room with ease)

I 8. _____ Why were the students weightless when the room became like the moon?
(any logical response; there is no gravity on the moon)

E 9. _____ Would you like to have a friend like this girl? Why?
(any logical response; yes, it would be fun to play with her)

V 10. _____ What does "instant" mean?
(right away; fast)

☐ Questions Missed

Retelling Notes

Writing Prompt: Write about what you would like to have imagination girl create for you.

Student Book copy is on page 42.

B 6867 (Grade 6) Say: "I'd like you to read out loud [silently]. Think about what you're reading because I'll ask you some questions about it when you're done. Please begin here." [Point to title.]

Lexile: 920

Keep Your Distance

		Substitution	Insertion	Omission	Reversal	Repetition	Self-Correction of Unacceptable Miscue	Meaning Change (Significant Miscue)
Elwood was considered the tough guy at	7							
Anderson Middle School. Everybody called	12							
him "Sky." They didn't dare call him by his	21							
full name because that riled him. He was	29							
colossal in size and looked like Mr. Wilson, his	38							
teacher, from far away. However, the moment	45							
you saw Elwood's shoes and faded, torn jeans,	53							
you knew who he was. Elwood felt insecure	61							
about his clothing and awkward appearance, so	68							
he tried to make up for it by shocking people	78							
with his unexpected rude behavior and rough	85							
attitude. He didn't have many friends, except	92							
Bob who lived in the same apartment complex.	100							
TOTAL								

Total Miscues ☐   Significant Miscues ☐

Word Recognition Scoring Guide		
Total Miscues	Level	Significant Miscues
0–1	Independent	0–1
2–4	Ind./Inst.	2
5	Instructional	3
6–9	Inst./Frust.	4
10 +	Frustration	5 +

Oral Reading Rate	Norm Group Percentile				
____)6000 WPM	☐ 90	☐ 75	☐ 50	☐ 25	☐ 10

B 6867 (Grade 6)

Keep Your Distance

T   1. _____   What is this passage about?
(a boy named Elwood)

F   2. _____   What was Elwood considered?
(a tough guy; bully)

F   3. _____   What school did he attend?
(Anderson Middle School)

F   4. _____   What kind of clothes did Elwood wear?
(faded, torn jeans; old clothes)

F   5. _____   What did Elwood look like?
(his teacher; Mr. Wilson; colossal in size; big)

F   6. _____   What did everybody call him?
(Sky)

F   7. _____   How did Elwood shock people?
(rude behavior; toughness)

I   8. _____   Why do you think Bob was Elwood's friend?
(any logical response; he lived in the same apartment complex)

E   9. _____   Would you be Elwood's friend if you went to Anderson Middle School? Why?
(any logical response; no because he seems mean; yes because he seems lonely)

V   10. _____   What does "riled" mean?
(irritated; made angry)

<table>
<tr><td>☐</td><td>Questions Missed</td></tr>
</table>

Comprehension Scoring Guide

Questions Missed	Level
0–1	Independent
1½–2	Ind./Inst.
2½	Instructional
3–4½	Inst./Frust.
5 +	Frustration

Retelling Notes

Retelling Rubric

Independent Level/Excellent
States central or key ideas
Identifies important facts
Retains the general sequence of events
Relates most of the content in an organized manner

Instructional Level/Satisfactory
States most central or key ideas
Identifies some important facts
Retains the general sequence of events
Relates an overall sense of the content

Frustration Level/Unsatisfactory
Provides bits of information in a haphazard manner
Little apparent organization

Writing Prompt: Write about a friend and why you enjoy spending time together.

Rubric for Writing Response

3	• Response is very closely related to prompt. • Response makes complete sense. • Response is well organized. • Response meets all age-appropriate spelling expectations and writing conventions.
2	• Response is related to prompt. • Response makes sense. • Response is organized in an acceptable manner. • Response meets most age-appropriate spelling expectations and writing conventions.
1	• Response is loosely related to prompt. • Some aspects of response make sense. • Response is not well organized. • Response lacks some age-appropriate spelling expectations and writing conventions.
0	• Response is unrelated to prompt. • Response does not make sense. • Response is poorly organized. • Response lacks most age-appropriate spelling expectations and writing conventions.

Student Book copy is on page 43.

B 3717 (Grade 7) Say: "I'd like you to read out loud [silently]. Think about what you're reading because I'll ask you some questions about it when you're done. Please begin here." [Point to title.]

Lexile: 1060

Looming Danger		Substitution	Insertion	Omission	Reversal	Repetition	Self-Correction of Unacceptable Miscue	Meaning Change (Significant Miscue)
		MISCUES						
The foreheads of the soldiers glistened	6							
with sweat as they struggled forward under the	14							
blazing sun of the tropics. This small band of	23							
soldiers sincerely felt that their leader was the	31							
salvation of their country. Their objective was to	39							
reach a distant army fort where they hoped to	48							
fire a rocket into the storeroom. This would	56							
cause the gunpowder in the fort to erupt like a	66							
tinderbox. A huge person bellowed an order	73							
from the leader as they trudged across the	81							
uninhabited land. The soldiers hoped their attack	88							
would scare enemy soldiers and inspire more	95							
local people to join them.	100							
TOTAL								

Total Miscues [ ]   Significant Miscues [ ]

Word Recognition Scoring Guide		
Total Miscues	Level	Significant Miscues
0–1	Independent	0–1
2–4	Ind./Inst.	2
5	Instructional	3
6–9	Inst./Frust.	4
10 +	Frustration	5 +

Oral Reading Rate	Norm Group Percentile
___ WPM)6000	☐ 90 ☐ 75 ☐ 50 ☐ 25 ☐ 10

B 3717 (Grade 7)

Looming Danger

T 1. _____ What is this passage about?
(soldiers planning to raid an army fort)

F 2. _____ What was the weather like?
(blazing sun; tropical; hot and sunny)

F 3. _____ How did the soldiers feel about their leader?
(they felt the leader was the salvation of their country; they liked him)

F 4. _____ What kind of land were they traveling through?
(uninhabited; tropics)

F 5. _____ What was the soldiers' objective?
(to reach a distant fort; to fire a rocket into the storeroom)

F 6. _____ What would be used to destroy the storeroom?
(a rocket)

F 7. _____ What did they hope their attack would accomplish?
(scare enemy soldiers; inspire local people to join them)

I 8. _____ In what country do you think this story took place? Why?
(any logical response that suggests a tropical climate)

E 9. _____ What dangers do you think might be involved for the soldiers in their attack?
(any logical response)

V 10. _____ What does "glistened" mean?
(to shine; to sparkle)

	Questions Missed

Comprehension Scoring Guide

Questions Missed	Level
0–1	Independent
1½–2	Ind./Inst.
2½	Instructional
3–4½	Inst./Frust.
5 +	Frustration

Retelling Notes

Retelling Rubric

Independent Level/Excellent
States central or key ideas
Identifies important facts
Retains the general sequence of events
Relates most of the content in an organized manner

Instructional Level/Satisfactory
States most central or key ideas
Identifies some important facts
Retains the general sequence of events
Relates an overall sense of the content

Frustration Level/Unsatisfactory
Provides bits of information in a haphazard manner
Little apparent organization

Writing Prompt: Write about someone in your life who is a good leader.

Rubric for Writing Response

3	• Response is very closely related to prompt. • Response makes complete sense. • Response is well organized. • Response meets all age-appropriate spelling expectations and writing conventions.
2	• Response is related to prompt. • Response makes sense. • Response is organized in an acceptable manner. • Response meets most age-appropriate spelling expectations and writing conventions.
1	• Response is loosely related to prompt. • Some aspects of response make sense. • Response is not well organized. • Response lacks some age-appropriate spelling expectations and writing conventions.
0	• Response is unrelated to prompt. • Response does not make sense. • Response is poorly organized. • Response lacks most age-appropriate spelling expectations and writing conventions.

Student Book copy is on page 44.

B 8183 (Grade 8) Say: "I'd like you to read out loud [silently]. Think about what you're reading because I'll ask you some questions about it when you're done. Please begin here." [Point to title.]

Lexile: 1060

In Transition

		Substitution	Insertion	Omission	Reversal	Repetition	Self-Correction of Unacceptable Miscue	Meaning Change (Significant Miscue)
		MISCUES						
The scarcity of nutritious food was	6							
commonplace in Eastern Europe where my	12							
parents grew up. Children began working	18							
before adolescence and attending school was	24							
considered a luxury. A "complete" education	30							
involved learning to grow, harvest, and prepare	37							
food—not the rigorous intellectual subjects	43							
we're taught in modern schools.	48							
Once my parents matured, they yearned	54							
for an enriched life in the United States: they	63							
immigrated, found suitable jobs, and flourished.	69							
However, they never transformed their	74							
traditional attitudes about education and don't	80							
consider advanced schooling a priority. How	86							
can I compel them to understand that my future	95							
aspirations necessitate a college degree?	100							
TOTAL								

Word Recognition Scoring Guide		
Total Miscues	Level	Significant Miscues
0–1	Independent	0–1
2–4	Ind./Inst.	2
5	Instructional	3
6–9	Inst./Frust.	4
10 +	Frustration	5 +

Total Miscues ☐   Significant Miscues ☐

Oral Reading Rate	Norm Group Percentile
____ WPM)6000	☐ 90 ☐ 75 ☐ 50 ☐ 25 ☐ 10

B 8183 (Grade 8)

In Transition

T 1. _____ What is this passage about?
(a child and his or her parents who have different attitudes about education)

F 2. _____ When did the author's parents start working?
(before adolescence; when they were young [either 1])

F 3. _____ How did the author's parents view school?
(it was a luxury; not a priority)

F 4. _____ What was important to learn in the author's family?
(how to grow, harvest, and prepare food [any 2]; to work)

F 5. _____ What prompted the author's parents to move to the United States?
(they yearned for an enriched life)

F 6. _____ What did the author's parents do in the United States?
(got jobs; flourished)

F 7. _____ What does the author want to do?
(continue to go to school; attend college; get a degree)

I 8. _____ What do the author's parents probably want the author to do?
(any logical response; get a job; help the parents)

E 9. _____ Do you think going to school is important? Why?
(any logical response; yes, people need education to get good jobs; no, school is boring)

V 10. _____ What is a "luxury"?
(something very nice that a person probably doesn't need or can't afford)

	Questions Missed

Comprehension Scoring Guide	
Questions Missed	Level
0–1	Independent
1½–2	Ind./Inst.
2½	Instructional
3–4½	Inst./Frust.
5 +	Frustration

Retelling Notes

Retelling Rubric

Independent Level/Excellent
States central or key ideas
Identifies important facts
Retains the general sequence of events
Relates most of the content in an organized manner

Instructional Level/Satisfactory
States most central or key ideas
Identifies some important facts
Retains the general sequence of events
Relates an overall sense of the content

Frustration Level/Unsatisfactory
Provides bits of information in a haphazard manner
Little apparent organization

Writing Prompt: Write about a difference of opinion you've had with an adult.

Rubric for Writing Response

3	• Response is very closely related to prompt. • Response makes complete sense. • Response is well organized. • Response meets all age-appropriate spelling expectations and writing conventions.
2	• Response is related to prompt. • Response makes sense. • Response is organized in an acceptable manner. • Response meets most age-appropriate spelling expectations and writing conventions.
1	• Response is loosely related to prompt. • Some aspects of response make sense. • Response is not well organized. • Response lacks some age-appropriate spelling expectations and writing conventions.
0	• Response is unrelated to prompt. • Response does not make sense. • Response is poorly organized. • Response lacks most age-appropriate spelling expectations and writing conventions.

Performance Booklet

Teacher Copy

Form C

Primary Uses:
- Oral Reading
- Initial Assessment

Other Uses:
- Silent Reading
- Listening Level
- Progress Monitoring

Note: This Performance Booklet is on the Basic Reading Inventory website.

BASIC READING INVENTORY PERFORMANCE BOOKLET

Jerry L. Johns, Laurie Elish-Piper, and Beth Johns

Form C

Student _____ Grade _____ Gender M F Date of Test _____

School _____ Examiner _____ Date of Birth _____

Address _____ Current Book/Level _____ Age _____

SUMMARY OF STUDENT'S READING PERFORMANCE

| Grade | Word Recognition | | | | | | Comprehension | | Reading Rate | |
| | Isolation (Word Lists) | | | | Context (Passages) | | Form C | | | |
	Sight	Analy-sis	Total	Level	Mis-cues	Level	Ques-tions Missed	Level	Words per Minute (WPM)	Norm Group Per-centile
Kb			/ 6							
Km			/ 9							
Ke			/12							
1b			/20							
1m										
1e										
2			/20							
3			/20							
4			/20							
5			/20							
6			/20							
7			/20							
8			/20							
9			/20							
10			/20							
11			/20							
12			/20							

ESTIMATE OF READING LEVELS

Independent _____   Instructional _____   Frustration _____

INFORMAL ANALYSIS OF ORAL READING

| Oral Reading Behaviors | Frequency of Occurrence | | | General Impact on Meaning | | |
	Seldom	Sometimes	Frequently	No Change	Little Change	Much Change
Substitutions						
Insertions						
Omissions						
Reversals						
Repetitions						

LISTENING LEVEL, FORM _____

Grade	1	2	3	4	5	6	7	8
Questions Missed								
Level								

ESTIMATED LISTENING LEVEL: _____

QUALITATIVE ANALYSIS OF BASIC READING INVENTORY INSIGHTS

General Directions: Note the degree to which the student shows behavior or evidence in the following areas. Space is provided for additional items.

Seldom   Always
Weak   Strong
Poor   Excellent

COMPREHENSION

Seeks to construct meaning
Makes predictions
Activates background knowledge
Possesses appropriate concepts and vocabulary
Monitors reading
Varies reading rate as needed
Understands topic and major ideas
Remembers facts or details
Makes and supports appropriate inferences
Evaluates ideas from passages
Understands vocabulary used
Provides appropriate definitions of words
Engages with passages
_____
_____

WORD IDENTIFICATION

Possesses numerous strategies
Uses strategies flexibly
Uses graphophonic information
Uses semantic information
Uses syntactic information
Knows high-frequency words automatically
Possesses sight vocabulary
_____
_____

ORAL AND SILENT READING

Reads fluently
Reads with expression
Attends to punctuation
Keeps place while reading
Reads at appropriate rate
Reads silently without vocalization
_____
_____

ATTITUDE AND CONFIDENCE

Enjoys reading
Demonstrates willingness to risk
Possesses positive self-concept
Chooses to read
Regards himself/herself as a reader
Exhibits persistence
_____
_____

Form C • Graded Word Lists • Performance Booklet • Student Book copy is on page 46.

List C Kb (Beginning Kindergarten)	Sight	Analysis
1. a*	_____	_____
2. to*	_____	_____
3. in*	_____	_____
4. can*	_____	_____
5. red*	_____	_____
6. big*	_____	_____

*denotes high-frequency word from Revised Dolch List

Number Correct _____ _____

Total _____

List C Km (Middle Kindergarten)	Sight	Analysis
1. up*	_____	_____
2. for*	_____	_____
3. you*	_____	_____
4. that*	_____	_____
5. see*	_____	_____
6. man	_____	_____
7. truck	_____	_____
8. look*	_____	_____
9. stop*	_____	_____

*denotes high-frequency word from Revised Dolch List

Number Correct _____ _____

Total _____

List C Ke (End Kindergarten)	Sight	Analysis
1. black*	_____	_____
2. bee	_____	_____
3. boy	_____	_____
4. cake	_____	_____
5. put*	_____	_____
6. said*	_____	_____
7. come*	_____	_____
8. good*	_____	_____
9. white*	_____	_____
10. school	_____	_____
11. day	_____	_____
12. have*	_____	_____

*denotes high-frequency word from Revised Dolch List

Number Correct _____ _____

Total _____

IMPORTANT NOTE: In kindergarten, the average student's experience with words in isolation is very limited, especially at the beginning of the school year. The number of words correct may depend more on the school's curriculum rather than the student's emerging skills. The number correct is not as important as the word attack strategies the student exhibits. The chart below is one way that teacher judgment can be used to quickly analyze a student's performance to better understand his or her strengths and weaknesses as an emergent reader.

Qualitative Analysis of Word List Responses (0 = not evident 1 = emerging 2 = evident)			
Uses initial sounds	0	1	2
Blends sounds	0	1	2
Recognizes vowels/vowel patterns	0	1	2
Knows high-frequency words by sight	0	1	2

List C 7141 (Grade 1)	Sight	Analysis	List C 8224 (Grade 2)	Sight	Analysis
1. ball	_____	_____	1. brave	_____	_____
2. new*	_____	_____	2. top	_____	_____
3. fast*	_____	_____	3. it's	_____	_____
4. has*	_____	_____	4. follow	_____	_____
5. with*	_____	_____	5. gold	_____	_____
6. children	_____	_____	6. front	_____	_____
7. work*	_____	_____	7. family	_____	_____
8. pet	_____	_____	8. knock	_____	_____
9. ready	_____	_____	9. count	_____	_____
10. much*	_____	_____	10. smell	_____	_____
11. came*	_____	_____	11. afraid	_____	_____
12. parade	_____	_____	12. done*	_____	_____
13. hen	_____	_____	13. silver	_____	_____
14. live	_____	_____	14. face	_____	_____
15. hear	_____	_____	15. visit	_____	_____
16. far*	_____	_____	16. mountain	_____	_____
17. thing	_____	_____	17. track	_____	_____
18. year	_____	_____	18. pile	_____	_____
19. hurry	_____	_____	19. been*	_____	_____
20. met	_____	_____	20. through*	_____	_____

*denotes high-frequency word from Revised Dolch List   *denotes high-frequency word from Revised Dolch List

Number Correct   _____   _____   Number Correct   _____   _____

Total   _____   Total   _____

Scoring Guide for Graded Word Lists			
Independent	Instructional	Inst./Frust.	Frustration
20 19	18 17 16	15 14	13 or less

Form C • Graded Word Lists • Performance Booklet • Student Book copy is on page 48.

List C 3183 (Grade 3)	Sight	Analysis	List C 5414 (Grade 4)	Sight	Analysis
1. pack	_____	_____	1. thunder	_____	_____
2. matter	_____	_____	2. friendship	_____	_____
3. hang	_____	_____	3. crickets	_____	_____
4. center	_____	_____	4. yesterday	_____	_____
5. chew	_____	_____	5. dozen	_____	_____
6. rule	_____	_____	6. telescope	_____	_____
7. pound	_____	_____	7. whiskers	_____	_____
8. danger	_____	_____	8. skunk	_____	_____
9. force	_____	_____	9. amount	_____	_____
10. history	_____	_____	10. nature	_____	_____
11. spend	_____	_____	11. level	_____	_____
12. wisdom	_____	_____	12. husky	_____	_____
13. mind	_____	_____	13. sight	_____	_____
14. adventure	_____	_____	14. distance	_____	_____
15. mental	_____	_____	15. hunger	_____	_____
16. harbor	_____	_____	16. figure	_____	_____
17. fault	_____	_____	17. medicine	_____	_____
18. pilot	_____	_____	18. ashamed	_____	_____
19. usually	_____	_____	19. saddle	_____	_____
20. though	_____	_____	20. anxious	_____	_____
Number Correct	_____	_____	Number Correct	_____	_____
Total		_____	Total		_____

Scoring Guide for Graded Word Lists			
Independent	Instructional	Inst./Frust.	Frustration
20 19	18 17 16	15 14	13 or less

Form C • Graded Word Lists • Performance Booklet • Student Book copy is on page 49.

List C 8595 (Grade 5)	Sight	Analysis	List C 6867 (Grade 6)	Sight	Analysis
1. brag	_____	_____	1. youngster	_____	_____
2. college	_____	_____	2. activity	_____	_____
3. tend	_____	_____	3. research	_____	_____
4. ditch	_____	_____	4. grizzly	_____	_____
5. bully	_____	_____	5. tornado	_____	_____
6. journal	_____	_____	6. ruffle	_____	_____
7. public	_____	_____	7. judgment	_____	_____
8. goblin	_____	_____	8. nylon	_____	_____
9. ransom	_____	_____	9. fable	_____	_____
10. remarkable	_____	_____	10. exact	_____	_____
11. ankle	_____	_____	11. decay	_____	_____
12. social	_____	_____	12. substitute	_____	_____
13. gym	_____	_____	13. wealthy	_____	_____
14. education	_____	_____	14. communicate	_____	_____
15. darling	_____	_____	15. assemble	_____	_____
16. muscle	_____	_____	16. economics	_____	_____
17. pouch	_____	_____	17. biscuit	_____	_____
18. barley	_____	_____	18. forbid	_____	_____
19. petticoat	_____	_____	19. attractive	_____	_____
20. invitation	_____	_____	20. pliers	_____	_____
Number Correct	_____	_____	Number Correct	_____	_____
Total		_____	Total		_____

Scoring Guide for Graded Word Lists			
Independent	Instructional	Inst./Frust.	Frustration
20 19	18 17 16	15 14	13 or less

Form C • Graded Word Lists • Performance Booklet • Student Book copy is on page 50.

List C 3717 (Grade 7)	**Sight**	**Analysis**	**List C 8183** (Grade 8)	**Sight**	**Analysis**
1. jazz	_____	_____	1. motive	_____	_____
2. puncture	_____	_____	2. function	_____	_____
3. fantastic	_____	_____	3. transplant	_____	_____
4. publication	_____	_____	4. impressive	_____	_____
5. derby	_____	_____	5. encircle	_____	_____
6. terminal	_____	_____	6. linoleum	_____	_____
7. hemisphere	_____	_____	7. investment	_____	_____
8. paralyze	_____	_____	8. fortify	_____	_____
9. environment	_____	_____	9. maximum	_____	_____
10. cantaloupe	_____	_____	10. detain	_____	_____
11. blockade	_____	_____	11. leaflet	_____	_____
12. ornamental	_____	_____	12. privacy	_____	_____
13. warrant	_____	_____	13. lubricant	_____	_____
14. bombard	_____	_____	14. oblong	_____	_____
15. typhoon	_____	_____	15. liberal	_____	_____
16. hypnotize	_____	_____	16. identification	_____	_____
17. browse	_____	_____	17. energetic	_____	_____
18. nasal	_____	_____	18. carburetor	_____	_____
19. tuberculosis	_____	_____	19. antiseptic	_____	_____
20. lacquer	_____	_____	20. infuriate	_____	_____
Number Correct	_____	_____	Number Correct	_____	_____
Total		_____	Total		_____

Scoring Guide for Graded Word Lists			
Independent	Instructional	Inst./Frust.	Frustration
20 19	18 17 16	15 14	13 or less

Form C • Graded Word Lists • Performance Booklet • Student Book copy is on page 51.

List C 4959 (Grade 9)	Sight	Analysis	List C 1047 (Grade 10)	Sight	Analysis
1. nationality			1. organism		
2. complex			2. tart		
3. bleach			3. ashtray		
4. comparable			4. consultant		
5. overwhelm			5. intolerable		
6. contraction			6. synthetic		
7. equivalent			7. conclusive		
8. conservative			8. diverse		
9. bewitch			9. premature		
10. insignificant			10. insufferable		
11. earthy			11. cater		
12. monogram			12. reformatory		
13. redeem			13. demolition		
14. amputate			14. disintegrate		
15. disastrous			15. hoax		
16. disband			16. granulate		
17. coronation			17. necessitate		
18. barracks			18. illegitimate		
19. abolition			19. gaseous		
20. vestibule			20. revue		
Number Correct			Number Correct		
Total			Total		

Scoring Guide for Graded Word Lists			
Independent	Instructional	Inst./Frust.	Frustration
20 19	18 17 16	15 14	13 or less

List C 1187 (Grade 11)	Sight	Analysis	List C 1296 (Grade 12)	Sight	Analysis
1. nonexistent	_____	_____	1. fusion	_____	_____
2. recession	_____	_____	2. modulate	_____	_____
3. prohibition	_____	_____	3. infectious	_____	_____
4. collaborate	_____	_____	4. delusion	_____	_____
5. philosophy	_____	_____	5. marginal	_____	_____
6. franchise	_____	_____	6. vulnerable	_____	_____
7. essence	_____	_____	7. inalienable	_____	_____
8. flagrant	_____	_____	8. fiscal	_____	_____
9. replenish	_____	_____	9. convene	_____	_____
10. anesthetic	_____	_____	10. avid	_____	_____
11. monotone	_____	_____	11. platitude	_____	_____
12. instigate	_____	_____	12. predecessor	_____	_____
13. cataract	_____	_____	13. amity	_____	_____
14. sedative	_____	_____	14. detonate	_____	_____
15. memoir	_____	_____	15. caste	_____	_____
16. dubious	_____	_____	16. atrophy	_____	_____
17. premonition	_____	_____	17. amenable	_____	_____
18. libel	_____	_____	18. omnibus	_____	_____
19. maladjustment	_____	_____	19. arable	_____	_____
20. claimant	_____	_____	20. meritorious	_____	_____
Number Correct	_____	_____	Number Correct	_____	_____
Total	_____		Total	_____	

Scoring Guide for Graded Word Lists			
Independent	Instructional	Inst./Frust.	Frustration
20 19	18 17 16	15 14	13 or less

Student Book copy is on page 54.

C Kb (Beginning K) Point to each word in the title as you read it. Then say: "Read this story about Ned. I'll ask you some questions about it when you're done."

Guided Reading Level: A

Ned		Substitution	Insertion	Omission	Reversal	Repetition	Self-Correction of Unacceptable Miscue	Meaning Change (Significant Miscue)
Ned will eat.	3							
Ned will dress.	6							
Ned will play.	9							
Ned will sleep.	12							
TOTAL								

Total Miscues ☐   Significant Miscues ☐

Word Recognition Scoring Guide		
Total Miscues	Level	Significant Miscues
0	Independent	0
—	Ind./Inst.	—
—	Instructional	—
1	Inst./Frust.	1
2 +	Frustration	2 +

Qualitative Analysis of Word Identification (0 = not evident 1 = emerging 2 = evident)			
Uses letter-sound relationships	0	1	2
Points to words while reading	0	1	2
Uses monitoring (rereads; corrects)	0	1	2
Knows high-frequency words	0	1	2
Possesses sight vocabulary	0	1	2
Exhibits persistence	0	1	2
Seems confident	0	1	2

Important Note: If the scoring guides are used, teacher judgment is especially important because of the length of the passage and the limited number of questions.

C Kb (Beginning K)

Ned

T 1. _____ What is this story about? [If student says "Ned," say "tell me more."]
(what Ned does; how Ned will eat, dress, play, and sleep)

F 2. _____ What's something else Ned does in the story?
(any one of the following: eat, dress, play, sleep)

I 3. _____ If you wanted to add more to the story, tell me what else Ned might do.
(any logical response; go to school; watch TV; go outside)

E 4. _____ Where do you think you would probably need to go to see Ned?
(any logical response; his house)

V 5. _____ What does the word "dress" mean when the story says, "Ned will dress"?
(any logical response; put on clothes)

Retelling Notes

Retelling Rubric

Independent Level/Excellent
States central or key ideas
Identifies important facts
Retains the general sequence of events
Relates most of the content in an organized manner

Instructional Level/Satisfactory
States most central or key ideas
Identifies some important facts
Retains the general sequence of events
Relates an overall sense of the content

Frustration Level/Unsatisfactory
Provides bits of information in a haphazard manner
Little apparent organization

☐ Questions Missed

Comprehension Scoring Guide	
Questions Missed	Level
0	Independent
1	Ind./Inst.
1½	Instructional
2	Inst./Frust.
2½ +	Frustration

Qualitative Analysis of Comprehension			
(0 = not evident 1 = emerging 2 = evident)			
Seeks to construct meaning	0	1	2
Understands topic and major ideas	0	1	2
Identifies facts or details	0	1	2
Evaluates ideas from story	0	1	2
Makes and supports appropriate inferences	0	1	2
Seems engaged with story	0	1	2

Writing Prompt: Write about something you do every day.

	Rubric for Writing Response
3	• Response is very closely related to prompt. • Response makes complete sense. • Response is well organized. • Response meets all age-appropriate spelling expectations and writing conventions.
2	• Response is related to prompt. • Response makes sense. • Response is organized in an acceptable manner. • Response meets most age-appropriate spelling expectations and writing conventions.
1	• Response is loosely related to prompt. • Some aspects of response make sense. • Response is not well organized. • Response lacks some age-appropriate spelling expectations and writing conventions.
0	• Response is unrelated to prompt. • Response does not make sense. • Response is poorly organized. • Response lacks most age-appropriate spelling expectations and writing conventions.

Important Note: If the scoring guides are used, teacher judgment is especially important because of the length of the passage and the limited number of questions.

Student Book copy is on page 55.

C Km (Middle K) Point to each word in the title as you read it. Then say: "Read this story about the babies. I'll ask you some questions about it when you're done."

Guided Reading Level: B

The Babies

		Substitution	Insertion	Omission	Reversal	Repetition	Self-Correction of Unacceptable Miscue	Meaning Change (Significant Miscue)
		MISCUES						
The baby will eat.	4							
The baby will play.	8							
The baby will crawl.	12							
The baby will cry.	16							
The baby will sleep.	20							
TOTAL								

Total Miscues ☐   Significant Miscues ☐

Word Recognition Scoring Guide		
Total Miscues	Level	Significant Miscues
0	Independent	0
—	Ind./Inst.	—
1	Instructional	1
2	Inst./Frust.	2
3 +	Frustration	3 +

Qualitative Analysis of Word Identification (0 = not evident 1 = emerging 2 = evident)			
Uses letter-sound relationships	0	1	2
Points to words while reading	0	1	2
Uses monitoring (rereads; corrects)	0	1	2
Knows high-frequency words	0	1	2
Possesses sight vocabulary	0	1	2
Exhibits persistence	0	1	2
Seems confident	0	1	2

Important Note: If the scoring guides are used, teacher judgment is especially important because of the length of the passage and the limited number of questions.

C Km (Middle K)

The Babies

T 1. _____ What is this story about? [If student says "the babies," say "tell me more."] (what babies do; babies will eat, play, crawl, cry, and sleep)

F 2. _____ What's something else the babies will do? (any one of the following: eat, play, crawl, cry, sleep)

I 3. _____ If you wanted to add more to the story, tell me what else the babies might do. (any logical response; take a bath, go for a ride)

E 4. _____ Where do you think you would probably need to go to see the babies? (any logical response; a house; the hospital; a daycare center)

V 5. _____ What does the word "crawl" mean? (any logical response; to move on hands and knees; student demonstrates how to crawl)

Retelling Notes

Retelling Rubric

Independent Level/Excellent

States central or key ideas
Identifies important facts
Retains the general sequence of events
Relates most of the content in an organized manner

Instructional Level/Satisfactory

States most central or key ideas
Identifies some important facts
Retains the general sequence of events
Relates an overall sense of the content

Frustration Level/Unsatisfactory

Provides bits of information in a haphazard manner
Little apparent organization

☐ Questions Missed

Comprehension Scoring Guide	
Questions Missed	Level
0	Independent
1	Ind./Inst.
1½	Instructional
2	Inst./Frust.
2½ +	Frustration

Qualitative Analysis of Comprehension			
(0 = not evident 1 = emerging 2 = evident)			
Seeks to construct meaning	0	1	2
Understands topic and major ideas	0	1	2
Identifies facts or details	0	1	2
Evaluates ideas from story	0	1	2
Makes and supports appropriate inferences	0	1	2
Seems engaged with story	0	1	2

Writing Prompt: Write about something you would like to do with a baby.

Rubric for Writing Response	
3	• Response is very closely related to prompt. • Response makes complete sense. • Response is well organized. • Response meets all age-appropriate spelling expectations and writing conventions.
2	• Response is related to prompt. • Response makes sense. • Response is organized in an acceptable manner. • Response meets most age-appropriate spelling expectations and writing conventions.
1	• Response is loosely related to prompt. • Some aspects of response make sense. • Response is not well organized. • Response lacks some age-appropriate spelling expectations and writing conventions.
0	• Response is unrelated to prompt. • Response does not make sense. • Response is poorly organized. • Response lacks most age-appropriate spelling expectations and writing conventions.

Important Note: If the scoring guides are used, teacher judgment is especially important because of the length of the passage and the limited number of questions.

Student Book copy is on page 56.

C Ke (End K) Point to each word in the title as you read it. Then say: "Read this story about a green frog. I'll ask you some questions about it when you're done."

Guided Reading Level: D

A Green Frog

		MISCUES						
	Substitution	Insertion	Omission	Reversal	Repetition	Self-Correction of Unacceptable Miscue	Meaning Change (Significant Miscue)
A green frog sits on a rock. 7							
It has big back legs. 12							
It can jump up. 16							
It can swim in the pond. 22							
It gets wet. 25							
TOTAL							

Total Miscues ☐   Significant Miscues ☐

Word Recognition Scoring Guide		
Total Miscues	Level	Significant Miscues
0	Independent	0
1	Ind./Inst.	—
2	Instructional	1
3	Inst./Frust.	2
4 +	Frustration	3 +

Qualitative Analysis of Word Identification (0 = not evident 1 = emerging 2 = evident)			
Uses letter-sound relationships	0	1	2
Points to words while reading	0	1	2
Uses monitoring (rereads; corrects)	0	1	2
Knows high-frequency words	0	1	2
Possesses sight vocabulary	0	1	2
Exhibits persistence	0	1	2
Seems confident	0	1	2

Important Note: If the scoring guides are used, teacher judgment is especially important because of the length of the passage and the limited number of questions.

C Ke (End K)

A Green Frog

T 1. _____ What is this story about? [If student says "a frog," say "tell me more."]
(a green frog jumps and swims in the pond)

F 2. _____ What's something else the frog does?
(any one of the following: sits on a rock; jumps up; swims in the pond; gets wet)

I 3. _____ If you wanted to add more to the story, tell me what else the frog might do.
(any logical response; eat; play)

E 4. _____ Where do you think you would probably need to go to see a green frog?
(any logical response; the pond; outside)

V 5. _____ What does the word "back" mean?
(any logical response; not the front; student points to show the back of something)

☐ Questions Missed

Comprehension Scoring Guide	
Questions Missed	Level
0	Independent
1	Ind./Inst.
1½	Instructional
2	Inst./Frust.
2½ +	Frustration

Qualitative Analysis of Comprehension			
(0 = not evident 1 = emerging 2 = evident)			
Seeks to construct meaning	0	1	2
Understands topic and major ideas	0	1	2
Identifies facts or details	0	1	2
Evaluates ideas from story	0	1	2
Makes and supports appropriate inferences	0	1	2
Seems engaged with story	0	1	2

Retelling Notes

Retelling Rubric

Independent Level/Excellent
States central or key ideas
Identifies important facts
Retains the general sequence of events
Relates most of the content in an organized manner

Instructional Level/Satisfactory
States most central or key ideas
Identifies some important facts
Retains the general sequence of events
Relates an overall sense of the content

Frustration Level/Unsatisfactory
Provides bits of information in a haphazard manner
Little apparent organization

Writing Prompt: Write about other animals that might be in the pond with the frog.

Rubric for Writing Response	
3	• Response is very closely related to prompt. • Response makes complete sense. • Response is well organized. • Response meets all age-appropriate spelling expectations and writing conventions.
2	• Response is related to prompt. • Response makes sense. • Response is organized in an acceptable manner. • Response meets most age-appropriate spelling expectations and writing conventions.
1	• Response is loosely related to prompt. • Some aspects of response make sense. • Response is not well organized. • Response lacks some age-appropriate spelling expectations and writing conventions.
0	• Response is unrelated to prompt. • Response does not make sense. • Response is poorly organized. • Response lacks most age-appropriate spelling expectations and writing conventions.

Important Note: If the scoring guides are used, teacher judgment is especially important because of the length of the passage and the limited number of questions.

Student Book copy is on page 57.

C 7141b (Beginning Grade 1) Point to each word in the title as you read it. Then say: "Read this story about a fun day. I'll ask you some questions about it when you're done."

Guided Reading Level: E

A Fun Day		MISCUES					Repetition	Self-Correction of Unacceptable Miscue	Meaning Change (Significant Miscue)
		Substitution	Insertion	Omission	Reversal				
"Here it comes!" said Tom.	5								
"I can see it," said Dan. "Here comes	13								
the band!"	15								
Tom jumped up and down. "Look at	22								
the man. He is tall. I can see his red hat."	33								
"Look!" said Dan. "I see a dog. The	41								
dog is big. The dog is brown and white."	50								
TOTAL									

Total Miscues [ ] Significant Miscues [ ]

Word Recognition Scoring Guide		
Total Miscues	Level	Significant Miscues
0	Independent	0
1–2	Ind./Inst.	1
3	Instructional	2
4	Inst./Frust.	3
5 +	Frustration	4 +

Qualitative Analysis of Word Identification (0 = not evident 1 = emerging 2 = evident)			
Uses letter-sound relationships	0	1	2
Points to words while reading	0	1	2
Uses monitoring (rereads; corrects)	0	1	2
Knows high-frequency words	0	1	2
Possesses sight vocabulary	0	1	2
Exhibits persistence	0	1	2
Seems confident	0	1	2

Important Note: If the scoring guides are used, teacher judgment is especially important because of the length of the passage and the limited number of questions.

C 7141b (Beginning Grade 1)

A Fun Day

F 1. _____ What is this story about? [If student
says "a fun day," say "tell me more."]
(Tom and Dan have a fun day; the boys
see a band and have fun)

F 2. _____ What was the first thing they saw?
(the band; a man)

I 3. _____ Why do you think Tom jumped up and
down?
(any logical response; he was excited;
he couldn't see)

E 4. _____ What were the children probably doing?
(any logical response; having fun;
listening to music; watching a parade)

V 5. _____ What is a "hat"?
(something you wear; something you
put on your head)

<table>
<tr><td colspan="2">**Retelling Notes**</td></tr>
</table>

<table>
<tr><td colspan="2">**Retelling Rubric**</td></tr>
<tr><td colspan="2">**Independent Level/Excellent**</td></tr>
<tr><td colspan="2">States central or key ideas
Identifies important facts
Retains the general sequence of events
Relates most of the content in an organized manner</td></tr>
<tr><td colspan="2">**Instructional Level/Satisfactory**</td></tr>
<tr><td colspan="2">States most central or key ideas
Identifies some important facts
Retains the general sequence of events
Relates an overall sense of the content</td></tr>
<tr><td colspan="2">**Frustration Level/Unsatisfactory**</td></tr>
<tr><td colspan="2">Provides bits of information in a haphazard manner
Little apparent organization</td></tr>
</table>

Writing Prompt: Write about a fun day you have had.

	Rubric for Writing Response
3	• Response is very closely related to prompt. • Response makes complete sense. • Response is well organized. • Response meets all age-appropriate spelling expectations and writing conventions.
2	• Response is related to prompt. • Response makes sense. • Response is organized in an acceptable manner. • Response meets most age-appropriate spelling expectations and writing conventions.
1	• Response is loosely related to prompt. • Some aspects of response make sense. • Response is not well organized. • Response lacks some age-appropriate spelling expectations and writing conventions.
0	• Response is unrelated to prompt. • Response does not make sense. • Response is poorly organized. • Response lacks most age-appropriate spelling expectations and writing conventions.

[ ] Questions
Missed

Comprehension Scoring Guide	
Questions Missed	Level
0	Independent
1	Ind./Inst.
1½	Instructional
2	Inst./Frust.
2½ +	Frustration

Qualitative Analysis of Comprehension			
(0 = not evident 1 = emerging 2 = evident)			
Seeks to construct meaning	0	1	2
Understands topic and major ideas	0	1	2
Identifies facts or details	0	1	2
Evaluates ideas from story	0	1	2
Makes and supports appropriate inferences	0	1	2
Seems engaged with story	0	1	2

Important Note: If the scoring guides are used, teacher judgment is especially important because of the length of the passage and the limited number of questions.

Student Book copy is on page 58.

C 7141m (Middle Grade 1) Point to each word in the title as you read it. Then say: "Read this story about the box. I'll ask you some questions about it when you're done."

Guided Reading Level: G

The Box		Substitution	Insertion	Omission	Reversal	Repetition	Self-Correction of Unacceptable Miscue	Meaning Change (Significant Miscue)
Ben went to see his friend Nan. He	8							
had a blue box. Nan saw the box, and	17							
asked, "What is in the blue box?"	24							
"I can not tell you," said Ben.	31							
Nan asked, "Is it a ball?"	37							
"No, it is not a ball," said Ben.	45							
"Is it a car?" asked Nan.	51							
"No, it is not a car," said Ben.	59							
"I know, it is an apple," said Nan.	67							
Ben looked in the box. There were	74							
two apples. One apple was green. One	81							
apple was red. He gave the red apple	89							
to Nan. Nan liked the apple. Ben was a	98							
good friend.	100							
TOTAL								

Total Miscues [   ]   Significant Miscues [   ]

Word Recognition Scoring Guide		
Total Miscues	Level	Significant Miscues
0–1	Independent	0–1
2–4	Ind./Inst.	2
5	Instructional	3
6–9	Inst./Frust.	4
10 +	Frustration	5 +

Oral Reading Rate	Norm Group Percentile				
_____ WPM)6000	☐ 90	☐ 75	☐ 50	☐ 25	☐ 10

C 7141m (Middle Grade 1)

The Box

T   1. _____   What is this story about?
(Ben's box; Nan guessing about the
box)

F   2. _____   Who did Ben see?
(Nan)

F   3. _____   What did Ben have with him?
(a box; apples)

F   4. _____   What color was the box?
(blue)

F   5. _____   What things did Nan think were in
the box?
(ball, car, apple [any 2])

F   6. _____   Which of those things were not in the
box?
(ball; car [either 1])

F   7. _____   How many apples were in the box?
(two)

I   8. _____   What color was the apple that Ben kept?
(green)

E   9. _____   Would you like Ben as your friend?
Why?
(any logical response)

V   10. _____   What does "good" mean?
(nice; friendly; kind)

[ ] Questions
Missed

Comprehension Scoring Guide	
Questions Missed	Level
0–1	Independent
1½–2	Ind./Inst.
2½	Instructional
3–4½	Inst./Frust.
5 +	Frustration

240

Retelling Notes

Retelling Rubric

Independent Level/Excellent
States central or key ideas
Identifies important facts
Retains the general sequence of events
Relates most of the content in an organized manner

Instructional Level/Satisfactory
States most central or key ideas
Identifies some important facts
Retains the general sequence of events
Relates an overall sense of the content

Frustration Level/Unsatisfactory
Provides bits of information in a haphazard manner
Little apparent organization

Writing Prompt: Write about something you could share with a friend.

	Rubric for Writing Response
3	• Response is very closely related to prompt. • Response makes complete sense. • Response is well organized. • Response meets all age-appropriate spelling expectations and writing conventions.
2	• Response is related to prompt. • Response makes sense. • Response is organized in an acceptable manner. • Response meets most age-appropriate spelling expectations and writing conventions.
1	• Response is loosely related to prompt. • Some aspects of response make sense. • Response is not well organized. • Response lacks some age-appropriate spelling expectations and writing conventions.
0	• Response is unrelated to prompt. • Response does not make sense. • Response is poorly organized. • Response lacks most age-appropriate spelling expectations and writing conventions.

Student Book copy is on page 59.

C 7141e (End Grade 1) Point to each word in the title as you read it. Then say: "Read this story about fun with leaves. I'll ask you some questions about it when you're done."

Guided Reading Level: J

Fun with Leaves		Substitution	Insertion	Omission	Reversal	Repetition	Self-Correction of Unacceptable Miscue	Meaning Change (Significant Miscue)
		MISCUES						
Bill had many leaves in his yard. He	8							
raked them into a pile, and Pat helped.	16							
Then Bill got a good idea. He jumped	24							
in that pile of leaves.	29							
"Wow! What fun!"	32							
"Let me jump," yelled Pat. He jumped	39							
in the leaves.	42							
Soon both boys were jumping. They	48							
threw leaves up into the air.	54							
Mother looked out and said, "I see	61							
two boys having fun, but it's time to come	70							
in for now."	73							
"See our big pile!" said Bill.	79							
"Where?" asked Mother.	82							
The boys looked around. The pile was	89							
not big now because the leaves were all	97							
over the yard.	100							
TOTAL								

Total Miscues [   ]   Significant Miscues [   ]

Word Recognition Scoring Guide		
Total Miscues	Level	Significant Miscues
0–1	Independent	0–1
2–4	Ind./Inst.	2
5	Instructional	3
6–9	Inst./Frust.	4
10 +	Frustration	5 +

Oral Reading Rate	Norm Group Percentile
_____ WPM)6000	☐ 90 ☐ 75 ☐ 50 ☐ 25 ☐ 10

C 7141e (End Grade 1)

Fun with Leaves

T 1. _____ What is this story about?
(boys raking and playing or jumping in leaves)

F 2. _____ Who was in this story?
(Bill and Pat; two boys; Mother)

F 3. _____ What was in the yard?
(leaves)

F 4. _____ What did the boys do with the leaves?
(raked them; jumped or dived in them; threw them about)

F 5. _____ What did Pat do?
(he jumped into the pile too; he helped to rake the leaves)

F 6. _____ What did Mother want the boys to do?
(come in to eat)

F 7. _____ What happened to the pile of leaves?
(it was all over the yard; the boys messed it up)

I 8. _____ What season do you think it was? Why?
(fall; any logical response)

E 9. _____ How do you think Mother felt about what the boys were doing?
(any logical response)

V 10. _____ What is "jumping"?
(to go up and down)

	Questions Missed

Comprehension Scoring Guide	
Questions Missed	Level
0–1	Independent
1½–2	Ind./Inst.
2½	Instructional
3–4½	Inst./Frust.
5 +	Frustration

Retelling Notes

Retelling Rubric

Independent Level/Excellent
States central or key ideas
Identifies important facts
Retains the general sequence of events
Relates most of the content in an organized manner

Instructional Level/Satisfactory
States most central or key ideas
Identifies some important facts
Retains the general sequence of events
Relates an overall sense of the content

Frustration Level/Unsatisfactory
Provides bits of information in a haphazard manner
Little apparent organization

Writing Prompt: Write about a time you had fun outside.

	Rubric for Writing Response
3	• Response is very closely related to prompt. • Response makes complete sense. • Response is well organized. • Response meets all age-appropriate spelling expectations and writing conventions.
2	• Response is related to prompt. • Response makes sense. • Response is organized in an acceptable manner. • Response meets most age-appropriate spelling expectations and writing conventions.
1	• Response is loosely related to prompt. • Some aspects of response make sense. • Response is not well organized. • Response lacks some age-appropriate spelling expectations and writing conventions.
0	• Response is unrelated to prompt. • Response does not make sense. • Response is poorly organized. • Response lacks most age-appropriate spelling expectations and writing conventions.

Student Book copy is on page 60.

C 8224 (Grade 2) Say: "I'd like you to read out loud [silently]. Think about what you're reading because I'll ask you some questions about it when you're done. Please begin here." [Point to title.]

Guided Reading Level: L; Lexile: 650

My Birthday

		Substitution	Insertion	Omission	Reversal	Repetition	Self-Correction of Unacceptable Miscue	Meaning Change (Significant Miscue)
		MISCUES						
I turn eight in two weeks. I have lots	9							
of ideas to make it the best birthday ever!	18							
First, I want my four best friends to spend	27							
the day with me. A big, black train will	36							
take us to a farm. The conductor will let	45							
me blow the whistle eight times. At the	53							
farm, we will see cows, ducks, and horses.	61							
Then we will have a picnic lunch with	69							
birthday cake. We will ride in a hot air	78							
balloon. Later, there will be a new bicycle	86							
in the back of our truck or a puppy	95							
waiting for me at home.	100							
TOTAL								

Total Miscues ☐   Significant Miscues ☐

Word Recognition Scoring Guide

Total Miscues	Level	Significant Miscues
0–1	Independent	0–1
2–4	Ind./Inst.	2
5	Instructional	3
6–9	Inst./Frust.	4
10 +	Frustration	5 +

Oral Reading Rate	Norm Group Percentile				
____)6000 WPM	☐ 90	☐ 75	☐ 50	☐ 25	☐ 10

C 8224 (Grade 2)

My Birthday

T   1. _____   What is this story about?
(a birthday party)

F   2. _____   How old will the child be?
(eight)

F   3. _____   Who will spend the day with the child?
(his or her best friends; four friends)

F   4. _____   Where will they go?
(to a farm)

F   5. _____   How will they get there?
(a big, black train)

F   6. _____   What are two things they will do?
(see animals; have a picnic lunch; eat
cake; go for a balloon ride [any 2])

F   7. _____   What does the child want for his or her
birthday?
(a bicycle or a puppy)

I   8. _____   Why might they blow the train whistle
eight times?
(any logical response; it was the
birthday child's age)

E   9. _____   Would you like a birthday party like
this? Why?
(any logical response)

V   10. _____   What is a "hot air balloon"?
(a big balloon people can ride in)

☐ Questions
   Missed

Comprehension Scoring Guide

Questions Missed	Level
0–1	Independent
1½–2	Ind./Inst.
2½	Instructional
3–4½	Inst./Frust.
5 +	Frustration

Retelling Notes

Retelling Rubric

Independent Level/Excellent
States central or key ideas
Identifies important facts
Retains the general sequence of events
Relates most of the content in an organized manner

Instructional Level/Satisfactory
States most central or key ideas
Identifies some important facts
Retains the general sequence of events
Relates an overall sense of the content

Frustration Level/Unsatisfactory
Provides bits of information in a haphazard manner
Little apparent organization

Writing Prompt: Write about what you want to do for your birthday.

Rubric for Writing Response

3	• Response is very closely related to prompt. • Response makes complete sense. • Response is well organized. • Response meets all age-appropriate spelling expectations and writing conventions.
2	• Response is related to prompt. • Response makes sense. • Response is organized in an acceptable manner. • Response meets most age-appropriate spelling expectations and writing conventions.
1	• Response is loosely related to prompt. • Some aspects of response make sense. • Response is not well organized. • Response lacks some age-appropriate spelling expectations and writing conventions.
0	• Response is unrelated to prompt. • Response does not make sense. • Response is poorly organized. • Response lacks most age-appropriate spelling expectations and writing conventions.

Student Book copy is on page 61.

C 3183 (Grade 3) Say: "I'd like you to read out loud [silently]. Think about what you're reading because I'll ask you some questions about it when you're done. Please begin here." [Point to title.]

Guided Reading Level: O; Lexile: 640

The Hungry Bear

		MISCUES Substitution	Insertion	Omission	Reversal	Repetition	Self-Correction of Unacceptable Miscue	Meaning Change (Significant Miscue)
The busy bees had been making honey all	8							
day. That night it was cool and damp. I had	18							
slept well until I heard a loud noise near my	28							
window. It sounded as if someone was	35							
trying to break into my cabin. As I moved	44							
from my cot, I could see something black	52							
standing near the window. In fright I knocked	60							
on the window. Very slowly and quietly the	68							
great shadow moved back and went away.	75							
The next day we found huge bear tracks.	83							
The bear had come for the honey the bees	92							
were making in the attic of the cabin.	100							
TOTAL								

Total Miscues ☐   Significant Miscues ☐

Word Recognition Scoring Guide

Total Miscues	Level	Significant Miscues
0–1	Independent	0–1
2–4	Ind./Inst.	2
5	Instructional	3
6–9	Inst./Frust.	4
10 +	Frustration	5 +

Oral Reading Rate	Norm Group Percentile				
_____ WPM $)6000$	☐ 90	☐ 75	☐ 50	☐ 25	☐ 10

C 3183 (Grade 3)

The Hungry Bear

T 1. _____   What is this story about?
(a bear trying to get honey; being scared)

F 2. _____   What had the bees been doing?
(making honey)

F 3. _____   Where were the bees making honey?
(in the attic of the cabin)

F 4. _____   What was the weather like?
(cool and damp)

F 5. _____   Why did the person in the story wake up?
(a bear; a loud noise at the window)

F 6. _____   What was found the next day?
(bear tracks)

F 7. _____   What did the bear want?
(honey)

I 8. _____   Why do you think the bear walked away?
(any logical response; it heard the knock)

E 9. _____   What might you do to keep the bear away?
(any logical response; remove the honey)

V 10. _____   What is an "attic"?
(a place way upstairs in your house where you put junk and stuff)

[ ] Questions Missed

Comprehension Scoring Guide	
Questions Missed	Level
0–1	Independent
1½–2	Ind./Inst.
2½	Instructional
3–4½	Inst./Frust.
5 +	Frustration

Retelling Notes

Retelling Rubric

Independent Level/Excellent
States central or key ideas
Identifies important facts
Retains the general sequence of events
Relates most of the content in an organized manner

Instructional Level/Satisfactory
States most central or key ideas
Identifies some important facts
Retains the general sequence of events
Relates an overall sense of the content

Frustration Level/Unsatisfactory
Provides bits of information in a haphazard manner
Little apparent organization

Writing Prompt: Write about a time you were scared.

	Rubric for Writing Response
3	• Response is very closely related to prompt. • Response makes complete sense. • Response is well organized. • Response meets all age-appropriate spelling expectations and writing conventions.
2	• Response is related to prompt. • Response makes sense. • Response is organized in an acceptable manner. • Response meets most age-appropriate spelling expectations and writing conventions.
1	• Response is loosely related to prompt. • Some aspects of response make sense. • Response is not well organized. • Response lacks some age-appropriate spelling expectations and writing conventions.
0	• Response is unrelated to prompt. • Response does not make sense. • Response is poorly organized. • Response lacks most age-appropriate spelling expectations and writing conventions.

Student Book copy is on page 62.

C 5414 (Grade 4) Say: "I'd like you to read out loud [silently]. Think about what you're reading because I'll ask you some questions about it when you're done. Please begin here." [Point to title.]

Guided Reading Level: R; Lexile: 880

The Soccer Game

		Substitution	Insertion	Omission	Reversal	Repetition	Self-Correction of Unacceptable Miscue	Meaning Change (Significant Miscue)
		MISCUES						
The score was tied with only two minutes	8							
left in the championship soccer game between	15							
rival teams, the Jets and Bombers. The ball	23							
was in the Jets' area, dangerously close to	31							
their goal. Rosa, a Jets midfielder, sprinted for	39							
the ball. She got there fast and delivered a	48							
tremendous kick, sending the ball sailing over	55							
the midline into Bomber territory.	60							
With an excited yell, Kim intercepted the ball	68							
and dribbled toward the Bomber goal. There	75							
was no time for mistakes. The shot must be	84							
perfectly placed. Kim faked right, then suddenly	91							
kicked left and scored just as the game ended!	100							
TOTAL								

Total Miscues [ ]   Significant Miscues [ ]

Word Recognition Scoring Guide		
Total Miscues	Level	Significant Miscues
0–1	Independent	0–1
2–4	Ind./Inst.	2
5	Instructional	3
6–9	Inst./Frust.	4
10 +	Frustration	5 +

Oral Reading Rate	Norm Group Percentile
___ WPM)6000	☐ 90 ☐ 75 ☐ 50 ☐ 25 ☐ 10

C 5414 (Grade 4)

The Soccer Game

T 1. _____ What is this passage about?
(a soccer game)

F 2. _____ How much time was left in the game?
(2 minutes)

F 3. _____ Tell me about the score near the end
of the game.
(it was tied)

F 4. _____ What was the name of the team Rosa
was on?
(Jets)

F 5. _____ What position did Rosa play?
(midfielder)

F 6. _____ When Rosa kicked the ball, where did
it go?
(over the midline; into Bomber
territory)

F 7. _____ Who scored the final goal of the game?
(Kim)

I 8. _____ Which team lost the game?
(Bombers)

E 9. _____ If you were the coach, what would you
tell your players to do?
(any logical response)

V 10. _____ What does "sailing" mean in this story?
(in the air; flying; soaring; to glide
through the air)

Questions Missed		

Comprehension Scoring Guide

Questions Missed	Level
0–1	Independent
1½–2	Ind./Inst.
2½	Instructional
3–4½	Inst./Frust.
5 +	Frustration

Retelling Notes

Retelling Rubric

Independent Level/Excellent
States central or key ideas
Identifies important facts
Retains the general sequence of events
Relates most of the content in an organized manner

Instructional Level/Satisfactory
States most central or key ideas
Identifies some important facts
Retains the general sequence of events
Relates an overall sense of the content

Frustration Level/Unsatisfactory
Provides bits of information in a haphazard manner
Little apparent organization

Writing Prompt: Write about a sport that you like to watch or play.

Rubric for Writing Response

3	• Response is very closely related to prompt. • Response makes complete sense. • Response is well organized. • Response meets all age-appropriate spelling expectations and writing conventions.
2	• Response is related to prompt. • Response makes sense. • Response is organized in an acceptable manner. • Response meets most age-appropriate spelling expectations and writing conventions.
1	• Response is loosely related to prompt. • Some aspects of response make sense. • Response is not well organized. • Response lacks some age-appropriate spelling expectations and writing conventions.
0	• Response is unrelated to prompt. • Response does not make sense. • Response is poorly organized. • Response lacks most age-appropriate spelling expectations and writing conventions.

Student Book copy is on page 63.

C 8595 (Grade 5) Say: "I'd like you to read out loud [silently]. Think about what you're reading because I'll ask you some questions about it when you're done. Please begin here." [Point to title.]

Guided Reading Level: V; Lexile: 1000

The Strange Gift

		MISCUES						
		Substitution	Insertion	Omission	Reversal	Repetition	Self-Correction of Unacceptable Miscue	Meaning Change (Significant Miscue)
Sherri sat quietly, staring at the tiny black	8							
and green slip of paper in her hand. She	17							
remembered how moved she had been when	24							
Maryann first gave it to her. Sherri knew her	33							
best friend was extremely poor and couldn't	40							
afford even a small gift for Sherri's twelfth	48							
birthday. She was surprised when Maryann	54							
pulled her aside and handed her a pretty,	62							
wrapped box with a tiny bow. Inside there was	71							
a ticket. Sherri was touched by her friend's	79							
gesture, but she never imagined that the slip of	88							
paper would be randomly drawn as the winner	96							
in their classroom raffle.	100							
TOTAL								

Total Miscues ☐   Significant Miscues ☐

Word Recognition Scoring Guide		
Total Miscues	Level	Significant Miscues
0–1	Independent	0–1
2–4	Ind./Inst.	2
5	Instructional	3
6–9	Inst./Frust.	4
10 +	Frustration	5 +

Oral Reading Rate	Norm Group Percentile	
⎯⎯⎯ WPM)6000	☐ 90 ☐ 75 ☐ 50 ☐ 25 ☐ 10	

C 8595 (Grade 5)

The Strange Gift

T   1. _____   What is this passage about?
(a birthday gift; a winning ticket)

F   2. _____   Who is Sherri's best friend?
(Maryann)

F   3. _____   How old is Sherri?
(eleven or twelve)

F   4. _____   Why did Sherri receive a gift?
(it was her birthday)

F   5. _____   Why was Sherri surprised?
(she didn't think Maryann could afford
a gift)

F   6. _____   What was the ticket for?
(a classroom raffle)

F   7. _____   What color was the ticket?
(black or green [either 1])

I   8. _____   Why do you think Maryann pulled her
aside to give her the gift?
(any logical response)

E   9. _____   How would you feel if you were Sherri?
Why?
(any logical response; happy; surprised;
thankful)

V   10. _____   What does "raffle" mean?
(a random drawing for a prize)

Questions Missed

Comprehension Scoring Guide

Questions Missed	Level
0–1	Independent
1½–2	Ind./Inst.
2½	Instructional
3–4½	Inst./Frust.
5 +	Frustration

Retelling Notes

Retelling Rubric

Independent Level/Excellent
States central or key ideas
Identifies important facts
Retains the general sequence of events
Relates most of the content in an organized manner

Instructional Level/Satisfactory
States most central or key ideas
Identifies some important facts
Retains the general sequence of events
Relates an overall sense of the content

Frustration Level/Unsatisfactory
Provides bits of information in a haphazard manner
Little apparent organization

Writing Prompt: Write about a gift you'd like to give a friend.

Rubric for Writing Response

3	• Response is very closely related to prompt. • Response makes complete sense. • Response is well organized. • Response meets all age-appropriate spelling expectations and writing conventions.
2	• Response is related to prompt. • Response makes sense. • Response is organized in an acceptable manner. • Response meets most age-appropriate spelling expectations and writing conventions.
1	• Response is loosely related to prompt. • Some aspects of response make sense. • Response is not well organized. • Response lacks some age-appropriate spelling expectations and writing conventions.
0	• Response is unrelated to prompt. • Response does not make sense. • Response is poorly organized. • Response lacks most age-appropriate spelling expectations and writing conventions.

Student Book copy is on page 64.

C 6867 (Grade 6) Say: "I'd like you to read out loud [silently]. Think about what you're reading because I'll ask you some questions about it when you're done. Please begin here." [Point to title.]

Lexile: 1030

Stranger at Willowbrook

		Substitution	Insertion	Omission	Reversal	Repetition	Self-Correction of Unacceptable Miscue	Meaning Change (Significant Miscue)
		MISCUES						
Joshua was attending Willowbrook School	5							
for the first time. As the five-minute warning	14							
bell rang, he hurried to math class and an	23							
unfamiliar voice inquired, "How's it going,	29							
Josh?" Startled, Joshua responded with a	35							
dismissive wave and continued rushing to	41							
classroom 203, still fairly mystified. During	47							
lunchtime, Joshua glimpsed the stranger in	53							
the cafeteria, but pretended not to notice. In	61							
the final period, Mrs. Nichols was taking	68							
attendance when Joshua recognized a familiar	74							
name. "Zach Wilson," Joshua contemplated, "I	80							
remember when we built block houses together	87							
in kindergarten!" Joshua happily realized that	93							
the stranger was actually a forgotten friend.	100							
TOTAL								

Word Recognition Scoring Guide		
Total Miscues	Level	Significant Miscues
0–1	Independent	0–1
2–4	Ind./Inst.	2
5	Instructional	3
6–9	Inst./Frust.	4
10 +	Frustration	5 +

Total Miscues [   ]   Significant Miscues [   ]

Oral Reading Rate	Norm Group Percentile
$\dfrac{}{)6000}$ WPM	☐90 ☐75 ☐50 ☐25 ☐10

C 6867 (Grade 6)

Stranger at Willowbrook

T 1. _____ What is this passage about?
(Joshua meets a forgotten friend; Joshua
figures out who the stranger is)

F 2. _____ What was the name of Joshua's school?
(Willowbrook)

F 3. _____ What startled Joshua?
(an unfamiliar voice; Zack; someone
saying "How's it going?" [any 1])

F 4. _____ Where was Joshua going when he first
heard the stranger?
(math class; room 203)

F 5. _____ Where else did Joshua see the stranger?
(in the cafeteria; at lunch; in the last
period)

F 6. _____ When did Joshua recognize the
stranger?
(during last hour; during Mrs. Nichol's
class; during attendance)

F 7. _____ What did Joshua and Zack do in
kindergarten?
(build block houses)

I 8. _____ Why do you think Joshua had trouble
remembering Zack?
(any logical response; he hadn't seen
him since kindergarten)

E 9. _____ How would you feel if you met a
forgotten friend? Why?
(any logical response; happy)

V 10. _____ What does "familiar" mean?
(known; seen before; recognize)

| | Questions
Missed |
|---|---|

Comprehension Scoring Guide

| Questions
Missed	Level
0–1	Independent
1½–2	Ind./Inst.
2½	Instructional
3–4½	Inst./Frust.
5 +	Frustration

Retelling Notes

Retelling Rubric

Independent Level/Excellent
States central or key ideas
Identifies important facts
Retains the general sequence of events
Relates most of the content in an organized manner

Instructional Level/Satisfactory
States most central or key ideas
Identifies some important facts
Retains the general sequence of events
Relates an overall sense of the content

Frustration Level/Unsatisfactory
Provides bits of information in a haphazard manner
Little apparent organization

Writing Prompt: Write about someone or
something you remember from a long time ago.

Rubric for Writing Response

| 3 | • Response is very closely related to prompt.
• Response makes complete sense.
• Response is well organized.
• Response meets all age-appropriate spelling expectations and writing conventions. |
|---|---|
| 2 | • Response is related to prompt.
• Response makes sense.
• Response is organized in an acceptable manner.
• Response meets most age-appropriate spelling expectations and writing conventions. |
| 1 | • Response is loosely related to prompt.
• Some aspects of response make sense.
• Response is not well organized.
• Response lacks some age-appropriate spelling expectations and writing conventions. |
| 0 | • Response is unrelated to prompt.
• Response does not make sense.
• Response is poorly organized.
• Response lacks most age-appropriate spelling expectations and writing conventions. |

Student Book copy is on page 65.

C 3717 (Grade 7) Say: "I'd like you to read out loud [silently]. Think about what you're reading because I'll ask you some questions about it when you're done. Please begin here." [Point to title.]

Lexile: 1130

Mountain Vacation

		MISCUES						
	Substitution	Insertion	Omission	Reversal	Repetition	Self-Correction of Unacceptable Miscue	Meaning Change (Significant Miscue)	
Every summer my family takes an extended	7							
vacation in the mountains near Pike's Peak.	14							
We all love to spend the temperate days hiking	23							
through dense forests watching for shy marmots	30							
and moose. My dad has a knack for selecting	39							
campsites close to running water and lakes.	46							
We get the chorus of a babbling brook to put us	57							
to sleep and a brisk plunge in the lake to wake	68							
us up. My annual problem of not having enough	77							
money for souvenirs has hopefully been solved	84							
this year. I instituted a strict plan of depositing	93							
every penny I earn into the bank.	100							
TOTAL								

Total Miscues ☐   Significant Miscues ☐

Word Recognition Scoring Guide		
Total Miscues	Level	Significant Miscues
0–1	Independent	0–1
2–4	Ind./Inst.	2
5	Instructional	3
6–9	Inst./Frust.	4
10 +	Frustration	5 +

Oral Reading Rate	Norm Group Percentile
‾‾‾‾‾ WPM)6000	☐ 90 ☐ 75 ☐ 50 ☐ 25 ☐ 10

C 3717 (Grade 7)

Mountain Vacation

T 1. _____ What is this passage about?
(a family vacation in the mountains)

F 2. _____ How often does this family go to the mountains?
(every summer; every year)

F 3. _____ What do they do in the mountains?
(hike; camp [either 1])

F 4. _____ What animals do they hope to see in the mountains?
(marmots; moose [either 1])

F 5. _____ What can they hear from their campsite?
(the babbling brook; water)

F 6. _____ What is the author's problem?
(he or she never has enough money to buy souvenirs)

F 7. _____ How does the author solve the problem?
(by putting his or her money directly into the bank)

I 8. _____ Why do you think the author hasn't had enough money for souvenirs in the past?
(any logical response; he or she spent it before vacation)

E 9. _____ Do you think a mountain vacation sounds like fun? Why?
(any logical response; yes, I like being outdoors; no, I hate to camp out)

V 10. _____ What are "temperate days"?
(days when it is not too warm, nor too cold to be outside)

Questions Missed

Comprehension Scoring Guide	
Questions Missed	Level
0–1	Independent
1½–2	Ind./Inst.
2½	Instructional
3–4½	Inst./Frust.
5 +	Frustration

Retelling Notes

Retelling Rubric

Independent Level/Excellent
States central or key ideas
Identifies important facts
Retains the general sequence of events
Relates most of the content in an organized manner

Instructional Level/Satisfactory
States most central or key ideas
Identifies some important facts
Retains the general sequence of events
Relates an overall sense of the content

Frustration Level/Unsatisfactory
Provides bits of information in a haphazard manner
Little apparent organization

Writing Prompt: Write about what you would like to do if you were in the mountains.

Rubric for Writing Response

3	• Response is very closely related to prompt. • Response makes complete sense. • Response is well organized. • Response meets all age-appropriate spelling expectations and writing conventions.
2	• Response is related to prompt. • Response makes sense. • Response is organized in an acceptable manner. • Response meets most age-appropriate spelling expectations and writing conventions.
1	• Response is loosely related to prompt. • Some aspects of response make sense. • Response is not well organized. • Response lacks some age-appropriate spelling expectations and writing conventions.
0	• Response is unrelated to prompt. • Response does not make sense. • Response is poorly organized. • Response lacks most age-appropriate spelling expectations and writing conventions.

Student Book copy is on page 66.

C 8183 (Grade 8) Say: "I'd like you to read out loud [silently]. Think about what you're reading because I'll ask you some questions about it when you're done. Please begin here." [Point to title.]

Lexile: 1130

A Scientist's Search

	MISCUES				Repetition	Self-Correction of Unacceptable Miscue	Meaning Change (Significant Miscue)
	Substitution	Insertion	Omission	Reversal			
Elizabeth, a dedicated scientist, worked — 5							
tirelessly in her extensive laboratory. She had — 12							
been given a stimulating suggestion in a letter — 20							
from an anonymous scholar. It indicated that — 27							
the key to ultimate success was in a radium — 36							
reaction that would activate the groundbreaking — 42							
medicine. Doing this would be a complex — 49							
procedure of reducing chemical compounds to — 55							
unearth the ideal combination. Ultimately, the — 61							
formula would be discovered, and Elizabeth — 67							
would have a monopoly on the mixture that — 75							
could immortalize humanity. Only she'd know — 81							
the precise amount in each valuable tablet, and — 89							
the eradication of death and disease would — 96							
make Elizabeth renowned everywhere. — 100							
TOTAL							

Total Miscues [ ]   Significant Miscues [ ]

Word Recognition Scoring Guide

Total Miscues	Level	Significant Miscues
0–1	Independent	0–1
2–4	Ind./Inst.	2
5	Instructional	3
6–9	Inst./Frust.	4
10 +	Frustration	5 +

Oral Reading Rate	Norm Group Percentile
WPM $\overline{)6000}$	☐ 90 ☐ 75 ☐ 50 ☐ 25 ☐ 10

255

C 8183 (Grade 8)

A Scientist's Search

T 1. _____ What is this passage about?
(a scientist searching for a medicine to
make people immortal)

F 2. _____ Where did the scientist get the idea for
the formula?
(in a letter from a scholar)

F 3. _____ Did Elizabeth know the scholar? Why?
(no, because he or she was anonymous)

F 4. _____ What was the key to the experiment?
(the radium reaction)

F 5. _____ What would the medicine do?
(make people immortal)

F 6. _____ Why would Elizabeth be powerful?
(only she would know the right amount
in each tablet)

F 7. _____ What would disappear because of the
medicine?
(death; disease)

I 8. _____ How do you think people would
probably react to this discovery? Why?
(any logical response)

E 9. _____ Do you think Elizabeth might be placed
in a dangerous position? Why?
(any logical response)

V 10. _____ What does "immortal" mean?
(to live forever; not to die)

☐ Questions
Missed

Comprehension Scoring Guide	
Questions Missed	Level
0–1	Independent
1½–2	Ind./Inst.
2½	Instructional
3–4½	Inst./Frust.
5 +	Frustration

Retelling Notes

Retelling Rubric

Independent Level/Excellent
States central or key ideas
Identifies important facts
Retains the general sequence of events
Relates most of the content in an organized manner

Instructional Level/Satisfactory
States most central or key ideas
Identifies some important facts
Retains the general sequence of events
Relates an overall sense of the content

Frustration Level/Unsatisfactory
Provides bits of information in a haphazard manner
Little apparent organization

Writing Prompt: Write about how it might feel to live forever.

Rubric for Writing Response

3	• Response is very closely related to prompt. • Response makes complete sense. • Response is well organized. • Response meets all age-appropriate spelling expectations and writing conventions.
2	• Response is related to prompt. • Response makes sense. • Response is organized in an acceptable manner. • Response meets most age-appropriate spelling expectations and writing conventions.
1	• Response is loosely related to prompt. • Some aspects of response make sense. • Response is not well organized. • Response lacks some age-appropriate spelling expectations and writing conventions.
0	• Response is unrelated to prompt. • Response does not make sense. • Response is poorly organized. • Response lacks most age-appropriate spelling expectations and writing conventions.

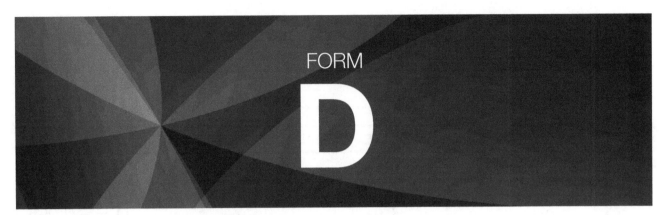

FORM D

Performance Booklet

Teacher Copy

Form D

Primary Uses:
- Silent Reading (Informational)

Other Uses:
- Oral Reading
- Progress Monitoring

Note: This Performance Booklet is on the Basic Reading Inventory website.

BASIC READING INVENTORY PERFORMANCE BOOKLET

Jerry L. Johns, Laurie Elish-Piper, and Beth Johns

Student _____   Grade _____ Gender M F   Date of Test _____

School _____   Examiner _____   Date of Birth _____

Address _____   Current Book/Level _____   Age _____

SUMMARY OF STUDENT'S READING PERFORMANCE

Grade	Word Recognition						Comprehension		Reading Rate	
	Isolation (Word Lists)				Context (Passages)		Form D			
	Sight	Analy-sis	Total	Level	Mis-cues	Level	Ques-tions Missed	Level	Words per Minute (WPM)	Norm Group Per-centile
Kb			/ 6							
Km			/ 9							
Ke			/12							
1b			/20							
1m										
1e										
2			/20							
3			/20							
4			/20							
5			/20							
6			/20							
7			/20							
8			/20							
9			/20							
10			/20							
11			/20							
12			/20							

ESTIMATE OF READING LEVELS

Independent _____   Instructional _____   Frustration _____

INFORMAL ANALYSIS OF ORAL READING

Oral Reading Behaviors	Frequency of Occurrence			General Impact on Meaning		
	Seldom	Sometimes	Frequently	No Change	Little Change	Much Change
Substitutions						
Insertions						
Omissions						
Reversals						
Repetitions						

LISTENING LEVEL, FORM _____

Grade	1	2	3	4	5	6	7	8
Questions Missed								
Level								

ESTIMATED LISTENING LEVEL: _____

QUALITATIVE ANALYSIS OF BASIC READING INVENTORY INSIGHTS

General Directions: Note the degree to which the student shows behavior or evidence in the following areas. Space is provided for additional items.

	Seldom / Weak / Poor			Always / Strong / Excellent

COMPREHENSION

Seeks to construct meaning

Makes predictions

Activates background knowledge

Possesses appropriate concepts and vocabulary

Monitors reading

Varies reading rate as needed

Understands topic and major ideas

Remembers facts or details

Makes and supports appropriate inferences

Evaluates ideas from passages

Understands vocabulary used

Provides appropriate definitions of words

Engages with passages

_____

_____

WORD IDENTIFICATION

Possesses numerous strategies

Uses strategies flexibly

Uses graphophonic information

Uses semantic information

Uses syntactic information

Knows high-frequency words automatically

Possesses sight vocabulary

_____

_____

ORAL AND SILENT READING

Reads fluently

Reads with expression

Attends to punctuation

Keeps place while reading

Reads at appropriate rate

Reads silently without vocalization

_____

_____

ATTITUDE AND CONFIDENCE

Enjoys reading

Demonstrates willingness to risk

Possesses positive self-concept

Chooses to read

Regards himself/herself as a reader

Exhibits persistence

_____

_____

Student Book copy is on page 68.

D Kb (Beginning K) Point to each word in the title as you read it. Then say: "Read this story about Mom. I'll ask you some questions about it when you're done."

Guided Reading Level: A

Mom		Substitution	Insertion	Omission	Reversal	Repetition	Self-Correction of Unacceptable Miscue	Meaning Change (Significant Miscue)
		MISCUES						
Mom is sitting.	3							
Mom is eating.	6							
Mom is driving.	9							
Mom is sleeping.	12							
TOTAL								

Oral Rereading:
Find and read out loud the sentence that tells what Mom is doing in a car.

Total Miscues ☐   Significant Miscues ☐

Word Recognition Scoring Guide		
Total Miscues	Level	Significant Miscues
0	Independent	0
—	Ind./Inst.	—
—	Instructional	—
1	Inst./Frust.	1
2 +	Frustration	2 +

Qualitative Analysis of Word Identification			
(0 = not evident 1 = emerging 2 = evident)			
Uses letter-sound relationships	0	1	2
Points to words while reading	0	1	2
Uses monitoring (rereads; corrects)	0	1	2
Knows high-frequency words	0	1	2
Possesses sight vocabulary	0	1	2
Exhibits persistence	0	1	2
Seems confident	0	1	2

Important Note: If the scoring guides are used, teacher judgment is especially important because of the length of the passage and the limited number of questions.

D Kb (Beginning K)

Mom

T 1. _____ What is this story about? [If student
says "Mom," say "tell me more."]
(what Mom does; Mom is sitting,
eating, driving, and sleeping)

F 2. _____ What's something else Mom does in the
story?
(any one of the following: sits, walks,
eats, sleeps)

I 3. _____ If you wanted to add more to the story,
tell me what else Mom might do.
(any logical response; work; cook;
clean; watch TV; shop)

E 4. _____ Where do you think you would probably
need to go to see Mom?
(any logical response; her house)

V 5. _____ What does the word "driving" mean?
(any logical response; to go somewhere
in a car; to make a car go)

Retelling Notes

Retelling Rubric

Independent Level/Excellent
States central or key ideas
Identifies important facts
Retains the general sequence of events
Relates most of the content in an organized manner

Instructional Level/Satisfactory
States most central or key ideas
Identifies some important facts
Retains the general sequence of events
Relates an overall sense of the content

Frustration Level/Unsatisfactory
Provides bits of information in a haphazard manner
Little apparent organization

Writing Prompt: Write about something you
would like to do with Mom.

	Rubric for Writing Response
3	• Response is very closely related to prompt. • Response makes complete sense. • Response is well organized. • Response meets all age-appropriate spelling expectations and writing conventions.
2	• Response is related to prompt. • Response makes sense. • Response is organized in an acceptable manner. • Response meets most age-appropriate spelling expectations and writing conventions.
1	• Response is loosely related to prompt. • Some aspects of response make sense. • Response is not well organized. • Response lacks some age-appropriate spelling expectations and writing conventions.
0	• Response is unrelated to prompt. • Response does not make sense. • Response is poorly organized. • Response lacks most age-appropriate spelling expectations and writing conventions.

☐ Questions
Missed

Comprehension Scoring Guide

Questions Missed	Level
0	Independent
1	Ind./Inst.
1½	Instructional
2	Inst./Frust.
2½ +	Frustration

Qualitative Analysis of Comprehension
(0 = not evident   1 = emerging   2 = evident)

Seeks to construct meaning		0	1	2
Understands topic and major ideas		0	1	2
Identifies facts or details		0	1	2
Evaluates ideas from story		0	1	2
Makes and supports appropriate inferences		0	1	2
Seems engaged with story		0	1	2

Important Note: If the scoring guides are used, teacher judgment is especially important because of the length of the passage and the
limited number of questions.

Student Book copy is on page 69.

D Km (Middle K) Point to each word in the title as you read it. Then say: "Read this story about the grass. I'll ask you some questions about it when you're done."

Guided Reading Level: B

In the Grass

	MISCUES						
	Substitution	Insertion	Omission	Reversal	Repetition	Self-Correction of Unacceptable Miscue	Meaning Change (Significant Miscue)
I see the dog in the grass. 7							
I see the cat in the grass. 14							
See the birds in the grass! 20							
TOTAL							

Total Miscues ☐   Significant Miscues ☐

Oral Rereading:
Find and read out loud the sentence that tells about the birds.

Word Recognition Scoring Guide		
Total Miscues	Level	Significant Miscues
0	Independent	0
—	Ind./Inst.	—
1	Instructional	1
2	Inst./Frust.	2
3 +	Frustration	3 +

Qualitative Analysis of Word Identification			
(0 = not evident 1 = emerging 2 = evident)			
Uses letter-sound relationships	0	1	2
Points to words while reading	0	1	2
Uses monitoring (rereads; corrects)	0	1	2
Knows high-frequency words	0	1	2
Possesses sight vocabulary	0	1	2
Exhibits persistence	0	1	2
Seems confident	0	1	2

Important Note: If the scoring guides are used, teacher judgment is especially important because of the length of the passage and the limited number of questions.

D Km (Middle K)

In the Grass

T 1. _____ What is this story about? [If student says "the grass," say "tell me more."] (the things I see in the grass; a dog, cat, and birds are in the grass]

F 2. _____ What's something else that is in the grass? (any one of the following: dog, cat, birds)

I 3. _____ If you wanted to add more to the story, tell me what else you might see in the grass. (any logical response; snake, mouse, bug, worm, rabbit)

E 4. _____ Where do you think you would probably need to go to see the grass? (any logical response; outside; the yard; the park; a field)

V 5. _____ What does the word "birds" mean? (any logical response; animals that have wings and can fly)

□	Questions Missed

Comprehension Scoring Guide	
Questions Missed	Level
0	Independent
1	Ind./Inst.
1½	Instructional
2	Inst./Frust.
2½ +	Frustration

Qualitative Analysis of Comprehension			
(0 = not evident 1 = emerging 2 = evident)			
Seeks to construct meaning	0	1	2
Understands topic and major ideas	0	1	2
Identifies facts or details	0	1	2
Evaluates ideas from story	0	1	2
Makes and supports appropriate inferences	0	1	2
Seems engaged with story	0	1	2

Retelling Notes

Retelling Rubric

Independent Level/Excellent
States central or key ideas
Identifies important facts
Retains the general sequence of events
Relates most of the content in an organized manner

Instructional Level/Satisfactory
States most central or key ideas
Identifies some important facts
Retains the general sequence of events
Relates an overall sense of the content

Frustration Level/Unsatisfactory
Provides bits of information in a haphazard manner
Little apparent organization

Writing Prompt: Write about something you have seen in the grass.

Rubric for Writing Response	
3	• Response is very closely related to prompt. • Response makes complete sense. • Response is well organized. • Response meets all age-appropriate spelling expectations and writing conventions.
2	• Response is related to prompt. • Response makes sense. • Response is organized in an acceptable manner. • Response meets most age-appropriate spelling expectations and writing conventions.
1	• Response is loosely related to prompt. • Some aspects of response make sense. • Response is not well organized. • Response lacks some age-appropriate spelling expectations and writing conventions.
0	• Response is unrelated to prompt. • Response does not make sense. • Response is poorly organized. • Response lacks most age-appropriate spelling expectations and writing conventions.

Important Note: If the scoring guides are used, teacher judgment is especially important because of the length of the passage and the limited number of questions.

Student Book copy is on page 70.

D Ke (End K) Point to each word in the title as you read it. Then say: "Read this story about Ted's dog. I'll ask you some questions about it when you're done."

Guided Reading Level: D

Ted's Dog

		MISCUES						
		Substitution	Insertion	Omission	Reversal	Repetition	Self-Correction of Unacceptable Miscue	Meaning Change (Significant Miscue)
Ted has a dog.	4							
His name is Ben.	8							
Ben is a big dog.	13							
He can jump up.	17							
Ted pets Ben.	20							
He is a fun dog.	25							
TOTAL								

Oral Rereading:
Find and read out loud the sentence that tells what the dog can do.

Total Miscues [ ]   Significant Miscues [ ]

Word Recognition Scoring Guide		
Total Miscues	Level	Significant Miscues
0	Independent	0
1	Ind./Inst.	—
2	Instructional	1
3	Inst./Frust.	2
4 +	Frustration	3 +

Qualitative Analysis of Word Identification			
(0 = not evident 1 = emerging 2 = evident)			
Uses letter-sound relationships	0	1	2
Points to words while reading	0	1	2
Uses monitoring (rereads; corrects)	0	1	2
Knows high-frequency words	0	1	2
Possesses sight vocabulary	0	1	2
Exhibits persistence	0	1	2
Seems confident	0	1	2

Important Note: If the scoring guides are used, teacher judgment is especially important because of the length of the passage and the limited number of questions.

D Ke (End K)

Ted's Dog

T 1. _____ What is this story about? [If student says "a dog" say "tell me more."]
(Ted's dog Ben; Ted's big dog)

F 2. _____ What's something else about Ted's dog in the story?
(any one of the following: he is big; he can jump up; Ted pets him; he is fun)

I 3. _____ If you wanted to add more to the story, tell me what else Ted might do with his dog.
(any logical response; go for a walk; play fetch; feed him; give him treats)

E 4. _____ Where do you think you would probably need to go to see Ted and his dog?
(any logical response; Ted's house; Ted's yard)

V 5. _____ What does the word "pets" mean in the story when it says "Ted pets Ben"?
(any logical response; to rub an animal's fur; to stroke an animal's fur)

	Questions Missed

Comprehension Scoring Guide

Questions Missed	Level
0	Independent
1	Ind./Inst.
1½	Instructional
2	Inst./Frust.
2½ +	Frustration

Qualitative Analysis of Comprehension
(0 = not evident   1 = emerging   2 = evident)

Seeks to construct meaning	0	1	2
Understands topic and major ideas	0	1	2
Identifies facts or details	0	1	2
Evaluates ideas from story	0	1	2
Makes and supports appropriate inferences	0	1	2
Seems engaged with story	0	1	2

Retelling Notes

Retelling Rubric

Independent Level/Excellent
States central or key ideas
Identifies important facts
Retains the general sequence of events
Relates most of the content in an organized manner

Instructional Level/Satisfactory
States most central or key ideas
Identifies some important facts
Retains the general sequence of events
Relates an overall sense of the content

Frustration Level/Unsatisfactory
Provides bits of information in a haphazard manner
Little apparent organization

Writing Prompt: Write about something you would like to do with a dog.

Rubric for Writing Response

3	• Response is very closely related to prompt. • Response makes complete sense. • Response is well organized. • Response meets all age-appropriate spelling expectations and writing conventions.
2	• Response is related to prompt. • Response makes sense. • Response is organized in an acceptable manner. • Response meets most age-appropriate spelling expectations and writing conventions.
1	• Response is loosely related to prompt. • Some aspects of response make sense. • Response is not well organized. • Response lacks some age-appropriate spelling expectations and writing conventions.
0	• Response is unrelated to prompt. • Response does not make sense. • Response is poorly organized. • Response lacks most age-appropriate spelling expectations and writing conventions.

Important Note: If the scoring guides are used, teacher judgment is especially important because of the length of the passage and the limited number of questions.

265

Student Book copy is on page 71.

D 7141b (Beginning Grade 1) Point to each word in the title as you read it. Then say: "Read this story about Pete's red ball. I'll ask you some questions about it when you're done."

Guided Reading Level: E

Pete's Red Ball

		MISCUES						
	Substitution	Insertion	Omission	Reversal	Repetition	Self-Correction of Unacceptable Miscue	Meaning Change (Significant Miscue)	
"I can not find my ball," said Pete. 8								
"My ball is a big ball. It is red." 17								
"Here is a ball," Rose said. "The ball 25								
is blue. It is little. It is not red." 34								
"I see a ball," said Pete. "It is red. 43								
It is big. It is my ball." 50								
TOTAL								

Oral Rereading:
Find and read out loud the sentence that tells what color Pete's ball is.

Total Miscuses [ ]   Significant Miscues [ ]

Word Recognition Scoring Guide		
Total Miscues	Level	Significant Miscues
0	Independent	0
1–2	Ind./Inst.	1
3	Instructional	2
4	Inst./Frust.	3
5 +	Frustration	4 +

Qualitative Analysis of Word Identification			
(0 = not evident 1 = emerging 2 = evident)			
Uses letter-sound relationships	0	1	2
Points to words while reading	0	1	2
Uses monitoring (rereads; corrects)	0	1	2
Knows high-frequency words	0	1	2
Possesses sight vocabulary	0	1	2
Exhibits persistence	0	1	2
Seems confident	0	1	2

Important Note: If the scoring guides are used, teacher judgment is especially important because of the length of the passage and the limited number of questions.

D 7141b (Beginning Grade 1)

Pete's Red Ball

T 1. _____ What is this story about? [If student says "a ball," say "tell me more."] (Pete has a big red ball; Pete loses then finds his big red ball)

F 2. _____ What did the ball Rose found look like? (blue and little)

I 3. _____ How did Pete know that the ball Rose found wasn't his? (any logical response; it was little and blue; it wasn't red or big)

E 4. _____ What kind of game do you think Pete might play with his ball? (any logical response)

V 5. _____ What is a "ball"? (any logical response; something you play with; it is round)

<table>
<tr><td>☐</td><td>Questions Missed</td></tr>
</table>

Comprehension Scoring Guide	
Questions Missed	Level
0	Independent
1	Ind./Inst.
1½	Instructional
2	Inst./Frust.
2½ +	Frustration

Qualitative Analysis of Comprehension (0 = not evident 1 = emerging 2 = evident)			
Seeks to construct meaning	0	1	2
Understands topic and major ideas	0	1	2
Identifies facts or details	0	1	2
Evaluates ideas from story	0	1	2
Makes and supports appropriate inferences	0	1	2
Seems engaged with story	0	1	2

Retelling Notes

Retelling Rubric

Independent Level/Excellent
States central or key ideas
Identifies important facts
Retains the general sequence of events
Relates most of the content in an organized manner

Instructional Level/Satisfactory
States most central or key ideas
Identifies some important facts
Retains the general sequence of events
Relates an overall sense of the content

Frustration Level/Unsatisfactory
Provides bits of information in a haphazard manner
Little apparent organization

Writing Prompt: Write about a game you would like to play with a ball.

Rubric for Writing Response	
3	• Response is very closely related to prompt. • Response makes complete sense. • Response is well organized. • Response meets all age-appropriate spelling expectations and writing conventions.
2	• Response is related to prompt. • Response makes sense. • Response is organized in an acceptable manner. • Response meets most age-appropriate spelling expectations and writing conventions.
1	• Response is loosely related to prompt. • Some aspects of response make sense. • Response is not well organized. • Response lacks some age-appropriate spelling expectations and writing conventions.
0	• Response is unrelated to prompt. • Response does not make sense. • Response is poorly organized. • Response lacks most age-appropriate spelling expectations and writing conventions.

Important Note: If the scoring guides are used, teacher judgment is especially important because of the length of the passage and the limited number of questions.

267

Student Book copy is on page 72.

D 7141m (Middle Grade 1) Point to each word in the title as you read it. Then say: "Read this story about Jill's egg. I'll ask you some questions about it when you're done."

Guided Reading Level: G

Jill's Egg		Substitution	Insertion	Omission	Reversal	Repetition	Self-Correction of Unacceptable Miscue	Meaning Change (Significant Miscue)
		MISCUES						
A white house was in the woods. Jill	8							
lived there. The sun made Jill happy. The	16							
air smelled clean. She took a walk.	23							
Jill found something along the road	29							
in the grass. It was round and white.	37							
"Oh!" said Jill. "What a nice egg.	44							
I'll take it home."	48							
Mother was home.	51							
She said, "Jill, you must keep the	58							
egg warm."	60							
Jill filled a box with rags. She set the	69							
egg in it. She put it near the stove.	78							
The next day Jill heard a sound	85							
she did not know.	89							
"Cheep!" A baby bird was born. Jill	96							
had a new pet.	100							
TOTAL								

Oral Rereading:
Find and read out loud the sentence that tells what mother told Jill to do with the egg.

Total Miscues [ ]   Significant Miscues [ ]

Word Recognition Scoring Guide		
Total Miscues	Level	Significant Miscues
0–1	Independent	0–1
2–4	Ind./Inst.	2
5	Instructional	3
6–9	Inst./Frust.	4
10 +	Frustration	5 +

Oral Reading Rate	Norm Group Percentile
‾‾‾‾‾ WPM)6000	☐ 90 ☐ 75 ☐ 50 ☐ 25 ☐ 10

D 7141m (Middle Grade 1)

Jill's Egg

T 1. _____ What is this story about?
(a girl named Jill who found an egg that hatched)

F 2. _____ Where did Jill live?
(in the woods; in a white house)

F 3. _____ What made Jill happy?
(the sun; finding an egg)

F 4. _____ What happened to Jill?
(she took a walk; she found an egg)

F 5. _____ Where did Jill find the egg?
(along the road in the grass)

F 6. _____ What happened to the egg?
(it hatched; a baby chick was born)

F 7. _____ What did Jill do to make the egg hatch?
(put it near the stove in a box; kept it warm)

I 8. _____ How do you think the egg got in the grass along the road?
(any logical response)

E 9. _____ What other things might Jill have found on her walk?
(any logical response; tracks; leaves; rocks)

V 10. _____ What is a "pet"?
(an animal to love, play with)

	Questions Missed

Comprehension Scoring Guide

Questions Missed	Level
0–1	Independent
1½–2	Ind./Inst.
2½	Instructional
3–4½	Inst./Frust.
5 +	Frustration

Retelling Notes

Retelling Rubric

Independent Level/Excellent
States central or key ideas
Identifies important facts
Retains the general sequence of events
Relates most of the content in an organized manner

Instructional Level/Satisfactory
States most central or key ideas
Identifies some important facts
Retains the general sequence of events
Relates an overall sense of the content

Frustration Level/Unsatisfactory
Provides bits of information in a haphazard manner
Little apparent organization

Writing Prompt: Write about things a pet bird can do.

Rubric for Writing Response

3	• Response is very closely related to prompt. • Response makes complete sense. • Response is well organized. • Response meets all age-appropriate spelling expectations and writing conventions.
2	• Response is related to prompt. • Response makes sense. • Response is organized in an acceptable manner. • Response meets most age-appropriate spelling expectations and writing conventions.
1	• Response is loosely related to prompt. • Some aspects of response make sense. • Response is not well organized. • Response lacks some age-appropriate spelling expectations and writing conventions.
0	• Response is unrelated to prompt. • Response does not make sense. • Response is poorly organized. • Response lacks most age-appropriate spelling expectations and writing conventions.

Student Book copy is on page 73.

D 7141e (End Grade 1) Point to each word in the title as you read it. Then say: "Read this story about the zoo. I'll ask you some questions about it when you're done."

Guided Reading Level: J

At the Zoo

MISCUES							
Substitution	Insertion	Omission	Reversal	Repetition	Self-Correction of Unacceptable Miscue	Meaning Change (Significant Miscue)	

Dan wanted to go to the zoo. He	8							
asked his mother. She said, "Yes." Dan	15							
had fun at the zoo. There were many	23							
animals he liked. One animal looked like it	31							
had two tails. It was an elephant. One had	40							
a nice back to ride on. It was a big turtle.	51							
Dan looked at many things. He saw many	59							
furry animals. He liked seeing them.	65							
It got dark. "Where is my mother?"	72							
he asked. Dan looked and looked for	79							
his mother. He was lost! He sat down and	88							
cried. Then Dan looked up. He saw	95							
his mother running to him!	100							
TOTAL								

Oral Rereading:

Find and read out loud the sentence that tells what Dan did when he was lost.

Total Miscues ☐   Significant Miscues ☐

Word Recognition Scoring Guide		
Total Miscues	Level	Significant Miscues
0–1	Independent	0–1
2–4	Ind./Inst.	2
5	Instructional	3
6–9	Inst./Frust.	4
10 +	Frustration	5 +

Oral Reading Rate	Norm Group Percentile
___)6000 WPM	☐ 90 ☐ 75 ☐ 50 ☐ 25 ☐ 10

D 7141e (End Grade 1)

At the Zoo

T   1. _____   What is this story about?
(a boy's trip to the zoo)

F   2. _____   Who went with Dan?
(his mother)

F   3. _____   What did Dan think he could do with the turtle?
(ride it)

F   4. _____   What other kinds of animals did Dan see at the zoo?
(furry animals; elephant)

F   5. _____   How did Dan think the elephant looked?
(like it had two tails)

F   6. _____   Why did Dan cry?
(he was lost; he was scared)

F   7. _____   What did Dan see when he looked up?
(his mother running to him)

I   8. _____   What do you think the furry animals were?
(any logical response; monkeys; bears; lions; tigers)

E   9. _____   What did you think the furry animals did?
(any logical response; ate; slept)

V   10. _____   What does "furry" mean?
(covered with fur; soft)

	Questions Missed

Comprehension Scoring Guide

Questions Missed	Level
0–1	Independent
1½–2	Ind./Inst.
2½	Instructional
3–4½	Inst./Frust.
5 +	Frustration

Retelling Notes

Retelling Rubric

Independent Level/Excellent
States central or key ideas
Identifies important facts
Retains the general sequence of events
Relates most of the content in an organized manner

Instructional Level/Satisfactory
States most central or key ideas
Identifies some important facts
Retains the general sequence of events
Relates an overall sense of the content

Frustration Level/Unsatisfactory
Provides bits of information in a haphazard manner
Little apparent organization

Writing Prompt: Write about a place you want to go.

Rubric for Writing Response

3	• Response is very closely related to prompt. • Response makes complete sense. • Response is well organized. • Response meets all age-appropriate spelling expectations and writing conventions.
2	• Response is related to prompt. • Response makes sense. • Response is organized in an acceptable manner. • Response meets most age-appropriate spelling expectations and writing conventions.
1	• Response is loosely related to prompt. • Some aspects of response make sense. • Response is not well organized. • Response lacks some age-appropriate spelling expectations and writing conventions.
0	• Response is unrelated to prompt. • Response does not make sense. • Response is poorly organized. • Response lacks most age-appropriate spelling expectations and writing conventions.

Student Book copy is on page 74.

D 8224 (Grade 2) Say: "I'd like you to read out loud [silently]. Think about what you're reading because I'll ask you some questions about it when you're done. Please begin here." [Point to title.]

Guided Reading Level: L; Lexile: 620

A Spider Friend

		MISCUES						
	Substitution	Insertion	Omission	Reversal	Repetition	Self-Correction of Unacceptable Miscue	Meaning Change (Significant Miscue)
A spider sat by a boy. The boy was — 9							
very afraid of it, but he should not have — 18							
been scared. The spider would not hurt — 25							
him because most spiders are friendly. — 31							
Spiders belong to a group of animals that — 39							
have eight legs. Spiders are not insects. — 46							
In the fall the mother spider lays — 53							
500 eggs, but only the strong baby spiders — 61							
live. **During spring they leave their nest.** — 58							
They eat flies, bugs, and ants. They also eat — 77							
insects that harm crops. Some large spiders — 84							
eat mice and birds. You should be able to — 93							
find a spider web where you live. — 100							
TOTAL							

Oral Rereading:
Find and read out loud the sentence that tells what spiders do in the spring.

Total Miscues [ ]   Significant Miscues [ ]

Word Recognition Scoring Guide		
Total Miscues	Level	Significant Miscues
0–1	Independent	0–1
2–4	Ind./Inst.	2
5	Instructional	3
6–9	Inst./Frust.	4
10 +	Frustration	5 +

Oral Reading Rate	Norm Group Percentile
_____ WPM)6000	☐ 90 ☐ 75 ☐ 50 ☐ 25 ☐ 10

D 8224 (Grade 2)

A Spider Friend

T   1. _____   What is this story about?
                (spiders)

F   2. _____   What did the spider do first in this
                story?
                (sat by a little boy)

F   3. _____   How many legs does a spider have?
                (eight)

F   4. _____   When do mother spiders lay their eggs.
                (in the fall)

F   5. _____   How many eggs does a mother spider
                lay?
                (about 500)

F   6. _____   When do baby spiders leave their nest?
                (in the spring)

F   7. _____   What do large spiders eat?
                (mice and birds [either 1])

I   8. _____   What happens to weak baby spiders?
                (any logical response; they die)

E   9. _____   Why do you think some people are
                afraid of spiders?
                (any logical response)

V 10. _____   What are "crops"?
                (any logical response; what farmers
                grow; corn; beans)

Questions Missed

Comprehension Scoring Guide

Questions Missed	Level
0–1	Independent
1½–2	Ind./Inst.
2½	Instructional
3–4½	Inst./Frust.
5 +	Frustration

Retelling Notes

Retelling Rubric

Independent Level/Excellent
States central or key ideas
Identifies important facts
Retains the general sequence of events
Relates most of the content in an organized manner

Instructional Level/Satisfactory
States most central or key ideas
Identifies some important facts
Retains the general sequence of events
Relates an overall sense of the content

Frustration Level/Unsatisfactory
Provides bits of information in a haphazard manner
Little apparent organization

Writing Prompt: Write about what you would do differently if you had eight legs.

Rubric for Writing Response

3	• Response is very closely related to prompt. • Response makes complete sense. • Response is well organized. • Response meets all age-appropriate spelling expectations and writing conventions.
2	• Response is related to prompt. • Response makes sense. • Response is organized in an acceptable manner. • Response meets most age-appropriate spelling expectations and writing conventions.
1	• Response is loosely related to prompt. • Some aspects of response make sense. • Response is not well organized. • Response lacks some age-appropriate spelling expectations and writing conventions.
0	• Response is unrelated to prompt. • Response does not make sense. • Response is poorly organized. • Response lacks most age-appropriate spelling expectations and writing conventions.

Student Book copy is on page 75.

D 3183 (Grade 3) Say: "I'd like you to read out loud [silently]. Think about what you're reading because I'll ask you some questions about it when you're done. Please begin here." [Point to title.]

Guided Reading Level: O; Lexile: 740

Big Star		MISCUES					Repetition	Self-Correction of Unacceptable Miscue	Meaning Change (Significant Miscue)
		Substitution	Insertion	Omission	Reversal				
The sun is important for life on earth	8								
because we need the sun for light, heat, and	17								
energy. If there was no sun, life on our	26								
planet earth would not exist. The sun is a	35								
star. It looks much larger than the stars you	44								
see in the night sky. It seems larger because	53								
it is a lot closer to the earth than the other	64								
stars. **It is actually about the same size as**	73								
other stars. Stars are big balls of energy in	82								
the form of gas. Our earth will continue to	91								
get energy from the sun for billions of years.	100								
TOTAL									

Oral Rereading:
Find and read out loud the sentence that tells how the sun compares to other stars.

Total Miscues ☐   Significant Miscues ☐

Word Recognition Scoring Guide		
Total Miscues	Level	Significant Miscues
0–1	Independent	0–1
2–4	Ind./Inst.	2
5	Instructional	3
6–9	Inst./Frust.	4
10 +	Frustration	5 +

Oral Reading Rate	Norm Group Percentile				
___ WPM)6000	☐ 90	☐ 75	☐ 50	☐ 25	☐ 10

D 3183 (Grade 3)

Big Star

T 1. _____ What is this story about?
(the sun)

F 2. _____ What does the sun give the earth?
(light, heat, energy [any 2])

F 3. _____ What would happen to life on earth
without the sun?
(it would not exist)

F 4. _____ What kind of object is the sun?
(a star)

F 5. _____ Why does the sun look larger than other
stars?
(because it is closer to the earth)

F 6. _____ What are stars made of?
(gas; big balls of energy)

F 7. _____ How long will earth get energy from
the sun?
(for billions of years)

I 8. _____ What would the earth be like without
the sun?
(any logical response; there would be
no life; cold; dark)

E 9. _____ Do you like the sun? Why?
(any logical response; it makes warm
days; it gives light)

V 10. _____ What does it mean to "exist"?
(to live; to be; to be real)

☐ Questions
Missed

Comprehension Scoring Guide	
Questions Missed	Level
0–1	Independent
1½–2	Ind./Inst.
2½	Instructional
3–4½	Inst./Frust.
5 +	Frustration

Retelling Notes

Retelling Rubric

Independent Level/Excellent
States central or key ideas
Identifies important facts
Retains the general sequence of events
Relates most of the content in an organized manner

Instructional Level/Satisfactory
States most central or key ideas
Identifies some important facts
Retains the general sequence of events
Relates an overall sense of the content

Frustration Level/Unsatisfactory
Provides bits of information in a haphazard manner
Little apparent organization

Writing Prompt: Write about what you might do
on a sunny day.

	Rubric for Writing Response
3	• Response is very closely related to prompt. • Response makes complete sense. • Response is well organized. • Response meets all age-appropriate spelling expectations and writing conventions.
2	• Response is related to prompt. • Response makes sense. • Response is organized in an acceptable manner. • Response meets most age-appropriate spelling expectations and writing conventions.
1	• Response is loosely related to prompt. • Some aspects of response make sense. • Response is not well organized. • Response lacks some age-appropriate spelling expectations and writing conventions.
0	• Response is unrelated to prompt. • Response does not make sense. • Response is poorly organized. • Response lacks most age-appropriate spelling expectations and writing conventions.

Student Book copy is on page 76.

D 5414 (Grade 4) Say: "I'd like you to read out loud [silently]. Think about what you're reading because I'll ask you some questions about it when you're done. Please begin here." [Point to title.]

Guided Reading Level: R; Lexile: 830

Amazing Plants

		MISCUES						
	Substitution	Insertion	Omission	Reversal	Repetition	Self-Correction of Unacceptable Miscue	Meaning Change (Significant Miscue)	
There are over three hundred thousand	6							
different varieties of plants. The oxygen we	13							
breathe comes from plants. Some plants grow	20							
bigger and live longer than animals, and	27							
plants grow in many sizes and shapes. **Some**	35							
plants are smaller than the period at the end	44							
of this sentence; therefore, these plants can	51							
only be viewed with a microscope. Other	58							
plants, like the giant pine, tower high in the	67							
sky. Most plants have stems and leaves.	74							
Plants can live in many places, and some	82							
even seem to grow out of rocks, while others	91							
live in water, old bread, or even old shoes!	100							
TOTAL								

Oral Rereading:

Find and read out loud the sentence that tells how to see very small plants.

Total Miscues [ ]   Significant Miscues [ ]

Word Recognition Scoring Guide		
Total Miscues	Level	Significant Miscues
0–1	Independent	0–1
2–4	Ind./Inst.	2
5	Instructional	3
6–9	Inst./Frust.	4
10 +	Frustration	5 +

Oral Reading Rate	Norm Group Percentile	
___)6000 WPM	☐ 90 ☐ 75 ☐ 50 ☐ 25 ☐ 10	

D 5414 (Grade 4)

Amazing Plants

T   1. _____   What is this passage about?
(plants)

F   2. _____   How many plants are there?
(over 300,000)

F   3. _____   Why are plants important to people?
(they provide oxygen)

F   4. _____   How small can plants be?
(smaller than a period at the end
of a sentence; so small you need a
microscope)

F   5. _____   What do most plants have?
(stems and leaves)

F   6. _____   According to the passage, where can
plants live?
(rocks; water; bread; shoes [any 2] or a
variety of places)

F   7. _____   What is used to view small plants?
(a microscope)

I   8. _____   Name a plant that would probably live
longer than most animals.
(any logical response; trees)

E   9. _____   What do you think would happen if all
the plants died? Why?
(any logical response; there would be no
life on earth; no oxygen)

V   10. _____   What is a "microscope"?
(a thing that makes small things seem
larger)

Questions Missed

Comprehension Scoring Guide

Questions Missed	Level
0–1	Independent
1½–2	Ind./Inst.
2½	Instructional
3–4½	Inst./Frust.
5 +	Frustration

Retelling Notes

Retelling Rubric

Independent Level/Excellent
States central or key ideas
Identifies important facts
Retains the general sequence of events
Relates most of the content in an organized manner

Instructional Level/Satisfactory
States most central or key ideas
Identifies some important facts
Retains the general sequence of events
Relates an overall sense of the content

Frustration Level/Unsatisfactory
Provides bits of information in a haphazard manner
Little apparent organization

Writing Prompt: Write about something besides a plant that you'd like to see under a microscope.

Rubric for Writing Response

3	• Response is very closely related to prompt. • Response makes complete sense. • Response is well organized. • Response meets all age-appropriate spelling expectations and writing conventions.
2	• Response is related to prompt. • Response makes sense. • Response is organized in an acceptable manner. • Response meets most age-appropriate spelling expectations and writing conventions.
1	• Response is loosely related to prompt. • Some aspects of response make sense. • Response is not well organized. • Response lacks some age-appropriate spelling expectations and writing conventions.
0	• Response is unrelated to prompt. • Response does not make sense. • Response is poorly organized. • Response lacks most age-appropriate spelling expectations and writing conventions.

Student Book copy is on page 77.

D 8595 (Grade 5) Say: "I'd like you to read out loud [silently]. Think about what you're reading because I'll ask you some questions about it when you're done. Please begin here." [Point to title.]

Guided Reading Level: U; Lexile: 900

Plane Flight

		Substitution	Insertion	Omission	Reversal	Repetition	Self-Correction of Unacceptable Miscue	Meaning Change (Significant Miscue)
		MISCUES						
Older airplanes were moved through	5							
the air by the use of propellers. Now, most	14							
planes are driven by large jet engines.	21							
Some fly faster than sound. **The first thing**	29							
you may notice about a plane is the wings	38							
that stick out on either side of its long	47							
body. Today jet planes land and take off	55							
from major airports every few seconds.	61							
People can travel several hundred miles	67							
in less than an hour. It can take travelers	76							
longer to retrieve their luggage than to fly	84							
to their destination. Planes have been	90							
much improved since the Wright brothers	96							
first flew in 1903.	100							
TOTAL								

Oral Rereading:
Find and read out loud the sentence that tells what you might first notice about a plane.

Total Miscues [ ]   Significant Miscues [ ]

Word Recognition Scoring Guide		
Total Miscues	Level	Significant Miscues
0–1	Independent	0–1
2–4	Ind./Inst.	2
5	Instructional	3
6–9	Inst./Frust.	4
10 +	Frustration	5 +

Oral Reading Rate	Norm Group Percentile
___ WPM)6000	☐ 90 ☐ 75 ☐ 50 ☐ 25 ☐ 10

D 8595 (Grade 5)

Plane Flight

T 1. _____ What is this passage about?
(airplanes; the development of planes through the years)

F 2. _____ What kind of engines do most airplanes have today?
(jet engines)

F 3. _____ How fast can some planes fly?
(faster than sound)

F 4. _____ How were older planes moved through the air?
(propellers)

F 5. _____ In what year did the Wright brothers fly?
(1903)

F 6. _____ According to this passage, how long does it take for people to fly several hundred miles?
(less than an hour)

F 7. _____ According to the passage, how often do airplanes land and take off from major airports?
(every few seconds)

I 8. _____ How do you think the Wright brothers felt after the first flight? Why?
(any logical response; happy)

E 9. _____ Do you think jet airplanes have changed our lives for the better? Why?
(any logical response)

V 10. _____ What is a "destination"?
(a place you are trying to get to)

Questions Missed

Retelling Notes

Retelling Rubric

Independent Level/Excellent
States central or key ideas
Identifies important facts
Retains the general sequence of events
Relates most of the content in an organized manner

Instructional Level/Satisfactory
States most central or key ideas
Identifies some important facts
Retains the general sequence of events
Relates an overall sense of the content

Frustration Level/Unsatisfactory
Provides bits of information in a haphazard manner
Little apparent organization

Writing Prompt: Write about what you would pack for a trip to Australia.

Rubric for Writing Response

3	• Response is very closely related to prompt. • Response makes complete sense. • Response is well organized. • Response meets all age-appropriate spelling expectations and writing conventions.
2	• Response is related to prompt. • Response makes sense. • Response is organized in an acceptable manner. • Response meets most age-appropriate spelling expectations and writing conventions.
1	• Response is loosely related to prompt. • Some aspects of response make sense. • Response is not well organized. • Response lacks some age-appropriate spelling expectations and writing conventions.
0	• Response is unrelated to prompt. • Response does not make sense. • Response is poorly organized. • Response lacks most age-appropriate spelling expectations and writing conventions.

Student Book copy is on page 78.

D 6867 (Grade 6) Say: "I'd like you to read out loud [silently]. Think about what you're reading because I'll ask you some questions about it when you're done. Please begin here." [Point to title.]

Lexile: 1020

Sunflowers

		Substitution	Insertion	Omission	Reversal	Repetition	Self-Correction of Unacceptable Miscue	Meaning Change (Significant Miscue)
One of the most amazing flowers in	7							
the Midwest is the sunflower. Legend says	14							
the flower got its name from its strange	22							
habit of turning its head in order to face	31							
the sun. The sunflower is a very strong	39							
plant, and it ranges in height from three to	48							
fifteen feet. The head of the sunflower is	56							
similar to that of a daisy, because both have	65							
an outer circle of wide petals and an inner	74							
circle of small brown flowers. **Seeds later**	81							
form from these small flowers. These seeds	88							
produce some of the most unique patterns	95							
found in the plant world.	100							
TOTAL								

Oral Rereading:

Find and read out loud the sentence that tells what happens to the brown flowers.

Total Miscues ☐   Significant Miscues ☐

Word Recognition Scoring Guide		
Total Miscues	Level	Significant Miscues
0–1	Independent	0–1
2–4	Ind./Inst.	2
5	Instructional	3
6–9	Inst./Frust.	4
10 +	Frustration	5 +

Oral Reading Rate	Norm Group Percentile				
_____ WPM 6000̅	☐ 90	☐ 75	☐ 50	☐ 25	☐ 10

D 6867 (Grade 6)

Sunflowers

T 1. _____ What is this passage about?
(sunflowers)

F 2. _____ How did the sunflower get its name?
(turning its head to face the sun)

F 3. _____ How tall is the sunflower?
(three to fifteen feet)

F 4. _____ What is on the outside of the sunflower?
(wide petals)

F 5. _____ What color is the inner circle of the
sunflower?
(brown)

F 6. _____ What is the head of the sunflower
similar to?
(daisy)

F 7. _____ What comes from the small flowers in
the middle?
(seeds)

I 8. _____ Would some sunflowers be taller than
you are? Why?
(any logical response)

E 9. _____ Why do you think a sunflower would be
considered a strong plant?
(any logical response; thick stem; tall)

V 10. _____ What does "unique" mean?
(any logical response; different)

[ ] Questions
Missed

Comprehension Scoring Guide	
Questions Missed	Level
0–1	Independent
1½–2	Ind./Inst.
2½	Instructional
3–4½	Inst./Frust.
5 +	Frustration

Retelling Notes

Retelling Rubric

Independent Level/Excellent
States central or key ideas
Identifies important facts
Retains the general sequence of events
Relates most of the content in an organized manner

Instructional Level/Satisfactory
States most central or key ideas
Identifies some important facts
Retains the general sequence of events
Relates an overall sense of the content

Frustration Level/Unsatisfactory
Provides bits of information in a haphazard manner
Little apparent organization

Writing Prompt: Write about something you think is amazing.

	Rubric for Writing Response
3	• Response is very closely related to prompt. • Response makes complete sense. • Response is well organized. • Response meets all age-appropriate spelling expectations and writing conventions.
2	• Response is related to prompt. • Response makes sense. • Response is organized in an acceptable manner. • Response meets most age-appropriate spelling expectations and writing conventions.
1	• Response is loosely related to prompt. • Some aspects of response make sense. • Response is not well organized. • Response lacks some age-appropriate spelling expectations and writing conventions.
0	• Response is unrelated to prompt. • Response does not make sense. • Response is poorly organized. • Response lacks most age-appropriate spelling expectations and writing conventions.

Student Book copy is on page 79.

D 3717 (Grade 7) Say: "I'd like you to read out loud [silently]. Think about what you're reading because I'll ask you some questions about it when you're done. Please begin here." [Point to title.]

Lexile: 1050

Native American Celebrations

		Substitution	Insertion	Omission	Reversal	Repetition	Self-Correction of Unacceptable Miscue	Meaning Change (Significant Miscue)
		MISCUES						
Native American Indians worshipped	4							
the power in natural things, such as the stars,	13							
moon, and the sun. At various times during	21							
the year, they would hold celebrations in	28							
honor of this power that they named the	36							
Great Spirit. On these occasions, they would	43							
have ceremonies of dancing and feasting.	49							
They would decorate their bodies and faces	56							
and dress themselves in their best clothes.	63							
A medicine man would lead them in the	71							
celebration that continued for several days.	77							
Native Americans gathered about the	82							
council fire and prayed that the Great	89							
Spirit's wish for them would be revealed	96							
by a natural sign.	100							
TOTAL								

Oral Rereading:
Find and read out loud the sentence that tells who led the celebration.

Total Miscues [ ]   Significant Miscues [ ]

Word Recognition Scoring Guide		
Total Miscues	Level	Significant Miscues
0–1	Independent	0–1
2–4	Ind./Inst.	2
5	Instructional	3
6–9	Inst./Frust.	4
10 +	Frustration	5 +

Oral Reading Rate	Norm Group Percentile
)6000 WPM	☐ 90 ☐ 75 ☐ 50 ☐ 25 ☐ 10

D 3717 (Grade 7)

Native American Celebrations

T   1. _____ What is this passage about?
(Indian worship; how Native Americans celebrated)

F   2. _____ What did the Native American Indians worship?
(the power in natural things; sun, moon, stars)

F   3. _____ Why did the Native Americans hold celebrations?
(to honor the Great Spirit)

F   4. _____ How did they decorate themselves for the celebrations?
(painted their faces and bodies; wore their best clothes)

F   5. _____ What did the medicine man do during the celebration?
(led them)

F   6. _____ What were the Native Americans doing at their celebrations?
(dancing, feasting, decorating themselves, and praying [any 2])

F   7. _____ What did they pray for?
(a sign from the Great Spirit)

I   8. _____ What sign do you think the Native Americans wanted from the Great Spirit?
(any logical response)

E   9. _____ Why do you think Native Americans worshipped things of nature?
(any logical response)

V   10. _____ What is meant by "reveal"?
(show; make known)

☐ Questions Missed

Comprehension Scoring Guide	
Questions Missed	Level
0–1	Independent
1½–2	Ind./Inst.
2½	Instructional
3–4½	Inst./Frust.
5 +	Frustration

Retelling Notes

Retelling Rubric

Independent Level/Excellent
States central or key ideas
Identifies important facts
Retains the general sequence of events
Relates most of the content in an organized manner

Instructional Level/Satisfactory
States most central or key ideas
Identifies some important facts
Retains the general sequence of events
Relates an overall sense of the content

Frustration Level/Unsatisfactory
Provides bits of information in a haphazard manner
Little apparent organization

Writing Prompt: Write about the kinds of things you'd like to celebrate.

	Rubric for Writing Response
3	• Response is very closely related to prompt. • Response makes complete sense. • Response is well organized. • Response meets all age-appropriate spelling expectations and writing conventions.
2	• Response is related to prompt. • Response makes sense. • Response is organized in an acceptable manner. • Response meets most age-appropriate spelling expectations and writing conventions.
1	• Response is loosely related to prompt. • Some aspects of response make sense. • Response is not well organized. • Response lacks some age-appropriate spelling expectations and writing conventions.
0	• Response is unrelated to prompt. • Response does not make sense. • Response is poorly organized. • Response lacks most age-appropriate spelling expectations and writing conventions.

Student Book copy is on page 80.

D 8183 (Grade 8) Say: "I'd like you to read out loud [silently]. Think about what you're reading because I'll ask you some questions about it when you're done. Please begin here." [Point to title.]

Lexile: 1090

Our Environment		Substitution	Insertion	Omission	Reversal	Repetition	Self-Correction of Unacceptable Miscue	Meaning Change (Significant Miscue)
		MISCUES						
Besides consuming plants and animals	5							
for food, people utilize the hides of animals	13							
for shoes, the wood from trees to construct	21							
houses, the fiber from the cotton plant to make	30							
skirts and shirts, and the wool from sheep to	39							
fashion suits and coats. Even the synthetic	46							
fibers that people use are constructed from	53							
matter found in the environment.	58							
People and the environment are	63							
interdependent, but that is not the entire story.	71							
Modern people can do much more; they can	79							
use science and technology to alter their	86							
environment. Because of their advanced	91							
brains, people can investigate and manipulate	97							
their precious environment.	100							
TOTAL								

Oral Rereading:
Find and read out loud the sentence that tells what two things people use to change their environment.

Total Miscues [ ]   Significant Miscues [ ]

Word Recognition Scoring Guide		
Total Miscues	Level	Significant Miscues
0–1	Independent	0–1
2–4	Ind./Inst.	2
5	Instructional	3
6–9	Inst./Frust.	4
10 +	Frustration	5 +

Oral Reading Rate	Norm Group Percentile
)6000 WPM	☐ 90 ☐ 75 ☐ 50 ☐ 25 ☐ 10

D 8183 (Grade 8)

Our Environment

T   1. _____ What is this passage about?
(people's interdependence with their
environment; how people use their
environment)

F   2. _____ What do modern people use to change
the environment?
(science and technology)

F   3. _____ Why are people able to investigate their
environment?
(they have a brain)

F   4. _____ What are synthetic fibers made from?
(matter found in the environment)

F   5. _____ What are some of the things in the
environment which people use?
(plants; animals; wood; cotton; wool
[any 2])

F   6. _____ What does the passage say people use to
make skirts and shirts?
(fiber from the cotton plant)

F   7. _____ According to the passage, what are the
hides of animals used for?
(shoes)

I   8. _____ What are some of the ways in which
people have changed the environment?
(any logical response)

E   9. _____ Do you think it's a good thing for
people to change their environment?
Why?
(any logical response)

V 10. _____ What does "synthetic" mean?
(any logical response; fake; unnatural;
made from several things put together)

	Questions Missed

Comprehension Scoring Guide	
Questions Missed	Level
0–1	Independent
1½–2	Ind./Inst.
2½	Instructional
3–4½	Inst./Frust.
5 +	Frustration

Retelling Notes

Retelling Rubric

Independent Level/Excellent
States central or key ideas
Identifies important facts
Retains the general sequence of events
Relates most of the content in an organized manner

Instructional Level/Satisfactory
States most central or key ideas
Identifies some important facts
Retains the general sequence of events
Relates an overall sense of the content

Frustration Level/Unsatisfactory
Provides bits of information in a haphazard manner
Little apparent organization

Writing Prompt: Write about a technology that
you find useful.

	Rubric for Writing Response
3	• Response is very closely related to prompt. • Response makes complete sense. • Response is well organized. • Response meets all age-appropriate spelling expectations and writing conventions.
2	• Response is related to prompt. • Response makes sense. • Response is organized in an acceptable manner. • Response meets most age-appropriate spelling expectations and writing conventions.
1	• Response is loosely related to prompt. • Some aspects of response make sense. • Response is not well organized. • Response lacks some age-appropriate spelling expectations and writing conventions.
0	• Response is unrelated to prompt. • Response does not make sense. • Response is poorly organized. • Response lacks most age-appropriate spelling expectations and writing conventions.

Performance Booklet

Teacher Copy

Form E

Primary Uses:

- Oral Reading
  (Informational)

Other Uses:

- Silent Reading
- Progress Monitoring

Note: This Performance Booklet is on the Basic Reading Inventory website.

BASIC READING INVENTORY PERFORMANCE BOOKLET

Jerry L. Johns, Laurie Elish-Piper, and Beth Johns

Student _____ Grade _____ Gender M F Date of Test _____

School _____ Examiner _____ Date of Birth _____

Address _____ Current Book/Level _____ Age _____

SUMMARY OF STUDENT'S READING PERFORMANCE

| Grade | Word Recognition | | | | | | Comprehension | | Reading Rate | |
| | Isolation (Word Lists) | | | | Context (Passages) | | Form E | | | |
	Sight	Analysis	Total	Level	Miscues	Level	Questions Missed	Level	Words per Minute (WPM)	Norm Group Percentile
Kb			/ 6							
Km			/ 9							
Ke			/12							
1b			/20							
1m										
1e										
2			/20							
3			/20							
4			/20							
5			/20							
6			/20							
7			/20							
8			/20							
9			/20							
10			/20							
11			/20							
12			/20							

ESTIMATE OF READING LEVELS

Independent _____ Instructional _____ Frustration _____

INFORMAL ANALYSIS OF ORAL READING

| Oral Reading Behaviors | Frequency of Occurrence | | | General Impact on Meaning | | |
	Seldom	Sometimes	Frequently	No Change	Little Change	Much Change
Substitutions						
Insertions						
Omissions						
Reversals						
Repetitions						

LISTENING LEVEL, FORM _____

Grade	1	2	3	4	5	6	7	8
Questions Missed								
Level								

ESTIMATED LISTENING LEVEL: _____

QUALITATIVE ANALYSIS OF BASIC READING INVENTORY INSIGHTS

General Directions: Note the degree to which the student shows behavior or evidence in the following areas. Space is provided for additional items.

Seldom   Always
Weak   Strong
Poor   Excellent

COMPREHENSION

Seeks to construct meaning
Makes predictions
Activates background knowledge
Possesses appropriate concepts and vocabulary
Monitors reading
Varies reading rate as needed
Understands topic and major ideas
Remembers facts or details
Makes and supports appropriate inferences
Evaluates ideas from passages
Understands vocabulary used
Provides appropriate definitions of words
Engages with passages

WORD IDENTIFICATION

Possesses numerous strategies
Uses strategies flexibly
Uses graphophonic information
Uses semantic information
Uses syntactic information
Knows high-frequency words automatically
Possesses sight vocabulary

ORAL AND SILENT READING

Reads fluently
Reads with expression
Attends to punctuation
Keeps place while reading
Reads at appropriate rate
Reads silently without vocalization

ATTITUDE AND CONFIDENCE

Enjoys reading
Demonstrates willingness to risk
Possesses positive self-concept
Chooses to read
Regards himself/herself as a reader
Exhibits persistence

Student Book copy is on page 82.

E Kb (Beginning K) Point to each word in the title as you read it. Then say: "Read this story about Dad. I'll ask you some questions about it when you're done."

Guided Reading Level: A

Dad		MISCUES							
		Substitution	Insertion	Omission	Reversal	Repetition	Self-Correction of Unacceptable Miscue	Meaning Change (Significant Miscue)	
Dad is sitting.	3								
Dad is eating.	6								
Dad is driving.	9								
Dad is sleeping.	12								
TOTAL									

Total Miscues [ ]   Significant Miscues [ ]

Word Recognition Scoring Guide		
Total Miscues	Level	Significant Miscues
0	Independent	0
—	Ind./Inst.	—
—	Instructional	—
1	Inst./Frust.	1
2 +	Frustration	2 +

Qualitative Analysis of Word Identification			
(0 = not evident 1 = emerging 2 = evident)			
Uses letter-sound relationships	0	1	2
Points to words while reading	0	1	2
Uses monitoring (rereads; corrects)	0	1	2
Knows high-frequency words	0	1	2
Possesses sight vocabulary	0	1	2
Exhibits persistence	0	1	2
Seems confident	0	1	2

Important Note: If the scoring guides are used, teacher judgment is especially important because of the length of the passage and the limited number of questions.

E Kb (Beginning K)

Dad

T 1. _____ What is this story about? [If student
says "Dad" say "tell me more."]
(what Dad does; Dad is sitting, eating,
driving, and sleeping)

F 2. _____ What's something else Dad does in the
story?
(any one of the following: Dad is sitting,
eating, driving, and sleeping)

I 3. _____ If you wanted to add more to the story,
tell me what else Dad might do.
(any logical response; work; cook;
clean; watch TV)

E 4. _____ Where do you think you would probably
need to go to see Dad?
(any logical response; his house)

V 5. _____ What does the word "sitting" mean?
(any logical response; to be in a chair;
student demonstrates sitting)

	Retelling Notes

Retelling Rubric

Independent Level/Excellent

States central or key ideas
Identifies important facts
Retains the general sequence of events
Relates most of the content in an organized manner

Instructional Level/Satisfactory

States most central or key ideas
Identifies some important facts
Retains the general sequence of events
Relates an overall sense of the content

Frustration Level/Unsatisfactory

Provides bits of information in a haphazard manner
Little apparent organization

	Questions Missed

Comprehension Scoring Guide	
Questions Missed	Level
0	Independent
1	Ind./Inst.
1½	Instructional
2	Inst./Frust.
2½ +	Frustration

Qualitative Analysis of Comprehension (0 = not evident 1 = emerging 2 = evident)			
Seeks to construct meaning	0	1	2
Understands topic and major ideas	0	1	2
Identifies facts or details	0	1	2
Evaluates ideas from story	0	1	2
Makes and supports appropriate inferences	0	1	2
Seems engaged with story	0	1	2

Writing Prompt: Write about something you would like to do with Dad.

Rubric for Writing Response	
3	• Response is very closely related to prompt. • Response makes complete sense. • Response is well organized. • Response meets all age-appropriate spelling expectations and writing conventions.
2	• Response is related to prompt. • Response makes sense. • Response is organized in an acceptable manner. • Response meets most age-appropriate spelling expectations and writing conventions.
1	• Response is loosely related to prompt. • Some aspects of response make sense. • Response is not well organized. • Response lacks some age-appropriate spelling expectations and writing conventions.
0	• Response is unrelated to prompt. • Response does not make sense. • Response is poorly organized. • Response lacks most age-appropriate spelling expectations and writing conventions.

Important Note: If the scoring guides are used, teacher judgment is especially important because of the length of the passage and the limited number of questions.

Student Book copy is on page 83.

E Km (Middle K) Point to each word in the title as you read it. Then say: "Read this story about feet. I'll ask you some questions about it when you're done."

Guided Reading Level: B

Feet		Substitution	Insertion	Omission	Reversal	Repetition	Self-Correction of Unacceptable Miscue	Meaning Change (Significant Miscue)
		MISCUES						
I see big feet.	4							
I see small feet.	8							
I see two feet.	12							
I see four feet.	16							
I see no feet!	20							
TOTAL								

Total Miscues ☐   Significant Miscues ☐

Word Recognition Scoring Guide		
Total Miscues	Level	Significant Miscues
0	Independent	0
—	Ind./Inst.	—
1	Instructional	1
2	Inst./Frust.	2
3 +	Frustration	3 +

Qualitative Analysis of Word Identification			
(0 = not evident 1 = emerging 2 = evident)			
Uses letter-sound relationships	0	1	2
Points to words while reading	0	1	2
Uses monitoring (rereads; corrects)	0	1	2
Knows high-frequency words	0	1	2
Possesses sight vocabulary	0	1	2
Exhibits persistence	0	1	2
Seems confident	0	1	2

Important Note: If the scoring guides are used, teacher judgment is especially important because of the length of the passage and the limited number of questions.

E Km (Middle K)

Feet

T 1. _____ What is this story about? [If student says "feet" say "tell me more."]
(different kinds of feet; big feet and small feet)

F 2. _____ What's something else the story says about feet?
(any one of the following: big feet, small feet, two feet, four feet, no feet)

I 3. _____ If you wanted to add more to the story, tell me what else you could write about feet.
(any logical response; feet are for walking, feet can be smelly)

E 4. _____ Where do you think you would probably need to go to see the feet in the story?
(any logical response; a zoo; outside)

V 5. _____ What does the word "small" mean?
(any logical response; tiny, not big)

Retelling Notes

Retelling Rubric

Independent Level/Excellent
States central or key ideas
Identifies important facts
Retains the general sequence of events
Relates most of the content in an organized manner

Instructional Level/Satisfactory
States most central or key ideas
Identifies some important facts
Retains the general sequence of events
Relates an overall sense of the content

Frustration Level/Unsatisfactory
Provides bits of information in a haphazard manner
Little apparent organization

	Questions Missed

Comprehension Scoring Guide

Questions Missed	Level
0	Independent
1	Ind./Inst.
1½	Instructional
2	Inst./Frust.
2½ +	Frustration

Qualitative Analysis of Comprehension
(0 = not evident   1 = emerging   2 = evident)

Seeks to construct meaning	0	1	2
Understands topic and major ideas	0	1	2
Identifies facts or details	0	1	2
Evaluates ideas from story	0	1	2
Makes and supports appropriate inferences	0	1	2
Seems engaged with story	0	1	2

Writing Prompt: Write about what you can do with your feet.

Rubric for Writing Response

3	• Response is very closely related to prompt. • Response makes complete sense. • Response is well organized. • Response meets all age-appropriate spelling expectations and writing conventions.
2	• Response is related to prompt. • Response makes sense. • Response is organized in an acceptable manner. • Response meets most age-appropriate spelling expectations and writing conventions.
1	• Response is loosely related to prompt. • Some aspects of response make sense. • Response is not well organized. • Response lacks some age-appropriate spelling expectations and writing conventions.
0	• Response is unrelated to prompt. • Response does not make sense. • Response is poorly organized. • Response lacks most age-appropriate spelling expectations and writing conventions.

Important Note: If the scoring guides are used, teacher judgment is especially important because of the length of the passage and the limited number of questions.

Student Book copy is on page 84.

E Ke (End K) Point to each word in the title as you read it. Then say: "Read this story about a spider. I'll ask you some questions about it when you're done."

Guided Reading Level: D

A Spider

A Spider		Substitution	Insertion	Omission	Reversal	Repetition	Self-Correction of Unacceptable Miscue	Meaning Change (Significant Miscue)
		MISCUES						
A spider can be big or little.	7							
It has eight legs.	11							
It has a head and tummy.	17							
It can spin a web. It eats bugs.	25							
TOTAL								

Total Miscues [ ]   Significant Miscues [ ]

Word Recognition Scoring Guide		
Total Miscues	Level	Significant Miscues
0	Independent	0
1	Ind./Inst.	—
2	Instructional	1
3	Inst./Frust.	2
4 +	Frustration	3 +

Qualitative Analysis of Word Identification			
(0 = not evident 1 = emerging 2 = evident)			
Uses letter-sound relationships	0	1	2
Points to words while reading	0	1	2
Uses monitoring (rereads; corrects)	0	1	2
Knows high-frequency words	0	1	2
Possesses sight vocabulary	0	1	2
Exhibits persistence	0	1	2
Seems confident	0	1	2

Important Note: If the scoring guides are used, teacher judgment is especially important because of the length of the passage and the limited number of questions.

E Ke (End K)

A Spider

T 1. _____ What is this story about? [If student says "a spider," say "tell me more."] (all about spiders; what spiders look like and what they do)

F 2. _____ What's something else the story says about spiders? (any one of the following: can be big or little, has eight legs, has a head and tummy, can spin a web, eats bugs)

I 3. _____ If you wanted to add more to the story, tell me what else the spider might do. (any logical response; it hangs from a web; it goes outside; it can scare some people)

E 4. _____ Where do you think you would probably need to go to see a spider? (any logical response; in a house; outside)

V 5. _____ What does the word "web" mean? (any logical response; something a spider makes to catch bugs; something a spider makes to walk or hang from)

	Questions Missed

Comprehension Scoring Guide	
Questions Missed	Level
0	Independent
1	Ind./Inst.
1½	Instructional
2	Inst./Frust.
2½ +	Frustration

Qualitative Analysis of Comprehension			
(0 = not evident 1 = emerging 2 = evident)			
Seeks to construct meaning	0	1	2
Understands topic and major ideas	0	1	2
Identifies facts or details	0	1	2
Evaluates ideas from story	0	1	2
Makes and supports appropriate inferences	0	1	2
Seems engaged with story	0	1	2

Retelling Notes

Retelling Rubric

Independent Level/Excellent
States central or key ideas
Identifies important facts
Retains the general sequence of events
Relates most of the content in an organized manner

Instructional Level/Satisfactory
States most central or key ideas
Identifies some important facts
Retains the general sequence of events
Relates an overall sense of the content

Frustration Level/Unsatisfactory
Provides bits of information in a haphazard manner
Little apparent organization

Writing Prompt: Write about what you would do if you saw a spider.

Rubric for Writing Response	
3	• Response is very closely related to prompt. • Response makes complete sense. • Response is well organized. • Response meets all age-appropriate spelling expectations and writing conventions.
2	• Response is related to prompt. • Response makes sense. • Response is organized in an acceptable manner. • Response meets most age-appropriate spelling expectations and writing conventions.
1	• Response is loosely related to prompt. • Some aspects of response make sense. • Response is not well organized. • Response lacks some age-appropriate spelling expectations and writing conventions.
0	• Response is unrelated to prompt. • Response does not make sense. • Response is poorly organized. • Response lacks most age-appropriate spelling expectations and writing conventions.

Important Note: If the scoring guides are used, teacher judgment is especially important because of the length of the passage and the limited number of questions.

Student Book copy is on page 85.

E 7141b (Beginning Grade 1) Point to each word in the title as you read it. Then say: "Read this story about fish. I'll ask you some questions about it when you're done."

Guided Reading Level: E

The Small Fish

	Substitution	Insertion	Omission	Reversal	Repetition	Self-Correction of Unacceptable Miscue	Meaning Change (Significant Miscue)
MISCUES							
There are two small fish. One is 7							
red and the other is blue. They live in 16							
the sea. They like to play. 22							
One day a big green fish came 29							
to the sea. It did not want to play. 38							
It wanted to eat the small fish. The 46							
big fish was hungry. 50							
TOTAL							

Total Miscues [ ]   Significant Miscues [ ]

Adapted from *Teaching Reading Pre-K–Grade 3* (3rd ed.) by Laurie Elish-Piper, Jerry L. Johns, and Susan Davis Lenski.

Word Recognition Scoring Guide		
Total Miscues	Level	Significant Miscues
0	Independent	0
1–2	Ind./Inst.	1
3	Instructional	2
4	Inst./Frust.	3
5 +	Frustration	4 +

Qualitative Analysis of Word Identification			
(0 = not evident 1 = emerging 2 = evident)			
Uses letter-sound relationships	0	1	2
Points to words while reading	0	1	2
Uses monitoring (rereads; corrects)	0	1	2
Knows high-frequency words	0	1	2
Possesses sight vocabulary	0	1	2
Exhibits persistence	0	1	2
Seems confident	0	1	2

Important Note: If the scoring guides are used, teacher judgment is especially important because of the length of the passage and the limited number of questions.

E 7141b (Beginning Grade 1)

The Small Fish

T 1. _____ What is this story about? [If student
             says "fish," say "tell me more."]
             (two small fish that almost get eaten by
             a big fish)

F 2. _____ What size was the green fish?
             (big)

I 3. _____ How do you think the small fish felt
             when they saw the big fish?
             (any logical response; afraid; scared)

E 4. _____ What do you think the red fish and the
             blue fish did when they saw the
             green fish?
             (any logical response; they swam away
             quickly; they hid)

V 5. _____ What does "play" mean?
             (any logical response; to have fun; to do
             a sport; to do a game)

Retelling Notes

Retelling Rubric

Independent Level/Excellent
States central or key ideas
Identifies important facts
Retains the general sequence of events
Relates most of the content in an organized manner

Instructional Level/Satisfactory
States most central or key ideas
Identifies some important facts
Retains the general sequence of events
Relates an overall sense of the content

Frustration Level/Unsatisfactory
Provides bits of information in a haphazard manner
Little apparent organization

☐ Questions
  Missed

Comprehension Scoring Guide	
Questions Missed	Level
0	Independent
1	Ind./Inst.
1½	Instructional
2	Inst./Frust.
2½ +	Frustration

Qualitative Analysis of Comprehension			
(0 = not evident 1 = emerging 2 = evident)			
Seeks to construct meaning	0	1	2
Understands topic and major ideas	0	1	2
Identifies facts or details	0	1	2
Evaluates ideas from story	0	1	2
Makes and supports appropriate inferences	0	1	2
Seems engaged with story	0	1	2

Writing Prompt: Write about different kinds of fish.

Rubric for Writing Response	
3	• Response is very closely related to prompt. • Response makes complete sense. • Response is well organized. • Response meets all age-appropriate spelling expectations and writing conventions.
2	• Response is related to prompt. • Response makes sense. • Response is organized in an acceptable manner. • Response meets most age-appropriate spelling expectations and writing conventions.
1	• Response is loosely related to prompt. • Some aspects of response make sense. • Response is not well organized. • Response lacks some age-appropriate spelling expectations and writing conventions.
0	• Response is unrelated to prompt. • Response does not make sense. • Response is poorly organized. • Response lacks most age-appropriate spelling expectations and writing conventions.

Important Note: If the scoring guides are used, teacher judgment is especially important because of the length of the passage and the limited number of questions.

Student Book copy is on page 86.

E 7141m (Middle Grade 1) Point to each word in the title as you read it. Then say: "Read this story about Blue. I'll ask you some questions about it when you're done."

Guided Reading Level: G

Blue

	Substitution	Insertion	Omission	Reversal	Repetition	Self-Correction of Unacceptable Miscue	Meaning Change (Significant Miscue)
			MISCUES				
One day Joe looked for his dog, Blue. 8							
Joe wanted to play ball with Blue. Joe looked 17							
in his room. He looked in the kitchen. He 26							
looked under the table. He looked on the 34							
couch. He looked all around the house. 41							
But Joe could not find Blue. 47							
Joe went outside. He called, "Blue! 53							
Come here, Blue!" Then he heard something. 60							
The sound led him to an old well. He looked 70							
down into the well. There was no water in 79							
the well. But there was his small black dog! 88							
Joe was happy he found Blue. Blue was 96							
happy to see Joe! 100							
TOTAL							

Total Miscues [ ]   Significant Miscues [ ]

Word Recognition Scoring Guide		
Total Miscues	Level	Significant Miscues
0–1	Independent	0–1
2–4	Ind./Inst.	2
5	Instructional	3
6–9	Inst./Frust.	4
10 +	Frustration	5 +

Oral Reading Rate	Norm Group Percentile
⎯⎯ WPM)6000	☐ 90 ☐ 75 ☐ 50 ☐ 25 ☐ 10

E 7141m (Middle Grade 1)

Blue

T   1. _____   What is this story about?
(Joe looking for Blue; a boy and his dog)

F   2. _____   What is this dog's name?
(Blue)

F   3. _____   What did Joe want to do?
(play ball)

F   4. _____   Where did Joe look for Blue?
(his room; the kitchen; under the table; on the couch; all around the house [any 1])

F   5. _____   What did Joe do when he couldn't find Blue in the house?
(went outside)

F   6. _____   What did Joe do when he heard something?
(he walked toward the well)

F   7. _____   How did Joe feel when he found Blue?
(happy)

I   8. _____   Why do you think Blue was in the well?
(any logical response; he fell; he was hiding from Joe)

E   9. _____   How do you think Joe will get Blue out of the well?
(any logical response)

V   10. _____   What is a "well"?
(a deep hole that water comes out of)

☐	Questions Missed

Comprehension Scoring Guide

Questions Missed	Level
0–1	Independent
1½–2	Ind./Inst.
2½	Instructional
3–4½	Inst./Frust.
5 +	Frustration

Retelling Notes

Retelling Rubric

Independent Level/Excellent
States central or key ideas
Identifies important facts
Retains the general sequence of events
Relates most of the content in an organized manner

Instructional Level/Satisfactory
States most central or key ideas
Identifies some important facts
Retains the general sequence of events
Relates an overall sense of the content

Frustration Level/Unsatisfactory
Provides bits of information in a haphazard manner
Little apparent organization

Writing Prompt: Write about something you could find in a well.

Rubric for Writing Response

3	• Response is very closely related to prompt. • Response makes complete sense. • Response is well organized. • Response meets all age-appropriate spelling expectations and writing conventions.
2	• Response is related to prompt. • Response makes sense. • Response is organized in an acceptable manner. • Response meets most age-appropriate spelling expectations and writing conventions.
1	• Response is loosely related to prompt. • Some aspects of response make sense. • Response is not well organized. • Response lacks some age-appropriate spelling expectations and writing conventions.
0	• Response is unrelated to prompt. • Response does not make sense. • Response is poorly organized. • Response lacks most age-appropriate spelling expectations and writing conventions.

Student Book copy is on page 87.

E 7141e (End Grade 1) Point to each word in the title as you read it. Then say: "Read this story about the moon. I'll ask you some questions about it when you're done."

Guided Reading Level: J

	MISCUES						
	Substitution	Insertion	Omission	Reversal	Repetition	Self-Correction of Unacceptable Miscue	Meaning Change (Significant Miscue)
The Moon							
The moon has a face. My friend says it is　10							
a man. I asked Miss Green. She said the moon　20							
face was made by big rocks that bumped　28							
and bumped. This made big holes. At night　36							
the holes look like a face. No one lives on the　47							
moon. It is too hot or cold to live there. It is　59							
hard to walk on the moon, too. I would be　69							
too light. I would go up into the sky.　78							
The moon seems to change from big to　86							
little and back again. I like to see it before　96							
I go to sleep.　100							
TOTAL							

Total Miscues ☐   Significant Miscues ☐

Word Recognition Scoring Guide		
Total Miscues	Level	Significant Miscues
0–1	Independent	0–1
2–4	Ind./Inst.	2
5	Instructional	3
6–9	Inst./Frust.	4
10 +	Frustration	5 +

Oral Reading Rate	Norm Group Percentile
___)6000 WPM	☐ 90 ☐ 75 ☐ 50 ☐ 25 ☐ 10

E 7141e (End Grade 1)

The Moon

T 1. _____ What is this story about?
(how the moon looks and changes)

F 2. _____ What did the friend say about the moon?
(it is a man)

F 3. _____ Who told the person in the story how the face was made?
(Miss Green)

F 4. _____ How were the holes in the moon made?
(big rocks bumped and bumped)

F 5. _____ What did the story say about why we can't live on the moon?
(it is too hot or cold; it is hard to walk [either 1])

F 6. _____ How does the moon seem to change?
(from big to little and back again)

F 7. _____ Why does the friend probably think the moon is a man?
(any logical response; it has a face)

I 8. _____ Why might it be too hot on the moon?
(any logical response; too close to the sun)

E 9. _____ What would you do if you could visit the moon in a spaceship?
(any logical response)

V 10. _____ What does "light" mean in the story?
(not heavy; doesn't weigh a lot)

	Questions Missed

Comprehension Scoring Guide

Questions Missed	Level
0–1	Independent
1½–2	Ind./Inst.
2½	Instructional
3–4½	Inst./Frust.
5 +	Frustration

Retelling Notes

Retelling Rubric

Independent Level/Excellent
States central or key ideas
Identifies important facts
Retains the general sequence of events
Relates most of the content in an organized manner

Instructional Level/Satisfactory
States most central or key ideas
Identifies some important facts
Retains the general sequence of events
Relates an overall sense of the content

Frustration Level/Unsatisfactory
Provides bits of information in a haphazard manner
Little apparent organization

Writing Prompt: Write about what you might like to do on the moon.

	Rubric for Writing Response
3	• Response is very closely related to prompt. • Response makes complete sense. • Response is well organized. • Response meets all age-appropriate spelling expectations and writing conventions.
2	• Response is related to prompt. • Response makes sense. • Response is organized in an acceptable manner. • Response meets most age-appropriate spelling expectations and writing conventions.
1	• Response is loosely related to prompt. • Some aspects of response make sense. • Response is not well organized. • Response lacks some age-appropriate spelling expectations and writing conventions.
0	• Response is unrelated to prompt. • Response does not make sense. • Response is poorly organized. • Response lacks most age-appropriate spelling expectations and writing conventions.

Student Book copy is on page 88.

E 8224 (Grade 2) Say: "I'd like you to read out loud [silently]. Think about what you're reading because I'll ask you some questions about it when you're done. Please begin here." [Point to title.]

Guided Reading Level: L; Lexile: 590

Weather		Substitution	Insertion	Omission	Reversal	Repetition	Self-Correction of Unacceptable Miscue	Meaning Change (Significant Miscue)
		MISCUES						
Weather is a word that tells people what	8							
conditions are like outside. The weather might	15							
be rainy, or it might be cold. The weather	24							
might be clear. Some people study the weather.	32							
They measure the temperature and how fast	39							
the wind blows, and they measure how much	47							
snow and rain fall.	51							
People use weather information to make plans.	58							
Farmers know when to plant crops. Sports teams	66							
plan when to play. Parents know what their	74							
children should wear to school. Children may	81							
decide whether they should play inside or outside.	89							
If bad weather is coming, people make plans	97							
to be safe.	100							
TOTAL								

Total Miscues [ ]   Significant Miscues [ ]

Word Recognition Scoring Guide		
Total Miscues	Level	Significant Miscues
0–1	Independent	0–1
2–4	Ind./Inst.	2
5	Instructional	3
6–9	Inst./Frust.	4
10 +	Frustration	5 +

Oral Reading Rate	Norm Group Percentile				
⎯⎯ WPM)6000	☐ 90	☐ 75	☐ 50	☐ 25	☐ 10

E 8224 (Grade 2)

Weather

T 1. _____ What is this story about?
             (weather)

F 2. _____ What is one kind of weather you read
             about?
             (rainy; cold; snow; clear)

F 3. _____ What are two parts of weather people
             can measure?
             (temperature; wind speed; snow fall;
             rain [any 2])

F 4. _____ What can farmers plan if they know
             the weather?
             (when to plant crops)

F 5. _____ What can sports teams plan by studying
             the weather?
             (when to play)

F 6. _____ What can parents know by studying
             the weather?
             (what clothes children should wear)

F 7. _____ What can people do if they know bad
             weather is coming?
             (make plans to be safe)

I 8. _____ What plans might your school make if
             a storm is coming?
             (any logical response; have children
             stay inside; cancel school)

E 9. _____ What kind of weather do you like best?
             Why?
             (any logical response)

V 10. _____ What does "temperature" mean?
              (how hot or cold something is)

Questions Missed

Comprehension Scoring Guide

Questions Missed	Level
0–1	Independent
1½–2	Ind./Inst.
2½	Instructional
3–4½	Inst./Frust.
5 +	Frustration

Writing Prompt: Write about your favorite kind of weather.

Rubric for Writing Response

3	• Response is very closely related to prompt. • Response makes complete sense. • Response is well organized. • Response meets all age-appropriate spelling expectations and writing conventions.
2	• Response is related to prompt. • Response makes sense. • Response is organized in an acceptable manner. • Response meets most age-appropriate spelling expectations and writing conventions.
1	• Response is loosely related to prompt. • Some aspects of response make sense. • Response is not well organized. • Response lacks some age-appropriate spelling expectations and writing conventions.
0	• Response is unrelated to prompt. • Response does not make sense. • Response is poorly organized. • Response lacks most age-appropriate spelling expectations and writing conventions.

Student Book copy is on page 89.

E 3183 (Grade 3) Say: "I'd like you to read out loud [silently]. Think about what you're reading because I'll ask you some questions about it when you're done. Please begin here." [Point to title.]

Guided Reading Level: O; Lexile: 580

		MISCUES						
Cricket Song		Substitution	Insertion	Omission	Reversal	Repetition	Self-Correction of Unacceptable Miscue	Meaning Change (Significant Miscue)
It is a summer night. I try to sleep, but a	11							
sound keeps waking me. It is a cricket. This	20							
bug does not sing with its mouth. The rough	29							
wings of the male cricket make sounds. He	37							
rubs his wings against each other.	43							
I try to find the bug, but it is hard. The sound	55							
does not come from one spot. It would also be	65							
hard to see the cricket because it can be as	75							
small as the nail on my thumb. Some people	84							
think the cricket brings luck. Maybe they know	92							
how to fall asleep to the cricket song.	100							
TOTAL								

Total Miscues ☐   Significant Miscues ☐

Word Recognition Scoring Guide		
Total Miscues	Level	Significant Miscues
0–1	Independent	0–1
2–4	Ind./Inst.	2
5	Instructional	3
6–9	Inst./Frust.	4
10 +	Frustration	5 +

Oral Reading Rate	Norm Group Percentile
___)6000 WPM	☐ 90 ☐ 75 ☐ 50 ☐ 25 ☐ 10

E 3183 (Grade 3)

Cricket Song

T 1. _____ What is this story about?
(how a cricket makes a song; a cricket)

F 2. _____ When does this story take place?
(night; summer)

F 3. _____ Why can't the person in the story sleep?
(a sound keeps him or her awake; the cricket song)

F 4. _____ How does the cricket make its sound?
(it rubs its wings together)

F 5. _____ What type of cricket makes this sound?
(male)

F 6. _____ Why was the cricket difficult to find?
(the sound didn't seem to come from one spot; the cricket is very small [any 1])

F 7. _____ What do some people think the cricket brings?
(luck)

I 8. _____ Why might only the male make this sound?
(any logical response; females don't have rough wings)

E 9. _____ How do you think you would feel if a cricket kept you awake? Why?
(any logical response; tired; angry)

V 10. _____ What does "nail" mean in this story?
(what's on your finger; part of finger that protects the tip)

[ ] Questions Missed

Comprehension Scoring Guide	
Questions Missed	Level
0–1	Independent
1½–2	Ind./Inst.
2½	Instructional
3–4½	Inst./Frust.
5 +	Frustration

Retelling Notes

Retelling Rubric

Independent Level/Excellent
States central or key ideas
Identifies important facts
Retains the general sequence of events
Relates most of the content in an organized manner

Instructional Level/Satisfactory
States most central or key ideas
Identifies some important facts
Retains the general sequence of events
Relates an overall sense of the content

Frustration Level/Unsatisfactory
Provides bits of information in a haphazard manner
Little apparent organization

Writing Prompt: Write about an insect you've seen.

	Rubric for Writing Response
3	• Response is very closely related to prompt. • Response makes complete sense. • Response is well organized. • Response meets all age-appropriate spelling expectations and writing conventions.
2	• Response is related to prompt. • Response makes sense. • Response is organized in an acceptable manner. • Response meets most age-appropriate spelling expectations and writing conventions.
1	• Response is loosely related to prompt. • Some aspects of response make sense. • Response is not well organized. • Response lacks some age-appropriate spelling expectations and writing conventions.
0	• Response is unrelated to prompt. • Response does not make sense. • Response is poorly organized. • Response lacks most age-appropriate spelling expectations and writing conventions.

Student Book copy is on page 90.

E 5414 (Grade 4) Say: "I'd like you to read out loud [silently]. Think about what you're reading because I'll ask you some questions about it when you're done. Please begin here." [Point to title.]

Guided Reading Level: R; Lexile: 860

Seaweed

		MISCUES						
	Substitution	Insertion	Omission	Reversal	Repetition	Self-Correction of Unacceptable Miscue	Meaning Change (Significant Miscue)	

Text	#	Substitution	Insertion	Omission	Reversal	Repetition	Self-Correction of Unacceptable Miscue	Meaning Change (Significant Miscue)
Some of the world's oldest plants grow	7							
underwater in the ocean. They are called algae or	16							
seaweed. Brown seaweed or kelp can be found	24							
in the coldest water. It contains a high amount of	34							
iodine and is often an ingredient in jelly and	43							
make-up. Red seaweed is found in the lower parts	53							
of the ocean. It has no roots, but uses hold-fasts to	65							
stick to the bottom of the ocean floor. Sometimes	74							
red seaweed is provided to cattle because of its	83							
nutritious value. Green algae lives in fresh water,	91							
and one-celled forms of this seaweed can swim.	100							
TOTAL								

Total Miscues ☐   Significant Miscues ☐

Word Recognition Scoring Guide		
Total Miscues	Level	Significant Miscues
0–1	Independent	0–1
2–4	Ind./Inst.	2
5	Instructional	3
6–9	Inst./Frust.	4
10 +	Frustration	5 +

Oral Reading Rate	Norm Group Percentile
____)6000 WPM	☐ 90 ☐ 75 ☐ 50 ☐ 25 ☐ 10

E 5414 (Grade 4)

Seaweed

T 1. _____ What is this passage about?
(different types of algae or seaweed;
plants)

F 2. _____ Where can some of the oldest plants
be found?
(in the ocean)

F 3. _____ What were two colors of seaweed
mentioned in the passage?
(brown; red; green [any 2])

F 4. _____ Where is brown seaweed found?
(in cold water)

F 5. _____ What is made from brown seaweed?
(jelly; make-up [either 1])

F 6. _____ What does red seaweed use instead of
roots to anchor itself?
(hold-fasts)

F 7. _____ How do some green algae move
around?
(they swim; hook onto something)

I 8. _____ What color is iodine? Why?
(brown; a shade of brown; it's made
from brown seaweed)

E 9. _____ What do you think is the most important
use of seaweed? Why?
(any logical response)

V 10. _____ What does "nutritious" mean?
(any logical response; good for you;
contains a lot of nutrients)

Questions Missed

Comprehension Scoring Guide

Questions Missed	Level
0–1	Independent
1½–2	Ind./Inst.
2½	Instructional
3–4½	Inst./Frust.
5 +	Frustration

Retelling Notes

Retelling Rubric

Independent Level/Excellent

States central or key ideas
Identifies important facts
Retains the general sequence of events
Relates most of the content in an organized manner

Instructional Level/Satisfactory

States most central or key ideas
Identifies some important facts
Retains the general sequence of events
Relates an overall sense of the content

Frustration Level/Unsatisfactory

Provides bits of information in a haphazard manner
Little apparent organization

Writing Prompt: Write about something in the ocean besides seaweed.

Rubric for Writing Response

3	• Response is very closely related to prompt. • Response makes complete sense. • Response is well organized. • Response meets all age-appropriate spelling expectations and writing conventions.
2	• Response is related to prompt. • Response makes sense. • Response is organized in an acceptable manner. • Response meets most age-appropriate spelling expectations and writing conventions.
1	• Response is loosely related to prompt. • Some aspects of response make sense. • Response is not well organized. • Response lacks some age-appropriate spelling expectations and writing conventions.
0	• Response is unrelated to prompt. • Response does not make sense. • Response is poorly organized. • Response lacks most age-appropriate spelling expectations and writing conventions.

Student Book copy is on page 91.

E 8595 (Grade 5) Say: "I'd like you to read out loud [silently]. Think about what you're reading because I'll ask you some questions about it when you're done. Please begin here." [Point to title.]

Guided Reading Level: U; Lexile: 910

All Kinds of Bubbles

		MISCUES						
	Substitution	Insertion	Omission	Reversal	Repetition	Self-Correction of Unacceptable Miscue	Meaning Change (Significant Miscue)
Soap bubbles can be exciting to play with on — 9							
a hot summer day. Dip your wand in the bottle — 19							
and blow gently or spin around quickly. This is — 28							
just one kind of bubble—you may have seen — 37							
other forms too. Large cardboard boxes may have — 45							
plastic bubble wrap inside to keep fragile objects — 53							
from breaking. These bubbles are fun to pop. — 61							
Another type of bubble can be found in fizzy — 70							
beverages. It is created when carbonated water is — 78							
mixed with sugar and flavors. When you blow — 86							
into a straw that is in soda, the forced air forms — 97							
many tiny bubbles. — 100							
TOTAL							

Total Miscues ☐   Significant Miscues ☐

Word Recognition Scoring Guide		
Total Miscues	Level	Significant Miscues
0–1	Independent	0–1
2–4	Ind./Inst.	2
5	Instructional	3
6–9	Inst./Frust.	4
10 +	Frustration	5 +

Oral Reading Rate	Norm Group Percentile
⎯⎯⎯ WPM)6000	☐ 90 ☐ 75 ☐ 50 ☐ 25 ☐ 10

E 8595 (Grade 5)

All Kinds of Bubbles

T 1. _____ What is this passage about?
              (different kinds of bubbles)

F 2. _____ What were some types of bubbles
              mentioned in the story?
              (soap; plastic; soda or pop [any 2])

F 3. _____ When did the story say you might play
              with soap bubbles?
              (on a hot day; on a summer day)

F 4. _____ Why is bubble wrap used in boxes?
              (to keep objects from breaking)

F 5. _____ Why is bubble wrap fun?
              (you can pop it)

F 6. _____ Tell me two things soda or pop is
              made of.
              (carbonated water; sugar; flavors
              [any 2])

F 7. _____ How did the passage say you could
              make bubbles in soda or pop?
              (blow into the straw; forced air forms
              bubbles)

I 8. _____ How are the kinds of bubbles mentioned
              in this story different?
              (any logical response)

E 9. _____ Which type of bubble would you prefer
              to play with? Why?
              (any logical response)

V 10. _____ What does "carbonated" mean?
              (full of bubbles)

	Questions Missed

Comprehension Scoring Guide	
Questions Missed	Level
0–1	Independent
1½–2	Ind./Inst.
2½	Instructional
3–4½	Inst./Frust.
5 +	Frustration

Retelling Notes

Retelling Rubric

Independent Level/Excellent
States central or key ideas
Identifies important facts
Retains the general sequence of events
Relates most of the content in an organized manner

Instructional Level/Satisfactory
States most central or key ideas
Identifies some important facts
Retains the general sequence of events
Relates an overall sense of the content

Frustration Level/Unsatisfactory
Provides bits of information in a haphazard manner
Little apparent organization

Writing Prompt: Write about things that are round besides bubbles.

	Rubric for Writing Response
3	• Response is very closely related to prompt. • Response makes complete sense. • Response is well organized. • Response meets all age-appropriate spelling expectations and writing conventions.
2	• Response is related to prompt. • Response makes sense. • Response is organized in an acceptable manner. • Response meets most age-appropriate spelling expectations and writing conventions.
1	• Response is loosely related to prompt. • Some aspects of response make sense. • Response is not well organized. • Response lacks some age-appropriate spelling expectations and writing conventions.
0	• Response is unrelated to prompt. • Response does not make sense. • Response is poorly organized. • Response lacks most age-appropriate spelling expectations and writing conventions.

Student Book copy is on page 92.

E 6867 (Grade 6) Say: "I'd like you to read out loud [silently]. Think about what you're reading because I'll ask you some questions about it when you're done. Please begin here." [Point to title.]

Lexile: 1050

Cave Icicles		Substitution	Insertion	Omission	Reversal	Repetition	Self-Correction of Unacceptable Miscue	Meaning Change (Significant Miscue)
It is common to see icicles formed when	8							
water drips off house roofs during winter time in	17							
frigid climates. The same process, when slowed	24							
down, explains how stone icicles can form in	32							
caves. Water dripping from the ceiling of a cave	41							
contains a common mineral called calcite. Little	48							
pieces of calcite sometimes stick to the cave	56							
ceiling or floor. After several years, small stone	64							
icicles begin to form. They grow less than an	73							
inch per year, and many do not get any longer	83							
than one foot. Differently colored icicles are	90							
created when the water contains elements of	97							
iron or copper.	100							
TOTAL								

Total Miscues [ ]   Significant Miscues [ ]

Word Recognition Scoring Guide		
Total Miscues	Level	Significant Miscues
0–1	Independent	0–1
2–4	Ind./Inst.	2
5	Instructional	3
6–9	Inst./Frust.	4
10 +	Frustration	5 +

Oral Reading Rate	Norm Group Percentile
WPM $\overline{)6000}$	☐ 90 ☐ 75 ☐ 50 ☐ 25 ☐ 10

E 6867 (Grade 6)

Cave Icicles

T 1. _____ What is this passage about?
(cave icicles; how stone icicles are
formed)

F 2. _____ At what rate do stone icicles build?
(less than an inch per year)

F 3. _____ Where does the water drip?
(from the ceiling; on the floor)

F 4. _____ What can the water contain?
(calcite; iron; copper; a mineral [any 2])

F 5. _____ How long does it take for a small stone
icicle to fully form?
(several years)

F 6. _____ What is the longest the icicles usually
get?
(one foot)

F 7. _____ How are colored icicles formed?
(when water contains iron or copper)

I 8. _____ How are stone and water icicles
different?
(any logical response; stone icicles form
slowly)

E 9. _____ Explain how you would prepare to find
stone icicles in a cave?
(any logical response)

V 10. _____ What does the word "created" mean?
(formed; made; developed)

	Questions Missed

Retelling Notes

Retelling Rubric

Independent Level/Excellent
States central or key ideas
Identifies important facts
Retains the general sequence of events
Relates most of the content in an organized manner

Instructional Level/Satisfactory
States most central or key ideas
Identifies some important facts
Retains the general sequence of events
Relates an overall sense of the content

Frustration Level/Unsatisfactory
Provides bits of information in a haphazard manner
Little apparent organization

Writing Prompt: Write about what it might be like to visit a cave.

Rubric for Writing Response

3	• Response is very closely related to prompt. • Response makes complete sense. • Response is well organized. • Response meets all age-appropriate spelling expectations and writing conventions.
2	• Response is related to prompt. • Response makes sense. • Response is organized in an acceptable manner. • Response meets most age-appropriate spelling expectations and writing conventions.
1	• Response is loosely related to prompt. • Some aspects of response make sense. • Response is not well organized. • Response lacks some age-appropriate spelling expectations and writing conventions.
0	• Response is unrelated to prompt. • Response does not make sense. • Response is poorly organized. • Response lacks most age-appropriate spelling expectations and writing conventions.

Student Book copy is on page 93.

E 3717 (Grade 7) Say: "I'd like you to read out loud [silently]. Think about what you're reading because I'll ask you some questions about it when you're done. Please begin here." [Point to title.]

Lexile: 1100

History of the Cornett

		Substitution	Insertion	Omission	Reversal	Repetition	Self-Correction of Unacceptable Miscue	Meaning Change (Significant Miscue)
		MISCUES						
Over 300 years ago in Medieval Germany,	7							
an instrument called the cornett was extremely	14							
popular, especially in church choirs. It was	21							
considered the most difficult wind instrument to	28							
play, requiring significant patience.	32							
The cornett is made from a curved piece of	41							
wood which is carved to make eight sides and	50							
then wrapped in leather. Six holes and one	58							
thumbhole are covered by different fingers to	65							
create notes, similar to a recorder. The	72							
mouthpiece is an ornamental metal or ivory cup	80							
that can be removed until the musician is ready.	89							
Cornetts still exist, but they are usually straight	97							
instead of curved.	100							
TOTAL								

Total Miscues ☐   Significant Miscues ☐

Word Recognition Scoring Guide		
Total Miscues	Level	Significant Miscues
0–1	Independent	0–1
2–4	Ind./Inst.	2
5	Instructional	3
6–9	Inst./Frust.	4
10 +	Frustration	5 +

Oral Reading Rate	Norm Group Percentile	
___ WPM)6000	☐ 90 ☐ 75 ☐ 50 ☐ 25 ☐ 10	

E 3717 (Grade 7)

History of the Cornett

T 1. _____ What is this passage about?
(how cornetts look; the history of the cornett)

F 2. _____ Where were cornetts popular?
(Germany)

F 3. _____ What kind of instrument is a cornett?
(wind; wooden)

F 4. _____ How many sides does it have?
(eight)

F 5. _____ How many holes does it have to sound notes?
(six; seven)

F 6. _____ What is wrapped on the outside of the cornett?
(leather)

F 7. _____ How has the cornett changed over the years?
(straight; not curved)

I 8. _____ Why might the instrument be difficult to play?
(any logical response; the mouthpiece might fall out; the sounds are hard to make correctly; curved)

E 9. _____ Why might the instrument be wrapped in leather?
(any logical response; to protect it; to make it easy to handle)

V 10. _____ What does "exist" mean?
(still around; still made)

[ ] Questions Missed

Comprehension Scoring Guide	
Questions Missed	Level
0–1	Independent
1½–2	Ind./Inst.
2½	Instructional
3–4½	Inst./Frust.
5 +	Frustration

Retelling Notes

Retelling Rubric

Independent Level/Excellent
States central or key ideas
Identifies important facts
Retains the general sequence of events
Relates most of the content in an organized manner

Instructional Level/Satisfactory
States most central or key ideas
Identifies some important facts
Retains the general sequence of events
Relates an overall sense of the content

Frustration Level/Unsatisfactory
Provides bits of information in a haphazard manner
Little apparent organization

Writing Prompt: Write about a musical instrument that you've seen or heard.

	Rubric for Writing Response
3	• Response is very closely related to prompt. • Response makes complete sense. • Response is well organized. • Response meets all age-appropriate spelling expectations and writing conventions.
2	• Response is related to prompt. • Response makes sense. • Response is organized in an acceptable manner. • Response meets most age-appropriate spelling expectations and writing conventions.
1	• Response is loosely related to prompt. • Some aspects of response make sense. • Response is not well organized. • Response lacks some age-appropriate spelling expectations and writing conventions.
0	• Response is unrelated to prompt. • Response does not make sense. • Response is poorly organized. • Response lacks most age-appropriate spelling expectations and writing conventions.

Student Book copy is on page 94.

E 8183 (Grade 8) Say: "I'd like you to read out loud [silently]. Think about what you're reading because I'll ask you some questions about it when you're done. Please begin here." [Point to title.]

Lexile: 1150

Sailing Explorers

		MISCUES						
	Substitution	Insertion	Omission	Reversal	Repetition	Self-Correction of Unacceptable Miscue	Meaning Change (Significant Miscue)
Over 400 years ago, European companies 6							
hired adventurous sailors to find new water routes 14							
so they could claim land and trade goods more 23							
effectively. An English company employed a sea 30							
captain named Henry Hudson to find a northeast 38							
passage between Europe and Asia. After many 45							
unsuccessful attempts blocked by polar ice, he 52							
was hired by the Dutch East India Trade Company. 61							
Hudson and his shipmates wanted to discover a 69							
better route. They headed towards the east coast 77							
of what is currently the United States and sailed 86							
up a river in New York. The river now carries 96							
Henry Hudson's last name. 100							
TOTAL							

Total Miscues [ ]   Significant Miscues [ ]

Word Recognition Scoring Guide		
Total Miscues	Level	Significant Miscues
0–1	Independent	0–1
2–4	Ind./Inst.	2
5	Instructional	3
6–9	Inst./Frust.	4
10 +	Frustration	5 +

Oral Reading Rate	Norm Group Percentile	
‾‾‾‾ WPM)6000	☐ 90 ☐ 75 ☐ 50 ☐ 25 ☐ 10	

E 8183 (Grade 8)

Sailing Explorers

T 1. _____ What is this passage about?
(Henry Hudson's travels; finding water routes)

F 2. _____ How many years ago did these events take place?
(over 300 years ago)

F 3. _____ Who hired sailors in this passage?
(English companies; Dutch companies [either 1])

F 4. _____ Why did the English and Dutch companies hire sailors?
(to find new water routes and trade more easily)

F 5. _____ Who was Henry Hudson?
(an English sea captain)

F 6. _____ What was Henry Hudson trying to locate?
(a northeast passage between Europe and Asia)

F 7. _____ Where did Hudson finally arrive in this passage?
(in the United States; Hudson River)

I 8. _____ Why do you think Hudson discontinued working for the English company?
(any logical response; unsuccessful mission; better opportunity with the Dutch Company; polar ice blocked his journey)

E 9. _____ Why did Hudson probably change direction from northeast to the United States?
(any logical response; bad weather; wind change)

V 10. _____ What does "course" mean?
(direction of travel; the way you head)

☐ Questions Missed

Comprehension Scoring Guide	
Questions Missed	Level
0–1	Independent
1½–2	Ind./Inst.
2½	Instructional
3–4½	Inst./Frust.
5 +	Frustration

Retelling Notes

Retelling Rubric

Independent Level/Excellent
States central or key ideas
Identifies important facts
Retains the general sequence of events
Relates most of the content in an organized manner

Instructional Level/Satisfactory
States most central or key ideas
Identifies some important facts
Retains the general sequence of events
Relates an overall sense of the content

Frustration Level/Unsatisfactory
Provides bits of information in a haphazard manner
Little apparent organization

Writing Prompt: Write about a trip you'd like to take.

	Rubric for Writing Response
3	• Response is very closely related to prompt. • Response makes complete sense. • Response is well organized. • Response meets all age-appropriate spelling expectations and writing conventions.
2	• Response is related to prompt. • Response makes sense. • Response is organized in an acceptable manner. • Response meets most age-appropriate spelling expectations and writing conventions.
1	• Response is loosely related to prompt. • Some aspects of response make sense. • Response is not well organized. • Response lacks some age-appropriate spelling expectations and writing conventions.
0	• Response is unrelated to prompt. • Response does not make sense. • Response is poorly organized. • Response lacks most age-appropriate spelling expectations and writing conventions.

FORM
LL

Performance Booklet

Teacher Copy

Form LL

Primary Uses:
- Silent Reading (Literary)

Other Uses:
- Oral Reading
- Progress Monitoring

Note: This Performance Booklet is on the Basic Reading Inventory website.

Miscue Summary Sheet for Forms LL and LI

MISCUES							
Substitution	Insertion	Omission	Reversal	Repetition	Self-Correction of Unacceptable Miscue	Meaning Change (Significant Miscue)	

Name _____ Date _____

Passage Title _____

Form _____

Total Miscues ☐   Significant Miscues ☐

BASIC READING INVENTORY PERFORMANCE BOOKLET

Jerry L. Johns, Laurie Elish-Piper, and Beth Johns

Student _____   Grade _____   Gender   M   F   Date of Test _____

School _____   Examiner _____   Date of Birth _____

Address _____   Current Book/Level _____   Age _____

SUMMARY OF STUDENT'S READING PERFORMANCE

Grade	Word Recognition		Comprehension		Oral Reading Rate		Silent Reading Rate
	Miscues	Level	Questions Missed	Level	Words per Minute (WPM)	Norm Group Percentile	Words per Minute (WPM)
3							
4							
5							
6							
7							
8							
9						■	
10						■	
11						■	
12						■	

ESTIMATE OF READING LEVELS

Independent _____   Instructional _____   Frustration _____

INFORMAL ANALYSIS OF ORAL READING

Oral Reading Behaviors	Frequency of Occurrence			General Impact on Meaning		
	Seldom	Sometimes	Frequently	No Change	Little Change	Much Change
Substitutions						
Insertions						
Omissions						
Reversals						
Repetitions						

LISTENING LEVEL

Form _____

Grade	Questions Missed	Level
3		
4		
5		
6		
7		
8		
9		
10		
11		
12		

ESTIMATED LEVEL: _____

GENERAL OBSERVATIONS

QUALITATIVE ANALYSIS OF BASIC READING INVENTORY INSIGHTS

General Directions: Note the degree to which the student shows behavior or evidence in the following areas. Space is provided for additional items.

	Seldom Weak Poor			Always Strong Excellent

COMPREHENSION

Seeks to construct meaning

Makes predictions

Activates background knowledge

Possesses appropriate concepts and vocabulary

Monitors reading

Varies reading rate as needed

Understands topic and major ideas

Remembers facts or details

Makes and supports appropriate inferences

Evaluates ideas from passages

Understands vocabulary used

Provides appropriate definitions of words

Engages with passages

_____

_____

WORD IDENTIFICATION

Possesses numerous strategies

Uses strategies flexibly

Uses graphophonic information

Uses semantic information

Uses syntactic information

Knows high-frequency words automatically

Possesses sight vocabulary

_____

_____

ORAL AND SILENT READING

Reads fluently

Reads with expression

Attends to punctuation

Keeps place while reading

Reads at appropriate rate

Reads silently without vocalization

_____

_____

ATTITUDE AND CONFIDENCE

Enjoys reading

Demonstrates willingness to risk

Possesses positive self-concept

Chooses to read

Regards himself/herself as a reader

Exhibits persistence

_____

_____

Danny and the Dragon

"Mother, there's a dragon after me! It won't go away!"	10
The next day when Danny went out, there it was again, roaring and blowing fire at	26
Danny. It was enormous and Danny felt miniature. "Leave me alone!"	37
Danny sprinted down the pathway to the river and hid behind a boulder to see if	53
the dragon was still coming—it was. He had to get rid of that dragon. He wandered	70
home through the woods and wanted a plan to trick the dragon.	82
In bed that evening, Danny developed his plan. He had to trick the dragon into	97
the river because he knew the dragon couldn't swim.	106
While it was still dark, Danny climbed out his window, got rope, and tiptoed away	121
from his house. Then he ran to the big boulder by the river and laid the rope across the	140
path. He tied one end of the rope to a tree and laid the other end on the ground behind	160
the big boulder. Danny ran home through the woods and noticed the dragon lying by	175
the door to his house. Danny climbed quietly in his window and waited patiently.	189
At morning light, Danny headed outside. Roaring, the dragon blew fire and leaped	202
at him. Danny dodged it and ran toward the river. He flew down the path, dove behind	219
the boulder, and grabbed the rope.	225
Down the path came the powerful dragon, until it tripped on the rope and crashed	240
into the river. The river carried it far, far away.	250

Total Miscues ☐   Significant Miscues ☐

Writing Prompt: Write about a place you feel safe.

Note: The rubric for evaluating the student's written response can be found in Appendix B.

Oral Reading Rate	Norm Group Percentile
WPM)15000	☐90 ☐75 ☐50 ☐25 ☐10

Word Recognition Scoring Guide		
Total Miscues	Level	Significant Miscues
0–3	Independent	0–2
4–12	Ind./Inst.	3–6
13	Instructional	7
14–24	Inst./Frust.	8–12
25 +	Frustration	13 +

LL 3183 (Grade 3) Say: "I'd like you to read out loud [silently]. Think about what you're reading because I'll ask you some questions about it when you're done. Please begin here." [Point to title.]

Danny and the Dragon

T 1. _____ What is this passage about?
               (how Danny gets rid of the dragon)

F 2. _____ When did Danny make his plan?
               (during the night)

F 3. _____ What was Danny's plan?
               (to trick the dragon)

F 4. _____ How did Danny get out of his house that night?
               (he climbed out his window)

F 5. _____ What did Danny do with the rope?
               (laid it across the path and tied it to a tree)

F 6. _____ Where was the dragon lying?
               (by the door to his house)

F 7. _____ What did the dragon do to Danny?
               (roared; blew fire; chased him; wouldn't leave him alone [any 2])

I 8. _____ What do you think happened to the dragon when it was in the river? Why?
               (any logical response; it drowned because it could not swim)

E 9. _____ What might be another plan you could use to get rid of the dragon?
               (any logical response)

V 10. _____ Explain what "tiptoed" means in this sentence: He tiptoed away from his house.
               (sneak; walk on tiptoes very quietly)

	Questions Missed

Comprehension Scoring Guide

Questions Missed	Level
0–1	Independent
1½–2	Ind./Inst.
2½	Instructional
3–4½	Inst./Frust.
5 +	Frustration

Retelling Rubric

Independent Level/Excellent
States central or key ideas
Identifies important facts
Retains the general sequence of events
Relates most of the content in an organized manner

Instructional Level/Satisfactory
States most central or key ideas
Identifies some important facts
Retains the general sequence of events
Relates an overall sense of the content

Frustration Level/Unsatisfactory
Provides bits of information in a haphazard manner
Little apparent organization

Retelling Notes

I Want to Fly

Jerry, looking up at the sky, promised himself, "I'm going to fly someday."	13
Jerry, a ten-year-old boy from a small neighborhood in Indiana, had dreamed of flying	29
since he was much younger. He wasn't just going to fly in an airplane—he was going to	47
fly like a hawk.	51
He spent endless hours watching hawks fly around. With their powerful wings they	64
built up speed, then could glide effortlessly. It was beautiful and breath-taking witnessing	78
them ride the air currents, and they made it look easy. "I'm going to fly."	93
As he climbed to the top of the cliff, Jerry's imagination was busy telling him how	109
exciting and fulfilling it would be. At the top he paused only for a moment; then he dove	127
off the cliff into the air. "This is wonderful! This is better than I ever imagined!" He	144
soared, dipped, and rose again, riding the air currents. Flying was even more exhilarating	158
than he had imagined.	162
When Jerry awoke, his concerned parents were standing beside the hospital bed.	174
"The doctor said you will be fine, but you will have to miss two weeks of school because	192
of your tonsil operation."	196
After Jerry's parents left, he thought for a moment, "I really felt like I was flying.	212
I felt cool air blowing through my hair, and I saw the vast landscape below me." Was it	230
a dream or not? If it was a dream, where did he get the brownish hawk feather he was	249
holding?	250

Total Miscues [ ]   Significant Miscues [ ]

Writing Prompt: Write about a future goal you have for yourself.

Note: The rubric for evaluating the student's written response can be found in Appendix B.

Oral Reading Rate	Norm Group Percentile
WPM)15000	☐ 90 ☐ 75 ☐ 50 ☐ 25 ☐ 10

Word Recognition Scoring Guide		
Total Miscues	Level	Significant Miscues
0–3	Independent	0–2
4–12	Ind./Inst.	3–6
13	Instructional	7
14–24	Inst./Frust.	8–12
25 +	Frustration	13 +

LL 5414 (Grade 4) Say: "I'd like you to read out loud [silently]. Think about what you're reading because I'll ask you some questions about it when you're done. Please begin here." [Point to title.]

I Want to Fly

T   1. _____   What is this passage about?
(Jerry wants to fly like a hawk)

F   2. _____   How old is Jerry?
(ten)

F   3. _____   Where did Jerry live?
(in a small town; in Iowa)

F   4. _____   What did Jerry spend hours watching?
(hawks flying)

F   5. _____   Why was Jerry in the hospital?
(he had a tonsil operation)

F   6. _____   Who came to visit Jerry?
(his parents)

F   7. _____   How much school will Jerry miss?
(two more weeks)

I   8. _____   Do you think Jerry really flew? Why?
(any logical response; no, he was dreaming; he imagined it; people can't fly)

E   9. _____   Where do you think the hawk feather came from?
(any logical response; he found it and brought it with him; his mom and dad brought it to him; it blew in his window)

V 10. _____   Explain what "landscape" means in this sentence: Jerry saw the landscape below him.
(a stretch of scenery)

Questions Missed

Comprehension Scoring Guide

Questions Missed	Level
0–1	Independent
1½–2	Ind./Inst.
2½	Instructional
3–4½	Inst./Frust.
5 +	Frustration

Retelling Rubric

Independent Level/Excellent
States central or key ideas
Identifies important facts
Retains the general sequence of events
Relates most of the content in an organized manner

Instructional Level/Satisfactory
States most central or key ideas
Identifies some important facts
Retains the general sequence of events
Relates an overall sense of the content

Frustration Level/Unsatisfactory
Provides bits of information in a haphazard manner
Little apparent organization

Retelling Notes

A Day in the Woods

Sue was visiting her grandparents' farm for a week and decided to have a picnic in the	17
forest. She packed a lunch with a peanut butter and jelly sandwich, a crispy apple, two	33
cookies, and cranberry juice. Sue put her lunch in her backpack and started out the door	49
when she remembered to run back into the house and bring Jennifer, her favorite doll.	64
Sue had an entertaining time in the forest, traveling on paths that animals had created.	79
After walking all morning, she was extremely hungry. Around noon she found a fallen tree	94
and sat on it to eat her lunch.	102
After eating, Sue found another faint animal trail that eventually led to a quiet spring.	117
She looked into the clear water and saw small fish swimming. She must remember to tell	133
her grandparents about the beautiful silvery fish in the spring.	143
Sue realized that it was time to start back to her grandparents' house, but she had	159
forgotten which way to travel. Just then she heard rustling in the bushes directly behind	174
her. She was frightened and started to run. The noise followed her as she ran and kept	191
getting closer, when all of a sudden something jumped at her! It was Rusty, her	206
grandparents' dog. Sue was so happy to see him she gave him a big hug.	221
Sue and Rusty returned to the family farm under the setting sun. Sue's grandparents	235
were worried about her. Sue promised never to go so deep into the forest again.	250

Total Miscues [ ]   Significant Miscues [ ]

Writing Prompt: Write about a time when you were lost or frightened.

Note: The rubric for evaluating the student's written response can be found in Appendix B.

Oral Reading Rate	Norm Group Percentile
___ WPM)15000	☐ 90 ☐ 75 ☐ 50 ☐ 25 ☐ 10

Word Recognition Scoring Guide		
Total Miscues	Level	Significant Miscues
0–3	Independent	0–2
4–12	Ind./Inst.	3–6
13	Instructional	7
14–24	Inst./Frust.	8–12
25 +	Frustration	13 +

LL 8595 (Grade 5) Say: "I'd like you to read out loud [silently]. Think about what you're reading because I'll ask you some questions about it when you're done. Please begin here." [Point to title.]

A Day in the Woods

T 1. _____ What is this passage about?
(a girl going for a walk in the woods and getting lost)

F 2. _____ What did Sue take with her?
(her doll, Jane; her lunch; her backpack [any 2])

F 3. _____ What did Sue bring to eat for her lunch?
(peanut-butter and jelly sandwich; an apple; two cookies; grape juice [any 2])

F 4. _____ Where did Sue eat her lunch?
(in the woods; on a fallen tree)

F 5. _____ What did Sue find in the woods?
(a fallen tree; animal trails; water; a spring; fish; Rusty [any 2])

F 6. _____ How did Sue decide where to go?
(she followed animal trails or paths)

F 7. _____ Why did Sue start running when she was in the woods?
(she heard rustling in the bushes)

I 8. _____ What do you think Sue thought was following her in the woods?
(any logical response; a wild animal)

E 9. _____ Why do you think Sue promised never to go so deep in the woods again?
(any logical response; because she had been so frightened; so she wouldn't get lost)

V 10. _____ Explain what "spring" means in this sentence: Sue saw fish swimming in a spring.
(a small stream of water coming from the earth; a little river; a little pond)

☐ Questions Missed

Comprehension Scoring Guide

Questions Missed	Level
0–1	Independent
1½–2	Ind./Inst.
2½	Instructional
3–4½	Inst./Frust.
5 +	Frustration

Retelling Rubric

Independent Level/Excellent
States central or key ideas
Identifies important facts
Retains the general sequence of events
Relates most of the content in an organized manner

Instructional Level/Satisfactory
States most central or key ideas
Identifies some important facts
Retains the general sequence of events
Relates an overall sense of the content

Frustration Level/Unsatisfactory
Provides bits of information in a haphazard manner
Little apparent organization

Retelling Notes

Lolly's Romp

During the springtime budding of cherry blossoms in the Pacific Northwest, | 11

Rebecca and her dog, Lolly, sit lazily on Lake Washington's waterfront. A temperate, | 24

refreshing breeze makes it too chilly for sunbathers or bicyclists, but delightfully | 36

perfect for Mallard ducks, who unintentionally gain Lolly's rapt attention. She plunges | 48

into the water and transforms into a magnificent huntress. Rebecca watches her paddling | 61

after the birds as they continually torment the canine, fluttering off the lake's surface | 75

and soaring barely beyond her reach, though she perseveres. "Lolly, come!" Rebecca | 87

bellows. Uncharacteristically, the focused hound disregards her owner's emphatic | 96

summons, and her tiny white head bounces with the wavelets, becoming progressively | 108

smaller. She's too distant now. It would be unimaginable to capture her by jumping in, | 123

so Rebecca sprints as nimbly as she can to the dock several hundred yards away. Despite | 139

it appearing uninhabited, there is a fellow there with an unpretentious motorboat, and | 152

when he notices Rebecca, she motions frantically to the vast expanse of water. "That | 166

your dog?" he inquires. She responds affirmatively. "Hop in," he commands, starting the | 179

engine. Rebecca imagines Lolly's head disappearing underneath the surface and not | 190

reemerging. "I can't understand why she's doing this. She usually obeys when I call." | 204

They approach, engine sputtering now. "Well, dogs are dogs, you know. They like to | 218

hunt." He maneuvers the vessel closer while Rebecca reaches out, clutches Lolly by the | 232

underarms, and heaves her into the dinghy. Dripping wet, Lolly gazes at Rebecca | 245

affectionately, not even breathing hard. | 250

Total Miscues [ ]   Significant Miscues [ ]

Writing Prompt: Write about an experience you've had with a stranger.

Note: The rubric for evaluating the student's written response can be found in Appendix B.

Oral Reading Rate	Norm Group Percentile
WPM 15000⟌	☐ 90 ☐ 75 ☐ 50 ☐ 25 ☐ 10

Word Recognition Scoring Guide		
Total Miscues	Level	Significant Miscues
0–3	Independent	0–2
4–12	Ind./Inst.	3–6
13	Instructional	7
14–24	Inst./Frust.	8–12
25 +	Frustration	13 +

LL 6867 (Grade 6) Say: "I'd like you to read out loud [silently]. Think about what you're reading because I'll ask you some questions about it when you're done. Please begin here." [Point to title.]

Lolly's Romp

T 1. _____ What is this passage about?
(a girl whose dog swims out too far and is rescued)

F 2. _____ What time of year does the story take place?
(springtime)

F 3. _____ What type of trees are blooming in the story?
(cherry)

F 4. _____ What is the name of the lake that Rebecca and her dog are visiting?
(Lake Washington)

F 5. _____ What does Lolly see that makes her jump into the water?
(Mallard ducks; ducks)

F 6. _____ Why doesn't Rebecca jump in the lake and swim out to get Lolly?
(She is too far out; it is too cold for people to swim)

F 7. _____ Who helps Rebecca rescue Lolly?
(a fellow; a man with a boat)

I 8. _____ Why do you think Rebecca runs to the boat dock even though it looks like no one is there?
(any logical response; she would look anywhere for help; the dock was closer to the dog)

E 9. _____ How would you help Rebecca if you didn't have a boat?
(any logical response; call to the dog; reassure her that the dog would swim back)

V 10. _____ Explain what "persevere" means in this phrase: Soaring barely beyond her reach, though she perseveres.
(to keep going; keep trying)

☐	Questions Missed

Comprehension Scoring Guide

Questions Missed	Level
0–1	Independent
1½–2	Ind./Inst.
2½	Instructional
3–4½	Inst./Frust.
5 +	Frustration

Retelling Rubric
Independent Level/Excellent
States central or key ideas
Identifies important facts
Retains the general sequence of events
Relates most of the content in an organized manner
Instructional Level/Satisfactory
States most central or key ideas
Identifies some important facts
Retains the general sequence of events
Relates an overall sense of the content
Frustration Level/Unsatisfactory
Provides bits of information in a haphazard manner
Little apparent organization

Retelling Notes

Glacier Climb

We marveled at the two ice climbers, their mysterious figures mere specks on the snow	15
600 feet above, and wondered, are they roped? No, they were both moving up, slowly, toward	31
the rock band below the summit. A rope between them would only ensure that if one person	48
fell, the other would too. A rope would only add security if one climber was anchored into the	66
ice, guiding the leader up from a protected position. These two were free soloing the route,	82
with no protection beyond the skillful placement of their spiked boots and tools.	95
I took photos, then holstered my camera and turned my attention back to the glacier, but	111
suddenly heard shouting. I looked to the west face: the top climber was sliding down,	126
accelerating, his ice axe hissing and spraying as it split the snow. It was impossible to judge the	144
time or distance he fell. He struggled to stop for a few long seconds before he lost control,	162
caught a spike and started tumbling down the face. Mark shouted, "Prepare to rescue!" We all	178
stood transfixed, but I carefully tracked him as he tumbled toward the crevasse, watching	192
closely to see where he would stop.	199
He hit the precipice with a sickening thud and disappeared. It was the highest of three	215
staggered fissures in his fall line. "Go! Go! Go!" Mark yelled. My rope team, 50 yards below	232
the crevasse, crossed under and climbed to the south, while another team traversed the slope	247
to the north.	250

Total Miscues [ ]   Significant Miscues [ ]

Writing Prompt: Write about something surprising you've experienced.

Note: The rubric for evaluating the student's written response can be found in Appendix B.

Oral Reading Rate	Norm Group Percentile
WPM ⟌15000	☐ 90 ☐ 75 ☐ 50 ☐ 25 ☐ 10

Word Recognition Scoring Guide		
Total Miscues	Level	Significant Miscues
0–3	Independent	0–2
4–12	Ind./Inst.	3–6
13	Instructional	7
14–24	Inst./Frust.	8–12
25 +	Frustration	13 +

LL 3717 (Grade 7) Say: "I'd like you to read out loud [silently]. Think about what you're reading because I'll ask you some questions about it when you're done. Please begin here." [Point to title.]

Glacier Climb

T   1. _____   What is this passage about?
                  (ice climbers witnessing a fall)

F   2. _____   How high up are the ice climbers?
                  (600 feet)

F   3. _____   What type of boots do ice climbers wear?
                  (spiked)

F   4. _____   What is the narrator doing just before he hears shouting?
                  (taking photos)

F   5. _____   How far did the ice climber fall?
                  (it was impossible to judge)

F   6. _____   What does Mark shout?
                  (Prepare to rescue; Go go go [either 1])

F   7. _____   How many rope teams rescue the fallen climber?
                  (two)

I   8. _____   Why is the narrator careful to watch the climber fall and see where he lands?
                  (any logical response; in order to locate and rescue him)

E   9. _____   What do you think might happen next in the story?
                  (any logical response; they rescue the climber)

V 10. _____   Explain what "crevasse" means in this sentence: I carefully tracked him as he tumbled toward the crevasse.
                  (a deep crack in a glacier)

	Retelling Rubric
Independent Level/Excellent	States central or key ideas
	Identifies important facts
	Retains the general sequence of events
	Relates most of the content in an organized manner
Instructional Level/Satisfactory	States most central or key ideas
	Identifies some important facts
	Retains the general sequence of events
	Relates an overall sense of the content
Frustration Level/Unsatisfactory	Provides bits of information in a haphazard manner
	Little apparent organization

Retelling Notes

☐ Questions Missed

Comprehension Scoring Guide

Questions Missed	Level
0–1	Independent
1½–2	Ind./Inst.
2½	Instructional
3–4½	Inst./Frust.
5 +	Frustration

The Angel of the Candy Counter

The Angel of the candy counter had found me out and was demanding extreme payment	15
for all the Snickers, Mounds, suckers, and Hershey bars. I had two huge cavities that were	31
rotten to the gums. The pain was well past the help of crushed aspirins or oil of cloves. Only	50
one thing could help me now, so I prayed earnestly that I'd be allowed to sit under the house	69
and have the entire building collapse on my jaw.	78
Since there was no dentist in Stamps, nor doctor either, for that matter, Momma had dealt	94
with other toothaches. She would try yanking them out with a string tied to the tooth and the	112
other end looped over her fist, as well as pain killers and prayer. In this case the medicine	130
proved ineffective. There wasn't enough enamel left to hook a string on, and the prayers were	146
being ignored because some demon was blocking their way.	155
I lived some days and nights in blinding pain, not so much toying with, as seriously	171
considering, the idea of jumping in the well. So Momma decided I had to be taken to a dentist.	190
The nearest dentist was in Mason, twenty miles away, and I was sure that I'd be dead long	208
before we reached half the distance. Momma said we'd go to Dr. Lincoln, and he'd take care	225
of me. She said we'd have to take the bus. I didn't know of anyone who'd been to see him,	245
but we had to go.	250

Adapted from *I Know Why the Caged Bird Sings* by Maya Angelou.

Total Miscues [ ]   Significant Miscues [ ]

Writing Prompt: Write about a time when you were in pain.

Note: The rubric for evaluating the student's written response can be found in Appendix B.

Oral Reading Rate	Norm Group Percentile
WPM $\frac{}{)15000}$	☐ 90 ☐ 75 ☐ 50 ☐ 25 ☐ 10

Word Recognition Scoring Guide		
Total Miscues	Level	Significant Miscues
0–3	Independent	0–2
4–12	Ind./Inst.	3–6
13	Instructional	7
14–24	Inst./Frust.	8–12
25 +	Frustration	13 +

Lexile: 1090

LL 8183 (Grade 8) Say: "I'd like you to read out loud [silently]. Think about what you're reading because I'll ask you some questions about it when you're done. Please begin here." [Point to title.]

The Angel of the Candy Counter

T   1. _____   What is this passage about?
(someone who has a toothache and has to go to the dentist)

F   2. _____   What remedies had already been tried to ease the pain?
(crushed aspirins; oil of clove; prayer [any 1])

F   3. _____   Why didn't Momma pull the teeth that were hurting?
(they were too rotten; there wasn't enough enamel to hook a string on)

F   4. _____   Why weren't the prayers being answered?
(a demon or devil was blocking their way)

F   5. _____   In what town did the narrator live?
(Stamps)

F   6. _____   How far was the nearest dentist from home?
(20 miles)

F   7. _____   What is the name of the dentist?
(Dr. Lincoln)

I   8. _____   What did this person think was responsible for the pain?
(candy; cavities)

E   9. _____   Why do you think Stamps had no dentist or doctor?
(any logical response; small town; poor town; the story takes place many years ago)

V   10. _____   Explain what "earnestly" means in this sentence: I prayed earnestly that the house would fall on my jaw.
(seriously; with determination)

☐ Questions
Missed

Comprehension Scoring Guide	
Questions Missed	Level
0–1	Independent
1½–2	Ind./Inst.
2½	Instructional
3–4½	Inst./Frust.
5 +	Frustration

Retelling Rubric
Independent Level/Excellent
States central or key ideas
Identifies important facts
Retains the general sequence of events
Relates most of the content in an organized manner
Instructional Level/Satisfactory
States most central or key ideas
Identifies some important facts
Retains the general sequence of events
Relates an overall sense of the content
Frustration Level/Unsatisfactory
Provides bits of information in a haphazard manner
Little apparent organization

Retelling Notes

Elizabeth Meets Darcy

Elizabeth watched for the first appearance of Pemberley Woods with some perturbation;	12
and when at length they turned in at the lodge, her spirits were in a high flutter.	29
The park was very large and contained great variety of ground. They entered it in one of	46
its lowest points, and drove for some time through a beautiful wood, stretching over a wide	62
extent.	63
Elizabeth's mind was too full for conversation, but she saw and admired every	76
remarkable spot and point of view. They gradually ascended for half a mile, and then found	92
themselves at the top of a considerable eminence, where the wood ceased, and the eye was	108
immediately captured by Pemberley House, situated on the opposite side of a valley, into	122
which the road with some abruptness wound. It was a large, handsome, stone structure,	136
standing well on rising ground, and backed by a ridge of high woody hills. She had never seen	154
a place for which nature had enhanced more, or where natural beauty had been so little	170
counteracted by an awkward taste. They were all of them warm in their admiration, and at the	187
moment she felt that to be mistress of Pemberley might be something!	199
They descended the hill, crossed the bridge, and drove to the door; and, while examining	214
the nearer aspect of the house, all her apprehensions of meeting its owner returned. As she	230
walked across the lawn, Elizabeth turned back to look again, and the owner himself suddenly	245
came forward from the road.	250

Adapted from *Pride and Prejudice* by Jane Austen.

Total Miscues ☐   Significant Miscues ☐

Writing Prompt: Write about a time when you were impressed with someone or something.

Note: The rubric for evaluating the student's written response can be found in Appendix B.

Oral Reading Rate	Norm Group Percentile
___ WPM)15000	☐ 90 ☐ 75 ☐ 50 ☐ 25 ☐ 10

Word Recognition Scoring Guide		
Total Miscues	Level	Significant Miscues
0–3	Independent	0–2
4–12	Ind./Inst.	3–6
13	Instructional	7
14–24	Inst./Frust.	8–12
25 +	Frustration	13 +

LL 4959 (Grade 9) Say: "I'd like you to read out loud [silently]. Think about what you're reading because I'll ask you some questions about it when you're done. Please begin here." [Point to title.]

Elizabeth Meets Darcy

T   1. _____   What is this passage about?
(Elizabeth going to Pemberley Woods)

F   2. _____   What did Pemberley House look like?
(large; handsome; a stone structure [any 1])

F   3. _____   Describe Pemberley Woods.
(large; a forest; hilly; valley; woody [any 2])

F   4. _____   How did the group feel about what they were seeing?
(warm in their admiration; excited; happy)

F   5. _____   What did they see when the woods ceased?
(Pemberley House)

F   6. _____   When did Elizabeth see the owner of Pemberley Woods?
(when she came up to the outside of the house; as she walked across the lawn)

F   7. _____   How did Elizabeth get to Pemberley Woods?
(drove)

I   8. _____   What does it mean when the story says that "Elizabeth's mind was too full for conversation"?
(any logical response; Elizabeth's mind was preoccupied with worry)

E   9. _____   Under what circumstances might someone be nervous about meeting the owner of a large mansion?
(any logical response)

V 10. _____   Explain what "ascended" means in this sentence: They gradually ascended for half a mile.
(went up)

	Questions Missed

Comprehension Scoring Guide

Questions Missed	Level
0–1	Independent
1½–2	Ind./Inst.
2½	Instructional
3–4½	Inst./Frust.
5 +	Frustration

Retelling Rubric
Independent Level/Excellent
States central or key ideas
Identifies important facts
Retains the general sequence of events
Relates most of the content in an organized manner
Instructional Level/Satisfactory
States most central or key ideas
Identifies some important facts
Retains the general sequence of events
Relates an overall sense of the content
Frustration Level/Unsatisfactory
Provides bits of information in a haphazard manner
Little apparent organization

Retelling Notes

Bookworm or Earthworm

To read or to weed is the challenging conundrum that confronts me whenever I have a	16
few spare minutes. Reading satisfies the wanderlust in me and affords the opportunity to	30
abandon the monotonous ruts of everyday life to traipse excitedly along mysterious trails in the	45
enchanting land of books. Lost in the magic of the printed page, I can cast off my customary	63
garments and array myself in the raiment of a victorious knight or a lacrosse superstar. No	79
longer shackled by the unforgiving chains of time and space, I shiver with Washington's	93
valiant soldiers in the piercing cold of Valley Forge and I kneel in reverent awe at Bethlehem's	110
manger. Is it any wonder that I am unable to resist the beckoning call of a good book?	128
My interest in weeding is probably the result of my interest in reading. This occupation	143
puts me on equal footing with those noble characters that I have respected in books. Few	159
chores are more intriguing to me than that of rescuing struggling plants from the greedy claws	175
of choking weeds. I like the feeling of the cold and damp earth as I eject intruding, strangling	193
roots. With the confident swagger of a conquering hero, I march triumphantly through our	207
flower garden, leaving grateful shrubs in my wake. Even the squirming worms wriggle their	221
gratitude for my righteous deed. Yes, recreation time is always debating time for me. The topic	237
of this secret controversy ever remains the same: to read or to weed?	250

Adapted from *Voyages in English* by Reverend Paul E. Campbell and Sister
Mary Donatus Macnickle. Copyrighted by Loyola University Press.

Total Miscues [ ]   Significant Miscues [ ]

Writing Prompt: Write about how you prefer to spend
your leisure time.
Note: The rubric for evaluating the student's written response
can be found in Appendix B.

Oral Reading Rate	Norm Group Percentile
____ WPM)15000	☐ 90 ☐ 75 ☐ 50 ☐ 25 ☐ 10

Word Recognition Scoring Guide		
Total Miscues	Level	Significant Miscues
0–3	Independent	0–2
4–12	Ind./Inst.	3–6
13	Instructional	7
14–24	Inst./Frust.	8–12
25 +	Frustration	13 +

LL 1047 (Grade 10) Say: "I'd like you to read out loud [silently]. Think about what you're reading because I'll ask you some questions about it when you're done. Please begin here." [Point to title.]

Bookworm or Earthworm

T   1. _____   What is this passage about?
(whether the author should read or weed)

F   2. _____   The author makes mention of casting off customary garments and dressing in the raiment of what?
(a victorious knight or soccer star [either 1])

F   3. _____   How did the author develop an interest in weeding?
(from an interest in reading)

F   4. _____   Where does the author weed?
(in the flower garden)

F   5. _____   What historical person was mentioned in the story?
(George Washington)

F   6. _____   What do the worms do to show their gratitude for the weeding of the garden?
(they wriggle)

F   7. _____   What chore, or job, is intriguing to the author?
(rescuing struggling plants from the greedy claws of choking weeds; simply weeding)

I   8. _____   What does the author probably mean by "reverent awe at Bethlehem's crib?"
(any logical response; the birth of Jesus)

E   9. _____   Reading satisfies the author's wanderlust. What satisfies wanderlust for you? Why?
(any logical response)

V 10. _____   Explain what "swagger" means in this phrase: With the confident swagger of a conquering hero.
(stride; strut)

[ ] Questions Missed

Comprehension Scoring Guide	
Questions Missed	Level
0–1	Independent
1½–2	Ind./Inst.
2½	Instructional
3–4½	Inst./Frust.
5 +	Frustration

Retelling Rubric
Independent Level/Excellent
States central or key ideas
Identifies important facts
Retains the general sequence of events
Relates most of the content in an organized manner
Instructional Level/Satisfactory
States most central or key ideas
Identifies some important facts
Retains the general sequence of events
Relates an overall sense of the content
Frustration Level/Unsatisfactory
Provides bits of information in a haphazard manner
Little apparent organization

Retelling Notes

American in Paris

On a brilliant day in May, in the year 1868, a gentleman was reclining at his ease on the	19
great circular divan which occupied the center of the Salon Carré, in the Museum of the	35
Louvre. He had taken serene possession of the softest spot of this commodious ottoman. With	50
his head thrown back and his legs outstretched, he was staring at Murillo's beautiful moon-	65
borne Madonna in profound enjoyment of his posture. He had removed his hat and flung down	81
beside him a little red guidebook and an opera glass. The day was warm; he was heated with	99
walking, and he repeatedly passed his handkerchief over his forehead with a somewhat wearied	113
gesture. His exertions on this particular day had been of an unwonted sort, and he had often	130
performed great physical feats which left him less jaded than his tranquil stroll through the	145
Louvre. He had looked at all the pictures to which an asterisk was affixed in those formidable	162
pages of fine print in his Baedeker guidebook; his attention had been strained and his eyes	178
dazzled, and he had sat down with an aesthetic headache. His physiognomy would have	192
sufficiently indicated that he was a shrewd and capable fellow. In truth, he had often sat up all	210
night over a bristling bundle of accounts and heard the cock crow without a yawn. But Raphael	227
and Titian and Rubens were a new kind of arithmetic, and they made him, for the first time in	246
his life, really wonder.	250

Note: Do not count the mispronunciation of proper nouns as significant miscues.

Adapted from *The American* by Henry James.

Total Miscues [ ]   Significant Miscues [ ]

Writing Prompt: Write about an activity that would be relaxing for you.

Note: The rubric for evaluating the student's written response can be found in Appendix B.

Oral Reading Rate	Norm Group Percentile
‾‾‾‾ WPM)15000	☐ 90 ☐ 75 ☐ 50 ☐ 25 ☐ 10

Word Recognition Scoring Guide		
Total Miscues	Level	Significant Miscues
0–3	Independent	0–2
4–12	Ind./Inst.	3–6
13	Instructional	7
14–24	Inst./Frust.	8–12
25 +	Frustration	13 +

339

LL 1187 (Grade 11) Say: "I'd like you to read out loud [silently]. Think about what you're reading because I'll ask you some questions about it when you're done. Please begin here." [Point to title.]

American in Paris

T   1. _____   What is this passage about?
(an American gentleman in the Louvre Museum)

F   2. _____   What is the gentleman holding in his hand?
(a handkerchief)

F   3. _____   What did the gentleman remove as he took his position on the ottoman?
(his hat)

F   4. _____   When does this story take place?
(1868; over one hundred years ago)

F   5. _____   What is he staring at?
(Murillo's Madonna; a painting)

F   6. _____   Describe the weather.
(warm)

F   7. _____   What kind of a book has he been reading?
(a red guidebook; Baedeker guidebook)

I   8. _____   What do you think the man's job was? Why?
(any logical response; accounting; some type of business)

E   9. _____   Why do you think Raphael, Titian, and Rubens made the gentleman wonder?
(any logical response)

V   10. _____   Explain what "physiognomy" means in this sentence: His physiognomy would have sufficiently indicated that he was a shrewd and capable fellow.
(outward appearance)

Questions
Missed

Comprehension Scoring Guide	
Questions Missed	Level
0–1	Independent
1½–2	Ind./Inst.
2½	Instructional
3–4½	Inst./Frust.
5 +	Frustration

Retelling Rubric
Independent Level/Excellent
States central or key ideas
Identifies important facts
Retains the general sequence of events
Relates most of the content in an organized manner
Instructional Level/Satisfactory
States most central or key ideas
Identifies some important facts
Retains the general sequence of events
Relates an overall sense of the content
Frustration Level/Unsatisfactory
Provides bits of information in a haphazard manner
Little apparent organization

Retelling Notes

Sacrifice

In the dazzling light of her dressing room, Li Jing deftly stroked on eyeliner and	15
contemplated her visage in the glass. She was esteemed for her lissome physique, her alluring	30
countenance, and her unrivaled ballet talent, but the diminutive mischief-maker from rural	43
China was never distant in her consciousness. Now, minutes before pirouetting on stage for	57
throngs of admirers, Li Jing felt more that little girl than the celebrated prima ballerina into	73
which she had unwittingly matured. She reclined on the nearby setee, lengthened her arms	87
overhead and closed her eyes. She ruminated on the impoverished family she forsook,	100
provoking intense contemplation about her resolutions. She heard, as luminous as daylight,	112
her unrelenting mother's admonition that she must go, regardless of how heartbroken it	125
made them both. But the utterance she heard now, which jolted her from her reverie, was the	142
stage manager summoning her forthwith to the proscenium.	150
At six, Li Jing was selected to attend the National Arts University—an extraordinary	164
opportunity to escape destitution, for which she was wholly appreciative. But she sometimes	177
felt uncherished, especially when families of other dancers frequented backstage delivering	188
flowers, congratulations, and tenderness. Was the defection to America, and the adoration and	201
prosperity she enjoyed, worth a lifetime of uncertainty about her mother's destiny? Orchestral	214
melodies intensified as Li Jing approached the wings and squinted through a tiny aperture in	229
the curtain to see the overflowing audience. This crowd was an enthusiastic but insubstantial	243
substitute for the familial affection she craved.	250

Total Miscues ☐   Significant Miscues ☐

Writing Prompt: Write about a notable performance or show you've seen.

Note: The rubric for evaluating the student's written response can be found in Appendix B.

Oral Reading Rate	Norm Group Percentile
$\frac{}{)15000}$ WPM	☐ 90 ☐ 75 ☐ 50 ☐ 25 ☐ 10

Word Recognition Scoring Guide		
Total Miscues	Level	Significant Miscues
0–3	Independent	0–2
4–12	Ind./Inst.	3–6
13	Instructional	7
14–24	Inst./Frust.	8–12
25 +	Frustration	13 +

LL 1296 (Grade 12) Say: "I'd like you to read out loud [silently]. Think about what you're reading because I'll ask you some questions about it when you're done. Please begin here." [Point to title.]

Sacrifice

T   1. _____ What is this passage about?
(a ballet dancer thinking about her past and family)

F   2. _____ Where does the story take place?
(America; dressing room; backstage; theatre [any 1])

F   3. _____ What kind of makeup is Li Jing applying in the story?
(eyeliner)

F   4. _____ What is Li Jing's occupation?
(prima ballerina; ballet dancer)

F   5. _____ What country is Li Jing from?
(China)

F   6. _____ What is the job title of the person who brings Li Jing to the stage on time?
(stage manager)

F   7. _____ What do the families of other dancers bring backstage to show their congratulations?
(flowers)

I   8. _____ Why do you think Li Jing peeks through the curtain to look at the audience?
(any logical response; she is curious)

E   9. _____ If you were required to perform on stage, what might make you nervous?
(any logical response; fear of failure)

V 10. _____ Explain what the word "aperture" means in this phrase: Approached the wings and squinted through the tiny aperture in the curtain.
(a hole; an opening)

<table>
<tr><td>☐</td><td>Questions
Missed</td></tr>
</table>

Comprehension Scoring Guide

Questions Missed	Level
0–1	Independent
1½–2	Ind./Inst.
2½	Instructional
3–4½	Inst./Frust.
5 +	Frustration

Retelling Rubric
Independent Level/Excellent
States central or key ideas
Identifies important facts
Retains the general sequence of events
Relates most of the content in an organized manner
Instructional Level/Satisfactory
States most central or key ideas
Identifies some important facts
Retains the general sequence of events
Relates an overall sense of the content
Frustration Level/Unsatisfactory
Provides bits of information in a haphazard manner
Little apparent organization

Retelling Notes

Performance Booklet

Teacher Copy

Form LI

Primary Uses:
- Silent Reading (Informational)

Other Uses:
- Oral Reading
- Progress Monitoring

Note: This Performance Booklet is on the Basic Reading Inventory website.

Miscue Summary Sheet for Forms LL and LI

MISCUES							
Substitution	Insertion	Omission	Reversal	Repetition	Self-Correction of Unacceptable Miscue	Meaning Change (Significant Miscue)	

Name _____ Date _____

Passage Title _____

Form _____

Total Miscues ☐   Significant Miscues ☐

BASIC READING INVENTORY PERFORMANCE BOOKLET

Jerry L. Johns, Laurie Elish-Piper, and Beth Johns

Student _____ Grade _____ Gender M F Date of Test _____

School _____ Examiner _____ Date of Birth _____

Address _____ Current Book/Level _____ Age _____

SUMMARY OF STUDENT'S READING PERFORMANCE

| Grade | Word Recognition | | Comprehension | | Oral Reading Rate | | Silent Reading Rate |
	Miscues	Level	Questions Missed	Level	Words per Minute (WPM)	Norm Group Percentile	Words per Minute (WPM)
3							
4							
5							
6							
7							
8							
9						███	
10						███	
11						███	
12						███	

ESTIMATE OF READING LEVELS

Independent _____ Instructional _____ Frustration _____

INFORMAL ANALYSIS OF ORAL READING

| Oral Reading Behaviors | Frequency of Occurrence | | | General Impact on Meaning | | |
	Seldom	Sometimes	Frequently	No Change	Little Change	Much Change
Substitutions						
Insertions						
Omissions						
Reversals						
Repetitions						

LISTENING LEVEL

Form _____

Grade	Questions Missed	Level
3		
4		
5		
6		
7		
8		
9		
10		
11		
12		

ESTIMATED LEVEL: _____

GENERAL OBSERVATIONS

QUALITATIVE ANALYSIS OF BASIC READING INVENTORY INSIGHTS

General Directions: Note the degree to which the student shows behavior or evidence in the following areas. Space is provided for additional items.

	Seldom / Weak / Poor			Always / Strong / Excellent

COMPREHENSION

Seeks to construct meaning

Makes predictions

Activates background knowledge

Possesses appropriate concepts and vocabulary

Monitors reading

Varies reading rate as needed

Understands topic and major ideas

Remembers facts or details

Makes and supports appropriate inferences

Evaluates ideas from passages

Understands vocabulary used

Provides appropriate definitions of words

Engages with passages

WORD IDENTIFICATION

Possesses numerous strategies

Uses strategies flexibly

Uses graphophonic information

Uses semantic information

Uses syntactic information

Knows high-frequency words automatically

Possesses sight vocabulary

ORAL AND SILENT READING

Reads fluently

Reads with expression

Attends to punctuation

Keeps place while reading

Reads at appropriate rate

Reads silently without vocalization

ATTITUDE AND CONFIDENCE

Enjoys reading

Demonstrates willingness to risk

Possesses positive self-concept

Chooses to read

Regards himself/herself as a reader

Exhibits persistence

Harris' Hawks

Most hawks hunt for prey alone. In New Mexico, there is a type of hawk called | 16

Harris' hawk. Harris' hawks work together as a team to catch their prey. This idea was | 32

interesting to a wildlife scientist. He decided to study these hawks. | 43

The first thing he had to do was catch one hawk in a group. He then put a radio | 62

transmitter on the bird's leg. This helped him keep track of where the bird went. He did | 79

this with one hawk from each group. | 86

The scientist went to a high place to watch the hawks. This took a lot of time and | 104

hard work. He discovered that most of the time the hawks caught rabbits. These were | 119

large rabbits that would be hard for one hawk to catch. The hawks worked together as a | 136

team so that they could catch their prey. Then they all shared the meal. | 150

The scientist watched as the hawks would stalk their prey. First, they would fly | 164

across a large area. Sometimes the hawks would sit in trees to watch the ground. When | 180

the hawks saw a rabbit, they would start following it. When the rabbit slowed down in | 196

an open place, the hawks would dive at it. The hawks would wait until the rabbit | 212

became tired to make their final dive. | 219

These hawks are very good at working as a team. This helps them to find food and | 236

stay alive. They have learned that it is very important to help each other. | 250

Total Miscues ☐   Significant Miscues ☐

Writing Prompt: Write about a time you used teamwork to accomplish something.

Note: The rubric for evaluating the student's written response can be found in Appendix B.

Oral Reading Rate	Norm Group Percentile
WPM $\frac{}{)15000}$	☐90 ☐75 ☐50 ☐25 ☐10

Word Recognition Scoring Guide		
Total Miscues	Level	Significant Miscues
0–3	Independent	0–2
4–12	Ind./Inst.	3–6
13	Instructional	7
14–24	Inst./Frust.	8–12
25 +	Frustration	13 +

LI 3183 (Grade 3) Say: "I'd like you to read out loud [silently]. Think about what you're reading because I'll ask you some questions about it when you're done. Please begin here." [Point to title.]

Harris' Hawks

T　1. _____　What is this passage about?
　　　　　　(what hawks do; what they eat; hawks that work together as a team to catch their prey)

F　2. _____　What is this type of hawk called?
　　　　　　(Harris' hawk)

F　3. _____　Where do these hawks live?
　　　　　　(New Mexico)

F　4. _____　Why do Harris' hawks work together as a team?
　　　　　　(to catch their prey; they are too small to work alone)

F　5. _____　What did the scientist do with the bird after he caught it?
　　　　　　(he put a radio transmitter on the bird's leg)

F　6. _____　Where did the scientist go to watch the hawks?
　　　　　　(to a high place)

F　7. _____　What type of animal did the hawks usually catch?
　　　　　　(rabbits)

I　8. _____　Why do you think the hawks would wait until the rabbit was in an open place before they would start diving at it?
　　　　　　(any logical response; because they could see it better; trees and bushes weren't in the way)

E　9. _____　If you were a scientist, what would you like to spend time studying? Why?
　　　　　　(any logical response)

V　10. _____　Explain what "prey" means in this sentence: Most hawks hunt for prey alone.
　　　　　　(animals hunted or seized for food, especially by another animal)

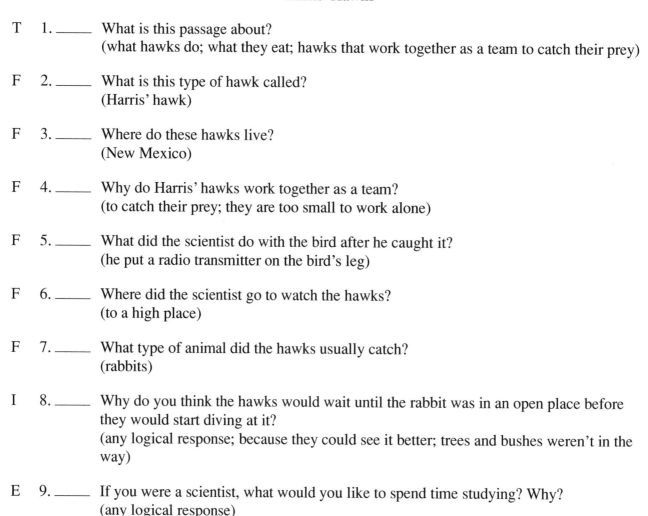

Questions Missed	

Comprehension Scoring Guide

Questions Missed	Level
0–1	Independent
1½–2	Ind./Inst.
2½	Instructional
3–4½	Inst./Frust.
5 +	Frustration

Retelling Rubric

Independent Level/Excellent
States central or key ideas
Identifies important facts
Retains the general sequence of events
Relates most of the content in an organized manner

Instructional Level/Satisfactory
States most central or key ideas
Identifies some important facts
Retains the general sequence of events
Relates an overall sense of the content

Frustration Level/Unsatisfactory
Provides bits of information in a haphazard manner
Little apparent organization

Retelling Notes

Early Travel

It was early winter when Martha and Johnny Stine began their journey. They were	14
traveling from Kansas to Colorado. When it was night, they set up camp wherever they	29
could. This type of trip was not easy. The year was 1891, which was before cars or	46
airplanes. Good roads were not available, so they traveled in a covered wagon pulled by	61
horses.	62
As time passed, the weather became colder. One night when they stopped to sleep,	76
it was six degrees below zero. The next night they were caught in a blizzard, so Martha	93
and Johnny stopped at a house to ask for directions. They were asked if they wanted to	110
spend the night there because of the blizzard, but Johnny didn't want to stay, although	125
Martha did. They continued on their journey in the blinding blizzard until they could no	140
longer see. The roads were covered with snow, and the horses couldn't be forced to	155
continue through the ice and snow any longer. Then they saw the shadow of a small cabin.	172
When they reached the cabin, it was locked. They pulled up beside the cabin in order to	189
get shelter from the wind and snow. Weary, they fell into a restless sleep. Martha felt very	206
depressed, because they were lost in a blizzard and tired from traveling.	218
Four days later they arrived at their destination, and Martha was so happy she cried.	233
It had been four weeks since they had started. Martha was happy to see the trip end.	250

Total Miscues [ ]   Significant Miscues [ ]

Writing Prompt: Write about an experience you've had with bad weather.

Note: The rubric for evaluating the student's written response can be found in Appendix B.

Oral Reading Rate	Norm Group Percentile
$\frac{}{)15000}$ WPM	☐90 ☐75 ☐50 ☐25 ☐10

Word Recognition Scoring Guide		
Total Miscues	Level	Significant Miscues
0–3	Independent	0–2
4–12	Ind./Inst.	3–6
13	Instructional	7
14–24	Inst./Frust.	8–12
25 +	Frustration	13 +

LI 5414 (Grade 4) Say: "I'd like you to read out loud [silently]. Think about what you're reading because I'll ask you some questions about it when you're done. Please begin here." [Point to title.]

Early Travel

T   1. _____   What is this passage about?
(Martha and Johnny Stine's trip by covered wagon in the winter)

F   2. _____   What state were the Stine's coming from and what state were they going to?
(they were traveling from Kansas to Colorado)

F   3. _____   What year did this passage take place?
(1891)

F   4. _____   Who wanted to stay at the house where they stopped and asked for directions?
(Martha)

F   5. _____   What did they discover about the cabin when they found it in a blizzard?
(it was locked)

F   6. _____   What was the temperature when they stopped to sleep one night?
(6 degrees below zero; below zero)

F   7. _____   How long did it take the Stine family from when they started their trip until they reached their destination?
(4 weeks)

I   8. _____   When they stopped at a house in the blizzard to ask for directions, they were asked if they wanted to spend the night there. Why do you think Johnny didn't want to stay?
(any logical response; he wanted to continue on; he was afraid of the strangers)

E   9. _____   If you were taking this trip with Martha and Johnny, what would you take with you? Why?
(any logical response; warm clothes; sleeping bag; food)

V 10. _____   Explain what "depressed" means in this sentence: Martha felt depressed when they were lost.
(sad; gloomy; low-spirited)

Questions	
Missed	

Comprehension Scoring Guide	
Questions	
Missed	Level
0–1	Independent
1½–2	Ind./Inst.
2½	Instructional
3–4½	Inst./Frust.
5 +	Frustration

Retelling Rubric
Independent Level/Excellent
States central or key ideas
Identifies important facts
Retains the general sequence of events
Relates most of the content in an organized manner
Instructional Level/Satisfactory
States most central or key ideas
Identifies some important facts
Retains the general sequence of events
Relates an overall sense of the content
Frustration Level/Unsatisfactory
Provides bits of information in a haphazard manner
Little apparent organization

Retelling Notes

Two Famous Brothers

Orville and Wilbur Wright invented and constructed the first successful airplane.	11
Orville flew it in December of 1903. These famous brothers had an interesting childhood.	25
In 1879, Wilbur was twelve and Orville was eight. Their father bought them a toy	40
helicopter made of paper, bamboo sticks, and cork after a trip to Ohio. They turned a stick	57
that twisted a rubber band, fastened it, and then tossed the helicopter into the air. Orville	73
and Wilbur reached to catch it before it fell. The toy helicopter flew several feet across the	90
room, and they played with it until it broke.	99
Orville had various plans for making money. He learned to make and fly kites, and he	115
made money by selling them to friends. By the time he was fourteen, he had a printing	132
press and business. Wilbur became interested in the business, and in a short time, they	147
published a weekly newspaper.	151
Bicycles became popular in the 1890s, but these early bikes were dangerous and	164
difficult to ride. The front wheel was five feet high, and the back wheel was eighteen	180
inches high. A new bicycle was then built with two wheels of equal size, similar to today's	197
bikes. The brothers rented a shop, and they began repairing and selling bicycles so now	212
they had two businesses.	216
One day Wilbur saw a photograph of a glider with a man hanging beneath the wings.	232
He showed it to Orville and that may have been the beginning of their serious talk of	249
flying.	250

Total Miscues [ ]   Significant Miscues [ ]

Writing Prompt: Write about an invention that could improve your life.

Note: The rubric for evaluating the student's written response can be found in Appendix B.

Oral Reading Rate	Norm Group Percentile
WPM)15000	☐ 90 ☐ 75 ☐ 50 ☐ 25 ☐ 10

Word Recognition Scoring Guide		
Total Miscues	Level	Significant Miscues
0–3	Independent	0–2
4–12	Ind./Inst.	3–6
13	Instructional	7
14–24	Inst./Frust.	8–12
25 +	Frustration	13 +

LI 8595 (Grade 5) Say: "I'd like you to read out loud [silently]. Think about what you're reading because I'll ask you some questions about it when you're done. Please begin here." [Point to title.]

Two Famous Brothers

T 1. _____ What is this passage about?
(Wilbur and Orville Wright; their childhood; two brothers)

F 2. _____ What are the names of the two famous brothers?
(Orville; Wilbur)

F 3. _____ What are the Wright brothers famous for?
(building and flying the first successful airplane)

F 4. _____ Who gave the brothers the toy helicopter?
(their father)

F 5. _____ What was the toy helicopter made of?
(paper; bamboo sticks; cork; a rubber band [any 2])

F 6. _____ Name one of the brothers' businesses.
(making and selling kites; publishing a newspaper; repairing and selling bicycles)

F 7. _____ What made early bikes dangerous and difficult to ride?
(the wheels were different sizes)

I 8. _____ Why do you think the newer bikes were better than the early bikes?
(any logical response; the wheels were of equal size)

E 9. _____ Why do you think Orville and Wilbur had more than one business?
(any logical response; they wanted to make money; they were interested in many things)

V 10. _____ Explain what "glider" means in this sentence: Wilbur saw a photograph of a glider.
(like an airplane; an airplane without a motor)

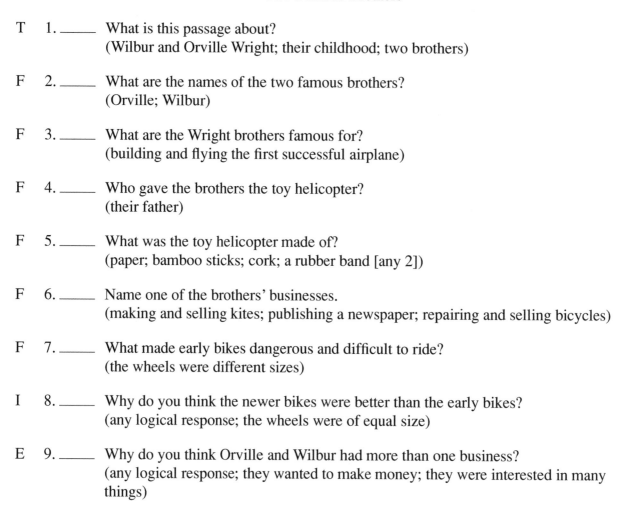

Questions Missed

Comprehension Scoring Guide	
Questions Missed	Level
0–1	Independent
1½–2	Ind./Inst.
2½	Instructional
3–4½	Inst./Frust.
5 +	Frustration

Retelling Rubric

Independent Level/Excellent
States central or key ideas
Identifies important facts
Retains the general sequence of events
Relates most of the content in an organized manner

Instructional Level/Satisfactory
States most central or key ideas
Identifies some important facts
Retains the general sequence of events
Relates an overall sense of the content

Frustration Level/Unsatisfactory
Provides bits of information in a haphazard manner
Little apparent organization

Retelling Notes

A Special Teacher

Many people are aware that Helen Keller was deaf and blind, but not as many people	16
know about Anne Sullivan. She taught Helen Keller to read and write and was her	31
companion for fifty years.	35
Anne Sullivan was born in 1866—more than 150 years ago. She was nearly blind	50
herself, and at the age of ten, she was sent to a poor house and separated from her family.	69
When Anne was fourteen, she was admitted to an institute for the blind in Boston. She had	86
several eye operations and was eventually able to learn to read.	97
When she was twenty-one, Anne was hired to teach Helen Keller, a seven year old	113
who was deaf and blind. Ann studied how to teach Helen Keller, and in March of 1887,	130
Anne went to Alabama to begin her new job. She even brought a doll for Helen.	146
Teaching Helen was extremely difficult because Anne had to spell out words on	159
Helen's hand through touch, and once Helen understood, she was finally able to learn	173
many words. When Helen wanted to know Anne's name, she spelled teacher in Helen's	187
hand. From that day on, Helen called Anne teacher, and Anne was also called a miracle	203
worker.	204
Anne was Helen's teacher and friend for fifty years. Near the end of Anne's life, her	220
eyesight became poor again, and she went blind. Fortunately, Anne knew all the letters in	235
braille—an alphabet blind people can read. When Anne died, she was called truly great.	250

Total Miscues [ ]   Significant Miscues [ ]

Writing Prompt: Write about a teacher and what you learned from him or her.

Note: The rubric for evaluating the student's written response can be found in Appendix B.

Oral Reading Rate	Norm Group Percentile
──── WPM)15000	☐90 ☐75 ☐50 ☐25 ☐10

Word Recognition Scoring Guide		
Total Miscues	Level	Significant Miscues
0–3	Independent	0–2
4–12	Ind./Inst.	3–6
13	Instructional	7
14–24	Inst./Frust.	8–12
25 +	Frustration	13 +

355

LI 6867 (Grade 6) Say: "I'd like you to read out loud [silently]. Think about what you're reading because I'll ask you some questions about it when you're done. Please begin here." [Point to title.]

A Special Teacher

T   1. _____   What is this passage about?
                  (Anne Sullivan; Helen Keller's teacher)

F   2. _____   How did Anne Sullivan gain her sight?
                  (she had many operations)

F   3. _____   What name did Helen call Anne?
                  (teacher)

F   4. _____   How old was Anne when she began teaching Helen?
                  (twenty-one)

F   5. _____   How long were Anne and Helen together?
                  (about fifty years)

F   6. _____   How did Anne teach Helen to spell words?
                  (Anne would spell out words on Helen's hand through touch)

F   7. _____   What did Anne take Helen when she first went to begin to teach her?
                  (a doll)

I   8. _____   Why do you think Anne decided to be a teacher for the blind?
                  (any logical response; she had once been blind, and knew how wonderful it was to learn to read)

E   9. _____   How do you think Helen Keller learned braille?
                  (any logical response; she taught herself)

V   10. _____   Explain what "braille" means in this sentence: Helen Keller taught Anne Sullivan braille.
                  (an alphabet composed of a series of raised bumps that allows blind people to read)

Retelling Rubric
Independent Level/Excellent
States central or key ideas
Identifies important facts
Retains the general sequence of events
Relates most of the content in an organized manner
Instructional Level/Satisfactory
States most central or key ideas
Identifies some important facts
Retains the general sequence of events
Relates an overall sense of the content
Frustration Level/Unsatisfactory
Provides bits of information in a haphazard manner
Little apparent organization

	Retelling Notes

☐	Questions Missed

Comprehension Scoring Guide	
Questions Missed	Level
0–1	Independent
1½–2	Ind./Inst.
2½	Instructional
3–4½	Inst./Frust.
5 +	Frustration

Have You Played This Game?

You might be one of about 500 million people who have played the best-selling board	16
game in the world. It is sold in 80 countries, is available in 26 languages, and over 200 million	35
games have been manufactured and sold. Say "Monopoly" and people of every age can	49
remember lively games with friends and family. How did this phenomenon start?	61
Charles B. Darrow, like most Americans, could not find a job during the Great	75
Depression. He started drawing a game board on his kitchen tablecloth, and soon he made	90
rules, property cards, and little houses and hotels. Evenings found Darrow with friends	103
and family playing his game. Soon news of the game spread by word of mouth, and people	120
asked Darrow for their own sets. Darrow made more games for his friends, and he sensed	136
that his game could actually become a job.	144
In 1934, Darrow took Monopoly to executives at Parker Brothers. They dismissed it for	158
52 design mistakes, but Darrow was confident he had a winning game. With a friend's help, he	175
created handcrafted sets and sold them at a Philadelphia department store. People loved the	189
game and orders soon flooded in, but Darrow knew he couldn't keep pace so he went to Parker	207
Brothers a second time. This time they accepted the game and quickly began mass production.	222
That first year, 1935, Monopoly was the best-selling game in America. Monopoly made	236
Darrow the first millionaire game designer, freeing him from worrying about a job again.	250

Total Miscues [ ]   Significant Miscues [ ]

Writing Prompt: Write about your favorite game and how to play it.

Note: The rubric for evaluating the student's written response can be found in Appendix B.

Oral Reading Rate	Norm Group Percentile
___ WPM)15000	☐ 90 ☐ 75 ☐ 50 ☐ 25 ☐ 10

Word Recognition Scoring Guide		
Total Miscues	Level	Significant Miscues
0–3	Independent	0–2
4–12	Ind./Inst.	3–6
13	Instructional	7
14–24	Inst./Frust.	8–12
25 +	Frustration	13 +

LI 3717 (Grade 7) Say: "I'd like you to read out loud [silently]. Think about what you're reading because I'll ask you some questions about it when you're done. Please begin here." [Point to title.]

Have You Played This Game?

T   1. _____   What is this passage about?
(how the game Monopoly was created)

F   2. _____   How popular is Monopoly?
(best-selling board game in the world; offered in 26 languages; sold in 80 countries; 500 million people have played it [any 1])

F   3. _____   Who created Monopoly?
(Darrow)

F   4. _____   Who were the first people to play Monopoly?
(Darrow; his friends; family [any 2])

F   5. _____   Why did Parker Brothers dismiss Monopoly?
(52 design mistakes; design mistakes)

F   6. _____   What did Darrow do next?
(he made sets and sold them to a Philadelphia department store)

F   7. _____   What did Parker Brothers do when Darrow went to them a second time?
(they accepted the game; they mass produced the game)

I   8. _____   Why do you think Monopoly was so popular during the Great Depression?
(any logical response; people were out of work; they had extra time; it made life more fun)

E   9. _____   Why do you think so many people like to play Monopoly?
(any logical response)

V 10. _____   Explain what "mass production" means in this sentence: This time they accepted the game and quickly began mass production.
(they made a lot of games exactly alike, very quickly)

	Retelling Rubric		Retelling Notes
	Independent Level/Excellent		
	States central or key ideas		
	Identifies important facts		
	Retains the general sequence of events		
	Relates most of the content in an organized manner		
	Instructional Level/Satisfactory		
	States most central or key ideas		
	Identifies some important facts		
	Retains the general sequence of events		
	Relates an overall sense of the content		
	Frustration Level/Unsatisfactory		
	Provides bits of information in a haphazard manner		
	Little apparent organization		

☐ Questions Missed

Comprehension Scoring Guide

Questions Missed	Level
0–1	Independent
1½–2	Ind./Inst.
2½	Instructional
3–4½	Inst./Frust.
5 +	Frustration

Friend of Lions

At the break of dawn, he rises from the bed that is placed just outside the door to his	19
hut. Dressed only in shorts and sandals, he sets out on his daily prowl of Kenya's Kora Game	38
Preserve in Eastern Africa, looking for lions.	44
George Adamson is not a big-game hunter; on the contrary, his days are spent trying to	61
preserve what few wild lions remain on this part of the African continent. The Kenyan	76
government closed Adamson's lion rehabilitation program after several people at his camp	88
were assaulted by the cats he considers the perfection of ageless beauty and grace. Now he	104
searches for the lions he returned from captivity and for their offspring. They come to him	120
when he calls, and he feeds them like pets. He also protects them from poachers.	135
In the late 1950s, when he was a government game warden, Adamson shot a man-eating	151
lioness who had a cub. The story of how he and his wife Joy raised the cub, Elsa, is told in the	173
book and the movie titled Born Free. This story brought the cause of wildlife conservation to	189
the attention of people in many countries around the world. It also raised $600,000 that has	205
been used for a variety of wildlife conservation projects.	214
Since Joy's death in 1980, Adamson has wandered the lonely landscape of this vast game	229
preserve. His long, flowing, golden hair and white beard make him appear like one of the	245
creatures he loves so much.	250

Total Miscues [ ]   Significant Miscues [ ]

Writing Prompt: Write about an animal that you find interesting.

Note: The rubric for evaluating the student's written response can be found in Appendix B.

Oral Reading Rate	Norm Group Percentile
WPM $\frac{}{)15000}$	☐ 90 ☐ 75 ☐ 50 ☐ 25 ☐ 10

Word Recognition Scoring Guide		
Total Miscues	Level	Significant Miscues
0–3	Independent	0–2
4–12	Ind./Inst.	3–6
13	Instructional	7
14–24	Inst./Frust.	8–12
25 +	Frustration	13 +

LI 8183 (Grade 8) Say: "I'd like you to read out loud [silently]. Think about what you're reading because I'll ask you some questions about it when you're done. Please begin here." [Point to title.]

Friend of Lions

T　1. _____　What is this passage about?
(a man who loves and protects lions)

F　2. _____　In what country does George Adamson live?
(Kenya)

F　3. _____　On what continent is Kenya located?
(Africa)

F　4. _____　What is the title of the book and the movie that tells the story of how the Adamsons raised a motherless lion cub?
(*Born Free*)

F　5. _____　In what way are the lions, to Adamson, just like household cats are to us?
(they will come to him when he calls; he feeds them like pets)

F　6. _____　How did *Born Free* aid the cause of wildlife conservation?
(it brought wildlife conservation to the attention of the world; it raised money for wildlife conservation projects)

F　7. _____　What was Adamson's job title at the time when he shot a man-eating lioness?
(he was a government game warden)

I　8. _____　Why do you think Adamson and his wife decided to raise Elsa, the motherless lion cub?
(any logical response; because they shot her mother; she was unable to survive without their help)

E　9. _____　Why do you think the authorities allow Adamson to live out in the wild, completely unprotected?
(any logical response; the lions are used to him; he is a friend of the lions)

V　10. _____　Explain what "poachers" means in this sentence: George Adamson protects lions from poachers.
(people who hunt fish or game illegally)

☐ Questions Missed	

Comprehension Scoring Guide	
Questions Missed	Level
0–1	Independent
1½–2	Ind./Inst.
2½	Instructional
3–4½	Inst./Frust.
5 +	Frustration

Retelling Rubric
Independent Level/Excellent
States central or key ideas
Identifies important facts
Retains the general sequence of events
Relates most of the content in an organized manner
Instructional Level/Satisfactory
States most central or key ideas
Identifies some important facts
Retains the general sequence of events
Relates an overall sense of the content
Frustration Level/Unsatisfactory
Provides bits of information in a haphazard manner
Little apparent organization

Retelling Notes

Ancient Destruction

Pompeii, an ancient city in Southern Italy, was settled in the 8th century B.C. It was	16
overtaken by the Romans in 310 B.C. and became part of the Roman Empire. During its first	33
five hundred years, Pompeii grew from a farming village to an important trading center. Then	48
in 62 A.D. an enormous earthquake hit the city, leaving it destroyed. The residents of the	64
city began rebuilding, but while they were in the middle of rebuilding the city temple, a more	81
lasting disaster arrived. Mount Vesuvius, a volcano which had been thought extinct, erupted in	95
79 A.D. covering Pompeii with hot lava.	102
Eye-witnesses watched Mount Vesuvius erupt as bright flames towered in the sky and	116
black smoke covered the sun. Volcanic ash and lava covered the city until almost no buildings	132
were left standing. As the volcanic eruption hit Pompeii, the universe seemed to fight against	147
the city sending lightning, earthquakes, and tidal waves. This attack lasted for three days,	161
killing all who had survived the volcano. When the dust settled, 15 feet of smoking debris	177
covered what had once been Pompeii.	183
Pompeii was completely buried under ashes, stone, and cinders for almost 2,000 years.	196
After the volcano, looters took what they could find from the city. Pompeii was forgotten until	212
the nineteenth century when the site was rediscovered and excavation began. Much has been	226
learned about the manners and customs of the ancient Romans. Today, visitors can walk	240
through Pompeii and view a city almost 3,000 years old.	250

Total Miscues [　]   Significant Miscues [　]

Writing Prompt: Write about a disaster you've heard about and how it made you feel.

Note: The rubric for evaluating the student's written response can be found in Appendix B.

Oral Reading Rate	Norm Group Percentile
‾‾‾‾‾ WPM)15000	☐ 90 ☐ 75 ☐ 50 ☐ 25 ☐ 10

Word Recognition Scoring Guide		
Total Miscues	Level	Significant Miscues
0–3	Independent	0–2
4–12	Ind./Inst.	3–6
13	Instructional	7
14–24	Inst./Frust.	8–12
25 +	Frustration	13 +

LI 4959 (Grade 9) Say: "I'd like you to read out loud [silently]. Think about what you're reading because I'll ask you some questions about it when you're done. Please begin here." [Point to title.]

Ancient Destruction

T 1. _____ What is this passage about?
(an ancient city, Pompeii, destroyed by a volcano and other natural forces)

F 2. _____ Where is Pompeii located?
(Italy; in Southern Italy)

F 3. _____ How was Pompeii first destroyed?
(by an earthquake)

F 4. _____ What was the name of the volcano that erupted?
(Mount Vesuvius)

F 5. _____ During the volcanic eruption, what other natural disasters happened at the same time?
(lightning; earthquakes; tidal waves [any 2])

F 6. _____ When was Pompeii rediscovered?
(in the nineteenth century; 200 years ago)

F 7. _____ How old is Pompeii today?
(almost 3,000 years old)

I 8. _____ What do you suppose the looters may have taken?
(any logical response)

E 9. _____ If a disaster destroyed where you live, what would be your thoughts, feelings, and actions?
(any logical response)

V 10. _____ Explain what "excavation" means in this sentence: Pompeii was forgotten until the nineteenth century when the site was rediscovered and excavation began.
(digging up; out; uncovering the city's ruins)

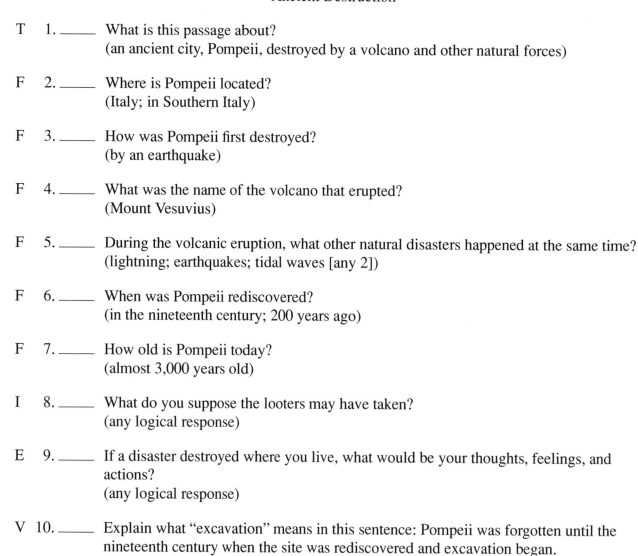

Questions Missed

Comprehension Scoring Guide	
Questions Missed	Level
0–1	Independent
1½–2	Ind./Inst.
2½	Instructional
3–4½	Inst./Frust.
5 +	Frustration

Retelling Rubric
Independent Level/Excellent
States central or key ideas
Identifies important facts
Retains the general sequence of events
Relates most of the content in an organized manner
Instructional Level/Satisfactory
States most central or key ideas
Identifies some important facts
Retains the general sequence of events
Relates an overall sense of the content
Frustration Level/Unsatisfactory
Provides bits of information in a haphazard manner
Little apparent organization

Retelling Notes

Beating the Bonk

Bonk describes the symptoms that occur when your body's carbohydrate stores are used	13
up as a result of sustained exercise. As you exercise, most of the fuel being burned is consumed	31
by your muscles. Both fats and carbohydrates can be used for this process. Fat, stored in fatty	48
tissue, is reduced to free fatty acids which are transported by the blood to the muscles. In	65
contrast, carbohydrates are stored within the muscles as glycogen. During exercise, individual	77
molecules of glycogen are removed and used as energy.	86
Your vital organs also need a continuous supply of fuel. Whether at rest or during	101
exercise, your brain and nervous system depend on blood glucose. The reason why they need	116
glycogen is because the cells of your nervous system don't store glycogen and can't use fat.	132
To meet energy requirements, your blood glucose levels must stay at the same levels. This job	148
is largely done by your liver, which contains large amounts of glycogen that can be converted	164
to glucose.	166
With the muscles and organs vying for glucose, lengthy exercise can drain the liver.	180
When blood glucose levels become too low to meet the fuel requirement of your central	195
nervous system, you begin to feel tired, irritated, and unhappy. In a word, you bonk.	210
Fortunately, you can remedy the bonk. When your blood glucose levels fall, you can	224
replenish them by eating or drinking something rich in carbohydrates. Carbohydrates are	236
quickly digested into glycogen, which is transported to the liver, muscles, and other organs.	250

Adapted from *Nutrition for Cyclists*. Rodale Press.

Total Miscues ☐   Significant Miscues ☐

Writing Prompt: Write about something you've done for exercise.

Note: The rubric for evaluating the student's written response can be found in Appendix B.

Oral Reading Rate	Norm Group Percentile
$\dfrac{\text{WPM}}{)15000}$	☐ 90 ☐ 75 ☐ 50 ☐ 25 ☐ 10

Word Recognition Scoring Guide		
Total Miscues	Level	Significant Miscues
0–3	Independent	0–2
4–12	Ind./Inst.	3–6
13	Instructional	7
14–24	Inst./Frust.	8–12
25 +	Frustration	13 +

LI 1047 (Grade 10) Say: "I'd like you to read out loud [silently]. Think about what you're reading because I'll ask you some questions about it when you're done. Please begin here." [Point to title.]

Beating the Bonk

T   1. _____   What is this passage about?
(what happens when you bonk and how to avoid it; what fuel the body uses; how a diet rich in carbohydrates can cure the bonk)

F   2. _____   What does it mean to bonk?
(to use up carbohydrates by exercise; to feel tired, irritated, unhappy; lose glycogen)

F   3. _____   What is used by your muscles for food?
(fats and carbohydrates [either 1])

F   4. _____   What is glycogen?
(the substance that is stored in muscles from carbohydrates; storage form of glucose; what gives you energy)

F   5. _____   Why does your body need glycogen?
(to meet energy requirements for your brain, muscles, and nervous system; so you can be active; so you won't bonk)

F   6. _____   According to the passage, what are the symptoms of low blood glucose levels?
(you feel tired, irritable, unhappy [any 2])

F   7. _____   How can you overcome bonking?
(by eating or drinking something rich in carbohydrates)

I   8. _____   Why do you think athletes should try to avoid bonking?
(any logical response; it slows performance)

E   9. _____   Based on this passage, if you were an athletic coach what advice about diet would you share?
(any logical response; a diet rich in carbohydrates)

V 10. _____   Explain what "vying" means in this phrase: With your muscles and organs vying for glucose. . . .
(wanting or needing; competing)

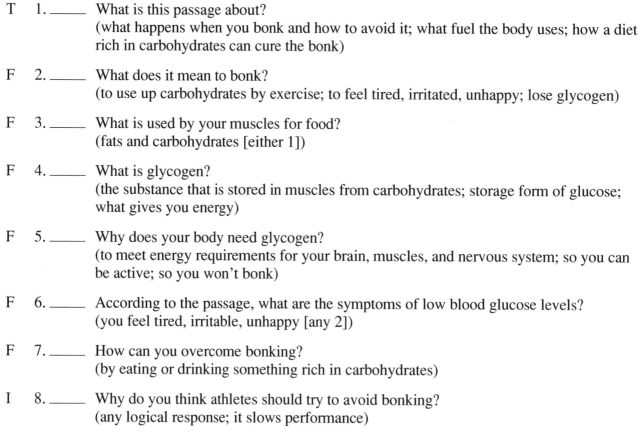

Questions Missed	

Comprehension Scoring Guide	
Questions Missed	Level
0–1	Independent
1½–2	Ind./Inst.
2½	Instructional
3–4½	Inst./Frust.
5 +	Frustration

Retelling Rubric

Independent Level/Excellent
States central or key ideas
Identifies important facts
Retains the general sequence of events
Relates most of the content in an organized manner

Instructional Level/Satisfactory
States most central or key ideas
Identifies some important facts
Retains the general sequence of events
Relates an overall sense of the content

Frustration Level/Unsatisfactory
Provides bits of information in a haphazard manner
Little apparent organization

Retelling Notes

Beards

The history of beards has been a topic of increasing curiosity in today's society. Early	15
man first cherished a beard for religious reasons; primitive races were convinced there was a	30
sacred connection between all parts of a man's body, including his hair, and his personality.	45
Hence, hair had to be carefully guarded from possible foes—this accounts for ancient man's	60
custom of burning hair clippings to prevent them from being used by his enemies for nefarious	76
purposes. Thus, the earliest beard was faith-conditioned and therefore meticulously cared for.	89
Ancient Egyptians used tongs, curling irons, dyes, and even gold dust to give their beards a	105
golden sheen.	107
In those days, shaving was considered perverted. It was a practice reserved for the	121
defeated adversary and the dangerously diseased; lepers were shaved to warn others of their	135
infection. Sometimes those in mourning also shaved as a symbol of vital sacrifice to the dead.	151
The whims of individual rulers also contributed to determining the fate of beards. For	165
example, Queen Elizabeth I, who disliked beards, taxed anyone sprouting a beard of more than	180
two weeks' growth—the amount of assessment depended upon the man's social standing. In	194
France, the beard became fashionable when it was the personal preference of the current king.	209
Francis I grew a beard to hide an ugly scar on his chin; his male subjects emulated the fashion.	228
During the eighteenth century, the Spaniards considered the beard to be in poor taste because	243
their king was unable to grow one.	250

Adapted from *How Did It Begin?* By R. Brasch.

Total Miscues [ ]   Significant Miscues [ ]

Writing Prompt: Write about the pros and cons of shaving.

Note: The rubric for evaluating the student's written response can be found in Appendix B.

Oral Reading Rate	Norm Group Percentile
$\frac{\quad\quad}{15000}$ WPM	☐ 90 ☐ 75 ☐ 50 ☐ 25 ☐ 10

Word Recognition Scoring Guide		
Total Miscues	Level	Significant Miscues
0–3	Independent	0–2
4–12	Ind./Inst.	3–6
13	Instructional	7
14–24	Inst./Frust.	8–12
25 +	Frustration	13 +

LI 1187 (Grade 11) Say: "I'd like you to read out loud [silently]. Think about what you're reading because I'll ask you some questions about it when you're done. Please begin here." [Point to title.]

Beards

T 1. _____ What is this passage about?
(history of beards)

F 2. _____ Name two of the major reasons men grew beards.
(any answer encompassing both religion and politics)

F 3. _____ Why did primitive man wear a beard?
(religious reasons; hair was sacred; there was a connection between all parts of man's body)

F 4. _____ Why did King Francis I grow a beard?
(to cover a scar on his chin)

F 5. _____ Why were lepers shaved?
(to warn others of their infectious disease)

F 6. _____ What did the ancient Egyptians use on their beards?
(tongs; curling irons; dyes; gold dust [any 2])

F 7. _____ Why did the Spaniards consider the beard to be in poor taste?
(their king was unable to grow one)

I 8. _____ Would men probably have beards during the reign of Queen Elizabeth I? Why?
(any logical response; no, she taxed anyone with a beard)

E 9. _____ What are some of the reasons that could account for the present popularity or unpopularity of beards?
(any logical response)

V 10. _____ Explain what "nefarious" means in this phrase: Man's custom of burning hair clippings to prevent them from being used by his enemies for nefarious purposes.
(evil; villainous; wicked; criminal)

☐ Questions Missed

Comprehension Scoring Guide	
Questions Missed	Level
0–1	Independent
1½–2	Ind./Inst.
2½	Instructional
3–4½	Inst./Frust.
5 +	Frustration

Retelling Rubric
Independent Level/Excellent
States central or key ideas
Identifies important facts
Retains the general sequence of events
Relates most of the content in an organized manner
Instructional Level/Satisfactory
States most central or key ideas
Identifies some important facts
Retains the general sequence of events
Relates an overall sense of the content
Frustration Level/Unsatisfactory
Provides bits of information in a haphazard manner
Little apparent organization

Retelling Notes

Earthquakes

Earthquakes can be devastating natural disasters. The infamous San Francisco earthquake	11
of 1906 caused over $200 million of damage, destroyed almost 30,000 buildings, and killed	25
about 450 persons. In Japan, the cities of Tokyo and Yokohama were leveled by the earthquake	41
of 1923 in which more than 140,000 persons were killed by falling buildings and fires, and	57
over a million people were left homeless—all in 30 seconds.	68
Hundreds of earthquakes occur every year throughout the world. Fortunately, few are as	81
destructive as those described above. The development of an accurate system for predicting	94
earthquakes would lessen the loss of life and property, but at present scientists can only study	110
these phenomena. The study of earthquakes is called seismology. Seismographs, instruments	121
sensitive to ground movement, are used to chart motions, and the Richter Scale is commonly	136
used to grade each earthquake's strength on a 1-to-10 scale.	148
We now know that earthquakes are created by sudden shifts that occur along faults deep	163
in the earth's crust. According to the Theory of Continental Drift, the earth's crust consists of	179
about twenty rigid sections, or plates, that are in continuous movement. This movement grinds	193
and presses rocks at the edge of the plates. If the pressure becomes too great, the rocks shift,	211
and the resulting movement sends energy, or seismic waves, to the Earth's surface. Most major	226
earthquakes occur along the edge of the plates, and the most damaging impact occurs at the	242
first surface-point reached by the seismic waves.	250

Total Miscues ☐   Significant Miscues ☐

Writing Prompt: Write about a phenomenon that you might like to study.

Note: The rubric for evaluating the student's written response can be found in Appendix B.

Oral Reading Rate	Norm Group Percentile
$\frac{\text{WPM}}{)15000}$	☐ 90 ☐ 75 ☐ 50 ☐ 25 ☐ 10

Word Recognition Scoring Guide		
Total Miscues	Level	Significant Miscues
0–3	Independent	0–2
4–12	Ind./Inst.	3–6
13	Instructional	7
14–24	Inst./Frust.	8–12
25 +	Frustration	13 +

LI 1296 (Grade 12) Say: "I'd like you to read out loud [silently]. Think about what you're reading because I'll ask you some questions about it when you're done. Please begin here." [Point to title.]

Earthquakes

T   1. _____   What is this passage about?
(earthquakes; scientific study of earthquakes; how earthquakes occur)

F   2. _____   This article named three cities where earthquakes have caused extensive damage. Name two.
(Tokyo; Yokohama; San Francisco [any 2])

F   3. _____   How many earthquakes occur throughout the world each year?
(hundreds)

F   4. _____   According to the article, what problems do earthquakes cause for people?
(people are killed; fires erupt; buildings fall [any 2])

F   5. _____   What is a seismograph?
(an instrument sensitive to ground movement)

F   6. _____   What is the purpose of a Richter Scale?
(to grade an earthquake's strength)

F   7. _____   How do earthquakes occur?
(a sudden shifting of rocks in the earth's crust sends seismic waves, or energy, to the surface of the earth; any reasonable explanation)

I   8. _____   What probably explains why so many people were killed in Japan's 1923 earthquake?
(any logical response; the earthquake occurred in two cities with large populations)

E   9. _____   What services would probably become most important to people who survive a major earthquake? Why?
(any logical response)

V   10. _____   Explain what "infamous" means in this sentence: The infamous San Francisco earthquake of 1906 caused over $200-million worth of damage.
(notorious; famously bad)

	Questions Missed

Comprehension Scoring Guide

Questions Missed	Level
0–1	Independent
1½–2	Ind./Inst.
2½	Instructional
3–4½	Inst./Frust.
5 +	Frustration

Retelling Rubric
Independent Level/Excellent
States central or key ideas
Identifies important facts
Retains the general sequence of events
Relates most of the content in an organized manner
Instructional Level/Satisfactory
States most central or key ideas
Identifies some important facts
Retains the general sequence of events
Relates an overall sense of the content
Frustration Level/Unsatisfactory
Provides bits of information in a haphazard manner
Little apparent organization

Retelling Notes

PART THREE

Early Literacy Assessments

Overview

Some students may experience difficulty with the easiest word lists and passages in the Basic Reading Inventory. The informal measures in Part 3 will be helpful to assess emergent reading behavior. For each measure, there are directions for you. Materials for the student are found in the separate student book. Two forms are available.

A Record Booklet for each form is provided for noting the student's responses and making other comments. These Record Booklets begin on page 379 and are also on the website.

Use the measures in Part 3 to gather insights about student behaviors that indicate the degree of movement toward what might be called conventional reading. Although there are numerals that can be attached to some of the measures, the major purpose of the assessments is to provide a means to gather qualitative judgments related to the student's current abilities. For example:

"Literacy Knowledge" helps determine the degree to which the student understands directionality in reading and concepts about letters, words, and punctuation.

"Wordless Picture Reading" provides the student with an opportunity to dictate a story based on pictures and then read it. During the reading, speech-to-print pointing can be assessed. Follow-up questions help determine the student's ability to locate several words and a specific sentence.

Tasks like "Phoneme Awareness" and "Phoneme Segmentation" have been identified as being among the best predictors of early reading acquisition (Yopp, 1995). Phonological awareness also seems to underlie the learning of letter-sound relationships and subsequent growth in reading.

 These assessments are intended to be used with emergent readers. Some of these students may be just beginning their schooling; others may be struggling readers throughout the grades. Select the assessments that will help you gain greater insights into students' emerging reading abilities so quality instruction and interventions can be provided.

Alphabet Knowledge

Overview

Alphabet Knowledge contains upper-case and lower-case letters of the alphabet in non-sequential order to help assess letter-identification ability.

Materials Needed:

Two 3" x 5" cards
Alphabet Knowledge in the student book (Form 1: p. 120; Form 2: p. 124)
Alphabet Knowledge in the Record Booklet (Form 1: p. 382; Form 2: p. 394)
Record Booklet cover (Form 1: p. 380; Form 2: p. 392)

Procedure

1. Duplicate the appropriate page of the Record Booklet.

2. Place the alphabet page before the student and ask him or her to identify any known letters. Say, **"Here are some letters. I want to see how many you know."** Encourage the student to say "pass" or "skip it" if a particular letter is not known.

3. Use the 3" x 5" cards to block off everything but the lines being read. If necessary, point to each letter with a finger.

4. As the student responds, use the Record Booklet to note correct (+) and incorrect responses. When responses are incorrect, record the actual response or D.K. (student doesn't know) above the stimulus letter. If the student self-corrects, write OK; self-corrections can be made at any time. See examples below:

Letter	*Meaning of Recording*
+ O	Identified correctly
DK H	Don't know
C S	Said C for S
B ok E	Said B for E but self-corrected

Scoring and Interpretation

Count the correct number of responses for the upper-case letters and the lower-case letters. Note the scores in the box on the record sheet and on the front of the Record Booklet. Based on the number of correct responses, make a judgment of the student's alphabet knowledge, and record an X on the continuum located on the cover page of the Record Booklet. Unknown letters or incorrect responses may help form the basis for instructional interventions.

For teaching strategies, consult Section 3.1 in Elish-Piper, Johns, and Lenski (2006) and/or 2.3 in Johns and Lenski (2014).

Writing

Overview

The student will demonstrate his or her ability to write words, letters, and sentences.

Materials Needed:

Pencil or pen
Paper (lined and unlined)
Writing in the Record Booklet (Form 1: p. 383; Form 2: p. 395)
Record Booklet cover (Form 1: p. 380; Form 2: p. 392)

Procedure

1. Give the student lined and unlined paper and a pencil or pen. If possible, have choices of paper and writing instruments.

2. Say, **"I'd like you to write some letters, words, and sentences."** Be patient and encouraging. You might want to ask the student to begin by writing his or her first name. If there is some success, try the last name.

3. After the student has finished, invite him or her to share what was written. Make mental notes or use the Record Booklet.

4. For the student who says "I can't write," you might ask him or her to print an X. Continue with a *few* other letters and perhaps names and numbers that the student may know. You might also suggest general categories of words: pets, colors, foods, things you can do.

Scoring and Interpretation

Informally evaluate the student's writing using the areas on the Writing page in the Record Booklet. Record an X on the continuum located on the cover page of the Record Booklet that represents your overall judgment.

For teaching strategies, consult the bonus chapter on the CD in Elish-Piper, Johns, and Lenski (2006).

Literacy Knowledge

Overview

This assessment contains questions you ask while sharing written material with the student. These questions will help you assess the student's knowledge of print directionality, letters, words, punctuation, and the like.

Materials Needed:

Remove and bind *New Shoes* (Form 1) or *A New Cat* (Form 2) at the back of the student book
Two 3" x 5" cards
Literacy Knowledge in the Record Booklet (Form 1: p. 384; Form 2: p. 396)
Record Booklet cover (Form 1: p. 380; Form 2: p. 392)

Procedure

1. Duplicate the appropriate pages of the Record Booklet.

2. Use *New Shoes* or *A New Cat* from the student book or secure some type of reading material that may be of interest to the student. The student will *not* have to read; rather, he or she will be given an opportunity to demonstrate understanding of how print works and basic knowledge of words, letters, and punctuation. Be sure the items on the test are appropriate for the type of reading material if you decide not to use *New Shoes* or *A New Cat*.

3. Say, **"I'd like you to show me some of the things you know about reading. You won't have to read."**

4. Begin with the first item in the Record Booklet and proceed through the test.

5. Stop if the student seems frustrated.

6. Note any relevant observations in the Record Booklet.

Scoring and Interpretation

1. Circle plus (+) for correct responses and minus (–) for incorrect responses.

2. Count the number of pluses and record the total in the box on the record sheet and on the front of the Record Booklet. The maximum score is 20.

Informally judge the student's knowledge of literacy concepts on the Literacy Knowledge page in the Record Booklet, and record an X on the continuum located on the cover of the Record Booklet. Areas of concern can be strengthened by the instructional program you design for the student.

For teaching strategies, consult Sections 2.1 and 2.2 in Elish-Piper, Johns, and Lenski (2006) and/or 2.2, 2.3, and 2.5 in Johns and Lenski (2014).

Wordless Picture Reading

Overview

Wordless picture reading will help assess the student's ability to tell a story using pictures.

Materials Needed:

Digital or tape recorder (optional)
One Wordless Picture Story in the student book (Form 1: p. 121; Form 2: p. 125)
Record Booklet cover (Form 1: p. 380; Form 2: p. 392)

Procedure

1. Show the student the entire page containing the wordless picture story.

2. Invite the student to look at each frame in order. Point to each frame in order as you say, **"I think you can use these pictures to tell me a story. Think about the story the pictures tell."** Give the student time to study the pictures.

3. Then ask the student to look at the pictures again and when ready, begin telling the story with the first picture (point to it). Say, **"Tell me your story from the pictures. Begin here. I'll write it for you."**

4. As the student tells the story, write the student's dictation on a copy of the record sheet of the wordless picture story or on a separate piece of paper. This is similar to what teachers do in a language experience activity. You may also want to record the student's story for later in-depth analysis.

5. After the student has finished dictating, have him or her read it aloud while pointing to the words. If the reading is similar to the text, mentally note miscues. If the text is "read" quite differently from the text, you may wish to write what the student says.

6. Following the student's reading, ask the student to point to several words in the text and to find where a particular sentence begins and ends.

Scoring and Interpretation

Make qualitative judgments regarding the student's ability to follow directions and the level of language used in telling the story. Look for evidence that the story connects to the pictures and the degree to which the student has a sense of story and any evidence that the student uses book language. Then record Xs that reflect your judgments on the continuums located on the cover of the Record Booklet.

For teaching strategies, consult Sections 2.1, 2.2, and 2.3 in Elish-Piper, Johns, and Lenski (2006) and/or 2.1 and 2.13 in Johns and Lenski (2014).

Auditory Discrimination

Overview

This test will help evaluate the student's ability to distinguish between words that differ in one phoneme (sound).

Materials Needed:

Auditory Discrimination in the Record Booklet (Form 1: p. 387; Form 2: p. 399)
Record Booklet cover (Form 1: p. 380; Form 2: p. 392)

Procedure

1. Prior to testing, practice the words on the list, saying them clearly in a normal voice.

2. Do not rush the student during the assessment. Place a ✓ in the appropriate column, total correct responses, and record the score in the box.

3. If the student misses a pair or asks for one to be repeated, move on to the next item and return to any such items at the conclusion of the test.

4. Facing the student, say:

   "Listen to the words I am about to say: fair-far.

   Do they sound exactly the same or are they different? (For young children, you may prefer the words 'alike' and 'not alike' in place of the words 'same' and 'different.')

   Yes, they are different.

   Listen to these two words: cap-cap.

   Are they the same or different?

   Now I am going to read you more pairs of words. I want you to tell me if they are the same or different. Do you understand what you are to do? Please turn your back to me and listen very carefully."

5. Say all the words distinctly but in a normal voice.

6. Be alert for students who do not understand the concepts "same" and "different."

Scoring and Interpretation

Note the number of correct responses, enter the total in the box, and enter this score on the front of the Record Booklet. Based on the score, make a judgment of the student's auditory discrimination ability, and record an X on the continuum located on the cover of the Record Booklet.

For teaching strategies, consult Section 3.2 in Elish-Piper, Johns, and Lenski (2006) and/or 2.4 and 2.6 in Johns and Lenski (2014).

Phoneme Segmentation

Overview

This test assesses the student's ability to segment phonemes or sounds in spoken words. This ability is strongly related to success in reading and spelling acquisition.

Note: This assessment was designed for use with English speaking kindergartners. It may also be used with older students experiencing difficulty in literacy acquisition.

Materials Needed:

Phoneme Segmentation in the Record Booklet (Form 1: p. 388; Form 2: p. 400)
Record Booklet cover (Form 1: p. 380; Form 2: p. 392)

Procedure

1. Duplicate the appropriate section of the Record Booklet.

2. With the student, say **"We're going to play a word game. I'm going to say a word and I want you to break the word apart. You are going to tell me each sound in the word in order. For example, if I say 'old,' you should say '/o/-/l/-/d/.'"** (Administrator: *Be sure to say the sounds, not the letters, in the word.*)

3. Then say: **"Let's try a few together."** The practice items are *ride, go*, and *man*. If necessary, help the student by segmenting the word for him or her. Encourage the student to repeat the segmented sounds. You could move a marker for each sound or drop a penny into a cup for each sound to highlight the segmentation.

4. During the test, feedback is provided to the student. You could nod or say "Right" or "That's right." If the student is incorrect, correct him or her. You should also provide the appropriate response.

5. Proceed through all 11 items. Circle those items that the student correctly segments. Incorrect responses may be recorded on the blank line following the item.

Scoring and Interpretation

The student's score is the number of items he or she correctly segments into all constituent phonemes. No partial credit is given. For example, *she* (item 5 in Form 1) contains two phonemes /sh/-/e/; *grew* (item 7 in Form 1) contains three phonemes /g/-/r/-/ew/; and *three* (item 15 in Form 2) contains three phonemes /th/-/r/-/ee/. If the student notes letter names instead of sounds, the response is coded as incorrect, and the type of error is noted in the Record Booklet. Such notes are helpful in understanding the student. Some students may partially segment, simply repeat the stimulus item, provide nonsense responses, or give letter names. Total the number of correct responses and place the score in the box on the record sheet and on the cover of the Record Booklet. Then make an overall judgment of the student's phoneme segmentation abilities. For further information on this test, see Hallie Kay Yopp, "A Test for Assessing Phonemic Awareness in Young Children," *The Reading Teacher, 49* (September 1995), 20–29. A wide range of scores is likely.

For teaching strategies, consult Section 3.2 in Elish-Piper, Johns, and Lenski (2006) and/or 2.7 in Johns and Lenski (2014).

Phoneme Awareness (Spelling)*

Overview

This brief spelling test will help assess the student's ability to associate letters with the sounds in words.

Materials Needed:

Pencil
Phoneme Awareness for the student (Form 1: p. 389; Form 2: p. 401)
Record Booklet cover (Form 1: p. 380; Form 2: p. 392)

Procedure

1. Say, **"I'm going to ask you to spell some words. Before you spell them, let's do a couple together."** Begin by modeling the spelling of *mat* by asking the student to think about what letter comes first, what next, and so on. You could say:
   "Let's begin with the word *mat*."
   "What letter comes first in *mat*?" If the student says *m*, write the *m* on the record sheet. If the student says an incorrect letter, say, **"No, it is an *m*."**
   Ask the student to say the word *mat* and ask, **"What else do you hear?"** If the student says *t*, write it on the record sheet with a space for the vowel. If necessary, correct the student by using a comment similar to that already mentioned.
   Ask, **"What else do you hear?"** If the student says *e*, say, **"No, it is an *a*."** Write the word and show it to the student.

2. Repeat the above process with *lip*. If the student is able to say the correct beginning letters for *mat* and *lip*, begin the test without any additional prompting.

3. Give the student the pencil and begin to dictate the 12 words in sentences. You may help once on the first letter for the words *back* and *feet*. No help should be given on the remaining words. The student can say the word out loud as it is being written. If the student asks how to form a letter and asks for it specifically, you may show the student how the letter is made.

4. Observe the spelling and ask the student to identify any letters that are unreadable.

5. If the student is unable to provide the correct initial consonant on *both* the sample words *and* the first two test words, stop the test.

6. The twelve words and sentences are:

1. back	I came back to school.	7. side	I'm at the side door.
2. feet	My feet are small.	8. chin	I hurt my chin.
3. step	I took a big step.	9. dress	You can dress yourself.
4. junk	I have junk in my desk.	10. peeked	I peeked in the box.
5. picking	I am picking up paper.	11. lamp	Turn off the lamp.
6. mail	Please mail the letter.	12. road	The road is bumpy.

Scoring and Interpretation

Count the number of correct responses and place the score in the box on the record sheet and on the front of the Record Booklet. Then make an overall judgment of the student's spelling. You may want to make separate judgments for "B" beginnings, "M" middles, and "E" ends. Be sure your focus is on sounds, not letters. For *junk*, both *j* and *g* would be considered correct. Record B, M, and E on the continuum located on the cover of the Record Booklet and use an X to represent your overall assessment.

For teaching strategies, consult Sections 3.2 and 3.3 in Elish-Piper, Johns, and Lenski (2006) and/or 2.4 in Johns and Lenski (2014).

*Based on the work of Darrell Morris.

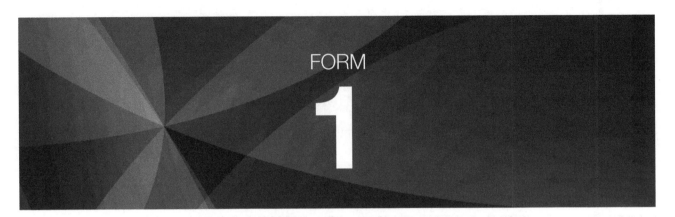

FORM

1

Early Literacy Assessments
Record Booklet

Teacher Copy

Note: This Performance Booklet is on the Basic Reading Inventory website.

Record Booklet for Early Literacy Assessments

Jerry L. Johns, Laurie Elish-Piper, and Beth Johns

Student _____ Grade _____ Gender M F Date of Test _____

School _____ Examiner _____ Date of Birth _____

Address _____ Current Book/Level _____ Age _____

Profile of Emergent Reader Behavior

	Low or Not Evident	Some	High or Very Evident

Alphabet Knowledge

_____/26 upper case

_____/28 lower case

Writing

Literacy Knowledge

_____/20

Wordless Picture Reading

sense of story

connects pictures

language use

reading dictation

Auditory Discrimination

_____/12

Phoneme Segmentation

_____/11

Phoneme Awareness

_____/12

Qualitative Analysis of Early Literacy Assessment Insights

General Directions: Note the degree to which the student shows behavior or evidence in the following areas. Space is provided for additional items.

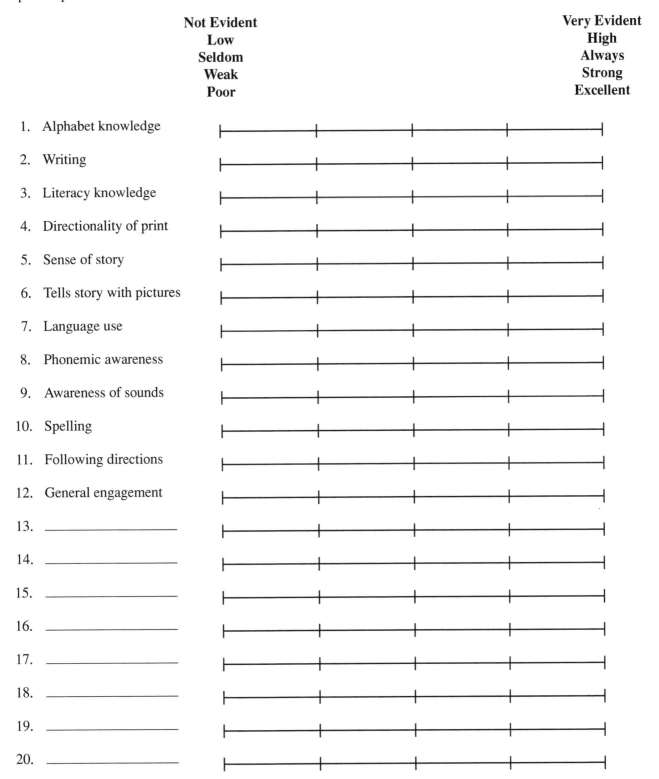

	Not Evident Low Seldom Weak Poor			Very Evident High Always Strong Excellent

1. Alphabet knowledge
2. Writing
3. Literacy knowledge
4. Directionality of print
5. Sense of story
6. Tells story with pictures
7. Language use
8. Phonemic awareness
9. Awareness of sounds
10. Spelling
11. Following directions
12. General engagement
13. _____
14. _____
15. _____
16. _____
17. _____
18. _____
19. _____
20. _____

Alphabet Knowledge

(Student Book copy is on page 120.)

Brief Directions: Present the alphabet sheet to the student. Use 3" x 5" cards to block off everything but the lines being read. If necessary, point to each letter with a finger. Then say, **"Here are some letters. I want to see how many you know."** Place a + above correctly identified letters. Record the student's responses for incorrect letters. Total correct responses, and record the score in the box.

O	H	S	E	G	P	
X	V	I	M	J	D	K
B	T	R	Z	F	N	
Y	Q	W	C	U	A	L

□ **Correct**

b	x	e	c	j	m	g
l	u	r	t	q	h	y
s	d	o	a	k	w	a
i	p	v	f	n	z	g

□ **Correct**

Observations, Comments, Notes, and Insights

Writing

(No student copy; supply paper and writing instruments.)

Brief Directions: Give the student paper and pencil. Ask the student to do some writing. Record qualitative judgments, observations, and insights below.

	Not Evident Low Seldom Weak Poor			Very Evident High Always Strong Excellent

Directionality

Left to right

Top to bottom

Writing

Scribbles or "cursivelike" scribbles

Letterlike formations

Repeated letters, numbers, words

Variety of letters, numbers, words

Knowledge of first (F) and last
    (L) name

Letter-Sound Relationships

Represents sounds heard at word
    beginnings

Represents sounds heard at word
    endings

Represents sounds heard in
    middles of words

Writing Conventions

Use of word boundaries

Use of punctuation

Overall Message Intent (check one)

_____ Student indicated no message intent.

_____ Student talked about but did not read or pretend to read what was written.

_____ Student was able to read what was written.

Teacher could make sense of writing independently. _____ yes _____ no

Observations, Comments, Notes, and Insights

Literacy Knowledge

(Student Book copy of *New Shoes*)

Brief Directions: Show *New Shoes* to the student. Say, **"I'd like you to show me some of the things you know about reading. You won't have to read."** Ask the following questions as *you* read the book to the student. Circle correct (+) or incorrect (–) responses. Total correct responses.

Page

	+	–	1. Hand the book to the child and say, **"Show me the front of this book."**
1	+	–	2. Say, **"Point to where I should start reading."** *Read page 1.*
2	+	–	3. Ask, **"Which way should I go?"** Check for knowledge of left to right. *Read first line of page 2.*
2/3	+	–	4. Ask, **"Where should I go after that?"** Check for knowledge of a return sweep to the left. *Read rest of page 2 and page 3.*
3	+	–	5. On page 3, point to the comma and ask, **"What's this or what's this for?"**
4	+	–	6. *Read text on page 4.* Point to a period and ask, **"What's this or what's this for?"**
5	+	–	7. *Read text on page 5.* Point to the exclamation mark and ask, **"What's this or what's this for?"**
6	+	–	8. *Read text on page 6.* Point to the question mark and ask, **"What's this or what's this for?"**
6	+	–	9. Point to a lower-case letter (m, y, s) and say, **"Find a capital letter like this, find an upper-case letter like this, or find the big one like this."** Repeat for each letter.
7	+	–	10. *Read text on page 7.* Say, **"Show me one letter."** (Two 3" x 5" cards may be useful for items 10–19.)
	+	–	11. Say, **"Now show me two letters."**
	+	–	12. Say, **"Show me only one word."**
	+	–	13. Say, **"Now show me two words."**
	+	–	14. Say, **"Show me the first letter of a word."**
	+	–	15. Say, **"Show me the last letter of a word."**
	+	–	16. Say, **"Show me a long word."**

+   –   17. Say, **"Show me a short word."**

+   –   18. Say, **"Show me a sentence."**

8–9   +   –   19. ***Read text on pages 8 and 9.*** Point to a capital letter (I, O, M) and say, **"Find a small letter like this or find a lower-case letter like this."** Repeat for each letter.

10   +   –   20. ***Read text on page 10.*** Close the book, and hand it to the child with back cover showing and say, **"Show me the title or show me the name of the book."**

☐ **Total Correct**

Qualitative Judgments of Literacy Knowledge

	Not Evident Low Seldom Weak Poor				Very Evident High Always Strong Excellent
Overall engagement	├	┼	┼	┼	┤
Understanding of print directionality	├	┼	┼	┼	┤
Knowledge of punctuation	├	┼	┼	┼	┤
Correspondence of upper-case with lower-case letters	├	┼	┼	┼	┤
Knowledge of *letter* and *letters*	├	┼	┼	┼	┤
Knowledge of *word* and *words*	├	┼	┼	┼	┤
Ability to frame a sentence	├	┼	┼	┼	┤

Observations, Comments, Notes, and Insights

Wordless Picture Reading

(Student Book copy is on page 121.)

Student's Dictation

Auditory Discrimination

(No student copy is needed.)

			Correct	Incorrect
1. bad	—	dad	_____	_____
2. buff	—	bus	_____	_____
3. watch	—	watch	_____	_____
4. ball	—	bowl	_____	_____
5. fall	—	fall	_____	_____
6. sink	—	think	_____	_____
7. lag	—	lad	_____	_____
8. tot	—	top	_____	_____
9. set	—	sit	_____	_____
10. foam	—	phone	_____	_____
11. rode	—	rode	_____	_____
12. lab	—	lad	_____	_____

Total Correct ☐

Phoneme Segmentation*

(No student copy needed.)

Directions: Today we're going to play a word game. I'm going to say a word and I want you to break the word apart. You are going to tell me each sound in the word in order. For example, if I say "old," you should say "/o/-/l/-/d/." (*Administrator: Be sure to say the sounds, not the letters, in the word.*) Let's try a few together.

Practice items: (*Assist the child in segmenting these items as necessary.*) ride, go, man

Test items: (*Circle those items that the student correctly segments; incorrect responses may be recorded on the blank line following the item.*) The correct number of phonemes is indicated in parentheses.

1. dog (3) _____

2. keep (3) _____

3. fine (3) _____

4. no (2) _____

5. she (2) _____

6. wave (3) _____

7. grew (3) _____

8. that (3) _____

9. red (3) _____

10. me (2) _____

11. sat (3) _____

Total Correct ☐

Adapted from Hallie Kay Yopp, "A Test for Assessing Phonemic Awareness in Young Children," *The Reading Teacher*, 49 (September 1995), 20–29.

Phoneme Awareness (Spelling)

(Teacher and student copy)

_____

_____

1. _____

2. _____

3. _____

4. _____

5. _____

6. _____

7. _____

8. _____

9. _____

10. _____

11. _____

12. _____

[ ] **Correct**　　　　_____ Beginnings (B)　　_____ Middles (M)　　_____ Ends (E)

Observations, Comments, Notes, and Insights

Early Literacy Assessments
Record Booklet

Teacher Copy

Note: This Performance Booklet is on the Basic Reading Inventory website.

Record Booklet for Early Literacy Assessments

Jerry L. Johns, Laurie Elish-Piper, and Beth Johns

Student _____ Grade _____ Gender M F Date of Test _____

School _____ Examiner _____ Date of Birth _____

Address _____ Current Book/Level _____ Age _____

Profile of Emergent Reader Behavior

	Low or Not Evident	Some		High or Very Evident

Alphabet Knowledge

_____/26 upper case

_____/28 lower case

Writing

Literacy Knowledge

_____/20

Wordless Picture Reading

sense of story

connects pictures

language use

reading dictation

Auditory Discrimination

_____/12

Phoneme Segmentation

_____/11

Phoneme Awareness

_____/12

Qualitative Analysis of Early Literacy Assessment Insights

General Directions: Note the degree to which the student shows behavior or evidence in the following areas. Space is provided for additional items.

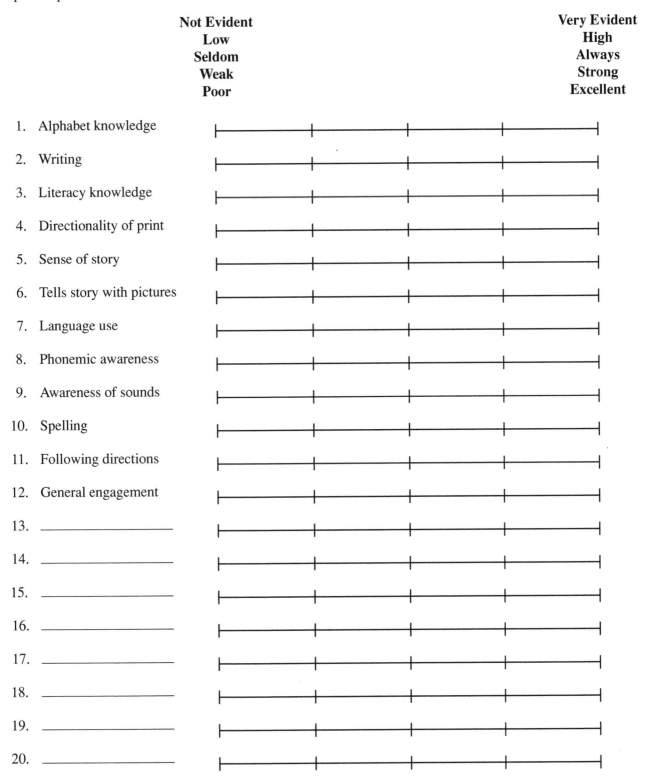

	Not Evident Low Seldom Weak Poor			Very Evident High Always Strong Excellent

1. Alphabet knowledge
2. Writing
3. Literacy knowledge
4. Directionality of print
5. Sense of story
6. Tells story with pictures
7. Language use
8. Phonemic awareness
9. Awareness of sounds
10. Spelling
11. Following directions
12. General engagement
13. _____
14. _____
15. _____
16. _____
17. _____
18. _____
19. _____
20. _____

Alphabet Knowledge

(Student Book copy is on page 124.)

Brief Directions: Present the alphabet sheet to the student. Use 3" x 5" cards to block off everything but the lines being read. If necessary, point to each letter with a finger. Then say, **"Here are some letters. I want to see how many you know."** Place a + above correctly identified letters. Record the student's responses for incorrect letters. Total correct responses, and record the score in the box.

X	V	I	M	J	D	K
O	H	S	E	G	P	
Y	Q	W	C	U	A	L
B	T	R	Z	F	N	

☐ **Correct**

l	u	r	t	q	h	y
b	x	e	c	j	m	g
i	p	v	f	n	z	g
s	d	o	a	k	w	a

☐ **Correct**

Observations, Comments, Notes, and Insights

Writing

(No student copy; supply paper and writing instruments.)

Brief Directions: Give the student paper and pencil. Ask the student to do some writing. Record qualitative judgments, observations, and insights below.

	Not Evident Low Seldom Weak Poor				Very Evident High Always Strong Excellent

Directionality

Left to right

Top to bottom

Writing

Scribbles or "cursivelike" scribbles

Letterlike formations

Repeated letters, numbers, words

Variety of letters, numbers, words

Knowledge of first (F) and last (L) name

Letter-Sound Relationships

Represents sounds heard at word beginnings

Represents sounds heard at word endings

Represents sounds heard in middles of words

Writing Conventions

Use of word boundaries

Use of punctuation

Overall Message Intent (check one)

_____ Student indicated no message intent.

_____ Student talked about but did not read or pretend to read what was written.

_____ Student was able to read what was written.

Teacher could make sense of writing independently. _____ yes _____ no

Observations, Comments, Notes, and Insights

Literacy Knowledge

(Student Book copy of *A New Cat*)

Brief Directions: Show *A New Cat* to the student. Say, **"I'd like you to show me some of the things you know about reading. You won't have to read."** Ask the following questions as *you* read the book to the student. Circle correct (+) or incorrect (−) responses. Total correct responses.

Page

	+	−	1. Hand the book to the child and say, **"Show me the front of this book."**
1	+	−	2. Say, **"Point to where I should start reading."** *Read page 1.*
2	+	−	3. Ask, **"Which way should I go?"** Check for knowledge of left to right. *Read first line of page 2.*
2/3	+	−	4. Ask, **"Where should I go after that?"** Check for knowledge of a return sweep to the left. *Read rest of page 2 and page 3.*
3	+	−	5. On page 3, point to the comma and ask, **"What's this or what's this for?"**
4	+	−	6. *Read text on page 4.* Point to a period and ask, **"What's this or what's this for?"**
5	+	−	7. *Read text on page 5.* Point to the exclamation mark and ask, **"What's this or what's this for?"**
5	+	−	8. *Read text on page 6.* Point to the question mark and ask, **"What's this or what's this for?"**
6	+	−	9. Point to a lower-case letter (t and i) and say, **"Find a capital letter like this, find an upper-case letter like this, or find the big one like this."** Repeat for each letter.
7	+	−	10. *Read text on page 7.* Say, **"Show me one letter."** (Two 3" X 5" cards may be useful for items 10–19.)
	+	−	11. Say, **"Now show me two letters."**
	+	−	12. Say, **"Show me only one word."**
	+	−	13. Say, **"Now show me two words."**
	+	−	14. Say, **"Show me the first letter of a word."**
	+	−	15. Say, **"Show me the last letter of a word."**
	+	−	16. Say, **"Show me a long word."**

+   –   17. Say, **"Show me a short word."**

+   –   18. Say, **"Show me a sentence."**

8–9   +   –   19. ***Read text on pages 8 and 9.*** Point to a capital letter (N, I, M) and say, **"Find a small letter like this or find a lower-case letter like this."** Repeat for each letter.

+   –   20. Close the book, and hand it to the child with back cover showing and say, **"Show me the title or show me the name of the book."**

☐ **Total Correct**

Qualitative Judgments of Literacy Knowledge

	Not Evident Low Seldom Weak Poor				Very Evident High Always Strong Excellent
Overall engagement	├	┼	┼	┼	┤
Understanding of print directionality	├	┼	┼	┼	┤
Knowledge of punctuation	├	┼	┼	┼	┤
Correspondence of upper-case with lower-case letters	├	┼	┼	┼	┤
Knowledge of *letter* and *letters*	├	┼	┼	┼	┤
Knowledge of *word* and *words*	├	┼	┼	┼	┤
Ability to frame a sentence	├	┼	┼	┼	┤

Observations, Comments, Notes, and Insights

Wordless Picture Reading

(Student Book copy is on page 125.)

Student's Dictation

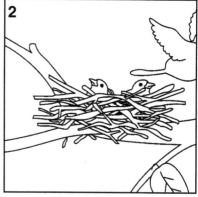

Auditory Discrimination

(No student copy is needed.)

			Correct	**Incorrect**
1. bed	—	bad	_____	_____
2. moth	—	moss	_____	_____
3. look	—	look	_____	_____
4. sick	—	sit	_____	_____
5. get	—	get	_____	_____
6. fan	—	tan	_____	_____
7. mug	—	mud	_____	_____
8. tip	—	tick	_____	_____
9. hit	—	sit	_____	_____
10. pick	—	pin	_____	_____
11. sold	—	sold	_____	_____
12. gnat	—	nap	_____	_____

Total Correct ☐

Phoneme Segmentation*

(No student copy needed.)

Directions: Today we're going to play a word game. I'm going to say a word and I want you to break the word apart. You are going to tell me each sound in the word in order. For example, if I say "old," you should say "/o/-/l/-/d/." *(Administrator: Be sure to say the sounds, not the letters, in the word.)* Let's try a few together.

Practice items: *(Assist the child in segmenting these items as necessary.)* ride, go, man

Test items: *(Circle those items that the student correctly segments; incorrect responses may be recorded on the blank line following the item.)* The correct number of phonemes is indicated in parentheses.

1. lay (2)   _____

2. race (3)   _____

3. zoo (2)   _____

4. three (3)   _____

5. job (3)   _____

6. in (2)   _____

7. ice (2)   _____

8. at (2)   _____

9. top (3)   _____

10. by (2)   _____

11. do (2)   _____

Total Correct   ☐

Adapted from Hallie Kay Yopp, "A Test for Assessing Phonemic Awareness in Young Children," *The Reading Teacher, 49* (September 1995), 20–29.

Phoneme Awareness (Spelling)

(Teacher and student copy)

_____

_____

1. _____

2. _____

3. _____

4. _____

5. _____

6. _____

7. _____

8. _____

9. _____

10. _____

11. _____

12. _____

☐ **Correct**   _____ Beginnings (B)   _____ Middles (M)   _____ Ends (E)

Observations, Comments, Notes, and Insights

PART FOUR

Appendices, References, and Index

Procedures for Eliciting and Evaluating Passage Retellings

How will this student retell the story?

Retelling Procedure 1*

Narrative Passages

1. Ask the student to retell the passage by saying: "Tell me about (name of passage) as if you were telling it to someone who has never heard it before."

2. Use the following prompts only when necessary:

   "What comes next?"

   "Then what happened?"

   If the student stops retelling and does not continue with the above prompts, ask a question about the passage that is based on that point in the passage at which the student has paused. For example, "What did the boys do after raking the leaves?"

3. When a student is unable to retell the story, or if the retelling lacks sequence and detail, prompt the retelling step by step. The following questions may be helpful:

   "Who was the passage about?"

   "When did the story happen?"

   "Where did the story happen?"

   "What was the main character's problem?"

   "How did he (or she) try to solve the problem? What was done first/next?"

   "How was the problem solved?"

   "How did the story end?"

*Adapted from: Morrow, L. M. (1985). Retelling stories: A strategy for improving young children's comprehension, concept of story structure, and oral language complexity. *The Elementary School Journal, 85*, 647–661.

Retelling Procedure 2*

Story Structure

General Directions: To evaluate passages for story structure, place a plus (+) next to the element if the student includes it. Include the number of points scored for each element based on retelling.

1. *Characters* (5 points)   _____

   Introduction of characters (2 points main characters, 1 point for each additional, total of 5 points)

2. *Setting* (5 points)   _____

   A time or place where the story happens (5 points)

   OR

   A general setting statement (5 points)

3. *Theme* (10 points) = gist   _____

   Initiating events that set the goal for the story

   OR

   A goal becomes evident for the main character to achieve or a problem is evident to solve

4. *Plot Episodes* (10 points)   _____

   Events leading toward accomplishing the goal or solving the problem (adjust maximum raw score to equal 10 based on number of events)

5. *Resolution* (10 points)   _____

   The problem is solved or goal is reached (8 points)
   The story is ended (2 points)

6. *Sequence* (10 points)   _____

   Story is told with elements in the structural order listed above (10 points if all in order; 6.6 points if 3 in order; 3.3 points if 2 in order; 1 point if 1 in order; 0 if none in order; omitted elements are not scored)

Total Points   _____

× 2

Retelling Score   ☐
(out of 100)

---

*Adapted from: Grant, J. (1984). Deciding what's important for readers to remember. Paper presented at the Annual Conference of the International Reading Association, Atlanta.

Retelling Procedure 3*

Expository Passages

Independent Level

Retelling will generally reflect:

1. the text structure
2. organization of how the material was presented
3. main ideas and details contained in the material

Instructional Level

Retelling will generally reflect:

1. less content than at an independent level
2. some minor misinterpretations and inaccuracies
3. organization that differs, in some respects, to the way it was presented in the material

Frustration Level

Retelling will generally be:

1. haphazard
2. incomplete
3. characterized by bits of information not related in any logical or sequential order

*Adapted from: Johnson, M. S., Kress, R. A., & Pikulski, J. J. (1987). *Informal reading inventories* (2nd ed.) Newark, DE: International Reading Association.

Summary Sheets and Rubric for Written Response

Even readers who practice in advance may make miscues.

Note: These summary sheets are on the Basic Reading Inventory website.

Miscue Summary Sheet for Forms LL and LI

MISCUES							
Substitution	Insertion	Omission	Reversal	Repetition	Self-Correction of Unacceptable Miscue	Meaning Change (Significant Miscue)	

Name _____ Date _____

Passage Title _____

Form _____

Total Miscues ☐   Significant Miscues ☐

From Jerry L. Johns, Laurie Elish-Piper, and Beth Johns, *Basic Reading Inventory* (12th ed.). Copyright © 2017 by Kendall Hunt Publishing Company (1-800-247-3458, ext. 6). May be reproduced for noncommercial educational purposes. Website: www.kendallhunt.com

Summary of Student's Oral Reading Performance on the Basic Reading Inventory

Student _____ Grade _____

Examiner _____ Date _____

SUMMARY OF STUDENT'S MISCUES IN ORAL READING			
Substitutions			
Different Beginnings	**Different Middles**	**Different Endings**	**Different in Several Parts**

Insertions	**Omissions**	**Repetitions**	**Miscellaneous**

Miscue Tally and Reading Behavior Summary Charts for the Basic Reading Inventory

Student _____ Grade _____

Examiner _____ Date _____

Directions: Record the number of miscues from all passages at the student's independent, instructional, and instructional/frustration levels. Total each category. Follow the same procedure for the other reading behaviors. Then make qualitative judgments about the student's reading and check the appropriate columns at the bottom of the cover page of the performance booklet.

Passages Read	Type of Miscue			
	Substitution	Insertion	Omission	Reversal
Kb				
Km				
Ke				
1b				
1m				
1e				
2				
3				
4				
5				
6				
7				
8				
TOTALS				

Passages Read	Other Reading Behaviors		
	Repetition	Self-Correction of Unacceptable Miscue	Meaning Change
Kb			
Km			
Ke			
1b			
1m			
1e			
2			
3			
4			
5			
6			
7			
8			
TOTALS			

Qualitative Summary of Miscues on the Basic Reading Inventory

Student _____ Grade _____

Examiner _____ Date _____

IMPORTANT NOTE:
Remember to only use miscues from the student's independent and instructional levels.

MISCUE	TEXT	GRAPHIC SIMILARITY			CONTEXT		Self-Correction of Unacceptable Miscues
		Beginning	Middle	End	Acceptable	Unacceptable	
Column Total							
Number of Miscues Analyzed							
Percentage							

PREDICTION STRATEGY

Graphic Similarity

B   M   E

100%
90
80
70
60
50
40
30
20
10

___% ___% ___%

Miscues Acceptable in Context

100%
90
80
70
60
50
40
30
20
10

___%

CORRECTION STRATEGY

Unacceptable Miscues Self-Corrected

100%
90
80
70
60
50
40
30
20
10

___%

Summary of Student's Comprehension Performance on the Basic Reading Inventory

Student _____ Grade _____

Examiner _____ Date _____

	ANALYSIS BY TYPE OF QUESTION									
	Fact		**Topic**		**Evaluation**		**Inference**		**Vocabulary**	
Grade	Oral	Silent	Oral	Silent	Oral	Silent	Oral	Silent	Oral	Silent
1m	__/6	__/6	__/1	__/1	__/1	__/1	__/1	__/1	__/1	__/1
1e	__/6	__/6	__/1	__/1	__/1	__/1	__/1	__/1	__/1	__/1
2	__/6	__/6	__/1	__/1	__/1	__/1	__/1	__/1	__/1	__/1
3	__/6	__/6	__/1	__/1	__/1	__/1	__/1	__/1	__/1	__/1
4	__/6	__/6	__/1	__/1	__/1	__/1	__/1	__/1	__/1	__/1
5	__/6	__/6	__/1	__/1	__/1	__/1	__/1	__/1	__/1	__/1
6	__/6	__/6	__/1	__/1	__/1	__/1	__/1	__/1	__/1	__/1
7	__/6	__/6	__/1	__/1	__/1	__/1	__/1	__/1	__/1	__/1
8	__/6	__/6	__/1	__/1	__/1	__/1	__/1	__/1	__/1	__/1
9	__/6	__/6	__/1	__/1	__/1	__/1	__/1	__/1	__/1	__/1
10	__/6	__/6	__/1	__/1	__/1	__/1	__/1	__/1	__/1	__/1
11	__/6	__/6	__/1	__/1	__/1	__/1	__/1	__/1	__/1	__/1
12	__/6	__/6	__/1	__/1	__/1	__/1	__/1	__/1	__/1	__/1
Ratio Missed	__/__	__/__	__/__	__/__	__/__	__/__	__/__	__/__	__/__	__/__
Percent Missed	__%	__%	__%	__%	__%	__%	__%	__%	__%	__%
Total Ratio Missed	__/__		__/__		__/__		__/__		__/__	
Total Percent Missed	__%		__%		__%		__%		__%	

	ANALYSIS BY LEVEL OF COMPREHENSION			
	Lower-Level Comprehension (Fact Questions Only)		**Higher-Level Comprehension (All Other Questions)**	
	Oral	Silent	Oral	Silent
Ratio Missed	__/__	__/__	__/__	__/__
Total Ratio Missed	__/__		__/__	
Total Percent Missed	__%		__%	

Informal Assessment of Comprehension Engagement on the Basic Reading Inventory at Middle-First Grade and Beyond

Student _____ Grade _____

Examiner _____ Date _____

	1m	1e	2	3	4	5	6	7	8	9	10	11	12
Correct responses especially full, fresh, or elaborated (numerals circled)*	___	___	___	___	___	___	___	___	___	___	___	___	___
Incongruent/incorrect responses **unrelated** to the passage in some meaningful, logical way (numerals with Xs)*	___	___	___	___	___	___	___	___	___	___	___	___	___

*Refers to numerals beside the comprehension questions in the performance booklet.

Informal Guidelines for Evaluating Engagement

1. More than one elaboration of a correct response per passage "can be taken as evidence of an alert mind that is engaged and being driven by meaning. It is too soon to say if any significant meanings can be attached to the absence of elaborations, or how much of this can be expected with different types of questions and formats" (Manzo & Manzo, 1993, p. 467).

2. More than three incongruent responses to comprehension questions are "an indication that engagement was weak and nonproductive" (Manzo & Manzo, 1993, p. 467).

Expert Noticing Observation Guide

Student _____ Grade _____

Examiner _____ Date _____

Question	Your Notes
What did you see the student do?	
Why is this important?	
What did you notice about the way the student responded to reading/writing/ discussion activities in terms of the knowledge, strategies, and dispositions necessary to perform the tasks?	
Why do you think the student responded this way?	
What do the student's responses tell you about how well the student understood the tasks?	
What did you learn about the student that will be helpful in planning an appropriate lesson or intervention?	

Class Summary Chart for the Basic Reading Inventory

Teacher _____ Grade _____

Examiner _____ Date _____

Student	Date	Levels				Consistent Strengths (+) and/or Weaknesses (−)												
						Comprehension					Word Recognition						
		Ind.	Inst.	Frust.	Lis.	Fact	Topic	Inference	Evaluation	Vocabulary	Substitutions	Corrections	Repetitions	Omissions	Punctuation	Phonics	Context

Rubric for Written Response

Student _____ Grade _____

Examiner _____ Date _____

Passage Title _____ Level _____

<table>
<tr><td colspan="2" align="center">Rubric for Writing Response</td></tr>
<tr><td>3</td><td>• Response is very closely related to prompt.
• Response makes complete sense.
• Response is well organized.
• Response meets all age-appropriate spelling expectations and writing conventions.</td></tr>
<tr><td>2</td><td>• Response is related to prompt.
• Response makes sense.
• Response is organized in an acceptable manner.
• Response meets most age-appropriate spelling expectations and writing conventions.</td></tr>
<tr><td>1</td><td>• Response is loosely related to prompt.
• Some aspects of response make sense.
• Response is not well organized.
• Response lacks some age-appropriate spelling expectations and writing conventions.</td></tr>
<tr><td>0</td><td>• Response is unrelated to prompt.
• Response does not make sense.
• Response is poorly organized.
• Response lacks most age-appropriate spelling expectations and writing conventions.</td></tr>
</table>

Note: This rubric is specifically intended for Form LL and Form LI, but it may be used with any of the forms.

Comments/Notes

References

Ackland, R. T. (1994). *Let's look at reading: Interactive professional development using informal reading inventories.* Retrieved from ProQuest Digital Dissertations. (AAT 9506465)

Adams, M. J. (1990). *Beginning to read: Thinking and learning about print* (a summary prepared by S. A. Stahl, J. Osborn, & F. Lehr). Champaign: University of Illinois.

Allington, R. L. (2005). The other five "pillars" of effective reading instruction. *Reading Today, 22,* 3.

Allington, R. L. (2012). *What really matters for struggling readers: Designing research-based programs* (3rd ed.). Boston: Pearson.

Allington, R. L., & McGill-Franzen, A. (1980). Word identification errors in isolation and in context: Apples vs. oranges. *The Reading Teacher, 33,* 795–800.

Allington, R. L., McCuiston, K., & Billen, M. (2015). What research says about text complexity and learning to read. *The Reading Teacher, 68*(7), 491–501.

Alvermann, D. E. (1985). Interfacing microcomputers with video-cassettes: A program for teaching the IRI. Paper presented at the meeting of the College Reading Association, Pittsburgh.

Anderson, B., & Joels, R. W. (1986). Informal reading inventories. *Reading Improvement, 23,* 299–302.

Antunez, B. (2002). Implementing reading first with English language learners. *Directions in Language and Education, 15.* Retrieved January 20, 2012 from http://www.ncela.gwu.edu/files/rcd/BE024311/15.pdf

Applegate, M. D., Quinn, K. B., & Applegate, A. J. (2004). *The critical reading inventory.* Columbus, OH: Merrill Prentice Hall.

Applegate, M. D., Quinn, K. B., & Applegate, A. J. (2008). *The critical reading inventory* (2nd ed.). Upper Saddle River, NJ: Pearson Education.

Bader, L. A. (1998). *Bader reading and language inventory* (3rd ed.). Upper Saddle River, NJ: Prentice-Hall.

Bader, L. A. (2002). *Bader reading and language inventory* (4th ed.). Columbus, OH: Merrill Prentice Hall.

Bader, L. A. (2005). *Bader reading and language inventory* (5th ed.). Upper Saddle River, NJ: Merrill Prentice Hall.

Bader, L. A. (2008). *Bader reading and language inventory* (6th ed.). New York: Pearson.

Bader, L. A. (2012). *Bader reading and language inventory* (7th ed.). New York: Pearson.

Barr, R., Blachowicz, C. L. Z., Bates, A., Katz, C., & Kaufman, B. (2007). *Reading diagnoses for teachers: An instructional approach* (5th ed.). Boston: Allyn & Bacon.

Bass, J. F., Dasinger, S., Elish-Piper, L., Matthews, M. W., & Risko, V. J. (2008). *A declaration of readers' rights: Renewing our commitment to students.* Boston: Allyn & Bacon.

Beaver, J., & Carter, M. (2011). *Development reading assessment* (2nd ed.). New York: Pearson.

Beldin, H. O. (1970). Informal reading testing: Historical review and review of the research. In W. K. Durr (Ed.), *Reading difficulties: Diagnosis, correction, and remediation* (pp. 67–84). Newark, DE: International Reading Association.

Berliner, D. C. (1981). Academic learning time and reading achievement. In J. T. Guthrie (Ed.), *Comprehension and teaching: Research reviews* (pp. 203–226). Newark, DE: International Reading Association.

Betts, E. A. (1936). *The prevention and correction of reading difficulties.* Evanston, IL: Row, Peterson and Company.

Betts, E. A. (1941). Reading problems at the intermediate grade level. *The Elementary School Journal, 40,* 737–746.

Betts, E. A. (1946). *Foundations of reading instruction.* New York: American Book Company.

Betts, E. A. (1949). Adjusting instruction to individual needs. In N. B. Henry (Ed.), *Reading in the elementary school* (pp. 266–280). The Forty-Eighth Yearbook of the National Society for the Study of Education, Part II. Chicago: The University of Chicago Press.

Betts, E. A., Everett, M., & Rodewald, F. (1936). Remedial reading. *Journal of Exceptional Children, 2,* 88–91.

Bieber, G., Hulac, D. M., & Schweinle, W. (2015). An independent evaluation of the technical features of the Basic Reading Inventory. *Journal of Psychoeducational Assessment, 33*(3), 199–209.

Bieber, G. A. (2011a). *The technical adequacy of the Basic Reading Inventory: An analysis of reliability and validity.* Retrieved from ProQuest Digital Dissertations. (AAT 3460570)

Bieber, G. A. (2011b). *Basic Reading Inventory: Accuracy data tables.* Unpublished manuscript.

Blanchard, J. S. (1985). *Computer-based reading assessment instrument.* Dubuque, IA: Kendall Hunt.

Block, C. C. (2003). *Literacy difficulties: Diagnosis and instruction for reading specialists and classroom teachers* (2nd ed.). Boston: Pearson.

Bolenius, E. M. (1919). *Teacher's manual of silent and oral reading.* Boston: Houghton Mifflin.

Botel, M. (1966). *Botel reading inventory.* Chicago: Follett Educational Corporation.

Bristow, P. S., Pikulski, J. J., & Pelosi, P. L. (1983). A comparison of five estimates of reading instructional level. *The Reading Teacher, 37,* 273–279.

Brittain, M. M. (1970). Informal reading procedures: Some motivational considerations. *The Reading Teacher, 24,* 216–219.

Brown, J., Goodman, K. S., & Marek, A. M. (Comps. and Eds.). (1996). *Studies in miscue analysis: An annotated bibliography.* Newark, DE: International Reading Association.

Brown, S. R. (1963). *A comparison of five widely used standardized reading tests and an informal reading inventory for a selected group of elementary school children.* Retrieved from ProQuest Digital Dissertations. (AAT 6404441)

Brozo, W. G., & Afflerbach, P. P. (2011). *Adolescent reading inventory, Grades 6–12.* Boston: Allyn & Bacon.

Burke, C. L., & Goodman, K. S. (1970). When a child reads: A psycholinguistic analysis. *Elementary English, 47,* 121–129.

Burkins, J. M., & Croft, M. M. (2010). *Preventing misguided reading: New strategies for guided reading teachers.* Newark, DE: International Reading Association.

Burns, P. C., & Roe, B. D. (1989). *Burns/Roe informal reading inventory* (3rd ed.). Boston: Houghton Mifflin.

Burns, P. C., & Roe, B. D. (1993). *Burns/Roe informal reading inventory* (4th ed.). Boston: Houghton Mifflin.

Burns, P. C., & Roe, B. D. (1999). *Informal reading inventory* (5th ed.). Boston: Houghton Mifflin.

Burns, P. C., & Roe, B. D. (2002). *Informal reading inventory* (6th ed.). Boston: Houghton Mifflin.

Burns, P. C., Roe, B. D., & Ross, E. P. (1996). *Teaching reading in today's elementary schools.* Boston: Houghton Mifflin.

Buros, O. K. (1972). *The seventh mental measurements yearbook.* Highland Park, NJ: The Gryphon Press.

Caldwell, J. (1985). A new look at the old informal reading inventory. *The Reading Teacher, 39,* 168–173.

Caldwell, J. S., & Leslie, L. (2005). *Intervention strategies to follow informal reading inventory assessment.* Boston: Allyn & Bacon.

Caldwell, J. S., & Leslie, L. (2009). *Intervention strategies to follow informal reading inventory assessment: So what do I do now?* (2nd ed.). New York: Pearson.

Caldwell, J. S., & Leslie, L. (2012). *Intervention strategies to follow informal reading inventory assessment: So what do I do now?* (3rd ed.). New York: Pearson.

Carnine, D. W., Silbert, J., Kame'enui, E. J., & Tarver, S. G. (2004). *Direct instruction reading* (4th ed.). Upper Saddle River, NJ: Pearson.

Carroll, J. B., Davies, P., & Richman, B. (1971). *Word frequency book.* Boston: Houghton Mifflin.

Carver, R. P. (1989). Silent reading rates in grade equivalents. *Journal of Reading Behavior, 21,* 155–166.

Christie, J. F. (1979). The qualitative analysis system: Updating the IRI. *Reading World, 18,* 393–199.

Cohn, M., & D'Alessandro, C. (1978). When is a decoding error not a decoding error? *The Reading Teacher, 32,* 341–144.

Conrad, L. L., & Shanklin, N. L. (1999). Using miscues to understand students' reading. *Colorado Reading Council Journal, 10,* 21–32.

Cooper, J. D., & Kiger, N. D. (2003). *Literacy: Helping children construct meaning* (5th ed.). Boston: Houghton Mifflin.

Cooper, J. D., & Kiger, N. D. (2011). *Literacy assessment: Helping teachers plan instruction*. Belmont, CA: Wadsworth.

Cooper, J. L. (1952). *The effect of adjustment of basal reading materials on reading achievement*. (Unpublished doctoral dissertation). Boston University, Boston.

Cooter, R. B., Jr., & Perkins, J. H. (2007). Looking to the future with *The Reading Teacher*: 900-year-old sheep and *Papa na come! The Reading Teacher, 61*, 4–7.

Cooter, R. B., Jr., Flynt, E. S., & Cooter, K. S. (2007). *Comprehensive reading inventory: Measuring reading development in regular and special education classrooms*. Upper Saddle River, NJ: Merrill Prentice Hall.

Cooter, R. B., Jr., Flynt, E. S., & Cooter, K. S. (2013). *The Flynt/Cooter comprehensive reading inventory—2: Assessment of K–12 reading skills in English & Spanish* (2nd ed.). New York: Pearson.

Council of Chief State School Officers & National Governors Association. (2010). *Common core state standards for English language arts & literacy in history/social studies, science, and technical subjects*. Retrieved June 3, 2011 from www.corestandards.org.

Cummins, C. (Ed.). (2006). *Understanding and implementing reading first initiatives*. Newark, DE: International Reading Association.

Cunningham, P. M., Hall, D. P., & Defee, M. (1991). Non-ability grouped, multilevel instruction: A year in a first-grade classroom. *The Reading Teacher, 44*, 566–571.

Dale, E., & O'Rourke, J. (1976). *The living word vocabulary: The words we know*. Elgin, IL: Dome.

D'Angelo, K., & Wilson, R. M. (1979). How helpful is insertion and omission miscue analysis? *The Reading Teacher, 32*, 519–520.

Dunkeld, C. G. (1970). *The validity of the informal reading inventory for the designation of instructional reading levels: A study of the relationships between children's gains in reading achievement and the difficulty of instructional materials*. Retrieved from ProQuest Digital Dissertations. (AAT 7114733)

Durrell, D. (1937). Individual differences and their implications with respect to instruction in reading. In G. M. Whipple (Ed.), *The teaching of reading* (pp. 325–356). The Thirty-Sixth Yearbook of the National Society for the Study of Education, Part I. Bloomington, IL: Public School Publishing Company.

Ekwall, E. E. (1974). Should repetitions be counted as errors? *The Reading Teacher, 27*, 365–367.

Ekwall, E. E. (1976). Informal reading inventories: The instructional level. *The Reading Teacher, 29*, 662–665.

Ekwall, E. E. (1986). *Ekwall reading inventory* (2nd ed.). Boston: Allyn & Bacon.

Ekwall, E. E., & Shanker, J. L. (1993). *Ekwall/Shanker reading inventory* (3rd ed.). Boston: Allyn & Bacon.

Elish-Piper, L., Johns, J. L., & Lenski, S. D. (2006). *Teaching reading pre-K–grade 3* (3rd ed.). Dubuque, IA: Kendall Hunt.

Emans, R. (1965). Teacher evaluation of reading skills and individualized reading. *Elementary English, 42*, 258–260.

Enz, B. (1989). *The 90% success solution*. Paper presented at the International Reading Association annual convention, New Orleans.

Estes, T. H., & Vaughan, J. L., Jr. (1973). Reading interest and comprehension: Implications. *The Reading Teacher, 27*, 149–153.

Evory, A. (Ed.). (1978). *Contemporary authors* (1st rev., vols. 33–36). Detroit: Gale Research Company, pp. 101–102.

Farr, R. (1992). Putting it all together: Solving the reading assessment puzzle. *The Reading Teacher, 4*, 26–37.

Felknor, C. (2000). Use of individual reading inventories with fourth-grade students on individual literacy plans. *Colorado Reading Council Journal, 11*, 15–17.

Felknor, C., Winterscheidt, V., & Benson, L. (1999). Thoughtful use of individual reading inventories. *Colorado Reading Council Journal, 10*, 10–20.

Ferroli, L. (2008). Criteria for interpreting word list reading performances with informal reading inventories. Unpublished study, Rockford College.

Ferroli, L., & Turmo, G. (2005–2006). Breaking the code of book levels and literacy stages. *Illinois Reading Council Journal, 34*(1), 28–33.

Fink, R. (2006). *Why Jane and John couldn't read—and how they learned: A new look at striving readers*. Newark, DE: International Reading Association.

Flynt, E. S., & Cooter, R. B., Jr. (1993). *Reading inventory for the classroom.* Scottsdale, AZ: Gorsuch Scarisbrick.

Flynt, E. S., & Cooter, R. B., Jr. (1995). *Reading inventory for the classroom* (2nd ed.). Scottsdale, AZ: Gorsuch Scarisbrick.

Flynt, E. S., & Cooter, R. B., Jr. (1998). *Reading inventory for the classroom* (3rd ed.). Upper Saddle River, NJ: Prentice-Hall.

Flynt, E. S., & Cooter, R. B., Jr. (1999). *English-Español reading inventory for the classroom.* Upper Saddle River, NJ: Prentice-Hall.

Flynt, E. S., & Cooter, R. B., Jr. (2001). *Reading inventory for the classroom* (4th ed.). Upper Saddle River, NJ: Prentice-Hall.

Flynt, E. S., & Cooter, R. B., Jr. (2004). *Reading inventory for the classroom* (5th ed.). Upper Saddle River, NJ: Merrill Prentice Hall.

Forman, J., & Sanders, M. E. (1998). *Project leap first grade norming study: 1993–1998.* Unpublished manuscript.

Fountas, I., & Pinnell, G. S. (2010). *The continuum of literacy learning, Grades pre-K–8* (2nd ed.). Portsmouth, NH: Heinemann.

Froese, V. (1974). Functional reading levels: From graded word lists? (Microfiche ED 102 520)

Fuchs, D., Fuchs, L. S., & Vaughn, S. (Eds.) (2008). *Response to intervention: A framework for reading educators.* Newark, DE: International Reading Association.

Gambrell, L. B., Wilson, R. M., & Gantt, W. N. (1981). Classroom observations of task-attending behaviors of good and poor readers. *Journal of Educational Research, 74,* 400–404.

Gates, A. I. (1935). *The improvement of reading* (Rev. ed.). New York: The Macmillan Company.

Gillet, J. W., & Temple, C. (1994). *Understanding reading problems: Assessment and instruction* (4th ed.). Glenview, IL: Scott, Foresman/Little Brown Higher Education.

Gillet, J. W., & Temple, C. (2000). *Understanding reading problems: Assessment and instruction* (5th ed.). New York: Addison Wesley Longman.

Gillet, J. W., Temple, C., & Crawford, A. N. (2004). *Understanding reading problems* (6th ed.). Boston: Allyn & Bacon.

Gillet, J. W., Temple, C. A., Temple, C. N., & Crawford, A. N. (2012). *Understanding reading problems: Assessment and instruction* (8th ed.). Boston: Allyn & Bacon.

Gillis, M. K., & Olson, M. W. (1985). *Elementary IRIs: Do they reflect what we know about text type/structure and comprehension?* Unpublished manuscript.

Goodman, K. S. (1965). A linguistic study of cues and miscues in reading. *Elementary English, 42,* 639–643.

Goodman, K. S. (1971). The search called reading. In H. M. Robinson (Ed.), *Coordinating reading instruction* (pp. 10–14). Glenview, IL: Scott, Foresman.

Goodman, K. S. (1973). Analysis of oral reading miscues: Applied psycholinguistics. In F. Smith (Ed.), *Psycholinguistics and reading* (pp. 158–176). New York: Holt, Rinehart and Winston.

Goodman, Y. M. (1972). Reading diagnosis—qualitative or quantitative? *The Reading Teacher, 26,* 32–37.

Goodman, Y. M., & Burke, C. L. (1972). *Reading miscue inventory manual: Procedure for diagnosis and evaluation.* New York: Macmillan.

Goodman, Y. M., & Marek, A. M. (1996). *Retrospective miscue analysis.* Katonah, NY: Richard C. Owen.

Goodman, Y. M., Watson, D. J., & Burke, C. L. (1987). *Reading miscue inventory: Alternative procedures.* New York: Richard C. Owen.

Graves, M. F., Juel, C., Graves, B. B., & Dewitz, P. (2011). *Teaching reading in the 21st century: Motivating all learners* (5th ed.). Boston: Allyn & Bacon.

Gray, W. S. (1916). Methods of testing reading II. *The Elementary School Journal, 16,* 281–298.

Gunning, T. G. (1998). *Assessing and correcting reading and writing difficulties.* Boston: Allyn & Bacon.

Gunning, T. G. (2000). *Creating reading instruction for all children* (3rd ed.). Boston: Allyn & Bacon.

Gunning, T. G. (2002). *Assessing and correcting reading and writing difficulties* (2nd ed.). Boston: Allyn & Bacon.

Gunning, T. G. (2003). *Creating literacy instruction for all children* (4th ed.). Boston: Allyn & Bacon.

Gunning, T. G. (2006). *Assessing and correcting reading and writing difficulties* (3rd ed.). Boston: Allyn & Bacon.

Gunning, T. G. (2008). *Creating literacy instruction for all students* (6th ed.). Boston: Allyn & Bacon.

Gunning, T. G. (2010a). *Assessing and correcting reading and writing difficulties* (4th ed.). Boston: Allyn & Bacon.

Gunning, T. G. (2010b). *Creating literacy instruction for all students* (7th ed.). Boston: Allyn & Bacon.

Haager, D., Klingner, J., & Vaughn, S. (2007). *Evidence-based reading practices for response to intervention.* Baltimore: Brooks.

Halladay, J. L. (2012). Revisiting key assumptions of the reading level framework. *The Reading Teacher, 66*(1), 53–62.

Hansen, J. (2004). *Tell me a story: Developmentally appropriate retelling strategies.* Newark, DE: International Reading Association.

Hardy, N. D., & Jerman, M. E. (1985). *Readability estimator.* Seattle: Berta-Max.

Harris, A. J., & Sipay, E. R. (1990). *How to increase reading ability* (9th ed.). New York: Longman.

Harris, T. L., & Hodges, R. E. (Eds.). (1981). *A dictionary of reading and related terms.* Newark, DE: International Reading Association.

Harris, T. L., & Hodges, R. E. (Eds.). (1995). *The literacy dictionary: The vocabulary of reading and writing.* Newark, DE: International Reading Association.

Hasbrouck, J., & Tindal, G. A. (2006). Oral reading fluency norms: A valuable assessment tool for reading teachers. *The Reading Teacher, 59*, 636–644.

Hasbrouck, J. E., & Tindal, G. (1992). Curriculum-based oral reading fluency norms for students in grades 2 through 5. *Teaching Exceptional Children, 24*, 41–44.

Hays, W. S. (1975). Criteria for the instructional level of reading. (Microfiche ED 117 665)

Helgren-Lempesis, V. A., & Mangrum, C. T., II. (1986). An analysis of alternate-form reliability of three commercially prepared informal reading inventories. *Reading Research Quarterly, 21*, 209–215.

Homan, S. P., & Klesius, J. P. (1985). A re-examination of the IRI: Word recognition criteria. *Reading Horizons, 26*, 54–61.

Hood, J. (1978). Is miscue analysis practical for teachers? *The Reading Teacher, 32*, 260–266.

Hunt, L. C., Jr. (1970). The effect of self-selection, interest, and motivation upon independent, instructional, and frustrational levels. *The Reading Teacher, 24*, 146–151, 158.

International Literacy Association. (2013). *Formative assessment: A position statement of the International Literacy Association.* Newark, DE: Author.

International Reading Association. (2000). *Making a difference means making it different* (A Position Statement). Newark, DE: Author.

International Reading Association. (2007). *Teaching reading well: A synthesis of the International Reading Association's research on teacher preparation for reading instruction.* Newark, DE: Author.

IOX. (1980). *Basic skills word list: Grades 1–12.* Los Angeles: IOX.

Jennings, J. H., Caldwell, J., & Lerner, J. W. (2006). *Reading problems: Assessment and teaching strategies* (5th ed.). Boston: Allyn & Bacon.

Johns, J., Lenski, S., & Berglund, R. (2011). *Essential comprehension strategies for the intermediate grades.* Dubuque, IA: Kendall Hunt.

Johns, J. L. (1976). Informal reading inventories: A survey among professionals. *Illinois School Research and Development, 13*, 35–39.

Johns, J. L. (1978). *Basic reading inventory.* Dubuque, IA: Kendall Hunt.

Johns, J. L. (1981). *Advanced reading inventory.* Dubuque, IA: Wm. C. Brown.

Johns, J. L. (1985). *Basic reading inventory* (3rd ed.). Dubuque, IA: Kendall Hunt.

Johns, J. L. (1986). *Computer-based advanced reading inventory* (Grade 7–College). DeKalb, IL: Northern Illinois University.

Johns, J. L. (1988). *Basic reading inventory* (4th ed.). Dubuque, IA: Kendall Hunt.

Johns, J. L. (1990a). Informal reading inventories: A holistic consideration of the instructional level. In N. D. Padak, T. V. Rasinski, & J. Logan (Eds.), *Challenges in reading* (pp. 135–140). Twelfth Yearbook of the College Reading Association. Provo, UT: College Reading Association.

Johns, J. L. (1990b). *Secondary & college reading inventory* (2nd ed.). Dubuque, IA: Kendall Hunt.

Johns, J. L. (1991). Emmett A. Betts on informal reading inventories (Open to Suggestion Column). *Journal of Reading, 34*, 492–493.

Johns, J. L. (Comp.). (1993). *Informal reading inventories: An annotated reference guide.* DeKalb, IL: Northern Illinois University.

Johns, J. L. (1994). *Basic reading inventory* (6th ed.). Dubuque, IA: Kendall Hunt.

Johns, J. L. (1996). Using informal reading inventories in classroom and clinic. In L. R. Putnam (Ed.), *How to become a better reading teacher: Strategies for assessment and intervention* (pp. 113–122). Columbus, OH: Merrill.

Johns, J. L. (1997). *Basic reading inventory* (7th ed.). Dubuque, IA: Kendall Hunt.

Johns, J. L. (2001). *Basic reading inventory: Pre-primer through grade twelve and early literacy assessments* (8th ed.). Dubuque, IA: Kendall Hunt.

Johns, J. L. (2005). *Basic reading inventory: Pre-primer through grade twelve and early literacy assessments* (9th ed.). Dubuque, IA: Kendall Hunt.

Johns, J. L. (2007). Monitoring progress in fluency: Possible unintended consequences. *Reading Today, 24*, 18.

Johns, J. L. (2008a). *Basic reading inventory DVD and CD.* Dubuque, IA: Kendall Hunt.

Johns, J. L. (2008b). *Basic reading inventory: Pre-primer through grade twelve and early literacy assessments* (10th ed.). Dubuque, IA: Kendall Hunt.

Johns, J. L. (2012). *Basic reading inventory: Pre-primer through grade twelve and early literacy assessments* (11th ed.). Dubuque, IA: Kendall Hunt.

Johns, J. L., & Berglund, R. L. (2002). *Strategies for content area learning* (2nd ed.). Dubuque, IA: Kendall Hunt.

Johns, J. L., & Berglund, R. L. (2010). *Fluency: Differentiated interventions and progress-monitoring assessments.* Dubuque, IA: Kendall Hunt.

Johns, J. L., & Berglund, R. L. (2011). *Strategies for content area learning* (3rd ed.). Dubuque, IA: Kendall Hunt.

Johns, J. L., & Daniel, M. C. (2010). *Spanish reading inventory* (2nd ed.). Dubuque, IA: Kendall Hunt.

Johns, J. L., & L'Allier, S. K. (2003). How well can teachers determine reading levels from an informal reading inventory? In M. B. Sampson, P. E. Linder, J. R. Dugan, & B. Brancato (Eds.), *Celebrating the freedom of literacy* (pp. 251–264). Twenty-Fifth Yearbook of the College Reading Association. Commerce, TX: College Reading Association.

Johns, J. L., & L'Allier, S. K. (2004). How preservice teachers score an informal reading inventory: Strengths and weaknesses. In J. R. Dugan, P. E. Linder, M. B. Sampson, B. Brancato, & L. Elish-Piper (Eds.), *Celebrating the power of literacy* (pp. 254–267). Twenty-Sixth Yearbook of the College Reading Association. Readyville, TN: College Reading Association.

Johns, J. L., & L'Allier, S. K. (2007). *Improving preservice teachers' ability to determine significant miscues when using an informal reading inventory.* Paper presented at the International Reading Association annual convention, Toronto.

Johns, J. L., & Lenski, S. D. (1997). *Improving reading: A handbook of strategies* (2nd ed.). Dubuque, IA: Kendall Hunt.

Johns, J. L., & Lenski, S. D. (2005). *Improving reading: Strategies and resources* (4th ed.). Dubuque, IA: Kendall Hunt.

Johns, J. L., & Lenski, S. D. (2019). *Improving reading: Strategies, resources, and Common Core connections* (6th ed.). Dubuque, IA: Kendall Hunt.

Johns, J., Lenski, S., & Berglund, R. (2011). *Essential comprehension for the intermediate grades.* Dubuque, IA: Kendall Hunt.

Johns, J. L., & Magliari, A. M. (1989). Informal reading inventories: Are the Betts criteria the best criteria? *Reading Improvement, 26*, 124–132.

Johns, J. L., & VanLeirsburg, P. (1990). Portfolio assessment: A survey among professionals. Literacy research report no. 1. DeKalb, IL: Northern Illinois University Reading Clinic.

Johns, J. L., & VanLeirsburg, P. (1992). How professionals view portfolio assessment. *Reading Research and Instruction, 32*, 1–10.

Johns, J. L., Elish-Piper, L., & Johns, B. (2017). *Basic reading inventory: Kindergarten through grade twelve and early literacy assessments* (12th ed.). Dubuque, IA: Kendall Hunt.

Johns, J. L., Garton, S., Schoenfelder, P., & Skriba, P. (1977). *Assessing reading behavior: Informal reading inventories* (An Annotated Bibliography). Newark, DE: International Reading Association.

Johns, J. L., L'Allier, S. K., & Johns, B. (2012). Making the most of informal reading inventories: Moving from purposeful assessment to targeted instruction. In E. T. Ortlieb & E. H. Cheek, Jr. (Eds.), *Literacy research, practice, and evaluation: Vol. 1* (pp. 39–72). Using informative assessments towards effective literacy instruction. Bingley, UK: Emerald Group.

Johns, J. L., Lenski, S. D., & Berglund, R. L. (2006). *Comprehension and vocabulary strategies for the elementary grades* (2nd ed.). Dubuque, IA: Kendall Hunt.

Johnson, M. S., & Kress, R. A. (1965). *Informal reading inventories*. Newark, DE: International Reading Association.

Johnson, M. S., Kress, R. A., & Pikulski, J. J. (1987). *Informal reading inventories* (2nd ed.). Newark, DE: International Reading Association.

Johnston, P. (1983). Prior knowledge and reading comprehension test bias (Technical Report No. 289). Champaign, IL: Center for the Study of Reading.

Johnston, P., & Allington, R. (1991). Remediation. In R. Barr, M. L. Kamil, P. B. Mosenthal, & P. D. Pearson (Eds.), *Handbook of reading research, volume II* (pp. 984–1012). New York: Longman.

Jorgenson, G. W. (1977). Relationship of classroom behavior to the accuracy of the match between material difficulty and student ability. *Journal of Educational Psychology, 69*, 24–32.

Kalmbach, J. R. (1986). Evaluating informal methods for the assessment of retellings. *Journal of Reading, 30*, 119–127.

Kender, J. P. (1966). *Analysis of factors associated with informal reading tests at the eighth grade level.* (Unpublished doctoral dissertation). University of Pennsylvania, Philadelphia.

Kender, J. P. (1970). Informal reading inventories. *The Reading Teacher, 24*, 165–167.

Kibby, M. W. (1995). *Practical steps for informing literacy instruction: A diagnostic decision-making model.* Newark, DE: International Reading Association.

Killgallon, P. A. (1942). *A study of relationships among certain pupil adjustments in language situations.* Retrieved from ProQuest Digital Dissertations. (AAT 0000560)

Klesius, J. P., & Homan, S. P. (1985). A validity and reliability update on the informal reading inventory with suggestions for improvement. *Journal of Learning Disabilities, 18*, 71–76.

Kragler, S. (1996). Vygotsky and at-risk readers: Assessment and instructional implications. In L. Dixon-Kraus (Ed.). *Vygotsky in the classroom: Mediated literacy instruction and assessment* (pp. 149–160). White Plains, NY: Longman.

Ladd, E. M. (1961). *A comparison of two types of training with reference to developing skill in diagnostic oral reading testing.* Retrieved from ProQuest Digital Dissertations. (AAT 6105648)

L'Allier, S. K. (2013). Lessons learned from research about informal reading inventories: Keys to data driven instructional recommendations. *Reading & Writing Quarterly, 29*(3), 288–307.

Lenski, S., Wham, M., Johns, J., & Caskey, M. (2011). *Reading and learning strategies* (4th ed.). Dubuque, IA: Kendall Hunt.

Lenski, S. D. (1998). *Schools that succeed on the IGAP reading test.* Bloomington, IL: Illinois Reading Council.

Lenski, S. D., & Johns, J. L. (2000). *Improving writing: Resources, strategies, and assessments.* Dubuque, IA: Kendall Hunt.

Lenski, S. D., Wham, M. A., & Johns, J. L. (1999). *Reading & learning strategies for middle & high school students.* Dubuque, IA: Kendall Hunt.

Leslie, L., & Caldwell, J. (1990). *Qualitative reading inventory.* Glenview, IL: Scott, Foresman/Little Brown Higher Education.

Leslie, L., & Caldwell, J. (1995). *Qualitative reading inventory—II*. New York: HarperCollins College Publishers.

Leslie, L., & Caldwell, J. (2001). *Qualitative reading inventory—3*. New York: Longman.

Leslie, L., & Caldwell, J. (2006). *Qualitative reading inventory—4*. Boston: Allyn & Bacon.

Leslie, L., & Caldwell, J. S. (2011). *Qualitative reading inventory—5*. Boston: Pearson.

Leslie, L., & Caldwell, J. S. (2016). *Qualitative reading inventory—6* (6th ed.). New York: Pearson.

Leu, D. J., Jr., & Kinzer, C. K. (1987). *Effective reading instruction in the elementary grades*. Columbus: Merrill.

Leu, D. J., Jr., & Kinzer, C. K. (1999). *Effective literacy instruction, K–8* (4th ed.). Upper Saddle River, NJ: Prentice-Hall.

Lipson, M. Y., & Wixson, K. K. (1991). *Assessment and instruction of reading disability*. New York: HarperCollins.

Lipson, M. Y., & Wixson, K. K. (2000). *Assessment and instruction of reading and writing difficulty: An interactive approach* (3rd ed.). Boston: Allyn & Bacon.

Lipton, A. (1972). Miscalling while reading aloud: A point of view. *The Reading Teacher, 25*, 759–762.

Lowell, R. E. (1970). Problems in identifying reading levels with informal reading inventories. In W. K. Durr (Ed.), *Reading difficulties: Diagnosis, correction, and remediation* (pp. 120–126). Newark, DE: International Reading Association.

Lutes, M. (2004). *The effects of reading and writing strategies on reading comprehension*. (Unpublished Master's Thesis). Southeast Missouri State University, Cape Girardeau.

Maginnis, G. H. (1978). Emmett Albert Betts. In J. F. Ohles (Ed.), *Biographical dictionary of American educators* (Vol. 1, pp. 125–126). Westport, CT: Greenwood.

Mahdavi, J. N., & Haager, D. (2007). Linking progress monitoring results to interventions. *Perspectives on Language and Literacy, 33*(2), 25–29.

Manderino, M., Berglund, R. L., & Johns, J. L. (2014). *Content area learning: Bridges to disciplinary literacy* (4th ed.). Dubuque, IA: Kendall Hunt.

Manning, J. C. (1995). Ariston Metron. *The Reading Teacher, 48*, 650–659.

Manzo, A. V., & Manzo, U. C. (1993). *Literacy disorders*. Fort Worth, TX: Harcourt Brace Jovanovich.

Manzo, A. V., & Manzo, U. C. (1995). *Teaching children to be literate*. Fort Worth, TX: Harcourt Brace College Publishers.

Manzo, A. V., Manzo, U. C., & McKenna, M. C. (1995). *Informal reading-thinking inventory*. Fort Worth, TX: Harcourt Brace College Publishers.

Marcell, B. (2007). Fluency to a fault: Put fluency in the passenger seat and let comprehension take the wheel. *Reading Today, 24*, 18.

Marzano, R. J., Larson, J., Tish, G., & Vodehnal, S. (1978). The graded word list is not a shortcut to an IRI. *The Reading Teacher, 31*, 647–651.

McCormick, S. (1987). *Remedial and clinical reading instruction*. Columbus: Merrill.

McCormick, S. (1995). *Instructing students who have literacy problems*. Englewood Cliffs, NJ: Prentice-Hall.

McCormick, S. (1999). *Instructing students who have literacy problems* (3rd ed.). Upper Saddle River, NJ: Prentice-Hall.

McCormick, S. (2003). *Instructing students who have literacy problems* (4th ed.). Upper Saddle River, NJ: Pearson Education.

McCormick, S. (2007). *Instructing students who have literacy problems* (5th ed.). Upper Saddle River, NJ: Prentice Hall.

McCracken, R. A. (1963). *The development and validation of the IRI for the individual appraisal of reading performance in grades one through six*. Retrieved from ProQuest Digital Dissertations. (AAT 6405659)

McCracken, R. A. (1966). *Standard reading inventory*. Bellingham, WA: Pioneer Printing.

McKenna, M. C., & Stahl, S. A. (2003). *Assessment for reading instruction*. New York: Guilford.

McNaughton, S. (1981). The influence of immediate teacher correction on self-corrections and proficient oral reading. *Journal of Reading Behavior, 13*, 367–371.

McTague, B. (1997). Lessons from reading recovery for classroom teachers. *Illinois Reading Council Journal, 25*, 42–49.

Micro Power & Light Co. (1995). *Readability calculations.* Dallas, TX: Author.

Millsap, L. N. (1962). *A study of teachers' awareness of frustration reading levels among their pupils in basal readers.* Retrieved from ProQuest Digital Dissertations. (AAT 6301081)

Morris, D. (2015). *Morris informal reading inventory: Preprimer through grade 8.* New York: Guilford.

Morris, D., Bloodgood, J., Perney, J., Frye, E., Kucan, L., Trathen, W., Ward, D., & Schlagal, R. (2011). Validating craft knowledge: An empirical examination of elementary-grade students' performance on an informal reading assessment. *Elementary School Journal, 112*(2), 205–233.

Morris, D., Trathen, W., Frye, E. M., Kucan, L., Ward, D., Schlagal, R., & Hendrix, M. (2013). The role of reading rate in the informal assessment of reading ability. *Literacy Research and Instruction, 52*(1), 52–64.

Morris, J. A. (1990). *An investigation of informal reading inventory scoring criteria with average second- and fourth-grade students.* Retrieved from ProQuest Digital Dissertations. (AAT 9034574)

Morrow, L. M. (1988). Retelling stories as a diagnostic tool. In S. M. Glazer, L. W. Searfross, & L. M. Gentile (Eds.), *Re-examining reading diagnosis and instruction* (pp. 128–149). Newark, DE: International Reading Association.

National Governors Association for Best Practices & Council of Chief School Officers [NGA Center & CCSSO] (2010). *Common Core State Standards for English language arts and literature in history/social studies, science, and technical subjects.* Washington, DC: Authors. Retrieved from www.corestandards.org/assets/CCSSI_ELA%20Standards.pdf

National Reading Panel. (2000). *Teaching children to read: An evidence-based assessment of the scientific research literature on reading and its implications for reading instruction.* Washington, DC: U.S. Department of Health and Human Services.

Newman, H. (1978). Oral reading miscue analysis is good but not complete. *The Reading Teacher, 31*, 883–886.

Nilsson, N. L. (2008). A critical analysis of eight informal reading inventories. *The Reading Teacher, 61*(7), 526–536.

Nilsson, N. L. (2013). The reliability of informal reading inventories: What has changed? *Reading & Writing Quarterly, 29*(3), 208–230.

Norton, D. E. (1992). *The impact of literature-based reading.* New York: Macmillan.

O'Connor, R. E., Bell, K. M., Harty, K. R., Larkin, L. K., Sacker, S. M., & Zigmond, N. (2002). Teaching reading to poor readers in the intermediate grades: A comparison of text difficulty. *Journal of Educational Psychology, 94*(3), 474–485.

Olson, M. W., & Gillis, M. K. (1985). *Text type and text structure: An analysis of three secondary informal reading inventories.* Unpublished manuscript.

Opitz, M. F. (2000). *Rhymes & reasons: Literature and language play for phonological awareness.* Portsmouth, NH: Heinemann.

Paris, S. G., & Carpenter, R. D. (2003). FAQs about IRIs. *The Reading Teacher, 56*, 578–580.

Paris, S. G., Paris, A. H., & Carpenter, R. D. (2002). Effective practices for assessing young readers. In B. M. Taylor & P. D. Pearson (Eds.), *Teaching reading: Effective schools, accomplished teachers* (pp. 141–160). Mahwah, NJ: Erlbaum.

Patty, D. L. (1965). *A comparison of standardized oral reading test scores and informal reading inventory scores.* Retrieved from ProQuest Digital Dissertations. (AAT 6513037)

Pearson, P. D. (2007). An endangered species act for literary education. *Journal of Literacy Research, 39*(2), 145–162.

Pearson, P. D. (2013). Research foundations of the Common Core State Standards in the English language arts. In S. B. Neuman & L. B. Gambrell (Eds.), *Quality reading instruction in the age of the Common Core Standards* (pp. 237–262). Newark, DE: International Reading Association.

Pehrsson, R. S. (1994). Challenging frustration level. *Reading & Writing Quarterly: Overcoming Learning Difficulties, 10*, 201–208.

Pikulski, J. J. (1974). A critical review: Informal reading inventories. *The Reading Teacher, 28*, 141–51.

Pikulski, J. J., & Shanahan, T. (1982). Informal reading inventories: A critical analysis. In J. J. Pikulski & T. Shanahan (Eds.), *Approaches to the informal evaluation of reading* (pp. 94–116). Newark, DE: International Reading Association.

Powell, W. R. (1970). Reappraising the criteria for interpreting informal inventories. In D. L. DeBoer (Ed.), *Reading diagnosis and evaluation* (pp. 100–109). Newark, DE: International Reading Association.

Powell, W. R. (1971). The validity of the instructional reading level. In R. E. Leibert (Ed.), *Diagnostic viewpoints in reading* (pp. 121–133). Newark, DE: International Reading Association.

Prior, S. M., & Welling, K. A. (2001). "Read in your head": A Vygotskian analysis of the transition from oral to silent reading. *Reading Psychology, 22*, 1–15.

Raphael, T. E. (1986). Teaching question-answer relationships. *The Reading Teacher, 39*, 516–520.

Raphael, T. E., & Au, K. H. (2005). QAR: Enhancing comprehension and test taking across grades and content areas. *The Reading Teacher, 59*, 206–221.

Recht, D. R. (1976). The self-correction process in reading. *The Reading Teacher, 29*, 632–636.

Reutzel, D. R., & Cooter, R. B., Jr. (2000). *Teaching children to read* (3rd ed.). Upper Saddle River, NJ: Prentice-Hall.

Reutzel, D. R., & Cooter, R. B., Jr. (2004). *Teaching children to read: Putting the pieces together* (4th ed.). Upper Saddle River, NJ: Pearson.

Reutzel, D. R., & Cooter, R. B., Jr. (2008). *Teaching children to read* (5th ed.). Upper Saddle River, NJ: Merrill Prentice Hall.

Richek, M. A., Caldwell, J. S., Jennings, J. H., & Lerner, J. W. (1996). *Reading problems: Assessment and teaching strategies* (3rd ed.). Boston: Allyn & Bacon.

Rinsky, L. A., & de Fossard, E. (1980). *The contemporary classroom reading inventory.* Dubuque, IA: Gorsuch Scarisbrick.

Rinsland, H. D. (1945). *A basic vocabulary of elementary school children.* New York: Macmillan.

Roe, B. D., & Burns, P. C. (2007). *Informal reading inventory* (7th ed.). Boston: Houghton Mifflin.

Roe, B. D., & Burns, P. C. (2011). *Informal reading inventory: Pre-primer to twelfth grade.* Belmont, CA: Wadsworth.

Roe, B. D., Smith, S. H., & Burns, P. C. (2009). *Teaching reading in today's elementary schools* (10th ed.). Belmont, CA: Wadsworth Cengage Learning.

Ross, P., & Gibson, S. A. (2010). Exploring a conceptual framework for expert noticing during literacy instruction. *Literacy Research and Instruction, 49*, 175–193.

Sakiey, E., & Fry, E. (1979). *3,000 instant words.* Highland Park, NJ: Drier Educational Systems.

Samuels, S. J. (2002). Reading fluency: Its development and assessment. In A. E. Farstrup & S. J. Samuels (Eds.), *What research has to say about reading instruction* (3rd ed., pp. 166–183). Newark, DE: International Reading Association.

Sattler, J. M. (2001). *Assessment of children: Cognitive approaches* (4th ed.). San Diego: Author.

Schell, L. M. (1982). The validity of the potential level via listening comprehension: A cautionary note. *Reading Psychology, 3*, 271–276.

Schell, L. M., & Hanna, G. S. (1981). Can informal reading inventories reveal strengths and weaknesses in comprehension subskills? *The Reading Teacher, 35*, 263–268.

Schlieper, A. (1977). Oral reading errors in relation to grade and level of skill. *The Reading Teacher, 31*, 283–287.

Shanahan, T. (2014). How and how not to prepare students for the new tests. *The Reading Teacher, 68*(3), 184–188.

Shanker, J. L., & Cockrum, W. (2010). *Ekwall/Shanker reading inventory* (5th ed.). Boston: Allyn & Bacon.

Shanker, J. L., & Cockrum, W. (2013). *Ekwall/Shanker reading inventory* (6th ed.). New York: Pearson.

Shanker, J. L., & Ekwall, E. E. (2000). *Ekwall/Shanker reading inventory* (4th ed.). Boston: Allyn & Bacon.

Shanker, J. L., & Ekwall, E. E. (2003). *Locating and correcting reading difficulties* (8th ed.). Columbus, OH: Merrill Prentice Hall.

Silvaroli, N. J. (1969). *Classroom reading inventory.* Dubuque, IA: Wm. C. Brown.

Silvaroli, N. J. (1994). *Classroom reading inventory* (7th ed.). Dubuque, IA: Wm. C. Brown.

Silvaroli, N. J. (1997). *Classroom reading inventory* (8th ed.). Dubuque, IA: Brown & Benchmark.

Silvaroli, N. J., & Wheelock, W. H. (2004). *Classroom reading inventory* (10th ed.). New York: McGraw Hill.

Smith, L., & Weaver, C. (1978). A psycholinguistic look at the informal reading inventory part I: Looking at the quality of reader's miscues: A rationale and an easy method. *Reading Horizons, 19*, 12–22.

Spache, G. D. (1976). *Diagnosing and correcting reading disabilities.* Boston: Allyn & Bacon.

Spichtig, A. N., Hiebert, E. H., Vorstius, C., Pascoe, J. P., Pearson, P. D., & Radach, R. (2016). The decline of comprehension-based silent reading efficiency in the United States: A comparison of current data with performance in 1960. *Reading Research Quarterly, 51*(2), 239–259.

Spiegel, D. L. (1995). A comparison of traditional remedial programs and reading recovery: Guidelines for success for all programs. *The Reading Teacher, 49*, 86–96.

Stieglitz, E. L. (1992). *The Stieglitz informal reading inventory.* Boston: Allyn & Bacon.

Stieglitz, E. L. (1997). *The Stieglitz informal reading inventory* (2nd ed.). Boston: Allyn & Bacon.

Sucher, F., & Allred, R. A. (1973). *Sucher-Allred reading placement inventory.* Oklahoma City: The Economy Company.

Tatham, S. M. (1978). Comprehension taxonomies: Their uses and abuses. *The Reading Teacher, 32*, 190–194.

Taylor, B. M., Pearson, P. D., Clark, K., & Walpole, S. (2002). Effective schools and accomplished teachers: Lessons about primary-grade reading instruction in low income schools. In B. M. Taylor & P. D. Pearson (Eds.), *Teaching reading: Effective schools, accomplished teachers* (pp. 3–72). Mahwah, NJ: Erlbaum.

Taylor, S. E., Frackenpohl, H., White, C. E., Nieroroda, B. W., Browning, C. L., & Birsner, E. P. (1979). *EDL core vocabularies in reading, mathematics, science, and social studies.* New York: EDL/McGraw-Hill.

Thorndike, E. L. (1934). Improving the ability to read. *Teachers College Record, 36*, 123–144.

Thorndike, E. L., & Lorge, I. (1944). *The teacher's word book of 30,000 words.* New York: Teachers College.

Tierney, R. J. (1998). Literacy assessment reform: Shifting beliefs, principled possibilities, and emerging practices. *The Reading Teacher, 51*, 374–390.

Torgesen, J. K. (2004). Lessons learned from research on interventions for students who have difficulty learning to read. In P. McCardle & V. Chhabra (Eds.), *The voice of evidence in reading research* (pp. 355–382). Baltimore: Paul H. Brooks.

Vacca, J. L., Vacca, R. T., & Gove, M. K. (1987). *Reading and learning to read.* Boston: Little, Brown.

Vacca, J. L., Vacca, R. T., & Gove, M. K. (1995). *Reading and learning to read* (3rd ed.). New York: HarperCollins College Publishers.

Vacca, J. L., Vacca, R. T., & Gove, M. K. (2000). *Reading and learning to read* (4th ed.). New York: Addison Wesley Longman.

Vacca, J. L., Vacca, R. T., Gove, M. K., Burkey, L. C., Lenhart, L. A., & McKeon, C. A. (2006). *Reading and learning to read* (6th ed.). Boston: Allyn & Bacon.

Vacca, J. L., Vacca, R. T., Gove, M. K., Burkey, L. C., Lenhart, L. A., & McKeon, C. A. (2012). *Reading and learning to read* (8th ed.). Boston: Allyn & Bacon.

Valencia, S. (1990). A portfolio approach to classroom reading assessment: The whys, whats, and hows. *The Reading Teacher, 34*, 338–340.

Valencia, S. W., & Buly, M. R. (2004). Behind test scores: What struggling readers *really* need. *The Reading Teacher, 57*, 520–531.

VanLeirsburg, P., & Johns, J. L. (1995). Portfolios: Teachers' perceptions and practices. *Michigan Reading Journal, 29*, 14–23.

Vygotsky, L. S. (1978). *Mind in society* (M. Cole, V. John-Steiner, S. Scribner, & E. Souberman, Eds.). Cambridge, MA: Harvard University Press.

Waldo, K. D. (1915). Tests in reading in Sycamore schools. *The Elementary School Journal, 15*, 251–268.

Walker, B. J. (1996). *Diagnostic teaching of reading: Techniques for instruction and assessment* (3rd ed.). Columbus: Merrill.

Walker, B. J. (2000). *Diagnostic teaching of reading* (4th ed.). Upper Saddle River, NJ: Prentice-Hall.

Walker, B. J. (2004). *Diagnostic teaching of reading: Techniques for instruction and assessment* (5th ed.). Upper Saddle River, NJ: Pearson.

Walker, B. J. (2008). *Diagnostic teaching of reading: Techniques for instruction and assessment* (6th ed.). Upper Saddle River, NJ: Pearson.

Walpole, S., & McKenna, M. C. (2006). The role of informal reading inventories in assessing word recognition (Assessment Column). *The Reading Teacher, 59*, 592–594.

Walter, R. B. (1974). History and development of the informal reading inventory. (Microfiche ED 098 539)

Wheat, H. G. (1923). *The teaching of reading.* Boston: Ginn.

Wheelock, W. H., & Campbell, C. J. (2011). *Classroom reading inventory* (6th ed.). New York: McGraw Hill.

Whipple, G. M. (Ed.). (1925). *Report of the National Committee on Reading.* The Twenty-Fourth Yearbook of the National Society for the Study of Education, Part I. Bloomington, IL: Public School Publishing Company.

Wilde, S. (2000). *Miscue analysis made easy.* Portsmouth, NH: Heinemann.

Williamson, L. E., & Young, F. (1974). The IRI and RMI diagnostic concepts should be synthesized. *Journal of Reading Behavior, 5*, 183–194.

Windell, I. (1975). Development and evaluation of a module to train special education teacher trainees to determine a pupil's instructional reading level. (Microfiche ED 111 142)

Woods, M. L., & Moe, A. J. (1985). *Analytical reading inventory* (3rd ed.). Columbus, OH: Merrill.

Woods, M. L., & Moe, A. J. (1989). *Analytical reading inventory* (4th ed.). Columbus, OH: Merrill.

Woods, M. L., & Moe, A. J. (1995). *Analytical reading inventory* (5th ed.). Columbus, OH: Merrill.

Woods, M. L., & Moe, A. J. (1999). *Analytical reading inventory* (6th ed.). Upper Saddle River, NJ: Prentice-Hall.

Woods, M. L., & Moe, A. J. (2003). *Analytical reading inventory* (7th ed.). Columbus, OH: Merrill Prentice Hall.

Woods, M. L., & Moe, A. J. (2007). *Analytical reading inventory* (8th ed.). Upper Saddle River, NJ: Pearson.

Woods, M. L., & Moe, A. J. (2014). *Analytical reading inventory: Comprehensive standards-based assessment for all students including gifted and remedial* (10th ed.). New York: Pearson.

Yopp, H. K. (1995). A test for assessing phonemic awareness in young children. *The Reading Teacher, 49*, 20–29.

Yopp, H. K., & Yopp, R. E. (2000). Supporting phonemic awareness development in the classroom. *The Reading Teacher, 54*, 130–143.

Zeigler, L. L., & Johns, J. L. (2005). *Visualization: Using mental images to strengthen comprehension.* Dubuque, IA: Kendall Hunt.

Zeno, S. M., Ivens, S. H., Millard, R. T., & Duvvuri, R. (1995). *The educator's word frequency guide.* Brewster, NY: Touchstone Applied Science Associates.

Photo Credits

Page xi, xiv, 21, 131: Courtesy of Suzi Hinrichs. Reprinted by permission.

Page xii, 27: Courtesy of Ryan Janisch. Reprinted by permission.

Page 3, 17: Courtesy of Jerry L. Johns. Reprinted by permission.

Page 10, 129: Courtesy of Beth Johns. Reprinted by permission.

Page 57, 117, 142, 405, 409: Courtesy of Lorena Lule. Reprinted by permission.

Page 62, 69: Courtesy of Laurie Elish-Piper. Reprinted by permission.

Index

Basic Reading Inventory Administration and Scoring Procedures

Jerry L. Johns, Laurie Elish-Piper, and Beth Johns

To determine a student's independent, instructional, and frustration levels, administer the graded word lists and graded passages included in the Basic Reading Inventory as follows:

WORD RECOGNITION IN ISOLATION: Select a graded word list at a reading level that will be easy for the student. Ask the student to pronounce the words at a comfortable rate. Record the student's responses in the sight column beside the corresponding word list in the performance booklet. The website provides downloadable versions of all performance booklets.

Return to mispronounced or unknown words for an attempt at analysis and note the student's responses in the analysis column. Administer successive word lists until the student is no longer able to achieve a total score of at least 14 correct words or until the student becomes frustrated.

Scoring: Total the correct responses in the sight and analysis columns. Consult the criteria on the scoring guide at the bottom of the word lists to determine a rough estimate of the reading level achieved on each graded word list. Judgment must be exercised at the kindergarten levels because of the limited number of words. Record the number-correct scores and the reading levels on the summary sheet of the performance booklet.

WORD RECOGNITION IN CONTEXT: Ask the student to read aloud the passage graded one level below the highest independent level achieved on the graded word lists. If desired, time the student's reading. As the student reads the passage, record all miscues such as omissions, repetitions, substitutions, and the like on the corresponding copy of the passage found in the performance booklet.

Scoring: Count the number of total miscues or significant miscues (those that affect meaning) in each graded passage.

To determine reading levels from the word recognition in context scores, consult the criteria on the scoring guide at the bottom of the passage. Judgment must be exercised at the kindergarten and beginning first-grade levels because of the limited number of words in these passages. Record the score and the reading levels on the summary sheet of the performance booklet.

COMPREHENSION: Ask the comprehension questions that accompany the passage in the performance booklet and record the student's responses. Continue administering graded passages until the student has many word recognition miscues or is unable to answer half the comprehension questions. Also, watch for behavior associated with frustration: lack of expression, word-by-word reading, excessive anxiety, and so on.

Scoring: Count the number of comprehension questions missed.

To convert these scores into reading levels, consult the criteria on the scoring guide at the bottom of the questions. Judgment must be exercised at the pre-primer levels because the limited number of questions may not permit precise measurement of comprehension. Record the scores and the reading levels on the summary sheet of the performance booklet.

Tabs for Basic Reading Inventory Manual

The tabs provided may be reproduced on card stock, cut out and placed in the manual of Basic Reading Inventory.

Overview	Administration and Scoring	Determining Reading Levels	Instructional Uses
11 Targeted Interventions	Development	Form A	Form B
Form C	Form D	Form E	Form LL
Form LI	Retelling Procedures	Summary Sheets	FAQs
Oral Reading Norms	Early Literacy Assessments	Six Clusters of Readers	

cut here →

cut here ↑